the Research Process

books & beyond

Myrtle S. Bolner

Gayle A. Poirier

second edition

The Research Process

Books and Beyond

SECOND EDITION

Myrtle S. Bolner
Louisiana State University

Gayle A. Poirier
Wayne State College

KENDALL/HUNT PUBLISHING COMPANY
4050 Westmark Drive   Dubuque, Iowa 52002

Formerly entitled *Library Research Skills Handbook*

Copyright © 1997, 2001 by Kendall/Hunt Publishing Company

ISBN 0-7872-7329-5

Printed in the United States of America

10 9 8 7 6 5 4 3 2 1

◆ Contents

Preface   vii
Acknowledgments   ix
How to Use This Book   xi
About the Authors   xiii

**1 Academic Libraries:
Materials and Services   1**
Introduction   2
The Academic Library   3
Formats of Information Sources   3
    Books   3
    E-Books   3
    CD-ROM Books   5
    Serials   5
    Dissertations and Theses   5
    Archives   6
    Vertical File   6
    Audio-Visual (A-V) Materials   6
    Electronic Sources   8
Arrangement of Library Materials   11
    Stacks   11
    Reference Department   12
    Reserve Department   12
    Periodical Department   12
    Newspaper Department   12
    Microform Department   12
    Audio-Visual Department   12
    Government Information
        Department   13
    Archives and Manuscripts
        Department   13
    Rare Books Department   13
    Special Collections   13
    Branch Libraries   13
Library Services   13
    Librarians   14
    Circulation   15
    Electronic Reference Services   15
    Library Instruction   15
    Interlibrary Loan   15
    Document Delivery   15
    Library Cooperatives   16
Exercises   17

2 The Research Paper   29
Introduction   30
What Is a Research Paper?   30
    Selecting a Topic   31
    Formulating a Thesis   32
    Preparing an Outline   32
    Finding Information:
        The Search Strategy   34
    Evaluating Sources   36
    Taking Notes   36
    Writing the Paper   37
    Documenting the Sources   37
Exercises   43

3 Evaluating Information Sources   53
Introduction   54
Understand the Sources   54
    Primary Sources   54
    Secondary Sources   55
    Popular and Scholarly Sources   55
Initial Approach   56
Applying Evaluation Criteria   56
Evaluating Internet Sources   57
Evaluative Reviews   57
Exercises   61

**4 Basic Search Techniques:
Electronic Sources   67**
Introduction   68
The Search Strategy   68
Information in Electronic Format   70
    Online Catalogs   70
    Databases   71
    Internet   72
Understanding Electronic Sources   72
    Bibliographic Information   72
    Full-Text Databases   73
Search Basics   73
    Commands   73
    Access Points   74
    Author Search   74

Title Search 75
Subject Search 75
Keyword Search 77
Exercises 83

5 Library Catalogs 87

Introduction 88
Classification Systems 88
   Dewey Decimal Classification
     System 89
   Library of Congress Classification
     System 89
   Superintendent of Documents
     Classification System 93
   United Nations Symbol Numbers 93
Call Numbers 93
Library Catalogs: Key to Access 96
   Materials That Might Not Be Found in
     Library Catalogs 96
   Format of Cataloged Materials 96
Card Catalog 97
   Printed Cards 97
   Arrangement of Cards in Catalog 97
Online Catalogs 99
   Using the Online Catalog to Find
     Information 99
   Online Catalogs (Text-Based): Sample
     Screens 100
   Periodical Indexes in an Integrated
     Online System 105
   Web-Based Catalogs 105
   Online Catalogs (Web-Based):
     Sample Screens 106
   Library Catalogs from Around
     the World 108
Exercises 109

6 The Internet 131

Introduction 132
What Is the Internet? 133
   An Overview 133
   How the Internet Works 134
Electronic Mail (E-Mail) 136
   E-Mail Addresses 136
LISTSERV 136
   Usenet News 136

File Transfer Protocol (FTP) 137
Gopher 137
World Wide Web 137
   What Is It? 137
   How Information on the Web
     Is Created 137
   Accessing the World Wide Web 138
   URL 138
   Connecting to the Web and
     Retrieving Information 139
Using Search Engines to Find Information
  on the Internet 140
   What Is a Search Engine? 141
   Developing a Search Strategy 141
   Types of Search Engines 141
   Performing a Search 142
   Search Engine Features 144
Evaluating Information Found on
  the Internet 144
Works Cited 145
Exercises 147

7 Reference Sources 157

Introduction 158
What Are Reference Sources? 158
Using Reference Sources 158
   Characteristics of Reference
     Sources 159
   Types of Reference Sources 160
   Selecting a Reference Source 161
   Finding Reference Sources 164
Evaluating Reference Sources 167
Selected Reference Sources by Type 167
   Almanacs and Yearbooks 168
   Atlases, Gazetteers, and
     Guidebooks 169
   Bibliographies 170
   Concordances 170
   Dictionaries 170
   Directories 172
   Encyclopedias 172
   Handbooks and Manuals 173
Selected Current Events Sources 173
Selected Internet Sites 174
Selected Print Reference Sources
  by Subject 176
Exercises 181

8 Periodicals   203

Introduction   204
Why Use Periodicals for Research?   204
Understanding Periodical Literature   204
   Types of Periodical Literature   205
   Subject Focus of Periodical
      Literature   205
   Format of Periodical Literature   206
Finding Information in Periodicals   206
   Indexes and Abstracts   206
   Databases   207
   Printed Indexes and Abstracts   210
   Newspaper Indexes/Databases   213
Selected Subject Indexes to Periodical
   Literature   215
Electronic Journals   217
Exercises   219

9 Government Information   245

Introduction   246
Government Information in the
   Research Process   246
United States Government Publications   247
   Format   248
   Depository Libraries   248
   Finding U.S. Government
      Information   249
State Government Information   255
   State Government Information on
      the Internet   255
Local Government Information   256
   Local Government Information on
      the Internet   256
International Organizations and Foreign
   Governments   256
   United Nations   257
   Other International Organizations and
      Foreign Governments   258
Exercises   259

10 Statistical Sources   273

Introduction   274
Why Use Statistics?   274
Finding Statistical Information   274
   Use the Internet   275
   Use an Index to Statistical Sources   276

   Use a Periodical Index   278
   Use the Library Catalog   279
Evaluating Statistical Sources   279
Selected Internet Sites for Statistics   283
   Guides   283
   General   283
   Selected Sites by Subject   284
Selected List of Print Statistical Sources   285
   General   285
   Subject   285
Exercises   289

11 Biographical Information   301

Introduction   302
Finding Biographical Information   302
   Internet   303
   Databases   303
   Biographical Indexes   306
   Biographical Dictionaries   309
   Library Catalogs   310
   Additional Sources for
      Biographical Information   311
Evaluating Biographical Information   312
Selected Internet Sites for Biographical
   Information   312
   Guides   312
   General   312
   Special Interests   312
Selected Print Sources for Biographical
   Information   313
   Indexes   313
   Biographical Dictionaries   314
Exercises   317

12 Book Reviews, Literary Criticism, and Literature in Collections   329

Introduction   330
Book Reviews   330
Literary Criticism   337
   Defining Terms   337
   Finding Literary Criticism   337
Literature in Collections (Anthologies)   342
   Finding Works Included in
      Anthologies   342
Exercises   349

Appendices 361

Appendix A   361
      Documenting Sources
        (MLA Style)   362
Appendix B   373
      Glossary   374
Appendix C   383
1. The Research Project   385
    1.1 Topic and Outline   385
    1.2 Developing a Search Strategy   387

    1.3 Works Consulted   389
    1.4 Research Project Worksheet   391
2. Pathfinder   393
3. Selecting and Evaluating Sources   397
    Example   401
4. Group Project   407

Index   411

◆ Preface

The evolution of civilization is really the story of learning. Beginning with the infancy of the universe, the first inhabitants gathered and used information just as they gathered food and other essentials of life. With the knowledge they gained, they were able to create new knowledge and make advancements that changed the way they lived. As the knowledge base has grown, so has the complexity of the *research process*—the process by which information is stored, retrieved, and used in the creation of new knowledge. Information can enlighten us as to the physical environment, the political and social order, the scientific and technical accomplishments, and, indeed, all aspects of life. Viewed in that light, it is clear that learning research skills is an essential part of the education process.

We live in an age in which we are constantly being bombarded by various information media ranging from books and journals to the Internet. It has become increasingly important that individuals recognize how information is created, organized, and disseminated and that they develop the ability to conduct research in a variety of media. Research today can be both amazingly simple and amazingly complex. Technology has played an important part in simplifying the way we locate information. At the same time it is quite easy for the researcher to be overwhelmed not only by the sheer volume of information but also by all the tools of research—especially those in less traditional formats such as the Internet.

It is our aim to provide a book that will serve a threefold purpose:

◆ make you aware of the different kinds of information that are available in libraries and beyond;
◆ provide you with a guide to the means of accessing information;
◆ help you evaluate and use information productively.

The authors recognize that along with basic retrieval skills you must acquire what is the most important ingredient for effective research—the ability to analyze and use information critically. Critical thinking in the context of research involves a certain attitude and disposition on the part of the information user, a willingness to challenge the propositions and assertions encountered as one taps the information sources. Most importantly, critical thinking calls for the testing of values and beliefs in the light of knowledge and evidence discovered in the course of an information search.

The book introduces you to the academic library and discusses the ways information is organized. It covers the principal tools for accessing information—library catalogs, the Internet, reference books, indexes, government publications, statistical sources, biographical sources, book reviews, literary criticism, and literature in collections. We have included many Internet sites and titles of reference books, indexes, and electronic databases on a variety of subjects. The more frequently used sources are described in some detail, while others are simply listed.

Earlier versions of this book were published under the titles *Library Research Skills Handbook* and *Books, Libraries, and Research*. This second edition of the present title reflects changes that have taken place over the last few years in information storage and retrieval, particularly on the Internet.

◆ Acknowledgments

We wish to thank the reference staff at Louisiana State University Libraries and at Wayne State College for suggestions. We are especially grateful to the library instruction staff at both institutions for their support and encouragement. Special thanks are due Denise Sokolowski, Librarian, University of Maryland, European Division, and her staff for their many excellent suggestions and continuing interest in the book.

◆ How to Use This Book

One of the most important skills you can acquire is the ability to find and use information. This is not only essential to achieving success in the classroom, but also necessary as part of the overall preparation for a lifetime of continuous learning. Recognizing that one of the best ways to acquire research skills is through specific instruction, many institutions provide formal courses that are designed to familiarize students with library resources and research techniques. In other instances, librarians and instructors cooperate to design research strategies that support classroom instruction.

This book is designed so that it may be used as a text in a formal course on developing research skills or as a guide to research by anyone seeking to learn how to locate and use information. While the chapters are arranged in a step-by-step progression that the authors have found useful in teaching research skills, they may be used out of sequence to suit individual needs and learning styles.

The book begins with an introduction to academic libraries and their resources and services, followed by a discussion of the research paper in Chapter 2. It contains explanations of plagiarism, copyright, and documentation forms. The next two chapters deal with two important research skills—evaluating resources and using basic search techniques. This foundation prepares you for the next two chapters—the online catalog and the Internet. The remaining chapters introduce you to various information sources: reference books, periodicals, government publications, statistical sources, biographies, book reviews, literary criticism, and literature in collections.

The exercises at the end of each chapter are designed to provide a review of the material covered in the chapter and to reinforce learning by providing hands-on experience with the information sources essential to successful research. Some chapters contain several exercises. It is expected that instructors will choose those exercises that they think are most appropriate. The authors have chosen to use the topic "women and employment" to illustrate the many facets of information retrieval. Where that topic was not appropriate to the sources under discussion, other subject headings were used.

The concept of using a research project to provide you with an opportunity to collect, organize, evaluate, and use information is the methodology that the authors have found to be effective in teaching research skills. Once you have mastered this technique, you will be able to vary your research activity according to subsequent demands, regardless of the topic involved.

◆ About the Authors

◆ Myrtle S. Bolner

Myrtle S. Bolner is Head of Reference Services at Louisiana State University Libraries. Prior to her current position, she was Head of the Business Administration/Government Documents Department at the LSU Libraries. Her professional experience includes four years as a teacher of high school English and twelve years as an instructor of Library Research Methods and Materials at LSU. She holds a Bachelor of Science in Education and a Master of Library Science from LSU. Bolner is the co-author of *Library Research Skills Handbook* (Kendall/Hunt, 1991) and *Books, Libraries, and Research* (Kendall/Hunt, 1979; 2nd ed. 1984; 3rd ed. 1987). Other publications include the *LLA Intellectual Freedom Manual* (Louisiana Library Association, 1986, 1994) and articles in the *LLA Bulletin* and *Government Publications Review.* She is the co-recipient of the 1990 GODORT/ALA Documents to the People Award for her contributions to the GPO/MARCIVE database, an online catalog of government publications. Bolner is a member of the American Library Association, the Southeastern Library Association, and the Louisiana Library Association.

◆ Gayle A. Poirier

Gayle A. Poirier is Documents/Reference Librarian at Conn Library, Wayne State College, Wayne, Nebraska. She also serves as Bibliographic Instruction Coordinator. At WSC she initiated a one-credit-hour course entitled Basic Research Skills, patterned on the Library Research Methods and Materials course she previously coordinated and taught at Louisiana State University. Before moving to Nebraska, Poirier served as Head of the Library Instruction Unit at the LSU Libraries. Prior positions include Adult Services Librarian, Columbine Public/School Library in Colorado; Head, Learning Media Center, Memphis State University; and Government Documents Librarian, Memphis State University. Poirier holds a Master of Library Science degree from the University of Oklahoma and a Master of Science in Curriculum and Instruction from Mankato State University. She is a member of the American Library Association and the Nebraska Library Association. Poirier has published several articles in *Research Strategies* in addition to co-authoring *The Research Process: Books and Beyond.*

Academic Libraries: Materials and Services

"I find that a great part of the information I have was acquired by looking up something and finding something else on the way."

FRANKLIN P. ADAMS

INTRODUCTION

Many of the assignments you receive as part of your experience in higher education will require you to use the library for research. To do this you must become familiar with its collections and services. You may be familiar with your high school or public library. You will find, however, that the college or university library is more complex and often larger than the library with which you may be familiar. It probably provides a greater variety of services, and it may use a different scheme for classifying its materials.

Over the last two decades technology has drastically changed the way we think of libraries. For many, the traditional notion of libraries as storehouses for books has been replaced by the image of a virtual library—that is, a library in which all the information is available electronically. In this image, if a building exists at all it is only to house computers and to provide a laboratory in which librarians, acting as information specialists, are engaged in creating information in digital format. Neither the traditional notion of a library as a storehouse for books nor the image of a virtual library is entirely true today. However, there is a certain amount of validity in each of these images. The library you are using probably no longer has a card catalog. In most academic libraries the card catalog has been replaced by an online catalog. Many libraries have canceled paper subscriptions to indexes and abstracts, replacing them with electronic versions. Although libraries have gotten rid of their card catalogs in favor of online catalogs and subscribe to online databases and other resources in electronic format, they continue to retain and purchase materials in traditional formats: paper, microfiche, microfilm, video cassette, and the like. And while it is true that technology has improved the ways we retrieve information, it has also added levels of complexity.

College and university libraries offer a variety of materials and services that are designed to support the teaching and research missions of the institution. As an information seeker, you will find it is helpful to know how materials are organized and arranged in libraries, what materials are available, and how to retrieve those materials. Although library arrangements and services vary from library to library, there are many elements that are common to all of them. This chapter gives an overview of the formats and arrangements of library materials and describes the various services commonly found in college and university libraries. In describing the formats of materials, the parts of a book are analyzed in detail; other information sources are treated with sufficient detail to provide you with an understanding of their physical properties.

◆ THE ACADEMIC LIBRARY

Whether you use a large university library, a public library, or a high school library you will find that the levels of materials and services available to you differ considerably. Libraries build their collections to meet the particular needs of their users; consequently, the collections found in an academic library will be different from those found in public libraries or in school libraries. For example, academic libraries probably do not purchase popular fiction, while a public library might collect heavily in this area. Academic libraries usually collect highly specialized reference materials in the sciences; the public library, unless it is a large research library, probably collects only popular science materials. High school libraries collect materials geared to the level of their students.

The mission of the college and university library is to provide books, periodicals, and other information-related materials and services to meet the research and instructional needs of the students and faculty. The rising costs of materials and new technologies make this difficult in all but the wealthiest institutions. The library is frequently hampered in this effort by financial constraints and by the destructive acts of those it seeks to serve. Mutilation and theft of library materials by patrons are major problems in college and university libraries. All such acts ultimately result in a decrease in the materials available and a lessening of services. It is incumbent on library users to share the responsibility of preserving library materials by seeing to it that such destructive acts do not occur.

◆ FORMATS OF INFORMATION SOURCES

The term *format* refers to the general physical quality or appearance of an information source. Thus, book format refers to printed pages of paper that are bound together. The book is still the most extensive way that information is stored, and it is the source that many of us still find the most "friendly." Other formats, such as photographs, magnetic recordings, video tapes, laser disks, CD-ROM, DVD (Digital Versatile/Video Disk), online databases and catalogs, and information from the Internet are being used with increasing frequency. You may not feel as comfortable with these sources as you do with books, but understanding the formats of the various information sources will help to dispel some of your fears about unfamiliar formats. Beyond that, developing skills in the intelligent use of information sources will save time and result in a more effective use of the source.

Books

The traditional book printed on paper consists of pages fastened together at one edge and covered with a protective cover. The first printed books consisted only of the cover and the text of the work. There were no title or introductory pages as in modern books. As printing evolved, publishers developed a uniform way to arrange the contents of books that greatly enhanced their usability. The most significant features are discussed in Table 1.1. (Some books may not have all the different parts described, and the order of their appearance may vary.)

E-Books

E-books are published in electronic format and available on the Internet. E-books from NetLibrary, a subscription service, can be checked out to allow exclusive viewing rights.

TABLE 1.1. ◆ Standard Features of Books

📖 **BOOK COVER:** The cover of the book holds the pages of the book together and protects them. The edge of the cover where the pages are bound together is called the spine. The short-title of the book, the author's name, the publisher, and, in the case of library books, the call number are printed on the spine. The front of the cover is often decorated. It may also give the author's name and the short-title of the book.

📖 **INTERIOR PAGES**

Preliminary Material

❑ **Title Page**

The title page is the first significant page in the book. It gives the following information:
- *Title:* The title page gives the full title of the book, including any subtitles or descriptive titles, e.g., *The Book: The Story of Printing and Bookmaking.* The title from the title page should be used in bibliographic citations.
- *Author:* The author's name and sometimes a list of credentials such as degrees, academic position, and, occasionally, the names of other works.
- *Editor, Compiler, Illustrator, or Translator:* The name of anyone other than the author who made a significant contribution to the book.
- *Edition:* Given if the book is other than a first edition. All copies of a book printed from one set of type make up an edition. Reprints are copies of the same edition printed at a later time. When any changes are made, it becomes a revised edition or a new edition.
- *Imprint:* The place of publication, the publisher, and the date of publication. These are usually found at the bottom of the title page although the publication date is sometimes omitted. The publication date identifies when a book was published. Only the place of publication, publisher, and date are needed for identification purposes in a bibliography. If there is no publication date, the copyright date is used in a bibliographic citation.

❑ **Copyright and Printing Information**

The back of the title page contains the following information:
- *Copyright:* The copyright grants legal rights to an author or publisher to sell, distribute, or reproduce a literary or artistic work. A small © before a date identifies it as the copyright date.
- *Printing history:* A list of different editions and printings of the work.

❑ **Table of Contents**

The table of contents lists in order the chapters or parts of the book and gives the pages on which they begin. Some books include a brief summary of each chapter listed.

❑ **Preface or Foreword**

Preface or foreword gives the author's purpose in writing the book and acknowledges those persons who have helped in its preparation.

❑ **Introduction**

The introduction differs from the preface or foreword in that it describes the subject matter of the book and gives a preliminary statement leading into the main contents of the book.

❑ **Illustrations**

The list of illustrations gives the pages on which illustrative material can be found. Illustrations might include pictures, maps, charts, etc.

Text and Notes

The main body of printed matter is the text of the book. It is usually divided into chapters or separate parts and may include explanatory material and identification of reference sources in the form of notes at the bottoms of the pages (footnotes) or at the ends of chapters (endnotes). In some books notes appear at the end of the book.

End Matter

❑ **Glossary**

A list with definitions of unfamiliar words or terms used in the text, usually at the end of the text.

❑ **Appendix**

Supplementary materials following the text such as tables, maps, questionnaires, or case studies.

❑ **Bibliography**

A list of all books, articles, and other materials the author used in writing the book. It may also include other sources that are relevant to the subject. The bibliography may appear at the end of each chapter or at the end of the book.

❑ **Index**

An alphabetical list of subjects discussed in the book. Some books have a separate name and/or author index.

CD-ROM Books

CD-ROM books are available in CD-ROM format.

Serials

A *serial* is a publication that is issued on a continuing basis at regularly stated intervals. The publication frequency varies: some serials are published each day (daily); others, once a week (weekly), every two weeks (biweekly), once a month (monthly), every two months (bimonthly), every three months (quarterly), twice a year (semiannually), or once a year (annually). Serials include periodicals (magazines and journals); newspapers; annuals and yearbooks; and the proceedings, transactions, memoirs, etc. of societies and associations.

◆ *Periodicals* are numbered consecutively and given volume designations so that several issues make up a volume. In many libraries, when a complete volume of a periodical has been accumulated, the issues are bound together in hard covers. These bound volumes may be shelved with other books by classification number, or they may be shelved in a separate periodical area. Some libraries acquire the current copies of periodicals in paper and the back issues on microform. *Periodicals* include *magazines* and *journals* that are issued at regular intervals, usually weekly, biweekly, monthly, bimonthly, or quarterly. *Magazines* contain popular reading, while *journals* are more scholarly.

◆ *E-journals* (electronic journals) are defined very broadly as those journals or magazines that are available over the Internet. The first e-journals appeared in the early 1990s and have proliferated at a phenomenal rate; currently there are thousands of journals and magazines available in electronic format and the trend for electronic publishing is expected to continue. Some of these are available exclusively online; others may have a print counterpart. Many libraries subscribe to e-journals and make them available through their home pages and in their online catalogs. The advantage of e-journals is that users do not have to come to the library in order to read available articles; rather they can access the journals from their home or office as long as they have a valid authorization to get to the database.

◆ *Newspapers* are usually published daily or weekly. They are printed on a type of paper called *newsprint* that does not last. For this reason, they are usually preserved on microfilm. The paper copies of newspapers are kept only until the microfilm copies arrive. Many newspapers are available on the Internet, some by subscription, others for free. For example, the *New York Times* is available at: http://www.nytimes.com/.

◆ *Annuals* and *yearbooks* are treated much as other book materials and shelved in the general collection or in the reference collection in a library. The proceedings, transactions, memoirs, etc. of a society or association are considered serials because they are usually published at regular intervals. The serial titles owned by a library are usually listed in the library's catalog but may also appear in a separate serials list that identifies those titles and issues that have been received in the library.

Dissertations and Theses

A *dissertation* is research that is conducted and written in partial fulfillment of the requirements for the doctoral degree at a university. A *thesis* is a research project completed in partial fulfillment of the requirements for the master's degree. At least one copy of the original of all the dissertations and theses written at a university are usually kept in the university library. Many libraries acquire microfilm copies of the theses and dissertations in order to preserve the original. Libraries may acquire dissertations and theses from other universities on microfilm.

Archives

Archives consist of both unpublished and published materials that have historical value, such as the public and private papers of notable persons or the records of an institution. The format of archival materials varies: for example, archives might include original manuscripts, letters, photographs, diaries, legal records, books, etc. (See Figure 1.1.) The materials found in archives may be likened to the items one frequently finds in the attics of old family homes: birth and marriage certificates, letters, and newspaper clippings that tell that family's story. Archives require special care and handling, and it is not unusual to find that access is limited to only serious researchers. Archival materials are also being preserved on microform, magnetic tapes, CD-ROM, DVD, and in digital form stored on computers. Many of the digitally stored materials are available over the Web. A notable example is the Library of Congress' *American Memory: Historical Collections for the National Digital Library*. As of this writing there are seventy archival collections that have been copied and stored in digital format. These collections can be accessed at: http://lcweb2.loc.gov/ammem/amhome.html

Vertical File

The vertical file (or pamphlet file) consists of pamphlets, brochures, newspaper and magazine clippings, pictures, maps, and other materials that are not suitable for cataloging and shelving along with the regular book collection. Vertical file materials are usually placed in manila folders and stored alphabetically by subjects in filing cabinets. The material placed in the vertical file is ephemeral in nature—that is, it has little, if any, lasting value and will soon be out-of-date. Therefore, the vertical file must be weeded, or cleared, from time to time to get rid of dated material. Much of the information kept in the vertical file might never appear in any other published form. Some libraries maintain a separate index of vertical file material.

Audio-Visual (A-V) Materials

Audio-visual materials include audio, video, and microform formats. A-V materials require special equipment for their use and are usually housed in separate areas of the library. The types of A-V materials are:

◆ *Audio* materials—records, audio cassettes, CD-ROM, DVD, and reel-to-reel tapes. The audio materials in most libraries include musical as well as spoken records.

◆ *Video* materials—microforms, video cassettes, slides, and synchronized slide-tapes.

◆ *Microforms*—printed materials that are reduced in size by photographic means and that can only be read with special readers. (See Figures 1.2 and 1.3.) There are several types of these photographically reduced materials:

—*microfilm* is print that is reproduced on a roll of 35 or 16 mm film;

—*microfiche* is a flat sheet of film, usually measuring four by six inches, on which separate pages of text are reproduced:

   ◆ *microprint* is the reproduction in positive form of a microphotograph. Microprint is printed on opaque paper, unlike microfilm and microfiche, which are printed or reproduced on film;

   ◆ *microcard* is a form of microprint, but its reduction is greater.

Microprints and microcards are no longer being distributed because of the difficulty in reproducing them on paper.

PLAN FOR THE GOVERNMENT OF THE WESTERN COUNTRY

A National Archives Facsimile

49

The Committee appointed to prepare a plan for the temporary government of the Western territory have agreed to the following resolutions.

Resolved, that the territory ceded or to be ceded by Individual states to the United states shall be formed into distinct states, bounded in the following manner as nearly as such cessions will admit, that is to say; Northwardly & Southwardly by parallels of latitude so that each state shall comprehend from South to North two degrees of latitude beginning to count from the completion of thirty one degrees North of the Equator: but any territory Northwardly of the 47th degree shall make part of the state next below. and Eastwardly & Westwardly they shall be bounded, those on the Missisipi by that river on one side and the meridian of the lowest point of the rapids of Ohio on the other; and those adjoining on the East by the same meridian on their Western side, and on their Eastern by the meridian of the Western cape of the mouth of the Great Kanhaway. And the territory Eastward of this last meridian between the Ohio, Lake Erie, & Pennsylvania shall be one state.

That the settlers within the territory so to be purchased & offered for sale shall, either on their own petition, or on the order of Congress, receive authority from them, with appointments of time and place for their free males of full age to meet together for the purpose of establishing a temporary government, to adopt the constitution & laws of any one of these states, so that such laws nevertheless shall be subject to alteration by their ordinary legislature, and to erect, subject to a like alteration, counties or townships for the election of members for their legislature.

That such temporary government shall only continue in force in any state until it shall have acquired 20,000 free inhabitants; when giving due proof thereof to Congress, they shall receive from them authority with appointments of time and place to call a Convention of representatives to establish a permanent constitution & government for themselves.

23. A Plan for the Government of the Western Country, March 1, 1784, *Papers of the Continental Congress No. 30, Other Reports of Committees of Congress on Indian Affairs and Lands in the Western Territory, 1776-88, I 49-51, Record Group 360, Records of the Continental and Confederation Congresses and the Constitutional Convention. Size of the original, Pages 49 and 50, 8⅞ x 7 in., page 51, 8¾ x 7⅛ in.*

In the hand of Thomas Jefferson. 3 pages.

Figure 1.1. A facsimile of a manuscript from the National Archives.

Libraries purchase microform materials in order to save valuable space and to acquire material not available in any other format. For example, the census records containing the names of persons are available from the National Archives and Records Administration only on microfilm. While it is more likely that newspapers and periodicals are acquired in microform format, it is not unusual to find books, especially out-of-print ones, on microfiche or microfilm.

Electronic Sources

Information in electronic format is available in a variety of formats—radio, television, video cassette, CD-ROM and DVD, etc. For the purposes of this discussion, electronic sources will be discussed only in the context of computer-assisted technologies. That is, to access information in these formats requires a computer and appropriate software. The most common electronic sources you are likely to encounter in a library are:

(1)   online catalogs,
(2)   online databases,
(3)   Internet,
(4)   CD-ROM and DVD, and
(5)   floppy disks.

The kind of information available in electronic format includes bibliographic information such as descriptions of books, periodical articles, and other literary works; raw data (e.g., statistics, census data, voting records); the full text of periodicals, books, and reports; and illustrative material such as maps and photographs. Telecommunications equipment is required for online databases, online catalogs, and Internet access. The equipment used to store and access information in electronic format consists of microcomputers, computer terminals, and disk players. In addition, software (computer programs) is necessary to run the various programs.

Following are descriptions of the various electronic sources:

◆   *Online catalog,* known as the OPAC (Online Public Access Catalog), is a computerized version of the traditional card catalog; it lists all of the items housed in the library or made available remotely through the Internet. The records are created in machine-readable format and are accessible by computer both within and beyond the library walls.

◆   *Online database* is a term used to describe information that is stored in a computer and retrieved by other computers through telephone lines and communication networks. There are thousands of online databases, providing nearly every type of information, both bibliographic and full text. Although commercial vendors are still the major producers of online databases, government agencies and professional and scholarly organizations also produce and disseminate them. The costs of accessing online databases vary, but in general, the benefits outweigh the costs. And many databases, including many produced by the federal government, are free. Some of the better known databases are: *InfoTrac, EBSCOhost, Academic Universe*, and *FirstSearch*.

◆   *Internet* is a global telecommunications network that links computers together by a unique IP (Internet Protocol) address, and that allows for the free exchange of information among them. The Internet contains all types of information: online catalogs, electronic journals, periodical databases, personal messages, and, in fact, any information that is computer generated can be found on the Internet. (For a full discussion of the Internet, see Chapter 6.)

Figure 1.2.
Microfilm reader.

Figure 1.3.
Microfiche reader.

Figure 1.4. Microform material, clockwise from top: microfilm, microcard, microfiche, and microprint.

Figure 1.5. Information in electronic format, clockwise from top: magnetic tape, compact disks, floppy disks.

- *CD-ROM* (Compact Disk, Read Only Memory) is a small (4.75 inches in diameter) plastic coated optical disk on which information can be stored. One disk is equal in contents to approximately 250,000 printed pages, or about 300 books. The information stored on a CD-ROM cannot be erased or altered, although it can be transferred to another utility such as a floppy disk or the hard drive on a computer. CD-ROM requires a microcomputer with appropriate software and a disk player to run the program. There are thousands of CD-ROM databases available. These include indexes, census data, corporation records, encyclopedias, government documents, statistics, maps, journal back files, and other literary works.

- *DVD* (digital versatile disk or digital video disk) is similar to a CD-ROM, except that it holds much more information—a minimum of 4.7GB (gigabytes) all the way up to 17GB, or enough for a full-length movie. Many experts believe that DVD will eventually replace CD-ROMs, as well as VHS video cassettes and laser discs. DVD technology is also much faster than that of CD-ROM.

The format of computer-generated material is different, at least in appearance although not in content, from traditional library sources. Computer technology is developing and changing at such a fast pace that it is not possible to predict what the format of electronic information will look like even in the very near future.

 ## ARRANGEMENT OF LIBRARY MATERIALS

While there is some uniformity of arrangement of the materials among college and university libraries, there are also many variations. Differences in arrangement among libraries is governed by a number of factors: size of the institution, educational mission, and availability of resources. Some schools have separate libraries for undergraduates; other schools have only one central library; many universities have a central library as well as branch libraries that serve various colleges or departments within the university.

In addition to locating library facilities on campus for maximum use, librarians are also concerned with arranging materials within the library. Most libraries arrange materials by function or by service provided. Typically, all the books are shelved together on shelves in what is called a stack area; non-book materials such as microforms and audio materials, are housed in other areas; and access services such as reference assistance, circulation, and interlibrary borrowing are provided at specially designated service desks. Many libraries provide guides to their collections and services; others have self-guided tours; and still others offer a computer-assisted or "virtual" tour of the library. These provide a good starting point in learning where materials are located and how they are arranged. The departments and areas listed below are typical of those found in most college and university libraries.

Stacks

The library's main collection of books is arranged by call number on rows of shelves called *stacks*. Libraries with large collections will have miles and miles of stacks. Some libraries have "closed" stacks to which only library staff and those with permission have access. Patrons present a "call slip" to a library attendant who gets the material. Having closed stacks reduces the loss of library material by theft and mutilation. It also reduces the number of books that are out of order in the stacks. In most libraries, however, books are shelved in "open" stacks where users are free to browse and select materials for themselves. Browsing is helpful in locating materials that the user might not have discovered in the library catalog. Some libraries have a combination of the two systems—the general stack areas are "open" while special collections are "closed." In some college and university libraries, stacks are open to faculty and graduate students, but closed to undergraduates.

The key to locating materials in the stacks or in other areas of the library is the *catalog*. When a library acquires a book or other information source, it is assigned a call number that determines where it will be located in the library. A catalog record is created that includes call number, author's name, title, publication information, and a note giving the size of the book and other descriptive information such as availability of maps, illustrations, and/or bibliographies. Subject headings are assigned in order to help the library user locate the book by its subject. The catalog record is placed in the library's catalog where it is available to library users.

Reference Department

One of the most useful collections in any library is the reference collection. This collection consists of encyclopedias, dictionaries, almanacs, handbooks, manuals, and indexes that are frequently used for finding information. It also contains reference tools in other formats such as CD-ROM and computers for accessing the Internet and specialized electronic databases. The reference department typically has open shelves that are systematically arranged, although some materials such as indexes may be shelved on separate index tables to facilitate their use. Highly used reference books may also be shelved in an area near the librarian's desk. Reference librarians familiar with this collection are available to help patrons find information in the reference area. As a rule, reference materials do not circulate and must be used in the reference area.

Reserve Department

The reserve department consists of materials that circulate for limited time periods, usually two hours or overnight. In many libraries, materials that can be copied, such as periodical articles and chapters or parts of books, are placed on electronic reserve. Students who are taking the courses for which the materials are reserved access the materials through secured Internet accounts.

Periodical Department

In many libraries periodicals (magazines and journals) are shelved together in one area for convenience of use. Other libraries have found that it is more desirable to have only the current periodicals in one area with the bound volumes in the stacks with other materials on the same subject.

Newspaper Department

Current newspapers may be housed with other periodical literature or kept in a separate area. Print copies of newspapers are kept for a limited period of time because they are printed on paper that does not last. Older copies are usually stored on microfilm.

Microform Department

Microform materials are usually housed in a separate area equipped with readers and copiers.

Audio-Visual Department

Audio-visual materials consist of recordings, cassette tapes, video cassettes, compact disks, films, and slides. These are usually kept in areas that are designed to accommodate these types of materials.

Government Information Department

Many university libraries serve as depositories for state, local, national, and international documents. These publications are frequently shelved together in a separate area. Some libraries locate state and local government documents in a documents room with national and international documents, but it is also quite common to house these materials in a distinct "state" room designed to preserve materials dealing with the particular state. Documents housed in separate areas are usually arranged by classification systems designed especially for those systems. For example, U.S. government documents are usually shelved by the Superintendent of Documents classification system.

Archives and Manuscripts Department

The archives department houses records and documents such as letters, manuscripts, diaries, personal journals, photographs, maps, and other materials that are of historical value. This area is staffed by archivists who are specifically trained in methods of acquisition and preservation of historical materials.

Rare Books Department

Many college and university libraries have books that are valuable because of their artistic and/or unique qualities or because they are old and no longer printed. Such books need protection and care in handling. They are housed in rooms or in branch libraries and are not allowed to circulate.

Special Collections

In fulfilling its research mission, a university library frequently has a number of highly specialized collections. The advantage of such collections is that they support the university's effort to become a center for research in particular subject fields. Examples of such collections might be African-American history, women's studies, or Asian studies.

Branch Libraries

Branch libraries consist of subject collections such as agriculture, business, chemistry, engineering, music, law, or architecture in libraries located away from the central library. These are conveniently located in buildings that serve the needs of students and faculty in a particular discipline.

 ## LIBRARY SERVICES

As more and more materials accumulate in libraries, the task of accessing stored information becomes more complex. While the introduction of computer technology into information handling has resulted in more efficient and faster methods of storing and retrieving information, it has not eliminated the need for basic library services. The services outlined below are representative of services offered in most academic libraries.

Librarians

An important and indispensable resource in any library is the librarian. In order to acquire, maintain, and disseminate the vast amount of information that is stored in libraries, trained personnel are needed. Most libraries require that their professional librarians have a master's degree or the equivalent from an American Library Association (ALA) accredited institution. Persons trained in librarianship or information sciences perform a variety of services: administrative, technical, and public.

◆ Administrators are concerned with the overall operation of the library and with the budget, staff, and physical plant.

◆ Technical service librarians are concerned with the acquisition, preparation, and maintenance of library materials. They are in charge of ordering and cataloging materials, serials check-in, sending materials to be bound, repairing damaged books, etc.

◆ Public service librarians are those who serve the patron directly as at a reference or circulation desk. They also select materials for the collection and provide outreach and instruction for the students and faculty.

Not everyone who works in a library is a professional librarian. Support staff such as clerks, paraprofessionals, and technicians help to maintain the library's services.

Library patrons are more familiar with public service librarians because these are the individuals with whom they come into contact when seeking assistance. Reference librarians are available to answer questions about the collection, to assist in using electronic reference tools, to help with search strategies, and generally to help locate and sort out information.

Reference Interview

When reference librarians are approached for assistance with a question that involves research, they conduct an informal reference interview to determine:

◆ the purpose of the research;
◆ the type of information desired (e.g., statistical, historical, etc.);
◆ specific questions to be answered, limitations (e.g., date, geographical, etc.);
◆ extent and findings of preliminary research.

It is important to ask appropriate questions during the reference interview and to be as specific as possible.

> **EXAMPLE** ■
>
> "Where can I find factual information on computer crimes among government workers?"
> **NOT**
> "Where are books on computers located?"

It is beneficial to conduct a preliminary search, such as searching the catalog, browsing, or looking up material in reference books, before approaching the reference desk for help. This enables you to focus on the type of information needed to deal with various aspects of the topic and then ask specific questions. It also gives the librarian a starting point from which to proceed in directing you to appropriate sources.

Circulation

Books and other materials are usually checked out from a centrally located desk that handles all matters dealing with the lending of library materials. In most libraries the circulation desk is located near the entrance or the exit of the library. Information regarding lending policies, fines, and schedules is available at the circulation desk. Many tasks such as checking books out and in, verifying circulation status, and sending out overdue and recall notices, once performed manually at the circulation desk, are now automated.

Electronic Reference Services

Electronic reference services are provided in a variety of ways:

(1) through acquisition of indexes and abstracts, reference books, and journals in electronic format;

(2) by identifying and providing access to free materials and services on the Internet; and

(3) by providing workstations, usually with print capabilities for accessing electronic information.

Most of the materials to which the libraries subscribe are now available over the Web, but some are in CD-ROM format. Reference librarians are responsible not only for selecting materials for purchase, but also for providing instruction and assistance in using the electronic resources.

Library Instruction

Library instruction is a service usually provided by reference librarians. It might include formal (for credit) courses, general orientation sessions, subject-related instruction, computer-assisted instruction, and individualized instruction. The reference librarians also prepare printed and online guides to the collection and to sources available on the Web.

Interlibrary Loan

The rising costs of library operations and acquisitions have forced more and more libraries to seek cooperation with other institutions in order to serve their patrons. Libraries lend each other books and other materials that are unavailable at the local library. The loans are for limited periods, and the costs of borrowing material (postage, handling, and duplication) are generally borne by the patron. If a lending library does not circulate an item, it may send photocopies. Patrons borrowing books are required to fill out forms giving accurate and complete information on the item they would like to borrow. This usually includes the author, title, publication information and a reference showing where the citation was found. Interlibrary loan is for specific titles only and not for subject requests such as "all the works on the Cold War."

Document Delivery

Document delivery is a library service that provides copies of materials from other libraries or vendors to users usually for a fee. It is usually administered by the interlibrary loan department. In some libraries, document delivery consists of the physical or electronic delivery of materials to the office or place of business of a library user. The term is also used to refer the concept of "documents on demand." Rather than subscribing to costly, low-use journals, the library subscribes to services that promise fast delivery of the articles. One of the largest document delivery services is the Colorado Alliance for Research Libraries (CARL). CARL is a database containing the full text of articles from several thousand journals. There is no charge to search the database, but if an individual or a library wants a copy of the article there is a charge, which includes the cost of reproducing and sending the article plus a copyright fee. The articles are usually sent by facsimile transmission (fax) to the individual or library requesting them.

Library Cooperatives

A practice that is prevalent among libraries today is that of forming cooperatives for the purpose of making holdings and services available to members and their patrons on a reciprocal basis. These groups are known by various names: library networks, information centers, or consortia. Some groups share general printed materials while others share specialized materials such as computing facilities, databases, periodicals, films, slides, and other audio-visual material.

Regional and state library systems, in which libraries in a geographical area share resources, are widespread throughout the United States. There are also national library networks in which members from different libraries all over the country cooperate to share resources. OCLC (Online Computer Library Center) is a national network with a variety of services ranging from shared cataloging to bibliographic searching. Members of OCLC may use its services to handle requests for interlibrary loan material, to catalog materials, and to help identify and locate materials.

Academic Libraries: Materials and Services

Instructor: _____ Course/Section: _____

Name: _____

Date: _____ Points: _____

Review Questions

1. How has technology changed the way we think of libraries?

2. What is meant by the term "format" in reference to information sources?

3. What is a serial?

   What is a periodical?

4. What is an e-journal?

5. What is the difference between a thesis and a dissertation?

6. What kinds of materials are included in audio-visual collections?

7. Name the forms of electronic information common to many libraries.

8. Which of the library materials discussed in this chapter are found in your library?

9. What are the differences between open and closed stacks in a library?

   What are the advantages and disadvantages of each?

10. What type of stack arrangement is used in your library?

11. What purpose does the reserve book department serve in the library?

12. What kinds of materials are found in an archives department?

13. Why is the reference librarian an important resource in the library?

14. What service does an interlibrary loan department perform for the library patron?

15. What are branch libraries? What are the branch libraries on your campus?

16. What is meant by the term "document delivery"?

17. Which of the library services discussed in this chapter does your library provide?

Academic Libraries: Materials and Services

Instructor: _____ Course/Section: _____

Name: _____

Date: _____ Points: _____

Parts of a Book

Using the library catalog or browsing the library stacks, select a book on a topic that interests you and examine its contents. Give the following information: (If you do not find some of these items, write NA (not applicable) in the blank.)

1. Call number:

2. Author's or authors' name(s): (If the book has an editor instead of an author, write "ed" after the name.)

3. Full title:

4. Place of publication: (Give first one listed.)

5. Publisher:

6. Edition (if given):

7. Date of latest copyright and publishing date:

8. Does the author state the purpose of the book? If so, state briefly what it is.

9. Is there an introduction? If so, identify two points made in the introduction.

10. Does the book have a table of contents?

11. Is there a list of maps or illustrations? If so, give pages.

12. Does the book have a bibliography? If so, give pages.

13. Does the book have an appendix? If so, what does it contain?

14. Does the book contain an index? If so, how many pages make up the index. What is its purpose?

15. Is there a glossary in the book? What is the purpose of a glossary?

16. Write a bibliographic citation for this book using the examples given in Appendix A.

Academic Libraries: Materials and Services

1

Instructor: _____ Course/Section: _____

Name: _____

Date: _____ Points: _____

Electronic Books

1. Go to each of the sites listed below. Describe what type of publications you find on the site.

    http://www.ipl.org/reading/books/

    http://chaucer.library.emory.edu/wwrp/index.html

    http://elf.chaoscafe.com/

    http://digital.library.upenn.edu/books/

    http://promo.net/pg/

2. From one of the sites in Question 1 select an e-book (a full-text book in electronic format). Compare the parts of an e-book with that of the paper copy of the book you reviewed in "Parts of a Book," Exercise 1.2. Which parts of the book described in Books in Chapter 1 are included in the online book you selected?

3.   What are the advantages of e-books?

What are the disadvantages?

Academic Libraries: Materials and Services

1

Instructor: _____ Course/Section: _____

Name: _____

Date: _____ Points: _____

Library Tour

Take a tour of your library and complete the exercise below. Write NA for any items that are not applicable for your library.

1. Look in the online catalog and locate a book on compulsive gambling and give the following information.

   a. Complete call number:

   b. Title of the book:

   c. Classification system:

   d. Where in the library is the book located?

2. Locate any reference book from the reference department and give the following information.

   a. Title of the book:

   b. Call number:

   c. Where in the reference area is it located? (e.g., reference stacks, ready reference, index tables)

3. Locate a book that has been assigned as reading for a course and give the following information.

   a. Title of the book:

   b. Course name and number for which the book is assigned:

4. Locate the latest copy of *U.S. News and World Report* and give the following information.

    a. Call number:

    b. Date of the issue and volume number:

    c. Title of one article from the issue:

    d. Inclusive pages of the article:

    e. Where in the library is it located?

5. Locate a copy of *U.S. News and World Report* that is five years old and give the following information.

    a. Call number:

    b. Date of the issue:

    c. Volume number:

    d. Title of one article from the issue:

    e. Inclusive pages of the article:

    f. Where in the library is it located?

6. Locate a recent issue of a newspaper from a city near your hometown (or any large city) and give the following information.

    a. Title of the newspaper:

    b. Date of the issue:

    c. Call number:

    d. In which department or area is it located?

7. Locate a U.S. government document and give the following information.

    a. Title of the document:

    b. Call number:

    c. In which department or area is it located?

8. Locate a recording of a musical work and give the following information.

    a. Title of the recording:

    b. Call number:

    c. In which department or area is it located?

9. Locate a computer workstation in the reference area. List five of the databases you can access on it.

    a.

    b.

    c.

    d.

    e.

Academic Libraries: Materials and Services

1

Instructor: _____ Course/Section: _____

Name: _____

Date: _____ Points: _____

Virtual Library Tour

Visit one of the "virtual library tours" on the Web sites below, or search "library virtual tour" using any search engine, and answer the questions that follow.

http://www.unmc.edu/library/virttour.html
http://tamu.edu/library/reference/virtual/tour00.html
http://juno.concordia.ca/tour/outline.html
http://www.lib.utc.edu/slide1.html

1. Go to the online catalog and locate a book on discrimination.
   Give the title, author, date, and call number of the work.

2. Is there a separate page linking to reference services and other departments in the library?
   If so, list the various departments here.

3. Is there a link to reserve books or a reserve collection?

4. Is there a library map on the page? Is it easy to understand?

5. How are the periodicals arranged in this library? Are they cataloged? Shelved alphabetically?
   Another system? All in one area, or shelved by call number within the stacks?

6. Where are the microforms housed? In a separate area? With periodicals?

7. Does this library have a government documents collection? If so, is it in a separate area, or combined with other cataloged material?

8. Is there a separate area for audio-visual material such as audio cassettes, video cassettes, etc.? If so, what name is given to this area?

9. Briefly compare the site to a printed library map or informational pamphlet. What are the advantages of the Web site? The disadvantages?

10. Based on what you have seen on the Internet tour, how does this library compare with your library? (For example, does it provide more materials? More services? Is it more attractive?)

2

The Research Paper

"The most original authors are not so because they advance what is new,
but because they put what they have to say
as if it had never been said before."

JOHANN WOLFGANG VON GOETHE

INTRODUCTION

Do you know what the Iditarod race is? Or have you ever wondered where you would find information on how to make cheese? Or, where you should go on your next vacation? Or, whether UFOs really do exist? Whether you go to an encyclopedia or other reference book, or you surf the Internet to find answers to these questions, you are doing research. Regardless of the objective, the research process consists of a systematic investigation to find information. For most of us, research consists of seeking out recorded knowledge—knowledge that is found in libraries or on the Internet. Most new knowledge is created by highly trained personnel in universities, in government, and in industry who conduct experiments or other types of original investigations. For the college student, research is an integral part of the learning process. Students are expected to prepare themselves for living by learning how to access information and how to use it efficiently and effectively. Instructors seeking to develop their students' information skills will usually rely on some type of formal research project—usually a formal essay requiring the student to use recorded knowledge. This can be a daunting experience, especially in light of the tremendous changes taking place in the way information is stored and retrieved. Some of the apprehensions related to doing research can be allayed once students learn how the research process works—how to organize and analyze information needs, how to locate and evaluate information, how to synthesize what is learned with original ideas and interpretations, and finally how to write and document the paper. This chapter will introduce you to the steps involved in researching and writing a research paper. Later chapters will concentrate on developing skills for finding and evaluating information in different types of resources.

◆ WHAT IS A RESEARCH PAPER?

The most common type of research project is the research paper, usually a formal essay based on an accumulation of facts gathered in the research process. The research paper offers the researcher an opportunity to examine issues, locate material relevant to an issue, digest, analyze, evaluate, and present the information with conclusions and interpretations. In preparing a research paper, you will do practical research in the library or on the Internet. You will not be expected to do the type of original research usually done by more advanced researchers. But your research paper will have an element of originality in that you will be putting together pieces of information from various sources in order to present a new view of a topic. For example, most people believe that the Democratic Party is more inclined to favor gun control than is the Republican Party. But what is the official view of the two parties on gun control? Are they in general agreement about the issue? And, if so, what does each espouse? Or is there disagreement among the members of each party on any aspects of gun control? Someone interested in this topic could examine the platforms of each party, look at the voting records and the arguments on the floors of the House and Senate, and find out what others outside of Congress have said on this topic. The writer of the paper would gather information from both primary and secondary sources and reach conclusions that would, in a sense, be new and original even though he or she used only recorded information.

▼ STEPS IN PREPARING A RESEARCH PAPER

It is helpful to approach the research paper assignment as a series of stages or steps. Some rather obvious steps are:

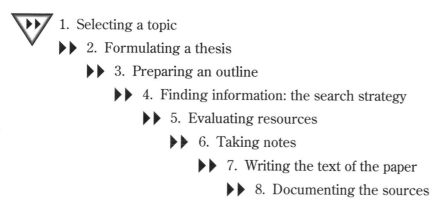

1. Selecting a topic
2. Formulating a thesis
3. Preparing an outline
4. Finding information: the search strategy
5. Evaluating resources
6. Taking notes
7. Writing the text of the paper
8. Documenting the sources

Selecting a Topic

Sometimes the initial step in the preparation of a research paper is the most challenging one. The selection of a topic is also the most crucial step in determining the success of the research paper. If your instructor assigns a topic, you need only determine how to proceed with the research. In most cases, however, you must choose your own topic. While this might tend to increase your apprehensions about the research paper, it also affords some exciting and rewarding possibilities. After all, research is about acquiring new knowledge and looking at information in new ways. The trick is to focus on a topic that interests you and to discover all the aspects that you want to work with. The best way to do this is to examine several possibilities systematically. Several overriding principles that should be considered in selecting a research topic are shown in Figure 2.1.

Most college research papers are fairly brief, usually between five and ten pages or roughly between 2,000 and 3,000 words. Thus it may be necessary to narrow the focus of an overly broad topic because it would not be possible to cover a broad general topic in so few words. Topics such as civil rights in the United States, World War II, and the pros and cons of abortion are much too broad to be covered in a short paper. The topic, "The Incidence of Divorce in My Home Town," is probably too narrow and too regional. It is best to focus first on a broader concept of a topic, then to narrow it to a manageable level. Often a preliminary search in one or more of the sources listed in Figure 2.2 will help you narrow the topic and at the same time help you determine if there is sufficient information available.

◆ Selecting a Topic	
Initial consideration	*Beware of topics that may be too*
◆ prior understanding of topic	◆ recent
◆ manageability of topic	◆ regional
◆ length of assignment/project	◆ emotional
◆ due date of assignment/project	◆ complex
◆ type of assignment/project	◆ broad
◆ availability of research materials	◆ narrow

Figure 2.1. Selecting a topic.

Figure 2.2. Sources to consult for a preliminary search on a topic.

Formulating a Thesis

After you have become somewhat familiar with the topic selected, the second step is to determine the *thesis* of the paper.

ASK YOURSELF

◆ What is the purpose of the paper?   ◆ What will be the focus?
◆ What is to be proven or shown in the paper?

The thesis statement is a concise statement of one or two sentences that provides a framework for the paper. The *search strategy*, or process to be used in locating information, is determined by the thesis since the information located must support the thesis. Some preliminary reading from one or two sources such as an encyclopedia article or a periodical article is probably sufficient to help formulate the thesis statement (see Figure 2.3).

Preparing an Outline

The third step in the process is to prepare a working outline that includes all facets of the topic to be investigated. The same preliminary sources used as a guide to narrow the topic and formulate the thesis statement are also helpful in compiling the outline. To be useful the outline should divide the thesis into a number of major points; each of the points should be further divided and subdivided until the writer can visualize the outline as a guide for research and as a skeleton for the final report. The process of subdividing should follow a logical sequence with related points grouped together (see Figure 2.4). The major points should be parallel, just as the subdivisions under each heading should be parallel. The main points in the outline should support the thesis statement. These should be assigned Roman numerals. The first subdivisions are given capital letters; the second, Arabic numbers; the third, lower-case letters. Use Arabic numbers in parenthesis if it is necessary to subdivide any further than this. Since each heading or subheading in the outline denotes a division, there must be more than one part if it is to be logical. Thus, if there is a I, there must be a II; if there is an A, there must be a B. The working outline is important to the search strategy since the search should be directed to the relevant points in the outline.

In the process of locating information, it is probable that other aspects of the topic not included in the working outline will be discovered and that the final outline will be changed and improved. As information is gathered the outline can be revised and new headings or subheadings added.

◆ Formulating a Thesis

Developing a Thesis

◆ Begin with a question—not an opinion. Don't just give the purpose of the paper.

◆ Conduct research to look for points that will shape or form an opinion.

◆ Final statement indicates that the thesis is supported by evidence. (Thesis statement should be brief—no more than three sentences.)

Sample Topic

The Glass Ceiling: Discrimination of Women in American Corporations

Initial Question

Does gender preference in American corporations prevent women from rising to positions of leadership on a par with men?

After Further Research

Does the "glass ceiling" really exist? Have women been denied promotions and salary benefits equal with men? Is there evidence to show that women have been grossly discriminated against in the business world? What factors prevent women from realizing their full potential in corporate America?

FINAL Thesis Statement

Despite the advances made by women during the last decade, women are still not on a par with men in the workplace. Women in the United States continue to face a glass ceiling preventing advancement to senior level management positions, especially in medium and large-sized corporations.

Figure 2.3. Formulating a thesis.

◆ Preliminary Topic Outline

Topic: The Glass Ceiling: Discrimination of Women in American Corporations

I. History
   A. Women in the labor force
      1. Traditional jobs
      2. The wage gap
   B. Men and traditional managerial and executive positions
   C. Reasons women historically denied parity with men

II. Sex discrimination in the workplace
   A. Case studies
   B. Statistics
   C. Sexual harassment

III. Legal interventions
   A. Civil Rights Act of 1964
   B. Reaffirmation by the Supreme Court in 1991 of the unlawfulness of sexual harassment as defined in Title VII
   C. The Glass Ceiling Commission

IV. Trends and issues
   A. Leveling the playing field
      1. Education
      2. Training and development
   B. Advances

Figure 2.4. Example of a preliminary topic outline.

Finding Information: The Search Strategy

Developing a Search Strategy

A search strategy is a plan of research. It usually involves two distinct phases:

1. analyzing the information you need, and
2. determining which search terms you should use to help you locate the information you need.

Figure 2.5 presents a brief overview of the factors you must focus on as you look for information.

Phase two involves selecting search terms to use in looking for information on your topic. Consult your thesis statement and your outline to come up with a list of key terms that will help guide your search. You might also think of related terms that are not on your list that might lead you to information on your topic. You should also include words that have broader or narrower meanings than your original terms. For example, the term "corporations" from the topic in the outline in Figure 2.6 might not be too useful in the research process; it would be more helpful to narrow the term to be more specific.

◆ What Do You Need to Know?	
Level of specificity	Do you need facts? opinions? background information? analyses? How much information do you need?
Time line	What is the time line of the information you need? Do you need an account of an event recorded at the time it happened? Does timeliness matter? Do you need current information? Or do you need a more historical presentation? Look at the date of the publication to determine currency and relevancy. For example, if you need information on the race riots in Tulsa, Oklahoma, in 1921, do you want newspaper articles written at the time of the event, or do you want articles written at any time since the event?
Focus	Do you need to focus on a specific subject area or discipline such as humanities, social science, or science? For example, if you were researching the causes of eating disorders among teenagers, would you look for information in scientific resources or would you look in the social sciences?
Level of scholarship	Do you need background information, or brief facts not backed by research? If so, you should use **popular** sources. If you need a more in-depth treatment, you should consult a **scholarly** source. (See Chapter 3 for a discussion of popular and scholarly sources.)
Type of information	Do you need an account of an event as it happened? **Primary** sources will allow you to get as close to an event or an account as possible. And although it does not provide analysis or interpretation, a primary source may be more factual. **Secondary** sources will provide analyses, explanations, or descriptions of primary sources. For a research paper, a good rule of thumb is to choose both primary and secondary sources when you have the opportunity. (See Chapter 3 for a discussion of the differences between primary and secondary sources.)

Figure 2.5. Analyzing your needs.

- ◆ BROAD TERM—CORPORATIONS
- ◆ NARROW TERM—EXECUTIVES
- ◆ NARROWER TERM—WOMEN EXECUTIVES

Figure 2.6. Determining search terms.

Use the sources listed in Figure 2.2 to help you select keywords. The *Library of Congress Subject Headings* (*LCSH*) would be especially helpful for finding appropriate terms.

Locating Appropriate Information Sources

Finally, you need to locate appropriate information sources. For this, you need to be somewhat familiar with the vast array of information sources that are available to you. Some of the materials you use will be located in the library in various formats such as paper, microform and CD-ROM. Others will be on the Internet. Later chapters of this book are devoted to analyzing the major sources to consult in the search process:

- ◆ the library catalog,
- ◆ the Internet,
- ◆ reference books,
- ◆ indexes and databases for periodical articles,
- ◆ government publications,
- ◆ biographical sources.

Asking for Help

Reference librarians can provide valuable assistance with research questions if they know what you are looking for. The key to getting assistance is knowing which questions to ask.

GUIDELINES FOR OBTAINING MAXIMUM HELP FROM THE LIBRARIAN

- ▼ Explain the purpose of the research.
- ▼ Give the assignment specifications—for example, length of paper, number of sources needed, and due date.
- ▼ Explain the level of difficulty of information you need—scholarly, technical, popular, easy-to-understand.
- ▼ Give the time framework—current, historical.
- ▼ Describe the kinds of sources needed—primary, secondary, or both.
- ▼ Ask for assistance for specific information that may be difficult to locate—statistics, dates, little-known facts.

◆ Guide to Selecting Sources		
Information	*Sources to Consult*	*Finding Aids*
Preliminary Ideas	*Library of Congress Subject Headings* magazine and journal articles	consult reference staff browse current periodicals Internet
Overview of Topic	general encyclopedias books periodicals	consult reference staff library catalog indexes and abstracts
Definitions	dictionaries	library catalog
Primary Sources	newspapers research reports manuscripts (archives) government publications	library catalog databases (e.g., *Academic Universe*) Internet
Secondary Sources	books magazine and journal articles subject encyclopedias	library catalogs indexes and abstracts databases
Facts	almanacs and yearbooks statistics government publications	library catalogs statistical indexes Internet
Current Information	newspapers magazines and journals	indexes and abstracts databases (e.g., *Academic Universe*)
Historical Information	books encyclopedias and reference books periodicals	library catalog browse reference shelves indexes and abstracts
Evaluative Sources	book reviews biographies	indexes to book reviews Internet

Figure 2.7. Selecting appropriate sources.

Evaluating Sources

You should evaluate each source that you locate for its suitability and its overall reliability. First of all, the information should be relevant to your thesis and the points covered in your outline. Further, is the information sufficiently up-to-date? Is the latest edition of a work available? Is the source reliable? Does the work reflect a particular prejudice? Use the criteria listed in Chapter 3 to evaluate the information you find.

Taking Notes

As you examine each source, you should take notes on all the important facts and opinions you might want to use in your paper. The best way to take notes is to use separate note cards or uniform sheets of paper for each topic that you locate. (If you are using a word processor, you need only create a separate document for each topic.) Each note card or note document should contain a heading that is keyed to a heading in your outline. As you take notes, it is best to paraphrase or summarize the words of the author, although sometimes direct quotations are needed for emphasis or for authoritativeness. In either case it is important to retain the author's intended meaning. Note the page or pages on which you found the information. Include all the essential bibliographic information: author or editor's name, title of the work, series (if any), publisher, date, and place of publication. It is helpful to include the call numbers of books and periodicals and the URL (Internet address) of materials found on the Web in case you need to go back to these.

Writing the Paper

Once you are satisfied that sufficient information has been gathered to support all the points in your outline, you can begin to write a first draft of the paper. Sort the notes so that they are grouped under topics that fit the headings in the outline. The research paper, by definition, is based primarily on evidence gathered from other sources. It demands a great deal of creativity to assimilate evidence and present it so that it gives the reader a new perspective. Allow yourself sufficient time for the actual writing. It may take several drafts to achieve the well-written research paper. As you write the paper, pay careful attention to all the elements of good writing: effective phrasing of ideas, good paragraph development, and logical flow of the paragraphs into a unified paper.

Documenting the Sources

Plagiarism

Plagiarism is the appropriation of ideas or the copying of the language of another writer without formal acknowledgment. Plagiarism is a serious violation of legal and ethical canons; yet many students who would not dare copy another's examination paper think nothing of "borrowing" ideas and even exact language from another writer without giving credit. This is not to say that you must document every single thing you write. Those ideas that evolved in your own mind, even though they are a result of your research, do not require documentation. Nor is it necessary to document facts considered common knowledge. Ordinarily you should not have difficulty determining what is common knowledge. Some facts will appear over and over in the readings. Well-known facts, such as the date of America's entry into World War I, require no documentation. Little-known facts, or facts about which you have no prior knowledge, such as details of President Wilson's peace proposals, would require documentation. If you have any doubt as to whether or not a fact is common knowledge, you should acknowledge the source.

Copyright

Copyright is the legal protection of any published or unpublished literary, musical, dramatic, pictorial or other audiovisual work, including publications and postings on the Internet. Copyright laws grant the owner the exclusive right to reproduce, sell, distribute, or display a work that he has created. No one else may make a copy or use any copyrighted works without explicit consent of the owner, except for "fair use" in education, research, and news reporting. Even so, there are limitations as to what can be copied and the extent of use of copied materials. For example, it is okay to copy an article for personal use; however, it is not okay to make multiple copies of the article for distribution. Works that are not copyrighted are said to be in the public domain. That is, anyone has the right to reproduce or use them without restriction. Certain government publications and works produced before 1923 are usually in the public domain. The terms of the copyright vary but most works produced after 1978 may be copyrighted for the life of the owner plus 70 years.

Copyright has taken on new significance with the advent of computer technology and the Internet. It is extremely easy, and tempting, to copy text and images from Web pages and to paste them into a document you might be creating. It is also tempting to use existing HTML coding to create Web pages. While you may use parts of a text if you document properly, you may not use the entire pages, or images, or HTML text without permission of the owner of the copyrighted material.

Documentation Style

It is expected that a research paper will be documented since by definition it includes ideas and facts gathered from other sources. To document a research paper means to acknowledge, or cite, the sources used or consulted. While there is no one "correct" form for documentation, convention dictates that in a formal research paper the writer must follow a prescribed style—one that is consistent throughout and that communicates clearly and accurately the sources that are being documented. Some scholarly disciplines recommend a style that is peculiar to that field. Your instructor may require that you use a certain style to document research for a particular assignment. The library has style manuals that provide models for documenting research. Many English composition textbooks contain a section on writing and documenting a research paper. You can also find style manuals on the Internet. The style manual that is used in this text is the *MLA Handbook for Writers of Research Papers*, hereafter referred to as the *MLA Handbook*. It is widely used in the humanities and social sciences. Table 2.1 is a selected list of style manuals useful for documenting your research. You should consult with your instructor in selecting one that is appropriate for your assignment.

Forms of Documentation

The citations used in documentation sources generally appear in two places in a research paper:

1. within the text, immediately following the sentence to which the citation refers, and
2. at the end of the paper in a "works cited" list or a bibliography.

TABLE 2.1. ◆ Style Manuals

The Chicago Manual of Style: The Essential Guide for Writers, Editors, and Publishers. 14th ed. Chicago: U of Chicago P, 1993.

Crane, Nancy C. "Bibliographic Formats for Citing Electronic Information." Based on *A Handbook for Citing Electronic Information.* 29 Oct 1997 University of Vermont. 23 Feb 2000 <http://www.uvm.edu/~ncrane/estyles/>.

Garner, Diane L., and Diane H. Smith. *The Complete Guide to Citing Government Information Resources: A Manual for Writers and Librarians.* Rev. ed. Chicago: ALA, 1993.

Gibaldi, Joseph. *MLA Handbook for Writers of Research Papers.* 5th ed. New York: MLA, 1999.

Li, Xia, and Nancy C. Crane. *Electronic Styles: A Handbook for Citing Electronic Information.* Rev. ed. Medford, NJ: Information Today, 1996.

Publication Manual of the American Psychological Association (APA). 4th ed. Washington: APA, 1994.

Turabian, Kate L. *A Manual for Writers of Term Papers, Theses, and Dissertations.* 6th ed. Chicago: U of Chicago P, 1996.

There are several acceptable methods of acknowledging the sources used within the text. These include:

1. parenthetical references,
2. notes, and
3. full bibliographic citation in the text.

Parenthetical References

The *MLA Handbook* (Sec. 4.2) recommends the use of parenthetical references in which citations in the text are keyed to a list of *Works Cited* as the preferred method for documenting sources used in a reference work. The *Works Cited* is a list with full bibliographic descriptions, sometimes referred to as bibliographic entries, of all the sources that were used and acknowledged in the text. The source in the text is identified by a brief reference in parenthesis to the corresponding reference in the list of *Works Cited*. Usually the author's last name and the page(s) cited in the text are sufficient for identification:

In the text of the paper:

```
"Women at the highest levels . . . comprise only 10% of senior managers
in Fortune 500 companies; less than 4% of the uppermost ranks of CEO,
president, executive vice president, and COO; and less than 3% of top
corporate earners" (Meyerson and Fletcher 126).
```

If the author is mentioned in the text, it is not necessary to repeat the author's name in the citation.

```
Meyerson and Fletcher contend that it took a revolution to get women
where they are today, but now a softer approach based on "small-wins" or
incremental changes that chip away at biases is needed to shatter the
glass ceiling (126).
```

In the Works Cited *list:*

```
Meyerson, Debra E., and Joyce K. Fletcher. "A Modest Manifesto for Shat-
    tering the Glass Ceiling." Harvard Business Review 78.1 (2000): 126-36.
```

If the parenthetical reference is to a work that is listed by title in *Works Cited*, use the title or a shortened form of the title. The reference "World for Women" is sufficient to identify the title and page reference for the article cited below. (Note that in research papers and unpublished manuscripts, words that are normally in italics, such as titles, are underlined.)

```
"A World for Women: Changes Affecting the Role of Women Over Time."
    The Economist. 31 Dec. 1999: 47+. InfoTrac: General BusinessFile ASAP.
    The Gale Group. LOUIS: Louisiana Library Network, Baton Rouge. 22 Feb.
    2000 <http://infotrac.galegroup.com/itweb/lln%5Falsu/>.
```

Notes

Some scholars, particularly in the arts and humanities, prefer to use *notes* to document sources used. Notes cited in the text may appear at the bottom of the page (footnotes) or at the end of the paper (endnotes). When notes are used for documentation, the documented material is indicated in the text with a *superscript* (a raised Arabic number) placed after the punctuation mark of material that is cited. The numbers are keyed to numbers in the notes. The first reference to the work contains full bibliographic information—author, title, and publication information. Subsequent references to the same work are cited in brief.

The note numbers should be consecutive throughout the paper. When endnotes are used for documentation, it is usually not necessary to include a separate bibliography or *Works Cited* list in the paper.

In the text of the paper:

. . . A number of government policies and a stronger business culture have resulted in a more favorable climate for women in business.[1]

. . . "When median earnings of women are compared with those of men of a similar age and similar levels of education, major fields of study, and occupational characteristics, however, the earnings gap narrowed progressively."[2] . . . Although affirmative action litigation has significantly increased hiring of women in lower echelons of government, female representation in higher positions such as city councilors or mayors was not significantly affected.[3]

In the footnotes or endnotes:

[1] Robert L. Nelson and William P. Bridges, <u>Legalizing Gender Inequality: Courts, Markets, and Unequal Pay for Women in America</u>, Structural Analysis in the Social Sciences, 16 (New York: Cambridge, 1999) 10.

[2] Daniel E. Hecker, "Earnings of College Graduates: Women Compared with Men," <u>Monthly Labor Review</u> 121.3 (1998), <u>EBSCOhost: Academic Search Elite</u>, LLN (Louisiana Library Network), Baton Rouge 22 Feb. 2000 <http://search.epnet.com/>.

[3] Nelson and Bridges 6.

The use of the terms *ibid.* (in the same place), *op. cit.* (in the work cited) and *loc. cit.* (in the place cited) is no longer recommended in most style manuals. Rather, the work being cited is identified with the relevant page numbers. In most cases the author's last name is sufficient to identify the work. If two or more different titles by the same author are being cited, the citation should include a shortened form of the title after the author's last name. References to Gwendolyn Mink's *The Wages of Motherhood* and her *Welfare's End* would be cited in subsequent references as follows:

[4] Mink, <u>Wages</u> 48.
[5] Mink, <u>Welfare's</u> 150.

Full Bibliographic Citation in the Text

Use a full bibliographic reference in the text to cite a source only when one or two references are cited.

The MLA advises against using complete citations in the text because it deprives the reader of the benefits of a list of works cited and interrupts the flow of the text (Gibaldi, Joseph. <u>MLA Handbook for Writers of Research Papers</u>, 3rd ed. New York: MLA, 1988, 182).

Works Cited

The *Works Cited* list identifies all the books, articles from periodicals, government documents, theses and dissertations, articles from reference books, information from the Internet, and other sources of information that were used in writing the paper. Each entry, referred to as a bibliographical entry, contains all the essential elements needed to identify the work—author, title, series, publication information, depending on the work being described. The *Works Cited* list is placed at the end of the paper. The term *Works Consulted* is used if the list includes additional works that were not cited in the text of the paper.

Items in the *Works Cited* section of the paper should be arranged alphabetically according to the last name of the author. If a work has more than one author, only the first name listed is inverted. If an item is listed by title rather than author, it is placed alphabetically by words in the title, excluding the initial articles *a, an,* or *the*. For example, *The Encyclopaedia Britannica* would be alphabetized by *Encyclopaedia*. If two or more entries have the same author, the author's name is not repeated. A three space line is used to indicate the omission of the name. The first line of each entry is placed in hanging *indentation*. That is, it begins five spaces to the left of the following lines in the entry. An example of a *Works Cited* list for a research paper on women and wages is provided in Table 2.2.

Bibliography

Another name for a *Works Cited* list is *a bibliography*. It is a broader term that encompasses other types of listings. For example, a bibliography may list works by one author (an *author* bibliography), or it may list works on a subject (a *subject* bibliography). A *selective* bibliography includes only some of the possible references, while a *complete* bibliography lists all the references available. Bibliographies with descriptive notes about each entry are called *annotated* bibliographies. The items in a bibliography may be grouped according to their form of publication. For example, books may be listed in one group and periodicals in a second group. Within each group, the items are arranged in alphabetical order.

TABLE 2.2. ◆ Sample Works Cited List

"Equal Rights Amendment." Encyclopaedia Britannica Online. 23 Feb. 2000 <http://www.search.eb.com/bol/topic?eu=33409&sctn=1#s_top>.

Federal Glass Ceiling Commission. "Good for Business: Making Full Use of the Nation's Human Capital." The Glass Ceiling Fact Finding Report. 8 Mar. 1996. Electronic Archive: The Glass Ceiling Commission. Catherwood Library, School of Industrial and Labor Relations, Cornell University. 23 Feb. 2000 <http://www.ilr.cornell.edu/library/e_archive/glassceiling/>.

Freedman, Marcia. Shifts in Labor Market Structure and Patterns of Occupational Training. 8 May 1996. Women's Studies Database. University of Maryland. 22 Feb. 2000 <http://www.inform.umd.edu/EdRes/Topic/WomensStudies/GenderIssues/WomenInWorkforce/ContingentLabor/Implications/freedman>.

Hecker, Daniel E. "Earnings of College Graduates: Women Compared with Men." Monthly Labor Review 121.3 (1998): 62+. EBSCOhost: Academic Search Elite. EBSCOhost Web. LLN (Louisiana Library Network), Baton Rouge. 22 Feb. 2000 <http://search.epnet.com/>.

Hill, Elizabeth T. "Marital History, Post-School-Age Training and Wages: Women's Experiences." Social Science Journal 31.2 (1994): 127-38.

Mink, Gwendolyn. <u>The Wages of Motherhood: Inequality in the Welfare State</u>. Ithaca: Cornell UP, 1995.

---. <u>Welfare's End</u>. Ithaca: Cornell UP, 1998.

Meyerson, Debra E., and Joyce K. Fletcher. "A Modest Manifesto for Shattering the Glass Ceiling." <u>Harvard Business Review</u> 78.1 (2000): 126-36.

<u>Negotiating the Glass Ceiling: Careers of Senior Women in the Academic World</u>. Ed. Miriam David and Diana Woodward. Washington: Falmer, 1998.

Nelson, Robert L., and William P. Bridges. <u>Legalizing Gender Inequality: Courts, Markets, and Unequal Pay for Women in America</u>. Structural Analysis in the Social Sciences, 16. New York: Cambridge UP, 1999.

"Number of Workers with Earnings..." <u>Statistical Abstract of the United States, 1991</u>. Table 656.

Phelan, Jo. "The Paradox of the Contented Female Worker: An Assessment of Alternative Explanations." <u>Social Psychology Quarterly</u> 57.2 (1994): 95-105.

Reskin, Barbara F., and Irene Padavic. <u>Women and Men at Work</u>. Thousand Oaks, CA: Pine Forge, 1994.

Sochen, June. "Women's Rights." <u>Compton's Encyclopedia</u>. 1991.

Stuhlmacher, Alice F., and Amy E. Walters. "Gender differences in Negotiation Outcome: A Meta Analysis." <u>Personnel Psychology</u> 52.3 (1999): 653-77. <u>ABI/INFORM Global</u>. ProQuest Direct, LOUIS: Louisiana Library Network, Baton Rouge 23 Feb. 2000 <http://proquest.umi.com/pqdweb>.

Taeuber, Cynthia M., ed. <u>Statistical Handbook on Women in America</u>. 2nd ed. Phoenix, AZ: Oryx, 1996.

Tang, Alisa. "Executive Women at the Top: Still a Very Lonely Club." <u>New York Times</u> 17 Nov. 1999, sec. G: 1.

United States. Dept. of Labor. Bureau of Labor Statistics. <u>What Women Earned in 1998</u>. Washington: GPO, 1999.

"A World for Women: Changes Affecting the Role of Women Over Time." <u>The Economist</u>. 31 Dec. 1999: 47+. <u>InfoTrac: General BusinessFile ASAP</u>. The Gale Group. LOUIS: Louisiana Library Network, Baton Rouge. 22 Feb. 2000 <http://infotrac.galegroup.com/itweb/lln%5Falsu/>.

The Research Paper

Instructor: _____ Course/Section: _____

Name: _____

Date: _____ Points: _____

Review Questions

1. Name the steps involved in writing a research paper.

    a.

    b.

    c.

    d.

    e.

    f.

    g.

    h.

2. What three things should be considered in developing a thesis?

    a.

    b.

    c.

3. What are the major information sources to consult when doing library research?

4. List four factors you should focus on when selecting sources for research.

    a.

    b.

    c.

    d.

5. Define plagiarism.

6. What is meant by copyright?

7. What is the purpose of documentation in a research paper?

8. Name and describe three methods of documenting a research paper.

   a.

   b.

   c.

9. What is the difference between a list of *Works Cited* and a list of *Works Consulted*?

The Research Paper

Instructor: _____ Course/Section: _____

Name: _____

Date: _____ Points: _____

Selelcting a Topic

The first step in writing a research paper is to select a topic. This exercise will help you focus on a topic and the aspect you want to research. Select a topic you might want to use for a 10-page research paper in one of your classes.

1.   Topic:

2.   Write questions or statements you can make about this topic today, based on what you already know about it.

a.

b.

c.

3.   Would you approach this topic from a social science, humanities, or science perspective? Explain.

4.   What keywords or terms might you use to find information on this topic?

5.   What kind of library materials might you use for this topic? (e.g., books, articles, statistics)

6. Would you expect to find mostly popular or scholarly sources?

7. Would you expect to find mostly primary or secondary sources on this topic?

The Research Paper

Instructor: _____ Course/Section: _____

Name. _____

Date: _____ Points: _____

Preliminary Research

Topic:

1. General background information: list sources used to find an overview of the topic.

2. Use *LCSH* (*Library of Congress Subject Headings*) to find:

   Main approved terms

   Narrow terms

   Broader terms

   Related terms

3. Perspective: What approach do you plan to take for this topic? (Humanities, social science, or science?)

4. Suggested search statement or phrase:

The Research Paper

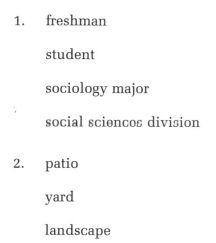

Instructor: _____ Course/Section: _____

Name: _____

Date: _____ Points: _____

Accessing Information: General to Specific

To begin searching for information, it is often necessary to consider several aspects of the topic. Practice arranging the following topics by placing them in numbered order from 1 to 4, with 1 being the most specific and 4 being the most general.

1. freshman

    student

    sociology major

    social sciences division

2. patio

    yard

    landscape

    barbeque pit

3. butterfly

    nature

    science

    entomology

4. Explorer

    automobiles

    Ford Motor Co.

    vehicles

Each of the terms below is very specific. For each, use two other terms that are general.

5.   penny loafer

6.   Dead Sea

The Research Paper

Instructor: _____ Course/Section: _____

Name: _____

Date: _____ Points: _____

Works Cited Exercise

Using the information provided below, prepare a list of citations as though you were preparing a *Works Cited* list for a research paper. Use the examples provided in Appendix A.

1. A definition of "vegetarianism" in a book entitled Mosby's Medical, Nursing, and Allied Health Dictionary, Edition 5, 1998, page 92, A4, copyright 1998 by Mosby-Year Book, Inc., of St Louis, Missouri.

2. A news report entitled "Vegetarian Dinosaurs," that is an article about new research on fossils of small dinosaurs discovered in China that shows mineral grains inside the rib cages. The article was written by Henry Fountain and appeared in The New York Times, December 7, 1999, page 5, section D, col 1.

3. An article entitled "Social Psychological and Structural Influences on Vegetarian Beliefs" by Linda Kalof, Thomas Dietz, and Gregory A. Guagnano in the journal, Rural Sociology, September 1999, volume 64, issue 3, page 500 and continued on other pages.

4. An article entitled "Vegetarianism in Young Women: Another Means of Weight Control?" by Simon M. Gilbody, Sara F.L. Kirk, and Andrew J. Hill in The International Journal of Eating Disorders, July 1999, volume 26, pages 87–90. The full text of the article is found in InfoTrac, Expanded Academic Index, available from River Oak Community College, Detroit. The URL is http://web2.infotrac.galegroup.com/. The article was accessed on the 3rd of June, 2000.

5. A book by Tarang Sheth and Tej Sheth entitled Why be a vegetarian?, published in 1995 by Jain Publishing Company, located in Fremont, California.

6. A government document, entitled Vegetarian Diets: the Pluses and the Pitfalls, by the Department of Health and Human Services, Public Health Services, Food and Drug Administration, in 1994, and published by the Government Printing Office in Washington, D.C.

7. A posting on a bulletin board by Reed Mangels on Tue Feb 8 14:36:02 2000, that you accessed on the 10th of June, 2000. The name of the group that hosts the bulletin board is the Vegetarian Resource Group. The URL for this particular posting is: http://www.vrg.org/feedback/ #SUBJECT.

3

Evaluating Information Sources

*"This is the best book ever written by any man on the wrong side
of a question of which he is profoundly ignorant."*

THOMAS B. MACAULAY

INTRODUCTION

As you do research you will find that the library has a lot to offer by way of information: books, periodical articles, reference materials, and access to the Internet. Never before has there been so much information available or so many ways to disseminate and retrieve it. Even as you read this, Web sites are being created, books and newspapers are being published, and new ways of storing and retrieving information are being developed. Many have characterized what is happening as "information overload." As someone looking for information, you will need to know not only how to locate information, but also how to evaluate the information that you locate. You will find that not all information sources are suitable for your research; nor is all information reliable. How critical are you? Can you tell the difference between propaganda and fact? Can you spot a hoax? Can you determine whether an author is "profoundly ignorant about the wrong side of a question"? Confronted with the wide array of print, electronic, oral, and visual resources available, you need to be able to make independent judgments about the suitability and the quality of the sources you locate. This chapter will provide you with criteria both for selecting appropriate materials and evaluating the materials you find.

◆ UNDERSTAND THE SOURCES

One of the first things you should be able to do as you locate and use information is to identify whether a source is a *primary* source or a secondary source and to understand the level of scholarship—whether the treatment of the topic is *popular* or *scholarly*. These concepts are critical to any evaluation of materials.

Primary Sources

Primary sources are firsthand accounts such as diaries, journals, letters—anything that is considered a direct source. That is, the author is actually a direct participant in or an observer of a research project or an event. It is also any raw data, such as census data or facts such as those gathered in a newspaper account. The test of whether or not something is a primary source is whether it is actual evidence without any interpretation or analysis beyond what the observer provided.

Secondary Sources

A secondary source, on the other hand, provides an analysis, an explanation, or a restatement of a primary source. Many secondary sources use primary sources to prove a point or to try to persuade the reader to hold a certain opinion.

For example, an article entitled "Methods of Pay Earnings: A Longitudinal Analysis" in *Industrial and Labor Relations Review* uses data from the National Longitudinal Survey of Youth, a primary source, to show level and variance of wages among workers.

Popular and Scholarly Sources

Popular sources are intended for general audiences who are not experts in the field. The information is presented in such a way that a wide range of readers or viewers can understand it. For example, if you are looking for an analytical treatment of the topic "effects of television violence on viewers' aggression," you are more likely to find the information you need in the *Psychological Bulletin* than in the popular magazine *Time*. An article on the subject in *Time* will not provide in-depth coverage of the subject. Because *Time* is aimed at a different audience, its approach is to provide readers with factual reporting, mostly devoid of analysis, and to be as brief as possible in its coverage. It might summarize the results of a study but would not provide the kind of in-depth analysis you might need. The *Psychological Bulletin* is a refereed journal; its purpose is to present the results of studies, experiments, surveys, or other types of research by its authors. An article in *Psychological Bulletin* is likely to provide an analytical approach that is backed by specific research and includes documentation. Keep in mind that each of the two levels of information might fill a different need.

Popular sources are not limited to magazines and journals. Reference books, books that you locate in the library's catalog, and Internet sources may also be popular or scholarly. *World Book Encyclopedia*, for example, is a general encyclopedia intended for a wide audience; the *Encyclopedia of Psychology* is a very specialized subject encyclopedia that has been written by authors selected for their expertise in the field.

INITIAL APPROACH

The first step for evaluating information takes place before you begin the actual search. You must begin any search with two basic questions.

 ASK YOURSELF

◆ What do I need to know?　◆ What sources are likely to provide the information I need?

◆　What Do You Need to Know?

It is best to approach this question by examining your information needs in light of five basic factors:

- level of specificity
- time line needed
- focus
- level of scholarship
- type of information

Figure 2.5 addresses this question in more detail.

◆　What Sources Are Likely to Provide the Information You Need?

Becoming proficient in finding information will require experience. Chapters 5 through 12 will introduce you to various information sources: books, Internet, periodical articles, encyclopedias, and government documents. As you develop skills in using these sources you will become more adept at matching your needs with the materials available to you. You should begin by examining the body of the source. Read the preface of a book to determine the author's purpose. Scan the table of contents and the index to get a broad overview of the material it covers. Peruse journals and magazines, reference book articles, and Internet sources to see if they contain the information you need. Note whether documentation and bibliographies are included that will lead to additional sources. Read the relevant parts of the book or article that specifically address your topic. As you locate sources of information you need to cast a more critical eye on the content. Are the sources reliable, fair, objective, lacking hidden motives? The next section of this chapter will provide you with some criteria to help you evaluate the worth of the information you locate.

APPLYING EVALUATION CRITERIA

The ability to determine the suitability and worth of a particular source is one of the most important research skills you can acquire. It is also one of the most difficult because you are dealing primarily with unknowns. The task is further complicated by the fact that there are so many different formats to deal with—books, periodicals, reference books, CD-ROMS, Internet resources. Most of the books and periodicals that you find in the library have already undergone some evaluative process. Publishers edit books and periodicals; articles in scholarly journals are "refereed" by peers in the field; librarians employ evaluative techniques in selecting materials for their collections. Information on the Internet, on the other hand, has not undergone any such selection process, so you will have to be especially vigilant when you use information found on the Internet. There is no single test that you can apply to determine whether a work is reliable or whether the contents are accurate or truthful. Instead, you must make a judgment based on a number of clues or indicators.

Table 3.1 is a set of criteria together with questions and discussion that can serve as a checklist to help you evaluate books, periodical articles or Internet information that you locate.

◆ EVALUATING INTERNET SOURCES

Anyone from anywhere in the world who has access to a computer and connectivity to the Internet can become a publisher. Individuals and groups are creating information on the Internet of every kind imaginable (articles, letters, facts, statistics, maps, family albums, teaching materials) and for purposes equally as varied—to inform, to sell, to teach, to persuade, or to dispel loneliness and boredom. This has resulted in a proliferation of information never before thought possible; some might argue that it has caused "information pollution." Information on the Internet ranges in quality from excellent to downright bad.

Unlike most print resources such as magazines, journals, and books that are subjected to some type of selection process (editing, peer review, library selection), information on the Internet is almost totally lacking in quality control. The onus rests with the user to determine the quality and reliability of information on the Internet. In any information that is posted on the Web there are some telltale signs that should lead you to suspect the credibility of the information: poor grammar, misspelling, or inflammatory words. Beyond the obvious things you should also be able to apply some criteria to determine the quality of a work. The same criteria that are listed in Table 3.1 can be used to evaluate Internet resources; however, because of the unique nature of information on the Internet, you need to apply a slightly different checklist (see Table 3.2).

◆ EVALUATIVE REVIEWS

You may be able to locate critical reviews of books in a reviewing source, such as *Book Review Index* or *Book Review Digest*. (See Chapter 12 to learn how to use these.) Book reviews may provide a more in-depth analysis than the one you are able to make by applying the criteria above. Book reviews may appear in journals dedicated solely to reviewing books, or they may appear in subject-based professional journals. Book reviews help answer such questions as whether the book makes a valuable contribution to the field, contains accurate information, or is overly biased or controversial. Articles in scholarly journals are refereed: that is, the authors' peers in the field have subjected them to critical review before publication. Many of the online databases will indicate whether or not a journal is refereed.

Evaluations of Web sites appear in many journals and magazines. Many Web pages list all of the awards they have won. For example, the page entitled "All the Virology on the WWW" has a separate page listing all of the awards it has received (http://www.virology.net/ATVaward.html). The authors of this page claim to be the "single site for virology information on the Internet." They list reviews as well as awards that will help you determine whether the claims are, indeed, well founded.

TABLE 3.1. ◆ Evaluating Print Material

Authoritativeness

Author
◆ What are the author's education, training, and level of expertise or experience in the field?
  Look for biographical information, the author's title, employment, position, and institutional affiliation.
◆ Are there other works in the same field by this author?
  Check the online catalog and databases on the same subject.
◆ What is the author's reputation or standing among peers?
  If a journal article, check to see if it is a refereed journal.
  If a signed article in a subject encyclopedia, read the preface to see how authors were selected.
◆ If the author is a corporation or an agency, is it one that is well known in the field?

Publisher
◆ Is the publisher well known in the field?
◆ Are there many works published by this publisher?
  Check the online catalog to find other books by the publisher.
◆ Does a university press publish the source?
◆ Is the publisher a professional organization?
  Generally one can assume that reputable publishers, professional associations, or university presses will publish high quality materials.

Comprehensiveness

◆ Are all aspects of the subject covered or have obvious facts been omitted?
  Examine the table of contents of books or peruse the article or Web source.
◆ Does the work update other sources or does it add new information?
  These questions may be difficult for the novice researcher to answer, but comparing information in one source with that in another may provide some answers. For example, compare the coverage of "black holes" in *World Book Encyclopedia* with the article on the same topic in *McGraw-Hill Encyclopedia of Science and Technology*.
◆ Is the source too elementary, too technical, too advanced, or just right for your needs?
◆ What type of audience is the author addressing?
◆ Is the information aimed at a specialized or a general audience?

Reliability

Objectives or Biased Treatment
◆ Do the facts support the author's viewpoint?
◆ Do you detect individual biases in the writing?
◆ Does the author use language that is designed to appeal to emotions and biases?
◆ What is the author's motive in writing the work?
  Knowing something about the author's background, training, and other works is useful in determining possible bias. Often this information can be obtained from biographical dictionaries and indexes. The periodical indexes and abstracts might be checked to see if the author has written biased literature or if there has been controversy surrounding his or her publications.
◆ Is the information that is presented fact or opinion?
  It is not easy to separate fact from opinion. Facts can usually be verified; opinions, though they may be based on factual information, are based on the author's interpretation of facts. Skilled writers can manipulate their opinions so as to make you think their interpretations are facts. Note whether the work is well researched and documented.

◆ Is the work propaganda?

We can recognize propaganda when it is in a leaflet that is handed out on the street corner, but can we recognize it in other media? Propaganda is material that is systematically distributed to advocate a point of view or a strongly held interest on an issue. Its purpose is to influence and change the opinions and behavior of others. Those who use propaganda tend to capitalize on events by playing on emotions and by exploiting human weaknesses and fears. However, all propaganda is not negative, especially when it is designed to accomplish good, such as a campaign to stop the use of drugs among teenagers or to combat neighborhood crimes. Politicians use propaganda when campaigning for public office; businesses use it to sell products. The need to recognize propaganda has taken on new meaning with the advent of the Internet. The Internet, as no other media in history, allows individuals from every walk of life and from throughout the world to put out messages that are designed to persuade and influence others to accept their point of view. You must be able to use your best judgment to distinguish propaganda from truly objective literature.

Accuracy

◆ Is the information correct, or are there obvious errors in the information?

It may be necessary to sample several sources to determine if there are inconsistencies in reporting such things as times, dates, and places. Statistical information is vulnerable to such inaccuracies, and one might do well to verify statistical information in more than one source whenever this is possible.

◆ Does the author cite the sources used?

◆ Does the author use primary or secondary sources?

Illustrations

◆ Does the work contain pictures, drawings, maps, or statistical tables that enhance its usefulness?

The use of illustrations not only makes a book or article more interesting, but also makes a significant contribution to the understanding of the materials being presented.

Currency

Date of Publication

◆ When was the work published?

◆ Is the information up-to-date or have discoveries been made or events taken place since the work was published?

To determine currency of information, you might check journal articles on the same topic to see if there have been new events or developments. On Web pages, the date of the last revision is usually at the bottom of the home page, or sometimes on every page.

◆ Is the source current or out-of-date for your topic?

Current information is needed in areas that undergo constant and frequent changes such as in the pure and behavioral sciences. On the other hand, material that was written many years ago is often more suitable for topics in history and literature than those written more recently.

TABLE 3.2. ◆ Evaluating Internet Information

Authoritativeness

Author
- ◆ Is the author's name listed on the page?
  In many instances Web pages are created by Web masters whose expertise is more in page design than in familiarity with the content of the page. Also beware of anonymity.
- ◆ Is the author qualified to write on this subject?
- ◆ Are his or her education, training, and/or experience in a field relevant to the topic that is covered?
  Look on the page for biographical information, such as the author's title or position.
- ◆ Has the author published in other formats?
- ◆ Is there a way to contact the author? (E-mail or other address provided?)
- ◆ If the author is an organization, is it one that is well known and respected?

Comprehensiveness

- ◆ Is this a summary of a topic or does it cover all aspects of the topic?
  It is not unusual to find postings that are just excerpts or summaries of another work in a printed source.
- ◆ Are the links annotated?
- ◆ Does the site offer a selected list of resources in a particular discipline or field or does it claim to offer a complete list?
- ◆ If a selected list is offered, does the author explain how the list of resources was chosen?
- ◆ Does the site refer to print and other non-Internet resources or just Internet resources?
- ◆ Is an explanation provided for use of particular criteria?

Reliability

- ◆ What is the origin of the source?
  Examine the source by checking the domain in the URL (Uniform Resource Locator) or Internet address. The domain name is the last part of the URL. The most common domains are "edu" for educational institutions, "gov" for government, "com" for commercial and "org" for organization. Countries outside of the United States use country codes as their domain names: for example, "ca" for Canada, and "fr" for France. Although government and education sites tend to be more reliable, information from commercial sites may also provide valid information. But keep in mind that commercial sites are probably more interested in selling you a product than in providing unbiased information.
- ◆ Does the site describe or provide the results of research or scholarly effort?
- ◆ Can the results be refuted or verified through other means—for example, in other research tools?
- ◆ Is advertising included on the site, and if so, does it affect the contents of the page?
- ◆ Does the page contain pictures, drawings, maps, or statistical tables that enhance its usefulness?
- ◆ Are there obvious signs of poor quality, such as bad grammar, colloquial speech, misspelled words, inflammatory words?

Currency

- ◆ When was the information posted or updated?
  On Web pages, the date of the last revision is usually at the bottom of the home page, or sometimes on every page.
- ◆ What are the inclusive dates of the information?

Exercise 3.1 Evaluating Information Sources

Instructor: _____ Course/Section: _____

Name: _____

Date: _____ Points: _____

Review Questions

1. Explain the difference between primary and secondary sources.

2. Give four examples of primary sources.

   a.

   b.

   c.

   d.

3. Give four examples of secondary sources.

   a.

   b.

   c.

   d.

4. Identify whether each of the following is a primary source or a secondary source.

   Biography of Woodrow Wilson
   Diary of a Vietnam soldier
   Letters of Dorothy Day
   Article in *Newsweek* on an interview with the two top presidential candidates
   Newspaper article describing the eruption of the volcano at Mount St. Helens
   Journal article on the history of the labor movement
   A congressional hearing on AIDS research
   A map of the Aegean Sea

5. What is meant by the term "level of scholarship"?

6. Explain the differences between popular and scholarly levels of information.

7. How would you go about determining whether materials you locate match your research needs?

8. Materials that you locate in libraries (or that libraries subscribe to online) have been subjected to some degree of evaluation. Describe to what extent this statement is correct.

9. How would you determine if a source meets each of the following criteria?

    Authoritativeness

    Comprehensiveness

    Reliability

    Currency

10. Why is so important that you evaluate information that you find on the Internet?

11. Name two sources that might help you evaluate books.

    a.

    b.

12. Name one way that information on the Internet is evaluated.

Evaluating Information Sources

3

Instructor: _____ Course/Section: _____

Name: _____

Date: _____ Points: _____

Evaluating Internet Sources

1. The following sites were pulled up from the Internet search engine Google on endangered species. Apply the checklist for Internet sources to evaluate each site. Write a brief comment presenting your evaluations.

    http://www.parascope.com/en/slips02.htm

    http://www.tnews.com/text/stupid_humans.html

    http://www.fs.fed.us/intro/testimony/19980430.html

    http://www.heritage.org/library/categories/regulation/lect559.html

    http://www.lib.umd.edu/UMCP/MCK/GUIDES/endangered_species.html

2. Each of the following sites relates to dust mites. Evaluate each and decide whether or not it would be useful to a research paper you are doing on that topic. Justify your answer.

    http://www.dustless.com/beta/allergies_mites.htm

    http://www.allerpet.com/

    http://www.ozemail.com.au/~lblanco/

    http://www.cellsalive.com/mite.htm

3.   There are a number of reviewing sources on the Internet, including the one listed below.

     http://www.zdnet.com/yil/filters/channels/reviews.html

     Go to this site and select a category that interests you. Give the URL for the top-rated site.

     Briefly state why the editors chose this site for top ranking.

     Give the URL for the lowest rated site.

     Briefly state why this received a lower evaluation.

4.   Using a search engine found at the site listed below, conduct a search on a topic that interests you or one that is assigned by your instructor.

     http://www.washburn.edu/ref_center/search/

     Locate a Web document, not just a site with links to information on your topic. Evaluate it using the criteria in the checklist.

5.   The two sites below deal with life expectancy. Which is the most credible? Explain your answer. Or do you consider neither to be credible? Explain your answer.

     http://www.deathclock.com/

     http://future.newsday.com/2/quiz.htm

Evaluating Information Sources

Instructor: _____ Course/Section: _____

Name: _____

Date: _____ Points: _____

Evaluating Print Sources

1. Locate a nonfiction book that interests you in the online catalog of your library or use a nonfiction book that you have read recently. Apply any of the evaluative criteria listed in the chapter to determine its merit.

    Give the following information.

    Author of the book:

    Title:

    Is this a primary or a secondary source?

    What is the level of scholarship? Popular or scholarly?

    Publisher of the book:

    Write a brief evaluation of the book based on the criteria listed in this chapter. For example, does the book include biographical information about the author? Is it sufficient to vouch for her or his authoritativeness? Explain.

2.   Locate a journal in your library and give the following information.

Author of an article in the journal:

Title of the article:

Title of the journal:

Publisher of the journal:

Is this a primary or a secondary source?

What is the level of scholarship? Popular or scholarly?

Write a brief evaluation of the journal article based on the criteria listed in this chapter.

Basic Search Techniques: Electronic Sources

"I don't pretend we have all the answers. But the questions are certainly worth thinking about."

ARTHUR C. CLARKE

INTRODUCTION

It has been said that access to information has never been so easy! Computer technology makes it possible to create, store, and retrieve information quickly and effectively. However, for the novice, the retrieval process can be daunting. We now have all types of information in electronic format: library catalogs, indexes and abstracts, and full-text books and journal articles. The information is available remotely from the Internet, or locally on CD-ROM. To compound the confusion, there is very little uniformity even among electronic sources that serve the same purpose, such as indexes and abstracts. Online catalogs, too, vary in the way searches are formulated and in the way that information is presented. The Internet offers a variety of search engines to help users locate information. The search commands in one source might be completely different from those in another; the way that the information appears on the screen in one electronic source may look altogether different on another screen, depending on the producer or the vendor. However, it is possible to acquire some basic search skills that will enable you to do research effectively, regardless of the source or type of electronic source.

This chapter will acquaint you with the "why's" and "how's" of searching various sources in electronic format. It outlines the steps in planning a search and shows some basic techniques for executing the steps. Chapter 5 focuses on understanding and interpreting information in library catalogs; Chapter 6 will give you greater insight into using search engines to get information on the Internet. Subsequent chapters will introduce you to various other information sources, much of which is available in electronic format. It is expected that the searching skills discussed here will be a springboard to use the myriad of available electronic information sources.

◆ THE SEARCH STRATEGY

In order to search a particular topic it is necessary to execute a search strategy that consists of the following steps.

STEPS TO EXECUTE A SEARCH STRATEGY

1. **Analyze your topic.**
   - ◆ Consider the appropriate disciplines or large subject areas for your topic.
   - ◆ What aspect of the topic are you looking for?
   - ◆ Under what discipline does it fall?
   - ◆ What are some concepts related to the topic that might cross disciplines?

2. **Identify standardized subject headings.**
   - ◆ Look in *LCSH (Library of Congress Subject Headings)*.
   - ◆ Check a thesaurus for discipline or subject related indexes and abstracts.
   - ◆ Look for a known item in the online catalog, such as an author in a field, and use the subject headings you locate.

3. **Identify keywords and terms that are not standardized subject headings.**
   - ◆ What words or terms most nearly describe the subject you are searching?
   - ◆ What are some synonyms?

4. **Combine subject headings or keywords to narrow or broaden your search.**

5. **Select the appropriate electronic source to use.**
   - ◆ Search the library's online catalog.
   - ◆ Look at the menu on the library's home page to see if indexes, abstracts, or full-text journals are available in electronic format.
   - ◆ Look at the menu on the library's home page for guides to Internet sites.
   - ◆ Check any print guides to bibliographic or full-text electronic sources.
   - ◆ Ask a reference librarian.

6. **Execute the search by typing in the commands on the computer's keyboard.**

7. **Evaluate the search results for appropriateness.**
   - ◆ The search results are sometimes called *hits*. If your search yields too many or too few hits, you might need to go back and modify it.

8. **Revise the search in light of your results.**
   - ◆ Consult a thesaurus or index (available in many electronic sources).
   - ◆ Narrow the search by combining search terms.
   - ◆ Broaden the search if the results are too limited.

◆ INFORMATION IN ELECTRONIC FORMAT

We have heard the phrase "information in electronic format." That phrase refers to any information that is created by a computer, stored electronically—either on a hard drive on the computer, on a disk (floppy, CD-ROM, or DVD), or on magnetic tape—and accessed by computer. The term *online* refers to information that is stored in a remote computer that is connected to the Internet and accessed on a local computer. Information in electronic format is available on a wide variety of subjects in all disciplines—science, social sciences, and humanities. It also includes three types of electronic information: online catalogs, databases, and information on the Internet. See Tables 4.1 and 4.2 for advantages and limitations of information in electronic format.

Online Catalogs

Most of us received our first introduction to information in electronic format with the online catalog, which lists the library's books, periodicals, and other materials. It has been commonplace in libraries since the mid-1980s. A discussion of online catalogs is found in Chapter 5.

TABLE 4.1. ◆ Advantages of Information in Electronic Format

◆ **Saves time.** It takes minutes or even seconds to search an entire database or several databases covering multiple years. To search the same indexes in paper copy might take hours or even longer, as each volume of the index would have to be searched separately.

◆ **More effective than searching a printed source.** It permits the searcher to link words and terms in a way that can never be done manually. Compare, for example, searching for a book in a card catalog. The search is limited to searching by the author's name, the title of the book, or the standardized subject heading. In an index to periodicals in paper format the access points are usually the same as in a card catalog by author, title, standardized subject heading. Information in electronic databases can be searched by keying in almost any element in the record, and "mixing and matching" keywords and terms.

◆ **More flexible than searching printed indexes and abstracts.** It is possible to search for words regardless of where they appear in the record. This is called *free-text searching* or *keyword searching*.

◆ **Possible to truncate or shorten terms.** All the variations of a term can be located.

◆ **Provides access to much more information than is available in the library.** Online databases through *EBSCOhost*, *Academic Universe*, or *INFOTrac* provide access to hundreds of journals; library networks provide access to the catalogs of other libraries in the network; the Internet makes available an endless amount and array of information.

◆ **Information is usually more up-to-date.** In an online catalog, records can be entered for materials as soon as they are ordered. Databases are updated frequently, sometimes daily. For example, in *Academic Universe*, a full-text database that includes hundreds of newspapers, information is available almost as soon as it is produced.

◆ **Possible to print material.** It is convenient and easy to print information retrieved as a result of a search in an electronic format.

◆ **Not always necessary to come to the library to find information.** Searching and retrieving information can be done from computers both inside and beyond the library—from offices, dormitories, and homes.

TABLE 4.2. ◆ Limitations of Information in Electronic Format
◆ **Sometimes the "logic" in electronic searching does not work.** For example, a search for articles on apricots in a database retrieved articles on the fruit as well as on a computer named "Apricot." This kind of result is called a "false hit'" or "false drop." Free-text searching is likely to yield more false drops than searching by controlled vocabulary. Full-text databases are more likely to yield false hits than are bibliographic databases.
◆ **Many databases do not include older information.** Most of the Wilson databases (see Chapter 8) go back to 1983 for bibliographic information and even more recent for full-text articles. In many databases, the information does not go beyond the last five to ten years. For example, you could use a database for current studies showing the effects of advertising on consumer preferences, but to find articles about consumer preference in the 1950s, you should consult a printed index from that period.
◆ **Information in electronic sources lacks standardization.** The screens of an online catalog in one library may not look at all like those in another library. This is because the software that runs the online system is different. Some libraries use NOTIS software; others use DRA (Data Research Associates), Innovative Interfaces, or some other system from a commercial vendor. A number of academic libraries have developed their own systems. CD-ROM and online databases also vary greatly in the way they are searched. For example, *Readers' Guide to Periodical Literature,* available online from SilverPlatter, does not use the same search commands as the same database available directly from the H.W. Wilson Company, its producer.
◆ **Not all of a library's electronic sources are available outside the library.** Some databases, especially those in CD-ROM or DVD formats, are available only in the library.

Databases

A *database* is a body of information in electronic format that is continuously updated. Databases are created and maintained by special software (known as a database management system) that stores and organizes data, provides a search mechanism for its retrieval, and guarantees some measure of security. Although online catalogs and information on the Internet are databases, the term is ordinarily used to refer to indexes, abstracts, full-text books and periodical articles, and images available either online or on CD-ROM or DVD. Just as with any information source stored in libraries, electronic databases are of two kinds: (1) bibliographic—citations or references to periodical articles, books, government reports, statistics, patents, research reports, conference proceedings, and dissertations, and (2) full text—the complete text of newspapers and periodicals, court cases, encyclopedias, research reports, books, and letters. A guide to databases is found in Chapter 8.

When indexes and abstracts in electronic format first became available, libraries would subscribe to services that would allow them to select the databases they wanted to search. The fees to search these sources varied. Some, such as DIALOG, were based on the time spent online plus the type of records retrieved. Others, such as *FirstSearch*, based charges on the number of search statements executed. Because of the fees involved, librarians usually took special training to learn how to search these databases and then conducted the search for the end-user. Since most libraries charged a fee based on the cost of the search, this service was limited to only a few who could afford to pay, usually faculty and graduate students. Although these services are still available from DIALOG and a few other vendors, it is more common today for libraries to subscribe to both bibliographic and full-text databases from providers or vendors and make them freely available to their registered users. Thus, the end-user must now learn how to search.

Internet

The Internet is a series of networks that connects computers of all types throughout the world, enabling users to communicate, find information, transfer data and program files, and access remote catalogs and databases such as those described above. Information available through the Internet is made accessible through a graphics interface known as the Web (World Wide Web). It allows users to read texts as well as to see images and hear sounds. The information includes a wide range of sources—some of it for a fee, but most of it free. This chapter introduces you to the basics that you need to understand in order to use search engines effectively. Chapter 6 provides a discussion on the Internet and the World Wide Web, including using specific search engines to find information.

 # UNDERSTANDING ELECTRONIC SOURCES

To make use of information in electronic format you need to understand a basic concept: some electronic sources contain the actual text of a document, while others contain only a description (bibliographic citation). Knowing this affects not only the way you search but also your results.

Bibliographic Information

In many ways bibliographic information in electronic format can be compared to the printed materials in libraries: card catalogs, indexes, and abstracts.

- They provide access to information in other sources: magazines, journals, and books.
- They organize the information in a systematic way.
- They provide several access points by which to locate the source.

As with access tools in paper format, each entry points to an individual source. The individual entries are called *records*. A bibliographic record in an electronic source has many of the same elements as its counterpart in paper format. The elements are divided into *fields,* each of which is labeled. The fields serve as access points by which to retrieve the record.

> **TYPICAL ONLINE CATALOG RECORD**
>
> **AUTHOR** [of the work being cited]
> **TITLE** [of the work cited]
> **EDITION**
> **PUBLISHER**
> **DATE**
> **PHYSICAL DESCRIPTION**
> **NOTES**
> **SUBJECTS**

(There may be other fields that are indexed, but they might not appear in the online catalog.)

TYPICAL BIBLIOGRAPHIC RECORD FOR A JOURNAL ARTICLE IN A PERIODICAL DATABASE

AN [Accession number]
TI [Titlo of articlo]
AU [Author of article]
IN [Author's institutional affiliation]
JN [Journal title or SO (source) in some databases]
IS [International Standard Serial Number]
LA [Language of the article]
PY [Publication year]
AB [Abstract]
DE [Subject descriptors or terms]

Full-Text Databases

Unlike bibliographic databases, full-text databases do not have labeled fields. Normally, with full-text databases, you can search only by using keywords that appear throughout the text or in titles, abstracts, headings, and notes. This may not be as precise as searching by controlled vocabulary or even keywords from labeled fields. It is possible to limit or qualify a search in full-text databases, but you need to be careful in phrasing the search lest you end up with more hits than you can manage. On the other hand, full-text searching can be very effective for narrow topics that might not be covered elsewhere. For example, the full text of a newspaper article might provide valuable information on events and persons that might never be named in a database that only has citations to the articles and not the full text. Scholars can use the full-text searching capabilities to find terms and concepts in electronic books.

 # SEARCH BASICS

Following are some basic search techniques that are common to most electronic databases. Remember that all electronic sources are not alike. In some, most notably text-based electronic sources accessed through Telnet rather than through the Web, you have to build your own search statements. Web-based databases and online catalogs have forms or templates where you can type in your search terms. Many have pull-down menus that allow you to select Boolean operators or other terms to limit or qualify your search.

Commands

While the computer is a powerful information storage and retrieval tool, it is also a very exacting one. To retrieve information, you need to select the appropriate electronic source and then type in a search request or a *command*. The computer then scans the source looking for an exact match of the search statement. If you misspell a word, the computer will look for a match of the misspelled word. Thus you will not get any hits unless the word is also misspelled in the database.

Although some Internet search engines recognize natural language, many online catalogs and databases do not. If the search query is "find the standard of living among people of Appalachia during the Great Depression," the search is not likely to yield anything because the computer is searching for an exact match of that statement. Some search engines on the Web allow natural language searching, but even these search only for the keywords in the statement. Most of the search engines in use today are designed in such a way as to permit searching on certain access points, to combine terms, and to limit terms.

EXAMPLE ■

For books *by* Hemingway   Search in the author field
For books *about* Hemingway   Search in the subject fields
For books *by* and *about* Hemingway   Search all the fields

Access Points

The key to access in any electronic source is identifying the concepts and terms you wish to search and applying basic search skills to achieve the desired results.

FOUR BASIC WAYS TO SEARCH AN ELECTRONIC SOURCE

◆ by author name   ◆ by subject of the work

◆ by title of the work   ◆ by keywords in the record

An explanation of each of these four methods of electronic searches follows, with examples of each. The examples illustrate searching in a typical text-based online catalog. Although the commands might vary slightly, the techniques can be applied to Web-based catalogs, online indexes and abstracts, and search engines available for searching the Web. With Web-based catalogs and databases, instead of identifying your type of search in the command line, you select the field or type of search from a template or pull-down menu. You then type the word or phrase in the form provided.

Author Search

An author search is restricted to searching only the author field. It necessarily involves a known element—either an author's name or part of the author's name. Some electronic sources allow you to truncate or shorten the author's name if you do not know the complete first name or correct spelling.

EXAMPLE ■

Type **a=[author's last name or a portion of the last name]**
   a=solzhenitayn or **a=solzhen** (for Solzhenitsyn)
   a=james hen   (For more common names, include at least some of the first name.)
   a=oneill eugene (Omit accent marks and all other punctuation in the author's name.)
   a=unesco   (An organization as author, also called a *corporate author.*)

Title Search

A title search is also a search for a known element—you know the title of a work or enough of the title to make it distinctive. To retrieve a title you must key in the title exactly as it appears in the title field (except that initial articles are usually omitted). If the first part of a title is sufficiently distinctive, it is not necessary to type in the full title. You only need to put in the first three or four words. In some online catalogs it is not necessary to type in the entire last word.

EXAMPLE ■

Type **t=[title or as much of the title of which you are certain]**

t=red badge of cour	(*Red Badge of Courage:* You need not include the entire title.)
t=man for all seasons	(*A Man for All Seasons:* Generally, omit initial articles "a," "an," "the," and foreign equivalents. Some systems accept articles.)
t=red white black	(*Red, White, and Black:* Omit all punctuation in the title.)
t=2 minutes to noon	(Write numbers in numeric form or spelled out, depending on how they appear in the original work.)
t=part time teacher	(Do not use hyphens; try as separate words or one word.)

Subject Search

Subject searching is usually recommended whenever possible because it gives a more precise search than keyword searching. A subject search here refers to using standardized subjects headings to search a record. The subject headings used in online catalogs are established by the Library of Congress and are listed in a multivolume publication, the *Library of Congress List of Subject Headings* (*LCSH*) (see Figure 4.1). It also gives alternative terms (refers from a term that is not used to one that is used), related terms, and terms used to broaden or narrow a search. The National Library of Medicine establishes headings that are appropriate for use in the medical sciences. In many periodical databases, the subject headings, or *descriptors* as they are sometimes called, are listed in a *thesaurus* or an index.

EXAMPLE ■

Type **s=[standardized subject heading]**
    s=afro american inventors

Standardized subject headings may be divided into parts, called subdivisions. To search for a subject heading with subdivisions, separate each part of the heading with two hyphens (--).

EXAMPLE ■

s=france--history
s=migraine--therapy
s=georgia--fiction

The mistake most people make with subject searching is that they think they can type in any word and the computer will pull up items on that subject. Although this does sometimes work, it is due more to chance than anything else. In subject searching, the terms must be keyed in exactly as they appear in the subject field(s). This may or may not be the terms you would use to describe the subject.

EXAMPLE ■

If you want books on:	You search under:
gun collecting	**firearms--collecting**
streetcars	**cable cars (streetcars)**
vitamin B3	**nicotinamide**
themes of folktales	**folklore--classification**

So how do you know what subject heading to use for your topic? When searching the online catalog, you can look in the *Library of Congress Subject Headings*. In doing a search in a periodical database, you should consult the thesaurus or index to determine appropriate terminology to use.

Sex discrimination (May Subd Geog)
  UF Discrimination, Sexual
      Gender discrimination
      Sexual discrimination
  BT Discrimination
      Sexism
  NT Radical therapy
      Sex discrimination against men
      Sex discrimination against women
      Sex discrimination in employment
      Sex of children, Parental preferences for
  --Law and legislation (May Subd Geog)
Sex discrimination against men
(May Subd Geog)
  UF Discrimination against men
      Men, Discrimination against
  BT Sex discrimination
Sex discrimination against women
(May Subd Geog)
  UF Discrimination against women
      Subordination of women
      Women, Discrimination against
  BT Feminism
      Sex discrimination
      Women's rights
  NT Purdah
  --Law and legislation (May Subd Geog)

Sex discrimination in consumer credit
(May Subd Geog)
Here are entered works on the difficulties encountered in obtaining consumer credit due to sex discrimination.
  BT Consumer credit
  --Law and Legislation (May Subd Geog)
Sex discrimination in criminal justice administration (May Subd Geog)
  BT Criminal justice, Administration of
      Discrimination in criminal justice
      administration
Sex discrimination in education
(May Subd Geog) [LC212.8-LC212.83]
  UF Education, Sex discrimination in
  BT Discrimination in education
  NT Sex discrimination in medical education
Sex discrimination in employment
(May Subd Geog) [HD6060-HD6060.5]
  BT Discrimination in employment
      Sex discrimination
  RT Sex role in the work environment
      Sexual division of labor
      Women--Employment

Figure 4.1. Library of Congress Subject Headings, 1995, p. 1710.

Keyword Search

Keyword searching is the term used to refer to free-text searching, or searching all the fields in a record.

GUIDELINES FOR USING KEYWORD SEARCHING

▼ When you are unsure about the order or spelling of all words in the title;

▼ When you don't know the author's name;

▼ When you don't know the precise subject heading used;

▼ When you want to link terms from different parts of a record such as an author's name with a word from a title;

▼ When you want to combine terms to narrow a topic or to limit a topic.

EXAMPLE

Type **k=[followed by a word, phrase, dates, or any term found in any indexed field within a record]**

In a keyword search, the computer looks at all the records and retrieves those that contain the word or phrase that you specify anywhere in the record. This is very important! If you type in the word "guns" in the online catalog, you are not only going to get books on guns, but books written by Walter Guns, a book titled *Guns or Butter* about Lyndon Johnson, or any other item that has the word "guns" somewhere in its record.

A keyword search is usually the only search that allows you to:

◆ truncate or shorten a search term;

◆ use Boolean and positional operators to combine search terms;

◆ use advance searching such as limiting a search to specific fields; or

◆ qualify a search according to certain specifications.

Keyword searching allows for flexibility in searching that you do not have with author, title, or subject searches. Below are outlined some of the techniques used in keyword searching.

Truncating Search Terms

In keyword searching it is possible to shorten a term by using a character such as a question mark (?) or, in some online catalogs and databases, an asterisk (*). This allows you to retrieve singular or plural forms or different spellings of a word or name in a single search.

EXAMPLE

k=colleg?
(Will match **college, colleges, collegial,** and **collegiate.**)

Avoid over-truncating search terms. Do not enter **const?** if you're searching for the term "constitution" as it will pull up too many terms.

Boolean Operators

Boolean operators are words used to make a logical search query. They enable you to broaden or narrow your search or link terms. Most databases use the basic Boolean operators: **and, or,** and **not.** When using any online catalog or database you should verify whether or not Boolean operators are used.

◆   **AND** searches for occurrences of all of the search terms in a single record.

> EXAMPLE ■
>
> **k=conservative and liberal and moderate**

◆   **OR** searches for records that contain any of the terms.

> EXAMPLE ■
>
> **k=conservative or liberal or moderate**

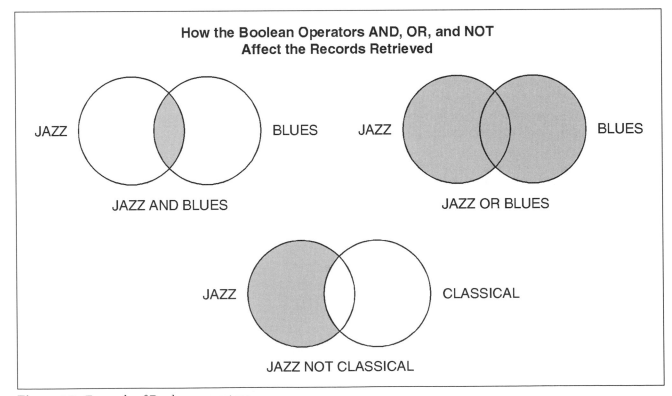

Figure 4.2. Example of Boolean operators.

◆ **NOT** searches for records that contain the first term but not the second term.

> EXAMPLE ■
>
> liberal **not** conservative

Nested Searches

Nesting is used to specify the order of the search. With nesting, parentheses are placed around words to make a single search statement.

> EXAMPLE ■
>
> **k=(fraud or evasion) and income tax**
> (Finds all records that have **fraud** and **income tax** and all those that have **evasion** and **income tax**.)
>
> An un-nested search:
> **k=fraud or evasion and income tax**
> (Finds all the records that have **fraud** (with or without income tax) and all those that have **evasion** and **income tax** in the same record.)

Positional Operators

Positional operators are used to refer to the order in which words appear in a record:

◆ **ADJ** searches for terms in the exact order in which they are typed. In many databases ADJ is the default operator, so there is no need to type it in.

> EXAMPLE ■
>
> **k=liberal democrat**
>   **OR**
> **k=liberal adj democrat**

◆ **ADJ#** finds terms in the order typed within a specified number of words of each other.

> EXAMPLE ■
>
> **k=conservative adj3 politics**
> (Finds records that contain the word "conservative" within three words of the word "politics.")

◆ **SAME** searches for terms in the same group of fields such as in any of the subject fields when there are multiple subject fields.

EXAMPLE ■

k=ultraviolet same radiation
Many systems do not require the use of the operator; rather, SAME is assumed.
k=ultraviolet radiation
(Retrieves the same results as **ultraviolet same radiation**.)

◆ **WITH** searches for records that contain the search terms, in any order, in the same field and in the same sentence of a field. A sentence is defined as any part of a field that ends with a period. If there are multiple subject fields, the two terms must appear together in only one subject field.

EXAMPLE ■

ultraviolet with radiation
(The two terms must appear in a single field, such as a single title field.)
NOTE: WITH is much more restrictive than SAME.

Variations of the SAME and WITH operators are NOT SAME and NOT WITH. These will retrieve records in which the first term occurs in the group of fields or in the same sentence (in the case of WITH), but the second term does not.

Limiting a Search to a Field

In keyword searching it is possible to limit a search to field or group of fields in a record, such as author, title, or subject.

In some online catalogs and databases a period must precede and follow the field code.

◆ .su.—to limit the search term to subject fields only
◆ .ti.—to limit the search term to title fields only
◆ .au.—to limit the search term to author fields only

EXAMPLE ■

k=bennett.au. and virtues.ti.
(A search for **Bennett** in the **author** field and **virtues** in the **title** field. Useful when only partial information is known.)

Some databases, such as those available from SilverPlatter, allow you to specify the field in the search statement. For example, if you recall that there is an article on the Surma tribe in Africa that was published in *National Geographic* but you do not recall the date, you can narrow your search to certain fields to locate it.

Surma in ti and (National Geographic) in so
   OR
surma.ti. and (National Geographic).so.
(In this example "ti" refers to the title field of the article, "so" refers to the source in which the article appears.)

Many databases have pull-down menus that allow you to limit your search to certain fields.

Qualifying a Search Term

Search terms may be further qualified by format, language, or date.

◆ **.fmt.**—to limit a search to a particular format:
b.fmt.=book
m.fmt.=music
s.fmt.=serials
p.fmt.=maps
f.fmt.=visuals
d.fmt.=computer file
u.fmt.=archives

k=plantations and u.fmt.
(Retrieves archival materials on plantations.)

◆ **.lng.**—to limit a search to items written in a particular language:
eng.lng.=English
spa.lng.=Spanish
fre.lng.=French

k=intelligence testing and eng.lng.
(Retrieves materials on intelligence testing in English.)

◆   **.DT1.**—to limit a search to a specific publication year:

Stopwords

Some words and abbreviations appear so frequently in records that a keyword search system does not search for them. These are called *stopwords*. Some common stopwords are:

a	from	same
an	in	the
and	not	to
by	of	with
for	or	

    Avoid use of all stopwords when constructing your keyword search statement. **AND, NOT, OR**, and **SAME** may be used only as Boolean or positional operators in a search.

The preceding explanation and examples have shown you how to formulate and execute a basic search using computer technology. While there appears to be no standardization among online catalogs, bibliographic and full-text databases, and Internet search engines there are a great number of search features that are common in most: use of truncation, use of Boolean logic, and the ability to limit or qualify a search. Although text-based and Web-based databases differ in the way search terms are formulated, the search basics discussed above apply to both. The information you learn here should help you to understand how computers translate your search request into retrieval of information, regardless of the interface or search engine used.

Basic Search Techniques

Instructor: _____ Course/Section: _____

Name: _____

Date: _____ Points: _____

Review Questions

1. What is meant by the term "information in electronic format"?

2. Define database as it is used in this chapter.

3. What is the difference between a bibliographic database and a full-text database?

4. Name four advantages of using an electronic database.

    a.

    b.

    c.

    d.

5. Name three limitations of information in electronic databases.

    a.

    b.

    c.

6. Explain what is meant by "records" as applied to an electronic source.

7. What are "fields" in electronic records?

8. Name four basic ways to search for information in an electronic source.

   a.

   b.

   c.

   d.

9. Explain the difference between a subject search and a keyword search.

10. What is meant by the term "truncating" as applied to searching?

11. What are Boolean operators?

12. Name the three Boolean operators and define each.

   a.

   b.

   c.

13. What is meant by the term "nesting" as applied to searching an online database?

14. What are "positional operators"?

   Name three positional operators.

   a.

   b.

   c.

15. What is meant by the term "limiting a search"?

16. Name three ways you can qualify a search.

   a.

   b.

   c.

Basic Search Techniques

4

Instructor: _____ Course/Section: _____

Name: _____

Date: _____ Points: _____

Electronic Searching

In the hypothetical problems below state the command you would use to execute the search.

Use: a=for author searches
     t=for title searches
     s= or subject searches
     k=for keyword search
     ? to truncate

For Questions 1–6 use Boolean or positional operators to state your commands:

> EXAMPLE ■
>
> Find all the information on using animals in experimentation
> Command:
>   **k=animal and experimentation**
>
> Find all the records with information on importing perfume from France
> Command:
>   **k=perfume and import? and France**

1. Find any records dealing with teaching reading to children with dyslexia.
   Command:

2. Find all the records that have information on reading and all the records that have information on dyslexia.
   Command:

3. Find the records that have information on reading, but eliminate those dealing with dyslexia.
   Command:

4. Find all the records that have reading in the same group of fields as dyslexia.
   Command:

5. Find all the records that have *dyslexia* and *reading* in the same sentence of a field.
    Command:

6. Find all the records where *country* appears within five words of music.
    Command:

Assume that you are using the online catalog in your library for problems 7–13.
Use the command: t=for a title search
    a=for an author search
    s=for a subject search
    k=for a keyword search

7. Find the periodical: *The American Journal of Mathematics.*
    Command:

8. Find all the works on the subject of *chemical warfare.*
    Command:

9. Find all the books by *Stephen King.*
    Command:

10. Find all the books about *Stephen King.*
     Command:

11. Find all books that have the word *cloning* in the record.
     Command:

12. Find all books with *cloning* as the established subject.
     Command:

13. Find a book dealing with *poverty* by an author whose last name is *Galbraith.*
     Command:

CHAPTER

5

Library Catalogs

"A place for everything, and everything in its place."
SAMUEL SMILES: *THRIFT* V.

INTRODUCTION

A library catalog is a listing of all the items available in a particular library—whether in tangible form (printed books, periodicals, CD-ROMs, etc.) or in Web-based form. Each record in a library catalog describes a particular item (book, video, map, audio tape, CD-ROM, or Internet site), and gives its location in the library or its address (URL) on the Internet. In order to provide access to its physical collections, libraries organize materials by classifying them and assigning specific location numbers or call numbers. In this way materials on similar subjects are grouped together on the shelves. This rationale has resulted in the development of uniform classification systems that are used by libraries throughout the world. Items available on the Internet are usually not given classification numbers; rather they are assigned subject headings and can be accessed by any of the searchable fields in the catalog—author, title, subject—or by keyword. This chapter will discuss some of the important things you need to know about using the catalog to find information.

◆ CLASSIFICATION SYSTEMS

The purpose of any classification system is to bring together comparable materials so they can be found easily and the library will have some logical arrangement. This also allows library patrons to browse the shelves in a given subject classification number or letter in order to find materials on that subject grouped together. In most libraries, books are classified and shelved in stack areas, while other materials may be grouped according to format, such as microforms, CD-ROMs, and audio-visual materials. These materials are usually assigned accession numbers that identify location, rather than numbers based on classification.

The two most commonly used classification systems in American libraries are the Dewey Decimal Classification System—commonly called Dewey or DC—and the Library of Congress Classification System—referred to as LC (see Figure 5.1). Many public libraries and small college libraries use the Dewey system while larger colleges and universities use the Library of Congress system.

All classification systems start with a general classification and then proceed to a more specific classification. Note that Dewey classifies all engineering in 620, while Library of Congress subdivides it into several branches (see Figure 5.2). The Library of Congress system is used in large libraries because its broader base allows room for expansion as new subjects are added to the fields of knowledge.

Materials covering one particular subject can be classified easily under that subject. However, when the item deals with more than one subject, it is classified under the largest subject covered or under what the catalogers feel is the most important subject. Subjects covered in the book that are not reflected in the call number selected by the cataloger are brought out by means of *subject headings*.

Libraries with extensive collections of materials published by the United States Government often use the *Superintendent of Documents* or *SuDocs* System to classify the publications. The system was devised by the Government Printing Office to organize the thousands of publications it issues annually.

In addition to the three major systems discussed above, libraries may also use other systems for classifying smaller special collections such as state documents, United Nations documents, or archives.

It is not necessary to learn all the details of the classification systems in order to use the library effectively, but you do need to be able to recognize which classification systems are used in your library and to understand the basic principles of each.

Dewey Decimal Classification System

The Dewey Decimal Classification System was originated by Melvil Dewey in the latter part of the 19th century. The system divides all knowledge into ten different classes. These ten primary classes are further subdivided into subclasses. Decimals are used to subdivide further. The example below illustrates how the addition of each decimal number to the whole number makes the classification more precise.

EXAMPLE ■

900	Geography and History
970	General history of North America
973	United States history
973.7	Civil War 1861–1865
973.71	Political and economic history (Civil War period)
973.73	Military operations
973.7349	Battle of Gettysburg
973.9	20th century 1901–
973.92	Later 20th century 1953–

Library of Congress Classification System

The Library of Congress Classification System was designed by the Library of Congress in the latter part of the 19th century solely for its own use. Because it is so comprehensive, it has been adopted by many other large libraries both in the United States and in other parts of the world.

MAJOR LIBRARY CLASSIFICATION SYSTEMS

DEWEY DECIMAL (DC)		LIBRARY OF CONGRESS (LC)		SUPERINTENDENT OF DOCUMENTS (SuDocs)		UNITED NATIONS SYMBOLS (UN)	
ex:	635.05 B35	ex:	B358 C.57 1985	ex:	L3.134/2:C83/2/983	ex:	ST/ESA/165
000	Generalities	A	General Works	A	Agriculture	A/	General Assembly
100	Philosophy/Psychology	B	Philosophy/Psychology/Religion	AE	Archives/Records	E/	Economic & Social Council
200	Religion						
		C	History—General	C	Commerce	S/	Security Council
300	Social Sciences	D	History—World	C.3	Census	T/	Trusteeship Council
400	Language	E	American History	D	Defense		
		F	Local American History	E	Energy	ST/	Secretariat
500	Natural Science/ Mathematics	G	Geography/Anthropology/Sports	ED	Education		
				EP	Environmental Protection	Other:	
		H	Social Sciences	FR	Federal Reserve		
600	Technology	HA	Statistics	GS	General Administration	CCPR/	Human Rights Committee
700	The Arts	HM	Sociology	HE	Health & Human Services		
				HH	Housing & Urban Development	DP/	UN Development Program
800	Literature/Rhetoric	J	Political Science	I	Interior		
900	Geography/History	K	Law	I19	US Geological Survey		
		L	Education	J	Justice		
		M	Music	JU	Judiciary		
		N	Fine Arts				
				L	Labor		
		P	Language/Literature	LC	Library of Congress		
		PR	English/Literature				
		PS	American Literature	NAS	National Aeronautics/Space		
				PR	President's Office		
		Q	Science				
		R	Medicine	S	State Department		
		S	Agriculture	SI	Smithsonian Institution		
		T	Technology				
		U	Military Science	T	Treasury		
		V	Naval Science	T22	Internal Revenue		
		Z	Bibliography/Library Science	TD	Transportation		
				VA	Veterans Administration		
				Y	Congress		
				Y4	Congressional Hearings		

Figure 5.1. Comparison of major library classification systems.

DEWEY DECIMAL

000	GENERALITIES
010	Bibliography
020	Library & Info Sciences
030	Gen Encyc Works
050	Gen Serials & Indexes
060	Gen Organiz & Museology
070	News Media, Jl, Publishing
080	General Collections
090	Manuscripts, Rare Books
100	PHIL & PSYCHOLOGY
110	Metaphysics
120	Epistemology, Creation
130	Paranormal Phen.
150	Psychology
160	Logic
170	Ethics
180	Ancient, Medieval, Oriental
190	Modern Western Phil.
200	RELIGION
210	Natural Theology
220	Bible
230	Christian Theology
240	Christian Moral/Devotional
250	Christ.Orders, Local Church
260	Christian Social Theology
270	Christian Church History
280	Christian Denom & Sects
290	Other, Comp. Religion
300	SOCIAL SCIENCES
310	General Statistics
320	Political Science
330	Economics
340	Law
350	Public Administration
360	Social Services, Admin.
370	Education
380	Commerce, Comm., Transp.
390	Customs, Etiquette, Folklore
400	LANGUAGE
410	Linguistics
420	English & Old English
430	Germanic Lang, German
440	Romance Languages, Fr
450	Italian, Rumanian
460	Spanish, Portuguese
470	Italic Languages, Latin
480	Hellenic Lang, Class. Greek
500	NATURAL SCIENCE
510	Mathematics
520	Astronomy & Allied Sci.
530	Physics
540	Chemistry & Applied Sci.
550	Earth Sciences
560	Paleontology, Paleozoology
570	Life Sciences
580	Botanical Sciences
590	Zoological Sciences
600	TECHNOLOGY
610	Medicine
620	Engineering
630	Agriculture
640	Home Economics
660	Chemical Engineering
670	Manufacturing
690	Buildings
700	THE ARTS
710	Civic & Landscape Art
720	Architecture
730	Plastic Arts, Sculpture
740	Drawing & Decorative Art
750	Painting & Paintings
760	Graphic Arts, Printmaking
770	Photography & Photographs
780	Music
790	Recreational & Perfm Art
800	LITERATURE
810	American
820	English & Old English
830	Germanic Languages
840	Romance Languages
860	Spanish & Portuguese
870	Italic, Latin
880	Hellenic, Classical Greek
890	Literature of Other Lang.
900	GEOG & HISTORY
910	Geography & Travel
920	Biography, Genealogy
930	Ancient History
940	Gen History of Europe
950	Gen Hist of Asia, Far East
960	Gen Hist of Africa
970	Gen Hist of North America
980	Gen Hist of South America
990	Gen Hist of Other Areas

LIBRARY OF CONGRESS

A	GENERAL WORKS
	Ger. Encyc, Ref Works
B	PHILOSOPHY/ RELIGION
C	HISTORY
CB	History of Civilization
CC	Archaeology
CD	Archives
CR	Heraldry
CS	Genealogy
CT	Biography (General)
D	HISTORY, World History
DA	Great Britain
DB	Austria
DC	France
DD	Other countries
E-F	HISTORY OF AMERICA
G	GEOG, ANTHRO, FOLK.
G	Geography
GB	Physical Geography
GC	Oceanography
GN	Anthropology
GR	Folklore
GV	Recreation
H	SOCIAL SCIENCES
HA	Statistics
HB	Economics
HM-HX	Sociology
J	POLITICAL SCIENCE
JC	Political Theory
JF-JQ	Constitutional History/ Public Administration
JS	Local Government
JX	International Law
K	LAW
L	EDUCATION
M	MUSIC
ML	Literature of Music
MT	Musical Instruction
N	FINE ARTS
NA	Architecture
NB	Sculpture
NC	Graphic Arts
ND	Painting
NK	Decorative Arts
P	LANGUAGE, LITERATURE
PA	Classical Languages
PC	Romance Languages
PD-PF	German Language
PJ-PL	Oriental Language
PN	Gen. and Comparative
PQ	Romance Literature
PR	English Literature
PS	American Literature
PT	Germanic Literature
PZ	Fiction in English, Juvenile
Q	SCIENCE
QA	Mathematics
QB	Astronomy
QC	Physics
QD	Chemistry
QE	Geology
QH	Natural History
QK	Botany
QL	Zoology
QM	Human Anatomy
QP	Physiology
R	MEDICINE
S	AGRICULTURE
SB	Plant Culture/Horticulture
SD	Forestry
SF	Animal Culture
SH	Fish Culture/Fisheries
SK	Hunting Sports
T	TECHNOLOGY
TA	Gen Engineering
TC	Hydraulic Engineering
TD	Sanitary/Municipal Engr.
TE	Highway Engineering
TF	Railroad Engineering
TH	Building Construction
TJ	Mechanical Engineering
TK	Electrical, Nuclear Engr.
TP	Chemical Technology
TR	Photography
TS	Manufacturing
TT	Handicrafts, Arts and Crafts
TX	Home Economics
U	MILITARY SCIENCE
V	NAVAL SCIENCE
Z	BIBLIOG LIBR. SCIENCE

Figure 5.2. Comparison of Dewey Decimal and Library of Congress Classification Systems.

The LC system has 21 different classes with numerous subdivisions under each class. Each primary class is designated by a single letter as illustrated in Figure 5.1. The first letter or group of letters is followed by a whole number that indicates a subdivision.

EXAMPLE ■

H	**Social sciences (General)**
HA	Statistics
Economics	
HB	Economic theory. Demography
HC-HD	Economic history and conditions
HE	Transportation and communications
HF	Commerce
HJ	Finance
Sociology	
HM	Sociology (General and theoretical)
HN	Social history. Social problems. Social reform
HQ	The family. Marriage. Women
HS	Societies: Secret, benevolent, etc. Clubs
HT	Communities. Classes. Races
HV	Social pathology. Social and public welfare. Criminology
HX	Socialism. Communism. Anarchism

The initial classification number can be subdivided further as shown in the three call numbers below.

EXAMPLE ■

HF	HF	HF
5686	5686	5686
.D7	.P3	.S75

Where HF=commerce
      5686=accounting
     .D7=drug stores
     .P3=petroleum industry
     .S75=steel industry

Although the system is based on the alphabet, not all of the letters have been used in either the main classes or the subclasses. These letters are reserved for new subjects, for the expansion of older subjects, or, in the case of **I** and **O**, to avoid confusion with the numbers one and zero.

Superintendent of Documents Classification System

The SuDocs system is used by the United States Government Printing Office to assign call numbers to government documents before they are sent to depository libraries. Libraries that serve as depositories for government publications usually establish separate collections arranged by SuDocs number. This system is an alphanumeric scheme based on the agency that issues the publication rather than on subjects, as in the case of Dewey or LC. The initial letter or letters designate the government agency, bureau, or department responsible for the publication. The letters are subdivided further to indicate subagencies.

Publications that are part of a series are assigned a number that designates a particular series. Each individual publication in the series is assigned a number or letter/number combination that identifies the individual title, volume, year, or issue number. This number follows a colon. The following example illustrates the elements in a typical SuDocs number.

EXAMPLE ■

C 3.134/2:C 83/2/995
Where   C=Issuing Department—Commerce Department
             3=Sub-agency—Bureau of the Census
             134/2—Series—Statistical Abstract Supplement
             C 83/2/995=Title and date—*County and City Data Book*, 1995

United Nations Symbol Numbers

United Nations publications are classified by series/symbol number designed by the UN library. Figure 5.1 shows the top level of the classification scheme. The numbers are divided further to indicate departments and series. The series symbol numbers are composed of capital letters in combination with numerical notations. The elements in the numbers are separated by slash marks.

EXAMPLE ■

The *Report on the World Social Situation* has the classification number:
ST/ESA/165.
Where   ST=United Nations Secretariat
             ESA=Department of International and Social Affairs
             165=series number

◆ CALL NUMBERS

The *call number* assigned to an item usually indicates its subject matter (classification), author, and title. The call number, either alone or in conjunction with an added location symbol, determines the location of the item in the library. For example, the book with the call number DS 69 .5 C5 would be shelved in the stacks, while a book with the call number Ref BF 311.G3 would be located in the reference area.

The following example identifies each element in a Dewey Decimal number.

EXAMPLE ■

976.3
D261Lo3
Where   976=Classification number
               D261=Author's initial and number
               Lo=First two letters of the book title
               3=Edition number

The example below identifies each element in a Library of Congress number.

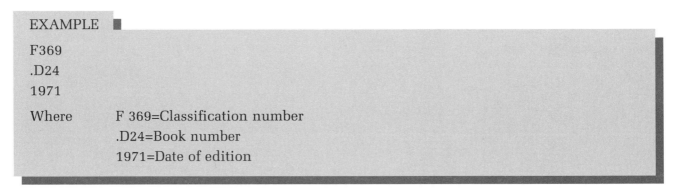

EXAMPLE ■

F369
.D24
1971

Where   F 369=Classification number
               .D24=Book number
               1971=Date of edition

In both the Dewey and LC systems, it is necessary to read the numbers/letters in the call numbers sequentially in order to locate books on the shelves. In Dewey, the number before the decimal point is always treated as a whole number or integer, while all of the numbers following the decimal point are treated as decimals. Although the decimal point may not appear physically in the call number, the book number is nevertheless treated as a decimal.

EXAMPLE ■

338   would be shelved before   338
A221i   A36

The following call numbers are arranged in correct order as they would stand on the shelf.

EXAMPLE ■

| 338 | 338 | 338.908 | 338.91 | 338.917 | 338.94 |
| A22li | A36 | F911r | B138e | R896y | R31c |

When locating a call number in LC, it is necessary to start with the letter combination and then proceed to the numbers. As with Dewey, the first set of numbers is treated as a whole number. The whole number or integer is followed either by a decimal point and numbers and/or one or more letter/number combinations. The remaining numbers are all treated as decimals.

PN	would be shelved before	PN
6		6
.S55		.S6

The next consideration when reading the call number is the letter/number combination that, in many cases, is followed by a third letter/number combination. All parts of the book numbers are read first alphabetically and then numerically as decimals. In many call numbers, the date of the book is added. When call numbers are exactly the same except for dates, as in the case with multiple editions, the books are arranged in chronological order. Notice in the second and third examples that the call numbers are exactly alike except for the 1967. The call number without the date is shelved before the one with the date. The example below illustrates LC call numbers in the correct order as they would stand on the shelf.

EXAMPLE ■

PN	PN	PN	PN	PN
6	56	56	56	57
.S55	.H63T5	.H63T5	.3	.A43L5
		1967	.N4J6	

The call numbers for documents are usually written horizontally unless there is not space on the spine of the book to write the numbers. In that case, the numbers are written vertically, with the break occurring at a punctuation mark.

EXAMPLE ■

A13.106/2-2:C 35

Documents with SuDocs call numbers are shelved in alphanumeric sequence. The numbers following periods are whole numbers as are the numbers following slashes or colons. The following example shows SuDocs numbers in shelf order.

EXAMPLE ■

A 2.113:C 35	A13.92:R 59	A13.92/2:F 29	A13.103:163

Many libraries have books housed in areas other than the regular stacks, and these areas are usually indicated by a symbol over the call number. For example, books on the reference shelves often will have the symbols "O" (for oversize), "R" or "Ref" (for Reference), or "RR" (for Ready Reference). It is necessary to check the library handbook or a chart of symbols to determine their meaning and location.

◆ LIBRARY CATALOGS: KEY TO ACCESS

The catalog is the key to the collections of any library. The catalog record gives the location of each item and provides a full description, including name of the author, complete title, edition, number of pages, size, publisher, place of publication, and date of publication. Thus, it is possible to learn a great deal about the item even before it is located in the library.

One of the most important elements on any cataloging record is the subject headings. These are the headings that are assigned to each item by catalogers. They are based on the *Library of Congress Subject Headings* (*LCSH*) (see Figure 4.1). It lists established or standardized terms used by the Library of Congress to describe the subject matter in cataloged materials. The standardized subject headings are used as subject headings in entries in both card and online catalogs. They must be searched exactly as they appear in *LCSH*. One advantage of subject searching is that the search results are likely to be much more on target than keyword searching. This is because professional catalogers assign the established subject headings after examining the work and determining its subject. The subject headings on the catalog record are important in the research process because they suggest related search terms that the researcher can use to find additional information on the topic.

Materials That Might Not Be Found in Library Catalogs

It is important to know what you will find in a library catalog as well as what you are not likely to find.

MATERIALS OFTEN NOT FOUND IN LIBRARY CATALOGS
◆ individual articles from magazines, journals, and newspapers;
◆ individual titles in series (although some individual titles may be cataloged);
◆ individual titles from anthologies; and
◆ government publications (varies with individual libraries).

Format of Cataloged Materials

When looking at catalog records you should recall that format is a consideration. The online catalog not only includes the books in the collection, but also identifies materials in a variety of formats. These include films, microfilm, microfiche, microprint, sound recordings, reel-to-reel tapes, videocassettes, maps, musical scores, CD-ROMs, online databases, and information found on the Internet.

The locations of material with special formats will be indicated on the catalog record. They usually have a location symbol such as "Film," "LP," "Recording," or "Tape" plus a sequence number instead of a classification number as a means of locating them. The number given with the location symbol is often an *accession number*. This means that as the materials are received by the library, they are assigned a number indicating their order of receipt. Sometimes a classification number and a location symbol are assigned to nonbook materials. Material available only on the Internet will have a note identifying the location as "Internet" or some similar notation, and will include the Internet address (URL) in a separate field.

◆ CARD CATALOG

Even though online catalogs are now the norm, the card catalog record remains a standard for understanding the information provided for each cataloged items. Traditional card catalogs consisted of index cards arranged alphabetically. A few libraries might still maintain catalogs in other formats, which include book catalogs, COM (Computer Output Microform), and CD-ROM catalogs.

Some libraries, because of the expense involved, cannot afford to change all of their records when they convert from one type of catalog to another. Therefore, records for older materials are left in one system, while those for newer materials are entered into the new system. A library changing from a card catalog to an online catalog might leave all of its records for materials cataloged before a certain date in the card catalog and enter only records for materials processed after that date into the online catalog. You will need to determine which type or types of catalogs the library is using in order to locate materials. This information is generally available in the library's handbook or from a reference librarian.

Printed Cards

Card catalogs consist of multiple drawers containing 3" x 5" printed cards arranged alphabetically by author, title, subject, and added entries. Added entries consist of cards for such things as editors, compilers, translators, illustrators, arrangers of music, and series. Practically every book, with the exception of fiction, has at least three cards in the catalog. These are: author, or main entry card; title card; and one or more subject cards. With printed cards, except for the top line, all the cards are identical. Figure 5.3 illustrates the author card for a particular work. The access points for this book are: author, joint author, title and two LC-established subject headings.

Cross reference cards are used to direct the card catalog user to the proper terminology or to additional sources of information. There are two kinds of cross reference cards—*see* and *see also*. The *see* reference directs the card catalog user from a subject heading or term that is not used to the synonymous term that is used (Figure 5.4). The *see also* reference card lists related subject headings under which more information can be found (Figure 5.5).

```
HD —— 1        2 —— Jongeward, Dorothy.
6058           3 ———— Affirmative action for women:  a practical guide [by]
J65            4    Dorothy Jongeward, Dru Scott, and contributors.  Reading, Mass., —— 5
               6 —— Addison-Wesley Pub. Co. [1973] ————————————————— 7
               8 —— xvi, 334 p.  Illus.  22 cm.
               9 —— Includes bibliographies.

               10a ——1. Women--Employment--United States.  2.  Discrimination in —— 10b
                    Employment--United States.  I. Scott, Dru, joint author.  II.  Title —— 10c

               11—— HD6058.J65          331.4'0973          73-10592 ———— 13
               12—— ISBN 0-201-03293-7                      MARC———— 14

     Library of Congress
```

1. Call number (Library of Congress class number and author number)
2. Author (first one listed on the title page)
3. Title of the book
4. Restatement of the authors' names
5. Place of publication
6. Publisher
7. Publication date
8. Physical description (preliminary paging, textual paging, note that it contains illustrations, size of book)
9. Notes (book includes bibliographies)
10. Tracings (traces cards in catalog for this book)
    10a Subject headings
    10b Joint author
    10c Title
11. Classification numbers assigned by the Library of Congress
12. International Standard Book Number
13. Library of Congress catalog number
14. MARC note (record available in Machine Readable Catalog (MARC) format)

Figure 5.3. Author or main entry card from a printed card catalog.

```
              DISCRIMINATION AGAINST WOMEN

                           see

              SEX DISCRIMINATION AGAINST WOMEN
```

Figure 5.4. Subject cross reference.

```
     DISCRIMINATION

     see also: Age discrimination; Civil rights; Discrimination in education; Discrimination in employment;
     Discrimination in housing; Discrimination in public accommodation; Minorities; Race discrimination;
     Sex discrimination; Toleration.
```

Figure 5.5. See also cross reference.

Arrangement of Cards in Catalog

There are two commonly used methods of alphabetizing—*letter by letter* and *word by word*. Dictionaries use letter-by-letter filing as do some indexes and encyclopedias. Cards in the card catalog are filed word by word. You need to be aware of differences in the two methods so that you will not miss entries in reference sources. The word-by-word method treats each word in a name, title, or subject heading as a separate unit, while the letter-by-letter method treats all the words in a name, title, or subject heading as if they were one unit. In other words, in the letter-by-letter method all the words in the heading are run together as if they were one word.

EXAMPLE ■

Word by Word	*Letter by Letter*
San Antonio	San Antonio
San Diego	Sanctuary
San Pedro	Sandalwood
Sanctuary	Sandblasting
Sand blasting	Sand, George
Sand, George	San Diego
Sandalwood	San Pedro

◆ ONLINE CATALOGS

Today most libraries have replaced the card catalog either entirely or in part by an automated catalog, usually referred to as an OPAC (Online Public Access Catalog). Online catalogs were made possible with the advent of MARC (machine readable catalog) records in 1965. MARC records are stored in electronic format and retrieved by the use of a computer. The Library of Congress developed the MARC format as a means of improving access to library information. Since that time it has been universally adopted by libraries throughout the world as a means for cataloging library materials.

Online catalogs may be described in one of two ways: access is through a host-based mode using Telnet software, or access is Web-based, directly through the Internet. With Telnet, all interaction is in the form of lines of text—hence, the term *text-based* is often used to refer to this mode. In the early days of online catalogs, terminals rather than personal computers were used to access catalogs. A terminal has a screen and a keyboard but lacks a processor. A terminal can only display data sent to it from another computer. Aside from only displaying text, it is activated only by a keyboard and does not respond to a mouse. Although most libraries no longer use terminals, they continue to provide Telnet access, which emulates a terminal. Others have switched to direct Internet access (or use both means of access). This type of catalog is called a WebPAC (Web Public Access Catalog). It has a graphic interface and can be activated by a mouse. Both Telnet and WebPAC are designed to make searching a library catalog simpler and more effective than using a card catalog.

Using the Online Catalog to Find Information

Access Points

The purpose of cataloging materials in a library is to describe certain elements of each item in the collection so that it can be identified and retrieved. The elements used in describing the work are the keys to access. In card catalogs the access points are called *entries*. In online records, they are called *fields*. The main access points in any online cataloging record are author, title, subject, and keyword. Each of these is discussed further in Chapter 4.

Searching the Online Catalog

The greatest advantage of an online catalog is that it provides access to library materials in ways not possible with a card catalog. Note that with the card catalog the access points are limited to author, title, and subject. The online catalog provides all of those access points plus keyword search capabilities. In addition to the public catalog, online systems may have other capabilities. These include the ability to:

◆ update the catalog on a daily basis;
◆ provide information concerning materials on order;
◆ provide circulation information, such as whether or not material has been checked out;
◆ provide information on periodical holdings; and
◆ access the database from remote locations, such as a faculty office, dormitory room, or home.

One of the problems with searching for information in online catalogs of libraries throughout the world is that libraries use different software packages, each of which has its own command language. Even so, there is much commonality among them. The basic search techniques discussed in Chapter 4 apply to searching online catalogs. In addition, most catalogs provide help screens and tutorials to show you how to find information. Once you become familiar with searching the online catalog in your library, you should not have difficulty searching any catalog. Figures 5.6–5.14 show results of searches in a text-based catalog.

Online Catalogs (Text-Based): Sample Screens

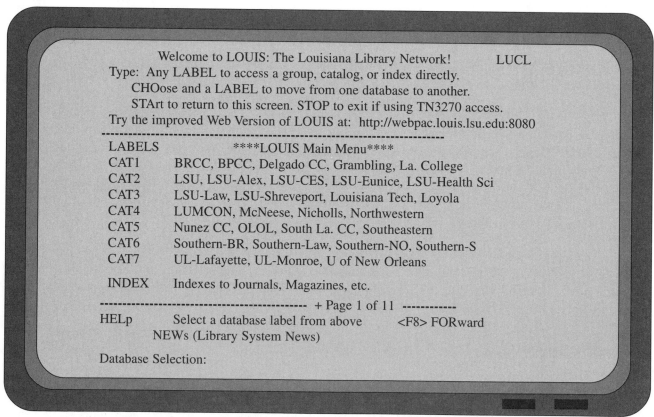

```
              Welcome to LOUIS: The Louisiana Library Network!          LUCL
     Type:  Any LABEL to access a group, catalog, or index directly.
        CHOose and a LABEL to move from one database to another.
        STArt to return to this screen. STOP to exit if using TN3270 access.
     Try the improved Web Version of LOUIS at:  http://webpac.louis.lsu.edu:8080
     -----------------------------------------------------------------
     LABELS              ****LOUIS Main Menu****
     CAT1       BRCC, BPCC, Delgado CC, Grambling, La. College
     CAT2       LSU, LSU-Alex, LSU-CES, LSU-Eunice, LSU-Health Sci
     CAT3       LSU-Law, LSU-Shreveport, Louisiana Tech, Loyola
     CAT4       LUMCON, McNeese, Nicholls, Northwestern
     CAT5       Nunez CC, OLOL, South La. CC, Southeastern
     CAT6       Southern-BR, Southern-Law, Southern-NO, Southern-S
     CAT7       UL-Lafayette, UL-Monroe, U of New Orleans

     INDEX      Indexes to Journals, Magazines, etc.

     ------------------------------------ + Page 1 of 11 ------------
     HELp       Select a database label from above      <F8> FORward
                NEWs (Library System News)

     Database Selection:
```

Figure 5.6. Introductory screen for a text-based online catalog. CAT# refers to the catalogs of member libraries in the network. INDEX is the access point to periodical indexes and abstracts available to authorized users.

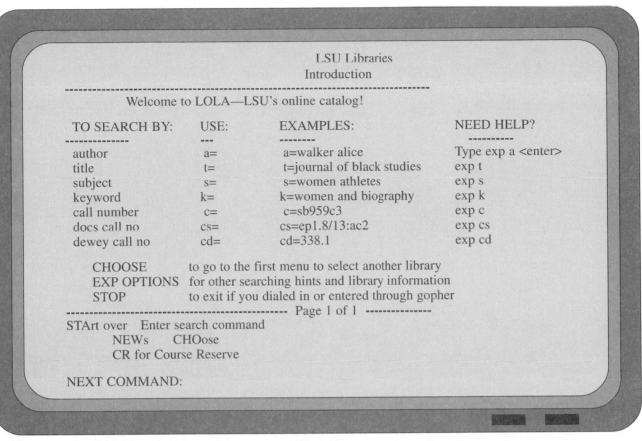

Figure 5.7. Introductory screen describing the commands to use in searching the online catalog.

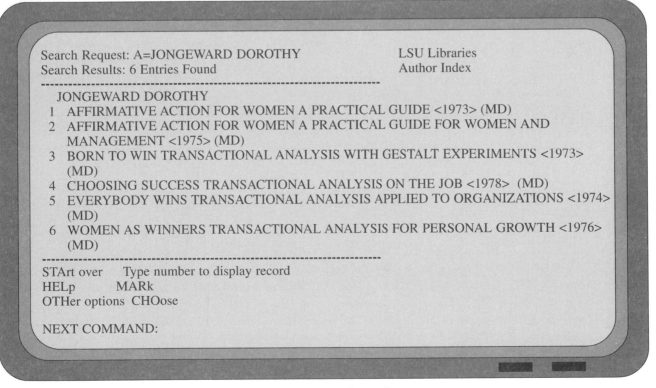

Figure 5.8. Author search. Notice that there are six entries for this author.

```
Search Request: A=JONGEWARD DOROTHY              LSU Libraries
BOOK - Record 1 of 6 Entries Found               Long View
-------------------------------------------------------------------
Author:      Jongeward, Dorothy.
Title:       Affirmative action for women: a practical guide [by] Dorothy
             Jongeward, Dru Scott, and contributors.
Publisher:   Reading, Mass., Addison-Wesley Pub. Co. [c1973]
Subjects:    Women--Employment--United States.
             Sex discrimination in employment--United States.
Other authors: Scott, Dru.
Description: xvi, 334 p. illus. 22 cm.
Notes:       Includes bibliographies.
-------------------------------------------------------------------
 LOCATION:              CALL NUMBER              STATUS:
 MIDDLETON              HD 6058 J65              Not checked out
------------------------------ Page 1 of 1 -----------------
STArt over   BRIef view   CHOose              <F6> NEXt record
HELp         INDex
OTHer options  MARk

NEXT COMMAND:
```

Figure 5.9. Long view of the first record in Figure 5.8. This was retrieved by typing the line number from the index screen, then typing "lon" in the command line for the long view of the record. Notice that it shows the established subject headings.

```
Search Request: T=AFFIRMATIVE ACTION              LSU Libraries
Search Results: 96 Entries Found                Title Guide
-----------------------------------------------------------------
 1  AFFIRMATIVE ACTION
 3  AFFIRMATIVE ACTION A COMPREHENSIVE RECRUITMENT MANUAL
 4  AFFIRMATIVE ACTION A REFERENCE HANDBOOK
 5  AFFIRMATIVE ACTION AFTER THE JOHNSON DECISION PRACTICAL GUIDANCE FOR
    PLANNING AND COMPLIANCE
 6  AFFIRMATIVE ACTION AN ANNOTATED BIBLIOGRAPHY
 7  AFFIRMATIVE ACTION AND EQUAL EMPLOYMENT A GUIDEBOOK FOR EMPLOYERS
 8  AFFIRMATIVE ACTION AND EQUAL EMPLOYMENT KNOXVILLE AND OAK RIDGE A REPORT
 9  AFFIRMATIVE ACTION AND EQUAL OPPORTUNITY ACTION INACTION REACTION
10  AFFIRMATIVE ACTION AND EQUAL PROTECTION HEARINGS BEFORE THE SUBCOMMITTEE
    ON THE CONSTITUTION OF THE COMMITTEE ON THE J
11  AFFIRMATIVE ACTION AND FEDERAL CONTRACT COMPLIANCE HEARING BEFORE THE
    SUBCOMMITTEE ON CIVIL AND CONSTITUTIONAL RIGHTS
12  AFFIRMATIVE ACTION AND JUSTICE A PHILOSOPHICAL AND CONSTITUTIONAL
    INQUIRY
---------------------------------- CONTINUED on next page ----
STArt over    Type number to begin display within index range
HELp  INDex                      <F8> FORward page
OTHer options  CHOose

NEXT COMMAND:
```

Figure 5.10. Title search. Shows the results of a title search: t=affirmative action. The screen displays all the first 12 of 96 titles that begin with "affirmative action."

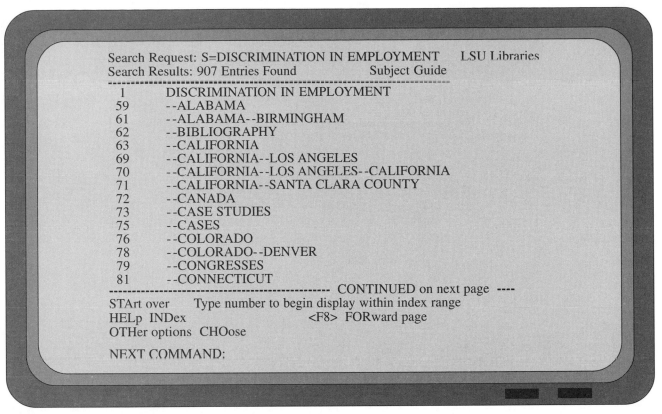

```
Search Request: S=DISCRIMINATION IN EMPLOYMENT     LSU Libraries
Search Results: 907 Entries Found                  Subject Guide
-------------------------------------------------------------------
    1         DISCRIMINATION IN EMPLOYMENT
   59         --ALABAMA
   61         --ALABAMA--BIRMINGHAM
   62         --BIBLIOGRAPHY
   63         --CALIFORNIA
   69         --CALIFORNIA--LOS ANGELES
   70         --CALIFORNIA--LOS ANGELES--CALIFORNIA
   71         --CALIFORNIA--SANTA CLARA COUNTY
   72         --CANADA
   73         --CASE STUDIES
   75         --CASES
   76         --COLORADO
   78         --COLORADO--DENVER
   79         --CONGRESSES
   81         --CONNECTICUT
-------------------------------------- CONTINUED on next page ----
STArt over    Type number to begin display within index range
HELp  INDex                          <F8> FORward page
OTHer options  CHOose

NEXT COMMAND:
```

Figure 5.11. Subject search.

```
Search Request: S=DISCRIMINATION IN EMPLOYMENT   LSU Libraries
Search Results: 907 Entries Found                Subject Index
-------------------------------------------------------------------
    DISCRIMINATION IN EMPLOYMENT
  1   *For Information on this Heading, Type 1

    DISCRIMINATION IN EMPLOYMENT
      *Search Also Under:
  2   AFFIRMATIVE ACTION PROGRAMS
  3   AGE DISCRIMINATION IN EMPLOYMENT
  4   BLACKLISTING LABOR
  5   EQUAL PAY FOR EQUAL WORK
  6   REVERSE DISCRIMINATION IN EMPLOYMENT
  7   SEX DISCRIMINATION IN EMPLOYMENT

    DISCRIMINATION IN EMPLOYMENT
  8   AFFIRMATIVE ACTION AND PUBLIC EMPLOYMENT COUNTY OF LOS ANGELES V
      DAVIS <1979> microfilm  (MD)
------------------------------------- CONTINUED on next page ----
STArt over    Type number to display record     <F8> FORward page
HELp       GUIde       CHOose
OTHer options  MARk

NEXT COMMAND:
```

Figure 5.12. Shows the results of requesting no. 1 from the subject search shown in Figure 5.11. Selecting no. 1 would retrieve a screen giving the scope of the subject. Nos. 1—7 are suggestions for additional subject headings.

```
Search Request: S=DISCRIMINATION IN EMPLOYMENT    LSU Libraries
BOOK—Record 8 of 907 Entries Found        Long View
-----------------------------------------------------------------------
Author:      Ackerman, David M.
Title:       Affirmative action and public employment [microform] : County
                 of Los Angeles v. Davis / David M. Ackerman.
Other titles: County of Los Angeles v. Davis.
Publisher:   [Washington, DC] : Library of Congress, Congressional Research
                 Service, 1979.
Subjects:    Minorities--Employment.
                 Discrimination in employment.
Series:      Major studies and issue briefs of the Congressional Research
                 Service. Supplement ; 1979-80, reel 1, fr. 0920.
Other authors: Library of Congress. Congressional Research Service.
Description: 5 p. ; 28 cm.
Notes:       Cover title.
                 "Date updated 05/24/79."
                 "Issue brief number IB78255."
------------------------------------------------- Page 1 of 3 -----------
STArt over    BRIef view    MARk        <F8> FORward page
HELp          INDex         CHOose      <F6> NEXt record
OTHer options GUIde                     <F5> PREvious record
NEXT COMMAND:
```

Figure 5.13. Long view of one of the titles resulting from the subject search shown in Figure 5.11.

```
Search Request: K=DISCRIMINATION AND WOMEN AND EMPLOY      LSU Libraries
Search Results: 338 Entries Found                  Keyword Index
-----------------------------------------------------------------------
      DATE   TITLE:                        AUTHOR:
  1   2000   On account of sex : an annotated bibliogra           MD
  2   1999   Gender and power in the workplace : analys Bradley, Harriet  MD
  3   1999   Gender at work : organizational change for Rao, Aruna        MD
  4   1999   The measurement of segregation in the labo Fluckiger, Yves   MD
  5   1999   Same or different : gender politics in the Fraser, Kay M     MD
  6   1999   Sexual harassment : analyses and bibliogra Argos, V. P       MD
  7   1999   Women and work : twenty-five years of gend Rees, Teresa L    MD
  8   1999   Women at war : gender issues of Americans Skaine, Rosemarie  MD
  9   1999   Women's figures : an illustrated guide to Furchtgott-Roth, D MD
 10   1998   Crimes of outrage : sex, violence and Vict D'Cruze, Shani    MD
 11   1998   Facts about pregnancy discrimination        GP
 12   1998   The Family and Medical Leave Act, the Amer                   GP
 13   1998   Mainstreaming equality in the European uni Rees, Teresa L    MD
 14   1998   One-eyed science : occupational health and Messing, Karen    MD
-------------------------------------------- CONTINUED on next page ----
STArt over    Type number to display record        <F8> FORward page
HELp          MARk
OTHer options CHOose

NEXT COMMAND:
```

Figure 5.14. Keyword search. Shows the results of a keyword search: k=discrimination and women and employment. The system only recorded part of the search request as it was too long; it actually searched for the word employment. Notice that the search resulted in 338 entries. The subject search s=discrimination in employment in Figure 5.11 retrieved 907 entries.

Periodical Indexes in an Integrated Online System

One of the capabilities of some of the software for online systems is the ability to manage bibliographic records for periodical indexes in the same database as the online catalog. Many of the text-based systems provide this capability.

ADVANTAGES OF HAVING PERIODICAL INDEXES AVAILABLE THROUGH THE SAME SYSTEM AS THE LIBRARY'S ONLINE CATALOG

▼ It provides the ability to do "one-stop shopping." The user can search one system for both books and periodical articles on a topic.

▼ Many of the systems provide a "hook to holdings." That is, after retrieving a citation, one can query the database to see if the library owns the periodical.

▼ The search techniques for the periodical articles are the same as those for books in the online catalog, thus providing a measure of standardization.

Web-Based Catalogs

Many online catalogs are now Web-based; they have a graphic interface, which is generally easier to use and easier to understand than the original Telnet versions. Web-based catalogs, sometimes known as WebPACs (Web Public Access Catalog), have labeled fields for each record and explicit onscreen instructions and capabilities. One main advantage of a Web-based catalog is the capability of "hot links" to Internet sites. That is, if you click on the URL in the catalog record you will go directly to the Internet site. This is extremely helpful to remote users, since they can now link directly from the online catalog to a Web-based document. It is also valuable to local and in-house users who can switch back and forth from cataloged information to full-text Web sites. You can compile bibliographies by downloading or exporting information, or you can insert information from the Internet directly into a word processing document while you have the information on the screen.

Figure 5.15 shows the first screen of the results of a search in a Web-based catalog for a journal entitled *Demography*. Figure 5.16 shows the record for the journal. Notice that the publication is available in the library in print, on microfilm, and online. The record provides "hot links" to the journal as well as to other subject headings and to other authors. Since this is a subscription, only authorized users will have access to the e-journal.

Online Catalogs (Web-Based): Sample Screens

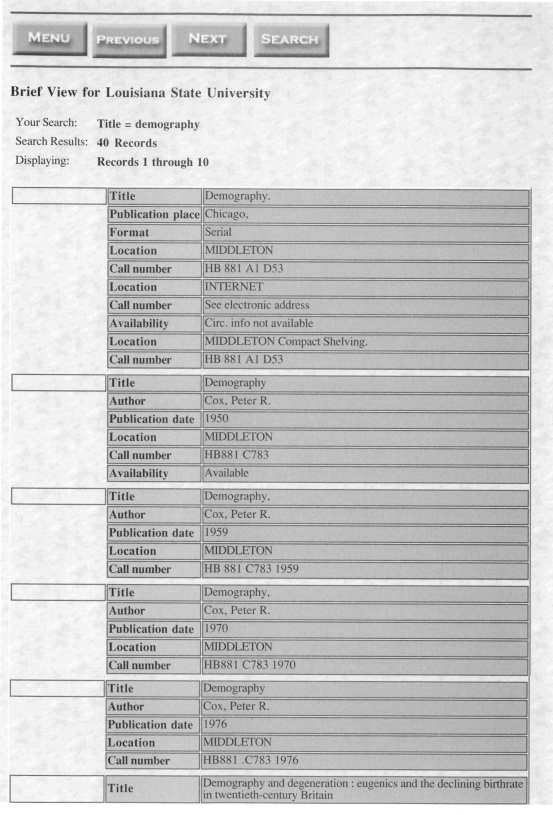

MENU	PREVIOUS	NEXT	SEARCH

Brief View for Louisiana State University

Your Search:	**Title = demography**
Search Results:	**40 Records**
Displaying:	**Records 1 through 10**

	Title	Demography.
	Publication place	Chicago,
	Format	Serial
	Location	MIDDLETON
	Call number	HB 881 A1 D53
	Location	INTERNET
	Call number	See electronic address
	Availability	Circ. info not available
	Location	MIDDLETON Compact Shelving.
	Call number	HB 881 A1 D53
	Title	Demography
	Author	Cox, Peter R.
	Publication date	1950
	Location	MIDDLETON
	Call number	HB881 C783
	Availability	Available
	Title	Demography,
	Author	Cox, Peter R.
	Publication date	1959
	Location	MIDDLETON
	Call number	HB 881 C783 1959
	Title	Demography,
	Author	Cox, Peter R.
	Publication date	1970
	Location	MIDDLETON
	Call number	HB881 C783 1970
	Title	Demography
	Author	Cox, Peter R.
	Publication date	1976
	Location	MIDDLETON
	Call number	HB881 .C783 1976
	Title	Demography and degeneration : eugenics and the declining birthrate in twentieth-century Britain

Figure 5.15. Title search in Web-based catalog.

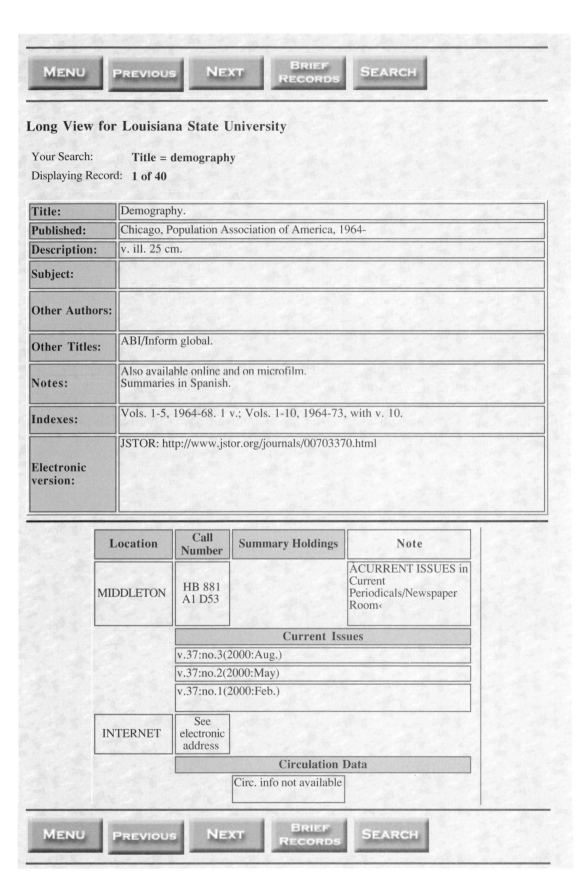

Figure 5.16. Record for e-journal *Demography*. Notice that it is also available in print and microfilm.

Library Catalogs from Around the World

Researchers have a great advantage in being able to search online catalogs from all over the world— from the Library of Congress (the national library of the United States) to the Bibliothèque Nationale (the national library of France). In many instances, they are able to find materials in a distant library that are not available locally. Most online catalogs are searched with the same search commands discussed earlier: author, title, subject, and keyword. Many have call number searching and other features. Although the search engines are not totally standardized, the search commands are easily recognized.

Some online catalogs now include options for ordering materials from other branches or libraries. The Nebraska State College Library System, which includes Wayne State College, Peru State College, and Chadron State College, provides access to all of the materials held by its members to students and faculty in all three colleges. Students and faculty can request material from any library in the consortium through their own campus network. Materials are then sent to their local library. Larger systems such as the Louisiana Library Network (LOUIS) and OhioLink have similar options. This additional access to materials provides patrons much-needed material that their local library does not have. Sharing of materials among libraries through inter-library loan programs has been in practice for many years, but the technology now allows patrons to request and receive materials directly, thus simplifying the procedures.

Taking this concept of shared resources one step further, *WorldCat,* the OCLC catalog of catalogs, is a database comprised of the holdings of more than 30,000 libraries in over 65 countries. Member libraries add cataloged materials to the database every 15 seconds, making this an excellent source for identifying and locating material. In addition to providing cataloging information for the item, *WorldCat* also lists libraries that hold the material, making interlibrary loan procedures much easier.

Library Catalogs

5

Instructor: _____ Course/Section: _____

Name: _____

Date: _____ Points: _____

Review Questions

1. Which classification system is used in most academic libraries in the United States?

2. How many main classes are found in the:

   a. Dewey Decimal classification system?

   b. Library of Congress classification system?

3. What does the class or classification number stand for in the call number in either the Dewey or the LC system?

4. What are the main differences between the Dewey Decimal and Library of Congress classification systems?

5. Why is it useful for researchers to become familiar with class letters and numbers in their subjects of interest?

6. Identify the correct classification systems for each of the following.

   | a. 341.7 Am26 | b. E 3.45/2:988 | c. ST/ESA/165 | d. F369 D 25 1960 |

   a.

   b.

   c.

   d.

7. What determines the location of a book in the library's collection?

8. Why are location symbols used in some libraries?

9. What is the purpose of the library catalog?

10. What is a card catalog?

11. How does a card catalog differ from an online catalog?

12. Name the three different kinds of catalog cards found for most material.

    a.

    b.

    c.

13. Which form of alphabetizing is used in a card catalog? In most dictionaries?

14. Name four access points to library resources in an online catalog.

    a.

    b.

    c.

    d.

15. What is the difference between a text-based catalog and a Web-based catalog?

16. How does keyword searching differ from subject searching?

17. What is the purpose of the *Library of Congress Subject Headings*?

Library Catalogs

Instructor: _____ Course/Section: _____

Name: _____

Date: _____ Points: _____

Understanding Classification Systems

1. Use Figure 5.2 to answer these questions about the Dewey Decimal classification system.

    a. What number range would include works on psychology?

    b. What number range would you use to find books on zoology?

    c. What number range would you use to find books written in the German language?

2. Use Figure 5.2 to answer these questions for the Library of Congress (LC) classification system.

    a. What general number would you use to find sociology books?

    b. What general number would you use to find reference books on medicine?

    c. In what call number range would you find periodicals on American history?

3. Use Figure 5.1 to answer these questions about the Superintendent of Documents (SuDocs) classification system.

    a. Give the names of three government agencies that are likely to publish information on drug abuse.

    b. Which agency of the government produces tax forms?

Library Catalogs

Instructor: _____ Course/Section: _____

Name: _____

Date: _____ Points: _____

Identifying Call Numbers

Listed below are three sets of call numbers. For each set, identify the classification system used and arrange each row of numbers within the set in shelf order. Place a number under the call number indicating the order.

Classification system:_____

PS	PR	PR	PQ	PR
559	5219	132	3939	5219
.R87R8	.R26Q3	.T8	.D37E4	1865
	1856			.R26L5
HT	HT	HT	HT	HT
393	393	393	393	393
.L616	.L62R323	.L62L52	.L62R52	.L6R52
KFL	KFL	KFL	KFL	KFL
112	45	45	211	30
.A2	.1	.A212	.Z9L68	.5
1820	.W35			.N48A3
				1910
TD	TD	TD	TD	TD
525	194	624	195	525
.L6S4	.5	.L8A53	.P4U555	.L3J48
	.E58		1978	

Classification system:_____

261	261	261	261	261
R51k	R6h	R13p	R13pr	R519g
828	828	828	828	828
M57p	M57	M57b	M5655	M152g
973.016	973.7349	973.41	973.8	973.8
W93	Ev26a	W277	G767ca	G767
341.6016	341.7	341.6016	341.63	341.67
W93	Am26	Am4	Am14c	Am35a

Classification system:_____

D301.6:177-19/988	D5.350:96943	D301.6:177-19/989
Y4.Ap6/6:L11/990/pt.2	Y3.T25: 2 W53	Y3 Ad6: 2F31
Al3.13:F39	Al3.13: W36/2/989	Al3.2: Si 3/7
HE20.3038:G28/988	HH1.108/a:N81c	HH1.2:R26/11
EP1.8:Su7/5	ED1.17:D84	ED1.4/2:45/5
ED1.308:D84	E3.2/2:Ut3/2	E3.2:C16/998

Library Catalogs

Instructor: _____ Course/Section: _____

Name: _____

Date: _____ Points: _____

Locating Material Using Classification Systems

Use Figure 5.1 to determine which type of classification system(s) is used in your library.

1. Select a number range in an area of interest to you (e.g., education would be 370 in Dewey Decimal, L in Library of Congress).

    What number did you select?

2. Go to the book stacks in your library and select a book from this general number range. Give the following information.

    Author:

    Title:

    Call number:

3. If your library catalogs periodicals, use this same general call number range to find a periodical. Give the following information.

    Title of the periodical:

    Call number (if given):

    Title of one article within the periodical:

4. Find a reference work using the same general number range. Give the following information.

    Author (if given):

    Title of the publication:

    Date of publication:

5. In the online catalog type in the call number of the book you selected in Question 2 above. What additional information did you receive about the book from the online catalog?

Library Catalogs

5
Instructor: _____ Course/Section: _____

Name: _____

Date: _____ Points: _____

Interpreting a Catalog Card

```
                    ARTIFICIAL INTELLIGENCE.
P           Moyne, John A.
37               Understanding language: man or machine / John A. Moyne.
.M69        --New York: Plenum Press, c1985.
1985             xvi, 357 p. ; ill. , 24 cm.--(Foundations of computer science)
            Bibliography: p. 325-345.
            Includes index.
            ISBN 0-306-41970-X


    1. Psycholinguistics.  2. Linguistics--Data processing.  3. Comprehension.
    4. Artificial intelligence.  5. Grammar, Comparative and general.  6. Formal
    languages.   I. Title. II. Series.
    P37.M69 1985                          401.9                   85-12341
                                                            AACR 2 MARC


Library of Congress
```

1. Use the information on the catalog card reproduced above to identify each of the following items.

    a. Call number of this book:

    b. Classification system used:

    c. Author/authors:

    d. Complete title of the work:

    e. Physical description of the work:

2. Is the work illustrated?

    How can you tell?

3.   Does it have a list of sources or references?

     How can you tell?

4.   List the subject headings used for this book.

5.   How are the assigned subject headings used in the research process?

6.   Name four other entries you could look under in the card catalog to find this work. Give the
     exact words you would use.

     a.

     b.

     c.

     d.

7.   Which type of record does this card represent?

     a.   Author entry
     b.   Title entry
     c.   Subject entry
     d.   Joint author
     e.   Corporate author
     f.   Series

8.   Write a complete bibliographic citation for this work. Use the bibliographic citation examples
     in Appendix A.

Library Catalogs

5

Instructor: _____ Course/Section: _____

Name: _____

Date: _____ Points: _____

Using the Library of Congress Subject Headings

Use the latest edition of the *LCSH* available in your library. List the subject headings and possible subheadings that are appropriate for a topic you have chosen. Write N/A (not applicable) where no information is available.

1. Topic selected:

2. Subject heading or headings found:

3. Was there a classification letter or number following any of the subject headings? If so, list them here.

4. List up to three subdivisions found under the topic.

   a.

   b.

   c.

5. List any used for (**UF**) terms.

6. List one related term (**RT**).

7. List one broad term (**BT**).

8. List one narrow term (**NT**).

Library Catalogs

5   Instructor: _____ Course/Section: _____

     Name: _____

     Date: _____ Points: _____

The Online Catalog

Select any three of the following **subjects**. Use your library catalog to determine whether or not the library has any books on these subjects.

drug abuse	computers	photography
airplanes	animal rights	environment
history of the church in Mexico	Kosovo	child development
alcoholism	journalism	social security
boxing	race cars	sports
crime and criminals	economic conditions in China	

1. Give the following information for each subject you selected.

    1st subject (name):

    Title of most recent work that you located on the subject:

    Commands or search terms used to look up information:

_____

    2nd subject (name):

    Title of most recent work that you located on the subject:

    Commands or search terms used to look up information:

_____

    3rd subject (name):

    Title of most recent work that you located on the subject:

    Commands or search terms used to look up information:

_____

2. Look up three **authors** from the list below in your library's catalog.

Anne Rice	Virginia Woolf	Mary Higgins Clark	John Grisham
Truman Capote	Stephen King	Maya Angelou	Michael Crichton
Sidney Sheldon	James Joyce	Walt Whitman	Oscar Wilde
Benjamin Franklin	Henry L. Mencken	Bill Gates	John F. Kennedy

Give the following information for the authors you selected.

1st author (name):

Title of most recent work that you located:

Commands or search terms used to look up information:

_____

2nd author (name):

Title of most recent work that you located:

Commands or search terms used to look up information:

_____

3rd author (name):

Title of most recent work that you located:

Commands or search terms used to look up information:

_____

3.   Look up two of the following **titles** in your library's online catalog.

MLA Handbook for Writers of Research Papers   Who's Who in America
Twentieth Century Authors   Julius Caesar
Silent Spring   Webster's New World Dictionary
Statistical Abstract of the United States   Arabian Nights

Give the following information for each of the titles.

1st title:

Call number:

Commands or search terms used to look up information:

_____

2nd title:

Call number

Commands or search terms used to look up information:

_____

4.   Look up each of the following **periodical and newspaper titles** in your library's online catalog. Write the call number next to the periodical.

Time   People Weekly

USA Today (newspaper)   JAMA (Journal of the American Medical Assn.)

The New York Times   Jet

5.   Does your library catalog indicate that any of these titles are located in a full-text database or
that it is available online as an e-journal? If so, indicate which ones.

6. Conduct a **keyword** search in your library's online catalog for three of the following topics.

an educational dictionary   a government document on divorce
effect of nuclear war on the environment   hurricane statistics
modern politics in France   alcoholism and divorce
books on pets other than dogs or cats   benefits of IRAs

Give the following information for each of the topics you selected.

1st topic:

Title of the most recent work you located:

Call Number:

Location:

Commands or search terms used to look up information:

2nd topic:

Title of the most recent work you located:

Call Number:

Location:

Commands or search terms used to look up information:

3rd topic:

Title of the most recent work you located:

Call Number:

Location:

Commands or search terms used to look up information:

Library Catalogs

5

Instructor: _____ Course/Section: _____

Name: _____

Date: _____ Points: _____

Online Catalog

Use the following sample screen from the online catalog at the LSU Libraries to respond to the questions below.

```
Search Request: S=WOMEN--EMPLOYMENT--UNITED STATES     LSU Libraries
BOOK - Record 416 of 495 Entries Found                  Long View
-------------------------------------------------------------------------------
Author:      Schneider, Dorothy.
Title:       The ABC-CLIO companion to women in the workplace / Dorothy
             Schneider and Carl J. Schneider.
Publisher:   Santa Barbara, Calif.: ABC-CLIO, c1993.
Series:      ABC-CLIO companions to key issues in American history and life.
Description: xxix, 371 p. ill. ; 27 cm.
Subjects:    Women--Employment--United States--History--Dictionaries
Other authors: Schneider, Carl J.
Other titles: Women in the workplace.
Notes:       Spin title: Women in the workplace.
             Includes bibliographical references (p. 323–356) and index.
LOCATION                    CALL NUMBER:                 STATUS:
MIDDLETON                   JD 6095 S34 1993             Not checked out
```

1. Who is the author of this work?

2. Name the publisher and the place of publication.

3. What is the date of publication?

4. Is the work illustrated?

    Justify your answer.

5. What subject headings are used for this work?

6. Is this work part of a series?

    How can you tell?

7. Would this book be an appropriate source for the topic "equal employment for women"? Explain your answer.

Use the following subject guide screen to answer the questions below.

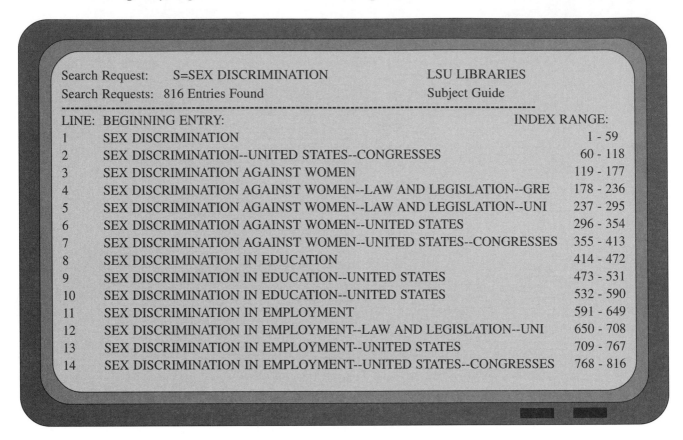

Search Request:	S=SEX DISCRIMINATION	LSU LIBRARIES
Search Requests:	816 Entries Found	Subject Guide

LINE:	BEGINNING ENTRY:	INDEX RANGE:
1	SEX DISCRIMINATION	1 - 59
2	SEX DISCRIMINATION--UNITED STATES--CONGRESSES	60 - 118
3	SEX DISCRIMINATION AGAINST WOMEN	119 - 177
4	SEX DISCRIMINATION AGAINST WOMEN--LAW AND LEGISLATION--GRE	178 - 236
5	SEX DISCRIMINATION AGAINST WOMEN--LAW AND LEGISLATION--UNI	237 - 295
6	SEX DISCRIMINATION AGAINST WOMEN--UNITED STATES	296 - 354
7	SEX DISCRIMINATION AGAINST WOMEN--UNITED STATES--CONGRESSES	355 - 413
8	SEX DISCRIMINATION IN EDUCATION	414 - 472
9	SEX DISCRIMINATION IN EDUCATION--UNITED STATES	473 - 531
10	SEX DISCRIMINATION IN EDUCATION--UNITED STATES	532 - 590
11	SEX DISCRIMINATION IN EMPLOYMENT	591 - 649
12	SEX DISCRIMINATION IN EMPLOYMENT--LAW AND LEGISLATION--UNI	650 - 708
13	SEX DISCRIMINATION IN EMPLOYMENT--UNITED STATES	709 - 767
14	SEX DISCRIMINATION IN EMPLOYMENT--UNITED STATES--CONGRESSES	768 - 816

8. How many entries were found for the search s=sex discrimination?

9. Which line number would be the most appropriate for:

    a. legal aspects of this topic?

    b. entries on sex discrimination in education?

    c. sex discrimination in education only in the United States?

    d. employment law regarding sex discrimination?

    e. conferences on sex discrimination in the United States?

    f. general books on sex discrimination?

Library Catalogs

5

Instructor: _____ Course/Section: _____

Name: _____

Date: _____ Points: _____

Using Remote Online Catalogs

Search the Library of Congress catalog located at http://catalog.loc.gov/ to retrieve one of the titles below.

MLA Handbook for Writers of Research Papers   *Who's Who in America*
Twentieth Century Authors   *Julius Caesar*
Silent Spring   *Webster's New World Dictionary*
Statistical Abstract of the United States   *Arabian Nights*

Which title did you select?

Look up this same title in the catalog of your own library.

1.   Compare the results of your search in the Library of Congress catalog with that found in your own online catalog.

     Is the information:

     a.   exactly the same?

     b.   different (be specific)?

2.   What classification system does the Library of Congress use?

3.   What classification system does your library use?

4.   If your library did not have a copy of this book, what library service could you use to request a copy from the Library of Congress or another library?

Search the Library of Congress catalog on a subject that interests you.

5.   What subject did you use?

6.   How many entries did you find?

7.   Were there any cross references (*see* or *see also* notes)? If so, what other terms were you referred to?

8.   Did you have to wait to enter the Library of Congress web site? If so, how long?

9.   Would you use this site again for research purposes? Why?

6

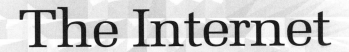

The Internet

"I used to think that cyberspace was fifty years away. What I thought was fifty years away, was only ten years away. And what I thought was ten years away . . . it was already here. I just wasn't aware of it yet."

BRUCE STERLING

INTRODUCTION

In a domain that we have come to call cyberspace, we find people from all walks of life and from throughout the globe communicating with one another, storing information, retrieving information, and producing new information. This is made possible by a technology known as the Internet. The Internet contains information from millions of sources, and is available to anyone with a computer and connections to an Internet service provider. Information on the Internet is of all kinds and is suitable for all levels of information seekers—from pre-school children to advanced researchers. It is a rich source of information that includes primary sources, providing new and original research, and secondary sources—bibliographies, biographies, directories, atlases, encyclopedias, dictionaries, periodical articles, and books.

ADVANTAGES OF INTERNET-BASED INFORMATION
OVER TRADITIONAL PAPER-BASED MATERIALS

▼ There is more information available than with a static collection housed in a building.

▼ Electronic resources have the potential of being more up-to-date than printed materials.

▼ Many electronic resources are searchable, enabling users to access and retrieve the exact information they need.

The unbridled nature of the Internet represents its best and worst features. The quantity of information on the Internet is enormous. It is of every stripe and hue, and runs the gamut from pure nonsense to the most highly respected research. Although Internet resources have the potential to be current, this is frequently not the case. Quite often individuals put information on the Internet for fun or perhaps as part of their current job responsibilities, but have no interest in keeping it up-to-date. This problem is further complicated because it is not always possible to tell whether an electronic resource is up-to-date. Many of the resources do not give a date of publication or a copyright date as do printed publications. But a more serious problem with information resources from the Internet is the lack of quality control. Although printed materials often have errors and inaccuracies, they are at least subjected to some measure of pre-publication evaluation by publishers. Further, librarians use established criteria for selecting printed materials for their libraries. Anyone can be a publisher on the Internet—from elementary school students to research scientists. For the most part, information on the Internet is not subject to any criteria to determine its accuracy or suitability for publication. **The user must be responsible for assessing the quality of the resources.** Table 3.2 provides criteria for evaluating any information resource and includes a checklist for evaluating resources on the Internet.

Accessing information on the Internet requires that you have some familiarity with computers—how to type, how to use word processors, and how to use a mouse. In addition, you need to develop skills for finding information by using a tool that has the potential of finding exactly what you need from a resource that is virtually limitless in possibilities. To become skilled in researching the Internet you need to understand what the Internet is, how it got started, why it is used, and how it works. This chapter answers some of those basic questions. It also provides an introduction to the tools available for exploring its services and resources. The Internet is a complex system requiring many levels of expertise to tap its full range of capabilities. This chapter is only an introduction to get you launched. As you use the Internet, you will find that experience is the best teacher.

◆ ## WHAT IS THE INTERNET?

The Internet is a vast series of networks connected via telephone lines, cables, and communications satellites. The metaphor that is most often used for the Internet is "information superhighway." That image is meant to convey a superhighway over which information travels. It is similar to the Interstate system in the U.S., which crisscrosses the country, connecting states and major cities. Connected to the super highways are smaller highways that are linked to rural roads and city streets. The "Interstate" highway of the Internet is a system of regional networks, which constitute the "backbone" of the system. Connected to the backbone are smaller networks serving particular geographic areas or organizations. Leading into these are small local networks and individual computers.

An Overview

In the 1960s, researchers from the U.S. Defense Department's Advanced Research Projects Agency (ARPA) began linking computers to each other through telephone hook-ups. ARPA was interested in designing a system that would support military research and at the same time provide a measure of security against partial cable outages. Previous computer networking efforts had required a single line between two computers. If something were to go wrong with the system, the entire network would be out of operation. The new system used a software program called Internet Protocol (IP) to send data in packets along a network of communication lines. Each piece of information was split into packets and transmitted from one network node to another until it reached its destination. There it could be reassembled by the computer into a readable message. With this system, researchers could exchange electronic mail (e-mail) and later were able to form discussion groups. Much of the early research for ARPANet was done at universities, where researchers soon realized what a powerful tool it was. They found ways to use ARPANet connections in order to communicate and exchange information with other researchers throughout the country (Krol 11).

In 1986, the National Science Foundation (NSF) provided funding for the creation of five super-computing networks. As more and more researchers connected to the networks, the system became overloaded. NSF again stepped in, upgrading the system to faster communication lines and faster computers. It promoted the widespread use of the Internet by providing funding to those institutions that planned to expand the development and use of the Internet. Until this time, access to the Internet had been limited to researchers in universities and a few government agencies. The five original networks were expanded to fifteen and use was extended to include thousands of colleges, research organizations, and government agencies. By 1988 the NSFNET had replaced ARPANet. In 1991, U.S. Senator Al Gore introduced the National Research and Educational Network (NREN) legislation that expanded NSFNET by extending use to K–12 schools, junior colleges, and community colleges. The legislation also included provisions for businesses to purchase part of the network for commercial use (Krol 15).

Academic research organizations once dominated the use and development of the Internet. Today, commercial networks such as America Online, CompuServe, and Prodigy are major providers of Internet services. They are experiencing competition from a growing number of companies—some local, others nationwide—that are working to provide subscribers direct access to Internet services. The use of the Internet by individuals from every walk of life has grown tremendously since 1991. We do not know exactly how many individual users access the Internet in a year, but a survey conducted in January, 2000, concluded that the number of Internet users over the age of 16 in the U.S. and Canada had reached 92 million, an increase of 13 million from a survey taken just 9 months earlier ("Internet"). Approximately 171 countries were connected to the Internet as of July 1999 (Zakon).

By mid-1994, the U.S. government had removed itself from any day-to-day control over the Internet. The Internet does not "belong" to anyone or any company. Anyone can connect to the Internet and anyone who wishes can "publish" on the Internet. The only "authority" rests with the Internet Society (ISOC). This is a nongovernmental, international organization with voluntary membership whose purpose is to promote global cooperation for the Internet and its working technologies. It is governed by a board that is responsible for setting policy and planning for the future.

Some portions of the Internet are subsidized, but each network is usually self-supporting and each pays for its connection. Commercial providers such as America Online (AOL), Prodigy, CompuServe, and a host of other companies pass their costs on to the user. Colleges and universities that provide access to their faculty and students not only pay the costs of network connections, they also incur large costs for hardware and software.

How the Internet Works

Networks

The basic element of the Internet is the network. A network consists of computers that are connected one to another through a communications channel. The channel may be an ordinary telephone wire, a fiber optic cable, or a high-speed microwave or satellite communications device.

TWO TYPES OF NETWORKS

◆ Local Area Network (LAN)—connects computers in a small geographic area over a single channel.

◆ Wide Area Network (WAN)—connects LANs, one to another over a wide geographic area.

The Internet is a WAN. It is composed of three levels of networks: national, regional and local. To send or receive information over the Internet an individual must be connected to a local network that, in turn, is connected to the other levels as shown in Figure 6.1. Messages sent to individuals within the same local area are routed directly to the recipient's computer via the local network. If the message is being sent to a computer at a distant location, it will be routed through the appropriate local and regional networks until it reaches its destination.

Information Transfer

The software used to send and receive information is called Transmission Control Protocol/Internet Protocol suite (TCP/IP). The Internet is often called a TCP/IP network, and for users to connect to the

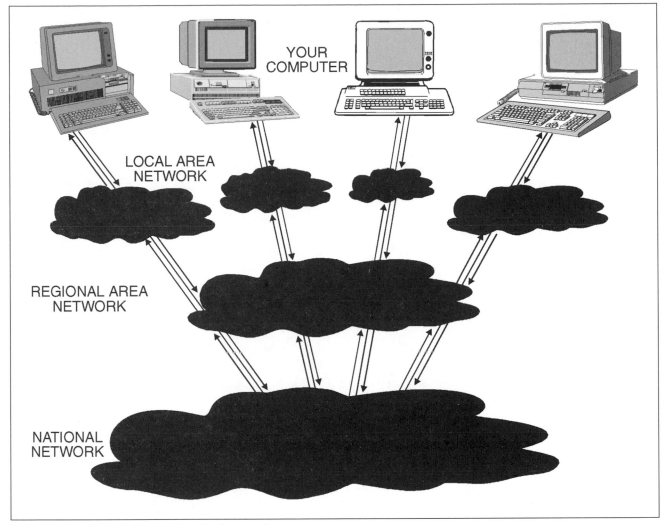

Figure 6.1. The Internet, a network of networks.

Internet they must connect to what is known as an IP address. The other key to information sharing on the Internet is the use of the client/server model of data transfer. In the client/server model one computer serves as a "host" machine that distributes information to a "client" machine that receives information. With the client/server model, client software is installed on a personal computer to perform such tasks as displaying menus to the screen, connecting to a remote computer, and saving files. The server or remote host computer performs tasks such as searching a database and transmitting the results to the client. All of the major Internet tools use the TCP/IP and the client/server model.

How to Connect to the Internet

Most college campuses have Internet connections, but if you are connecting from home you will need a dial-up modem or a high-speed cable connection. For direct access to the Internet you will also need an Internet provider. There are a growing number of commercial Internet providers offering a wide range of services to subscribers. Some of the better known are America Online, CompuServe, AT&T, Sprint, and Prodigy. There are also a number of Internet providers that give free access to the Internet. The tradeoff is that the providers put advertising on the pages.

Note: A list of Internet providers may be found on the Internet at: **http://thelist.com.**

◆ ELECTRONIC MAIL (E-MAIL)

Electronic mail (e-mail) is a feature of the Internet that allows you to send or receive mail electronically. With e-mail you can send a message to any person with an e-mail account anywhere in the world. Mail delivered in this way is extremely fast, usually arriving at its destination within seconds of having been sent. E-mail functions support LISTSERV discussion groups where you can share information with people around the world.

▼ E-MAIL PROCEDURES

1. Logon to the computer and activate the e-mail software.

▶▶ 2. The system will prompt you for the address of the person to whom you are sending mail.

▶▶ 3. Create the message. (Be sure to proofread the message before sending it. Once a message has been sent it is not always possible to retrieve it.)

▶▶ 4. Send the message.

E-Mail Addresses

The e-mail address is based on a user ID (assigned to you by the Internet provider) within the domain at a specific institution.

THE TOP-LEVEL DOMAINS ON THE INTERNET			
EDU	educational institution	ORG	organization
COM	commercial organization or a business	MIL	military organization
GOV	government agency	NET	network resources

◆ LISTSERV

LISTSERVs are a combination of e-mail and Discussion Groups. You must formally subscribe to a LISTSERV in order to receive and send mail. Once you have subscribed you will automatically receive mail that is sent by any other member of the list. To subscribe to a LISTSERV you must first find the address of the list to which you wish to subscribe. Then send a message to that address by placing the following message in the body:

subscribe [name of LISTSERV] [your real name (not your e-mail ID)]

Usenet News

There are thousands of Usenet newsgroups that are designed to serve as electronic forums for discussion, debate, questions, and distribution of software, images, sounds, and other information. The newsgroups' messages are distributed to computer sites all over the world. Each computer site accumulates the messages and redistributes them to its own subscribers. Subscribers can read the articles posted to the Usenet newsgroups, reply to articles, post new articles, save articles, or forward them by via e-mail to others. Newsgroups are listed by categories that define the subject. For example, "soc.culture.fr" deals with social issues related to French culture.

 FILE TRANSFER PROTOCOL (FTP)

File transfer protocol (FTP) allows you to transfer files of all kinds over the Internet. There are special software utilities to handle file transfer. Two of the most widely used are WS-FTP and CuteFTP.

 GOPHER

Gopher is a technology that was developed at the University of Minnesota to handle text files on the Internet. Today Gopher is rarely used except on a few servers that still have large text files.

 WORLD WIDE WEB

What Is It?

The World Wide Web (WWW or Web) is a facet of the Internet that was developed by scientists at CERN, a research institute located in Switzerland. The idea was to develop a tool that would be an improvement on existing technologies such as Gopher. They created Hypertext Transfer Protocol (HTTP), which standardized communication between servers and clients. With the Web, a searcher can follow a thread that will lead to documents and files wherever they might be. The Web also has the capability of presenting information in graphic format: pictures, images, maps, charts, and animations. The World Wide Web is now the primary Internet tool, and in fact, to most people, the Internet is the Web.

How Information on the Web Is Created

The main way that information gets on the Web is through the creation of Web sites. A Web site is any location on the Internet that contains information. Each Web site has its unique address. (See *URL* below.) A *home page*, or a *Web page*, is typically the top level of information at a Web site. It contains links to other Web sites in its collection. For example, http://lib.lsu.edu is the home page for the LSU Libraries. A home page can also be the page that individuals, businesses, or organizations create about themselves.

Information on Web pages is created by the use of *hypertext* or *hypermedia* that allows links to and from files located on servers anywhere on the Internet. In a hypertext document, words, phrases, or images are highlighted in order to point to a different document where more information pertaining to that word can be found. When the user selects a highlighted word or phrase, a second document is opened. (To select a highlighted word or phrase using a mouse interface, the user places the mouse over the highlighted section and clicks the mouse button.) The second document may contain links to other related documents. The linked documents may all be located at different sites, all of which will be transparent to the user as he/she moves through the Web.

Hypertext documents are created by using Hypertext Markup Language (HTML). With HTML the words and phrases are written as normal text but special format codes, called tags, are used to set fonts and colors and to insert images. Certain tags are also used to create links to other Web pages. Many of the pages that you see on the Web contain animation and imaginative graphic creations. These are probably created using special coding languages such as *Java*, which is a powerful tool used to exploit the graphic and audio potential of the Internet. There are a number of Web authoring software programs that allow even the novice to create imaginative and artistic Web pages. Recent versions of word processing software such as Microsoft Word, WordPerfect, and WordPro allow you to convert any document into hypertext. That is, you can prepare Internet-ready materials as easily as you can write a letter or an essay.

Accessing the World Wide Web

The World Wide Web is accessed by means of a browser—a powerful tool that allows you to navigate the Web by pointing and clicking on highlighted words or images (hot links or hyperlinks). The browser then retrieves the selected information from a remote computer and displays it on your screen. This information might be a picture, a movie, text, or sound, or it might be a connection to a Gopher, Usenet Newsgroup, or a Telnet or FTP site. The browser uses the Uniform Resource Locator (URL), which is the address for the link you selected.

There are two types of browsers—text-based and graphical user interface (GUI). With a text-based browser, you can view only the text, while with a GUI browser you can see images.

Mosaic was the first browser to use a graphical interface. It was widely used during the late 1980s and early 1990s, but lately has been replaced by Netscape and Internet Explorer, both of which use features similar to those developed by Mosaic. Mosaic developed software that made it possible to point to hypertext links, display images, and play sounds.

Netscape and *Internet Explorer* are the most widely used Web browsers. They are easy to use and highly versatile. Both can be downloaded free from the Internet. The address for Netscape is http://netscape.com; for Internet Explorer, it is http://www.microsoft.com. At the top of either screen is a standard menu bar and a tool bar with frequently used commands. The block just below the toolbar shows the Internet address (URL) of the document that is currently displayed. A new address can be typed in at any time to change the page. Beneath that is the screen with graphics and hypertext links. Both browsers have features that allow for e-mail, chat, downloading, and the creation of personal home pages.

URL

To go directly to a specific source you must know the URL (Uniform Resource Locator). The URL is a unique global Internet identifier used on the World Wide Web. It allows any document anywhere on the Internet to be accessed by any browser. The URL is comparable to someone's address that gives the country, state, city, street, and house number. URLs are composed of several parts including the Internet access protocol, the location, and the file.

Listings of URLs can be found in a great number of places, including subject guides and directories on the Internet. You can create a special directory on your computer of addresses to frequently visited sites. In Netscape this is called "Bookmarks." In Internet Explorer it is called "Favorite Places." To save the address of a Netscape site that is currently displayed on the screen:

◆   click on the **Bookmarks** button on the menu bar;
◆   click on **Add Bookmark**.

The location of that site will be placed at the bottom of your bookmark list.

To retrieve a site from your Bookmark site:

◆   click on the **Bookmarks** button on the menu bar;
◆   move to the address you want to retrieve.

The **Favorite Places** button in Internet Explorer operates in a similar fashion. Keep in mind that URLs may change and even disappear.

Connecting to the Web and Retrieving Information

To connect to the Internet you will need to connect through an Internet service provider, either from your home or through one available at your institution. The following procedures are based on using a Netscape browser that is installed on a computer that you are using.

STEPS TO RETRIEVE INFORMATION ON THE INTERNET

1. **Connect to the Internet.**

   Click on the Netscape icon (picture symbol).

2. **Go to a URL.**

   From the default page (this will be the default page from Netscape or whatever page has been set up as the default page on the computer you are using) type the URL in the "Location" space below the "Menu" bar. For example, type

   http://www.yahoo.com

3. **Follow links.**

   From the Yahoo main page, select a topic and click on it.
   Type a search statement in the box that is displayed on the Yahoo page.
   When it returns the results, click on a site that is described.
   This will take you to the next Web page.

   > Usually links will be displayed in one color; previously followed links, in a different color. This helps you to avoid clicking on previously searched links. To return to Yahoo's main page, or to go to any previously visited page, click on BACK on the menu bar until you get to the page.

4. **Print information.**

   Click the print button in the toolbar or click on the "File" button and select **Print**.

5. **Exit Netscape.**

   Click on FILE in the menu bar.
   Click on EXIT.

◆ USING SEARCH ENGINES TO FIND INFORMATION ON THE INTERNET

You now know what the Internet is, how much information is available on the Internet, how it gets there, and how to connect to the Internet and retrieve information. This next section will concentrate on finding the appropriate information on the Internet—that is, information that matches your needs. Searching the Internet can be time-consuming and confusing. You have seen how much information is available and how varied it is. To further complicate matters, there are many ways to go about finding information on the Internet. You can search the databases for which your college or university buys a subscription, or you can search the vast amount of free information that is available on the Web. Other chapters are devoted to finding information in specific types of sources—reference works, periodical databases, and government sources. This discussion will focus on using search engines to find information that is free on the Web.

What Is a Search Engine?

A search engine is a utility that searches the entire Internet, a site, or a database for terms that you select. Although *search engine* is really a general class of programs that employs a search mechanism, the term is used here to describe systems like Alta Vista, Google, and Excite that enable users to search for documents and USENET newsgroups on the Web. Typically, a search engine works by sending out a program called a *spider,* or a *robot,* to scan the area to be searched and to retrieve as many documents as possible that correspond to the search request.

Using a search engine to find specific information can be rewarding; at the same time it can be frustrating. Because it is searching so much information, it is likely to return an unmanageable number of results. In addition, there are many search engines and new ones appear regularly. As with any information search, it is important to plan ahead to know which tools to use to achieve the best results.

Developing a Search Strategy

Before you begin any search you should develop a search strategy.

 ASK YOURSELF

◆ Is your topic likely to be found on the Internet?
The Internet is an excellent source for information related to:

Government at all levels	Business	Computers	Engineering
Geography	Travel	Recreation	Biography
Entertainment News	Popular Culture	Arts	Literature

◆ Do you need current or historical information?
Normally, you can expect to find information that is current on the Internet, but you need to be aware that this is not necessarily the case. You need to always check the date of information you find posted on the Internet. You will also find material that is in the public domain; that is, it is older than 75 years, and the copyright has expired.

◆ Decide on which keywords you will use to search for the information you need.

◆ Decide which type of search engine is more appropriate to use for your search.

◆ Evaluate any source you locate. (See the checklist in Table 3.2 for evaluating Internet information.)

Types of Search Engines

While you do not need to learn how to use every search engine, it is helpful to be able to identify some of the more popular ones and to understand the differences among them. As you begin to search the Internet, you will, no doubt, develop one or two favorites and will also learn which ones work best for different information needs.

There are essentially four types of search engines. See Figure 6.2 for examples of search engines.

◆ A **mediated search engine**, also known as a **directory search engine**, searches for information by categories. It is a hierarchical search that starts with a broad subject heading and searches for more specific topics that fall within those categories. This type of search engine searches descriptors that have been placed in a predefined database established by the creators. Yahoo and Lycos are among the more popular search engines of this type.

◆ A **keyword search engine** searches for information through the use of keywords. It sends out a spider, or a robot, that searches for keywords that appear in special fields, called *meta tags*. Since it is searching a much larger database than a directory type search engine, it will gather more information. However, it is more likely to retrieve information that is not relevant. Alta Vista, Google, and Excite are examples of keyword search engines.

    Some search engines combine mediated and keyword searching. They search first in the directory and then move to a keyword search. You can browse in the directory, select a category to search, view the results and then proceed to more specific keyword terms. As you narrow the search you will get fewer but more relevant hits.

◆ A **meta-search engine** (sometimes called a **multi-search engine**) searches a number of search engines in tandem. The search is conducted using keywords employing commonly used operators or plain language. The program then lists the hits either by search engine or by integrating the results into a single listing. The search method it employs is known as a "meta search." It has the advantage of searching over a large number of other search engines, but it is not considered to be as effective as some of the keyword search engines. Dogpile is an example of a meta-search engine.

◆ A **subject search engine** is a mediated search engine dedicated to specific broad subject areas. Findlaw and GovBot are typical of subject specific search engines.

Performing a Search

As new search engines are being developed on a continuing basis, so are changes being made to existing search engines. The search features that one sees today could very well be gone tomorrow. However, it is true that practically all of the major search engines support searching using Boolean operators in one form or another. For example, some search engines use plus (+) or minus (–) symbols to indicate the Booleans AND and NOT, respectively. Search features of a few of the major search engines are shown in Figure 6.3. Review Chapter 4 to remind yourself of basic techniques for searching using Boolean and positional operators.

◆ Different Types of Search Engines

Mediated or Directory	Keyword or Unmediated	Meta-search or Multi-search	Subject
About.com	AltaVista	BigHub	Argos (History)
Ask Jeeves	Excite	Brightgate	BPubs.com (Business)
Beaucoup	Fast	Dogpile	FindLaw (Legal)
LookSmart	Google	Infind	GovBot (Government)
Lycos	HotBot	IxQuick	Health A–Z
Northern Light	Magellan	Profusion	PsychCrawler
Yahoo	Webcrawler	RedSearch	Star Wars

Figure 6.2. Search engines by type.

The search tips below apply to most search engines, but you usually will be better served by first going to the "help" features or "search tips" of individual search engines.

Keyword Search

GUIDELINES TO CONDUCT A SUCCESSFUL KEYWORD SEARCH

▼ Analyze your topic and be as specific as possible.

Request exactly what you are looking for.

For example, if you want information on the harmful effects of diet pills, you want to use all the terms in your search statement—diet/pills/harmful/effects, not just "diet" or "diet pills."

▼ Use Boolean operator AND (or the plus (+) symbol) to narrow a search.

> EXAMPLE ■
>
> Diet and pills and harmful and effects
> **OR**
> diet +pills +harmful +effects

▼ Use the Boolean operator NOT (or the minus (–) symbol) to eliminate pages that have one word on them but not another.

> EXAMPLE ■
>
> You may want to find information about "jazz," but you want to eliminate those pages that have information on the Utah Jazz.
> Jazz not utah
> **OR**
> Jazz -Utah

Phrase Search

A search for keywords retrieves pages that have all the words in your search statement, but the words may not necessarily be near each other. For example, if you did a search on the census forms for the year 2000 (2000 +census +forms) you could get a page that mentions 2000 in one place, census in another, and forms in still another. All of the words in your search statement would appear on the page, but they still might not match your needs. You can do a phrase search to avoid this problem. With a phrase search, you tell the search engine to retrieve the terms in your search statement in the exact order in which you requested them. In most search engines, this is done by enclosing the phrase in quotation marks; others use parentheses.

> EXAMPLE ■
>
> "2000 census forms"
> **OR**
> (2000 census forms)

The search will retrieve pages that have all the words and in the exact order shown above. With some search engines, such as Google, the AND is implied; a search for 2000 census forms without the quotation marks would yield different results from one enclosed in quotation marks.

Natural Language Search

Natural language searching allows you to post a query in the form of a question instead of by keyword or subject. With natural language searching, you simply state your search in the form of a question. For example, if you type: Is acupuncture effective for the relief of pain?, the search engine would ignore common words such as "is," "for," "the," and "of" and find articles containing the words "acupuncture," "effective," "relief," and "pain."

With natural language searching, the search is based on:

◆ the recognition and weighting of usual word combinations, such as "homeless shelters," "United States," or "Third World";

◆ exact matching of search terms to article titles;

◆ proximity of search words in an article; and

◆ the number of times the search terms occurs in each article.

Search results are ranked with those meeting most of the criteria above ranked higher. Natural language searching is good for beginners and for children, but usually it is not as effective as keyword or subject searching.

More Information

Some search engines might be case sensitive, and others might not allow certain types of searches. Still others might have advanced search features that allow you to limit your search in much the same way as you would in an online catalog. For updates on search engines and their features, go to Search Engine Watch (searchenginewatch.com) or look at the help features on individual search engine pages.

Search Engine Features

Figure 6.3 shows some of the important features for a few of the most popular search engines. The information is current as of May, 2000. Recall that the Internet is fluid—anything listed here is subject to change.

 EVALUATING INFORMATION FOUND ON THE INTERNET

It is important to keep in mind that for the most part the sources on the Internet are not subject to standards for reliability and quality. Use the criteria for evaluating information from the Internet found in Table 3.2.

◆ Search Engine Features

Search Engine	Boolean	Plus/ Minus	Phrase*	Natural Language	Stemming	Case Sensitive
AltaVista	no	yes	Q	yes	yes	no
Excite	yes	yes	P	no	no	no
Fast**	no	yes	Q	yes	no	no
Galaxy	yes	no	Q	no	yes	no
GO-Infoseek *	yes	no	Q	no	no	yes
Google	automatic AND	yes	Q	no	yes	no
HotBot**	yes (also, automatic AND)	no	Q	no	no	no
Lycos	yes	no	Q	no	no	no
Magellan	yes	yes	P	no	no	no
Mama	no	yes	Q	no	no	no
Northern Light**	yes	yes	Q	yes	yes	no
Snap	no	yes	Q	no	no	no
Web Crawler	yes	yes	Q	no	no	yes
Yahoo	yes	yes	Q	no	yes	no

*For Phrase searching   Q= uses quotation marks to indicate exact phrase.
                                     P= uses parentheses to indicate exact phrase.
**Provides a form for advanced searching.

Figure 6.3. Search engine features.

◆ Works Cited

Internet Demographic Highlights. *The CommerceNet/Nielsen Internet Demographic Survey.* April 1999. 4 Apr. 2000 <http://www.commerce.net/research/stats/april99.html>.

Krol, Ed. *The Whole Internet User's Guide and Catalog.* 2nd. ed. Sebastopol, CA: O'Reilly, 1994.

Zakon, Robert Hobbes. *Hobbes' Internet Timeline v5.0.* 1999. 4 April 2000 <http://www.isoc.org/guest/zakon/Internet/History/HIT.html>.

The Internet

6

Instructor: _____ Course/Section: _____

Name: _____

Date: _____ Points: _____

Review Questions

1. Name four advantages of information on the Internet for college students.

   a.

   b.

   c.

   d.

2. How did the Internet originate?

3. Who owns the Internet?

   Who pays for the Internet?

4. What are networks?

5. What is an Internet service provider?

6. What is e-mail?

7. What is a LISTSERV?

8. What is the World Wide Web?

9. Who can "publish" information on the Web?

10. What is a search engine?

11. Explain what is meant by a URL.

12. What is a home page?

13. Name four different types of search engines. Explain how they differ.

    a.

    b.

    c.

    d.

14. Explain the difference between a subject search and a keyword search on the Internet.

15. What is natural language searching?

6

Instructor: _____ Course/Section: _____

Name: _____

Date: _____ Points: _____

Finding Information on the Internet

The Internet provides current news sources as well as information on many subjects. Search the Internet for each of the following using the LSU Libraries home page as a starting point.

To get there type in http://www.lib.lsu.edu in your browser's location bar.

Search for Current News

1. Select "Ready Reference" on the LSU Library's home page
    Click on "Newspapers"; then click on "NANDO TIMES."
    Click on a category of news that interests you. Which category did you select?

2. Give the title of one article you find.

3. Briefly summarize the article.

4. Go back to the "Newspaper" page and click on another newspaper that interests you.
    Give the URL for this entry.

Search for Specific Information

Return to the "Ready Reference" page of the LSU Libraries' home page. Click on "My Virtual Reference Desk." Locate the following information.

5. List three people who were born on your birthday.
    (Search: http://www.scopesys.com/anyday/)

6. Where would you find the local weather report for today? Give the URL.

7. Find a review of the book *The Ground Beneath Her Feet* by Salman Rushdie. Give the URL.

Return to the LSU Libraries' home page.

8. Assume that you want to use one of the "subject guides" to find information on the stock market. Explain the steps you need to take get to the page that contains links to information on the stock market.

9. Give the URL for a site that contains useful information on the stock market.

Return to the LSU Libraries' home page.

10. Click on "Internet Searching." Select any search engine to help you find the text of the Declaration of Independence.
    Which search engine did you use?

11. Was it difficult to find the Declaration of Independence? Explain your answer.

12. Give the URL for a site that gives you the text of the Declaration of Independence.

The Internet

Instructor: _____ Course/Section: _____

Name: _____

Date: _____ Points: _____

Comparing Search Engines

Select a topic of your choice to use in the following three searches, or choose from the list below.

gun control	Medicare	distance running	distance education
school testing	unemployment	the millennium	Kennedy Space Center

1. What topic did you select?

2. Go to http://www.lycos.com and answer the following questions.

    a. Does the page contain advertising?

    b. If so, is it annoying or obtrusive? Explain.

    c. Describe any features on the page that you find interesting or useful.

    d. Is there a list of subject categories?

    e. If so, is there a category that is appropriate for the topic you selected above? If so, which is it?

    f. If you find an appropriate category for your subject, continue searching until you find a site that contains information that would be useful to you. Give the URL for the site.

    g. Select one Web document from the site that would be relevant to your topic and print out the first page. Attach the printout to your assignment.

3. Go to http://www.google.com and answer the following questions.

    a. Does the page contain advertising?

    b. If so, is it annoying or obtrusive? Explain.

   c. Describe any features on the page that you find interesting or useful.

   d. Is there a list of subject categories?

   e. If not, how would you find information on your topic?

   f. Use the method you describe in Question 3.e to locate a site that contains information that would be useful to you. Give the URL for the site.

   g. Select one Web document from the site that would be relevant to your topic and print out the first page. Attach the printout to your assignment.

4. Go to http://www.dogpile.com and answer the following questions.

   a. Does the page contain advertising?

   b. If so, is it annoying or obtrusive? Explain.

   c. Describe any features on the page that you find interesting or useful.

   d. Is there a list of subject categories?

   e. If so, is there a category that is appropriate for your topic? If so, which category is it?

   f. If you find an appropriate category for your subject, continue through different levels until you find a site that contains information that would be useful to you. Give the URL for the site.

   g. Select one Web document from the site that would be relevant to your topic and print out the first page. Attach the printout to your assignment.

5. Compare the three Web sites in terms of their helpfulness in finding information for your topic (e.g., ease of use or relevancy of materials found). Which of the three did you find most useful? Why?

6. Would you use this same search engine for another search? Why?

The Internet

6

Instructor: _____ Course/Section: _____

Name: _____

Date: _____ Points: _____

Finding Factual Information on the Internet

Go to the LSU Libraries' home page (http://www.lib.lsu.edu) and click on "Ready Reference." From this page select a link that will provide answers to each of the questions below.

1. Which link did you select? Give the URL.

2. What do the initials NAACP stand for?

3. What is the toll-free telephone number for Air France airlines?

4. What are the top three national universities, according to the *U.S. News Online* survey?

5. List the current Chiefs of State for:

    a. China

    b. Mexico

    c. Yemen

6. What is the symbol for *Libra*? What does it mean?

7. What is the American dollar equivalent of 100 Belgian francs?

The Internet

Instructor: _____ Course/Section: _____

Name: _____

Date: _____ Points: _____

Comparing Types of Search Engines

Assignment: Find out whether Vitamin C is effective in the prevention and treatment of the common cold.

Search by Subject

1. Look up topics relating to the assignment using the Galaxy search engine (http://www.galaxy.com/); select the most appropriate category for your assignment. Which subject category did you select?

2. Stop after the first level and type in a search statement in the box near the top of the page. What query did you type in the search box? (Give the exact command.)

3. How many hits did you get?

4. Were any of them helpful in answering your query? Explain briefly.

5. Give the URL for one of the sites you found.

Search by Keyword

6. Look up topics related to the assignment in the Alta Vista search engine. (http://www.altavista.com/)

   What query did you type in the search box? (Give the exact command.)

7. How many hits did you get?

8. Were any of them helpful in answering your query? Explain briefly.

9. Give the URL for one of the sites you found.

Search by Natural Language

10. Look up topics related to the assignment in the Ask Jeeves search engine. (http://www.askjeeves.com/)

    What query did you type in the search box? (Give the exact command.)

11. How many hits did you get?

12. Were any of them helpful in answering your query? Explain briefly.

13. Give the URL for one of the sites you found.

---

14. Which of the three methods of searching was the most effective? Explain.

Reference Sources

"Knowledge is of two kinds: we know a subject ourselves, or we know where we can find information upon it."

SAMUEL JOHNSON

INTRODUCTION

Reference sources are useful in the research process for a number of reasons: they provide background information, they provide facts or specific details on a subject, and they point to other sources of information. Reference services have changed dramatically with the introduction of computers and the Internet. With access to worldwide information literally at your fingertips 24 hours a day, you might find that many of your reference questions can now be answered with the click of a button without having to visit your local library. However, in many instances, and particularly for research papers, you will find that some of the reference sources that would prove helpful are available only in the library. Libraries continue to provide access to a combination of sources—some in print and others in electronic format such as CD-ROM that are not available remotely. Any information retrieval, whether in paper or electronic format, is more effective if you are familiar with the sources that provide that information. This chapter seeks to identify the major reference sources, regardless of format, and to help you sharpen your skills in finding and using them.

◆ WHAT ARE REFERENCE SOURCES?

Reference books are housed in a separate area in the library. They usually provide quick answers to questions or specific facts, such as the address of the local Congressional representatives, the number of alcohol-related deaths in a given year, a short biography of Malcolm X, or a brief interpretation of the poem "The Love Song of J. Alfred Prufrock" by T.S. Eliot. Certain nonbook materials are also used for reference. These include information in electronic format such as CD-ROMs, online catalogs and databases, and information in other formats such as microforms, videocassettes, and the Internet.

Several characteristics distinguish traditional reference material from other materials in library collections.

- ◆ They are designed to be consulted rather than being read straight through (reference).
- ◆ They may provide facts and figures in an easy-to-find format.
- ◆ They may provide concise information to frequently asked questions.
- ◆ They may contain valuable information for particular subject areas.
- ◆ They may serve as guides to information.
- ◆ They do not circulate but remain in the library for access to all.

◆ USING REFERENCE SOURCES

Reference works can serve a variety of purposes. In the beginning of the research process, general encyclopedias and dictionaries can highlight specific major aspects of a topic. A subject bibliography might provide references to information that has already been gathered on a topic. For example, the *United States Government Documents on Women, 1800–1990: A Comprehensive Bibliography* by Mary Ellen Huls would be useful in reviewing the topic of women and discrimination in employment. An article in *Compton's Encyclopedia* entitled "Women's Rights" gives a narrative of the history of women in the workforce and highlights the inequality in wages that continues to exist. Most encyclopedias give bibliographies for further reading. Subject reference books provide more in-depth information on a particular aspect of a topic. Statistics and facts are often found in one-volume reference works such as almanacs or yearbooks. While many statistical sources and periodical indexes, abstracts, and databases are often housed in the reference area, they will be discussed in other chapters.

Characteristics of Reference Sources

Some characteristics of reference works that you should look for to determine their suitability for research are discussed below.

Scope of Coverage

The scope of the reference work must match that of the research question. Does the work include sufficient material to answer the question? Is there sufficient detail to cover all the points needed for an answer? There are several ways to determine the scope of a work.

1. The introduction, the preface, and the table of contents all tell something about the scope or coverage of the work and about the author's intent. Manuals or instruction books that accompany nonbook materials serve the same purpose as the introductory pages of books.

2. The title of a work will help to determine its scope. Subject reference works tend to give greater coverage to the topics that they cover than more general works. The title of the work often provides clues to the contents. The text itself might be perused to determine the extent of details and the type of coverage.

Timeliness

The *copyright date*, revision date, or last update notification for Web documents should be used to determine whether or not the information contained in the source is current. The contents of a reference book are about a year older than the copyright date since it takes approximately a year before a book is published. The publication date and any revised edition dates are found on the reverse side of the title page of a work. A revised edition with a new copyright may indicate only minor changes. The terms "completely revised edition" or "enlarged edition" are indicative of more extensive revisions.

Arrangement

Reference works may be arranged or organized in three ways.

1. Alphabetically: Subjects or words appear in simple alphabetical order. Dictionaries are typically arranged in this fashion. Some reference books arranged in alphabetical order often include a separate index to help locate subtopics within the work. For example, *Webster's New World Dictionary* has a single alphabetical arrangement without a separate index while *World Book Encyclopedia* includes a separate index volume.

2. Topically: Subjects are listed in order by broad categories. Reference works arranged by topics almost always have a separate index that is used to find specific subjects within the broad categories. *The Encyclopedia of Crime and Justice* and *Sociological Abstracts* are examples of this type of arrangement.

3. Chronologically: Subjects are listed by date or time periods. Historical works such as Langer's *Encyclopedia of World History* are arranged by time periods.

Author

Knowing something about the author can be useful for determining the reliability of information. Occasionally reference books are written by one author, but more often, they are the work of several authors under the direction of an editor. Individual articles are usually signed by the author or authors responsible. Often the author's full name is given along with a brief biographical note indicating education, professional position, and a list of the author's other works. Sometimes that information appears elsewhere in the book or even in a separate volume if the work is a multivolume one. In *The New Encyclopaedia Britannica*, for example, only the author's initials appear at the end of the article; the full name and biographical information are found in a separate volume. On Web-based documents, some authorship or ownership is usually provided on the initial page of the source.

Bibliographies

Bibliographies are helpful in providing the researcher with a list of materials for further consideration. They also tell the reader that the author has researched the topic, which is an indication of the reliability of the information. Bibliographies may be found at the end of each article, at the end of a section in some topically arranged works, at the end of the entire work, or perhaps as an appendix to the work.

Cross References

Cross references include *see* and *see also* references that direct the reader to similar or related topics. The *see* reference guides the reader from a term that is not used to one that is used. A *see also* reference suggests other terms to consult for additional information. Both of these are useful in gathering information.

Types of Reference Sources

Reference sources fall into two broad categories: (1) general, and (2) subject.

General—Materials that are general in scope provide information in one source on a wide variety of topics. *The New Encyclopaedia Britannica* and *World Almanac* are examples of general reference sources.

Subject—Subject reference sources cover a single subject field or a group of related subjects. The *New Grove Dictionary of Musical Instruments* and *Black's Law Dictionary* are examples of reference works that are devoted to single subject areas. *The Encyclopedia of the Social Sciences* covers education, psychology, sociology, business and other subjects.

Both general and subject reference sources can be further categorized as being direct or indirect sources of information. A *direct source* provides the information in such a way that it is not necessary to consult another source. An *indirect source* serves as a guide to information that is located in other sources.

DIRECT ACCESS	INDIRECT ACCESS
almanacs	abstracts
biographical dictionaries	bibliographies
dictionaries	concordances
directories	indexes
encyclopedias	
gazetteers	
guidebooks	
handbooks	
manuals	
yearbooks	

Each year thousands of reference materials are published. Librarians select those sources that will be of greatest value to their library users. The reference collection is necessarily diverse, consisting of various types of reference sources designed to yield different kinds of information. Figure 7.1 briefly defines the various types of reference sources that are standard for most libraries.

Selecting a Reference Source

As you can see from the preceding discussion the collection of materials found in a typical library and on the Internet varies widely both in content and in format. Whether you are looking for quick facts or conducting extensive research, there are several strategies to use in selecting the best source to help you locate information. You should begin the search by analyzing the question to determine what sort of information is needed. Then you need to determine which reference sources are most likely to have the information you need.

Determine the Type of Reference Source

Knowing something about the types of reference sources can save you from having to guess where to look for information. Many of the types of reference books listed in Figure 7.1 may already be familiar to you. The definitions will help you to become familiar with those that you have not used before. Figure 7.2 illustrates several types of sources that might be used for the topic discrimination of working women.

Determine the Subject Area (Discipline)

The next step in selecting appropriate reference sources for a topic is to determine the subject category. It is often necessary to examine the topic from its broadest aspect or discipline—humanities, social sciences, or sciences. For example, to find an encyclopedia article specifically about discrimination of women in the workplace, you are likely to find materials that will be more on target in an encyclopedia of the social sciences than in a general encyclopedia. Further, you may need to change the search terms to consider broader aspects of the topic. For information on types of discrimination against women in jobs you should look up "women" or "discrimination" rather than "jobs." Most subjects can be grouped into broad disciplines such as those shown in Figure 7.3.

There are indexes, abstracts, and reference works in all three major subject disciplines. To select the most appropriate sources, first you must determine how the topic is to be approached. In developing a research statement, it is extremely helpful to determine the focus of your topic. For example, how would you plan to treat the topic of women and discrimination?

TYPES OF REFERENCE SOURCES

ABSTRACT an index that lists citations of works as well as a summary of each item (ex. *Psychological Abstracts, ERIC, ABI/INFORM*)

ALMANAC usually a one-volume work with statistics and a compilation of specific facts (ex. *World Almanac and Book of Facts,* and *Information Please Almanac, Atlas and Yearbook*)

ATLAS a book of maps and geographical information (ex. *Atlas of American History*)

BIBLIOGRAPHY a compilation of sources of information; provides literature on a specific subject or by a specific author (ex. *Books in Print* and *Bibliography of Nursing*)

BIOGRAPHICAL DICTIONARY sources of information about the lives of people; short entries (ex. *Current Biography* and *Who's Who in America*)

CONCORDANCE an alphabetical listing of keywords or phrases found in the work of an author or work in a collection of writings (ex. *Strong's Exhaustive Concordance of the Bible*)

DICTIONARY defines words and terms; confirms spelling, definition, and pronunciation; used to find out how words are used; helps to locate synonyms and antonyms and to trace the origin of words (ex. *Webster's Dictionary* and *Black's Law Dictionary*)

DIRECTORY lists names and addresses of individuals, companies, organizations, and institutions (ex. *Encyclopedia of Associations* and *Foundation Directory)*

ENCYCLOPEDIA covers knowledge or branches of knowledge in a comprehensive, but summary fashion; useful for providing facts and giving a broad survey of a topic; written by specialists (ex. *Encyclopedia Americana* and *World Book Encyclopedia*)

GAZETTEER a dictionary of geographical places (no maps) (ex. *Webster's New Geographical Dictionary*)

GUIDEBOOK provides detailed descriptions of places; intended primarily for the traveler; geographical facts plus maps (ex. *Baedeker's guidebooks to various countries*)

HANDBOOK treats one broad subject in brief, or gives a brief survey of a subject (ex. *Handbook of Literature* and *Benet's Reader's Encyclopedia*)

INDEX lists citations to periodical articles, books, and proceedings, and tells where they can be found (*see* Chapter 8. ex. *Readers' Guide to Periodical Literature* and *New York Times Index*)

MANUAL a specific work that tells how to do something, such as how something operates; descriptions of the inner workings of an organization (ex. *Chilton's Car Repair, MLA Handbook,* and *U.S. Government Organizational Manual*)

YEARBOOK covers the trends and events of the previous year; may be general in coverage, limited to one subject, or restricted to one geographical area (ex. *Britannica Book of the Year*)

Figure 7.1. Types of reference sources.

TOPIC: DISCRIMINATION OF WORKING WOMEN		
Needed information		**Appropriate reference sources**
overview article	------------ consult ------------	subject or general encyclopedia
current statistics	------------ consult ------------	statistical handbook, yearbook, almanac, *Statistical Abstract of the United States*
biographical information	------------ consult ------------	biographical index or biographical dictionary, library catalog
contemporary accounts	------------ consult ------------	periodical indexes, Internet, online databases
definition of legal terms	------------ consult ------------	dictionary, legal dictionary

Figure 7.2. Sample reference sources for a selected topic.

HUMANITIES	SOCIAL SCIENCES	SCIENCE
Architecture	Anthropology	Agriculture
Art	Business	Biology
Classical Studies	Criminal Justice	Chemistry
History	Economics	Computer Science
Journalism	Education	Engineering
Literature	Geography	Environment
Music	History	Health
Philosophy	Law	Mathematics
Poetry	Management	Medicine
Religion	Political Science	Petroleum
	Psychology	Physics
	Social Work	
	Sociology	

Figure 7.3. Selected subjects within disciplines.

APPROACH	DISCIPLINE
Women and employment	Social Sciences
The way that discrimination against women is reflected in literature	Humanities
The ability of women to handle the same physical jobs as men	Science

Finding Reference Sources

Once you have analyzed your research topic and determined the appropriate subject areas to use for finding information, the next step is to actually locate the appropriate sources.

GUIDELINES TO LOCATE REFERENCE SOURCES

▼ use the library catalog,

▼ browse the reference shelves,

▼ consult a guide to reference books,

▼ consult the reference sources on the Internet, and

▼ ask the reference librarian for assistance.

Library Catalog

Use the library catalog when you know the title of a reference source, but not its location, or to find titles of works when you know only the subject. If you do not find the topic, it may be because it is too specific or it may be that the topic is not used as a subject in the catalog.

The *Library of Congress Subject Headings (LCSH)* (see Chapter 4, Figure 4.1) suggests related terms, narrow terms, and broader terms to be used in locating topics in the library catalog. In finding reference sources, it is often necessary to broaden the topic (see Figure 7.4).

The terms "use" and "used for" in the *LCSH* indicate the proper terminology to be used in locating a subject heading. Reference books are listed in the library catalog by subject and then by the type of reference book. The examples below illustrate various subdivisions of a subject.

HISTORY--BIBLIOGRAPHY

HISTORY--DICTIONARIES

HISTORY--DIRECTORIES

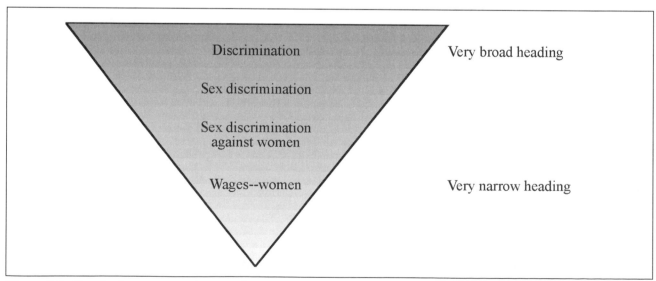

Figure 7.4. Broadening or narrowing a topic.

HISTORY--HANDBOOKS, MANUALS, ETC.
HISTORY--INDEXES
HISTORY--YEARBOOKS

Many of the types of reference sources listed in Figure 7.1 can be located by using a keyword approach.

Browse the Reference Shelves

Class numbers may be found in the library catalog or sometimes in the *LCSH*. For example, to locate reference works on the topic of women, you could browse the reference stacks under the general class number range for women. Relevant works such as *Statistical Handbook on Women in America* (Ref HQ1420.T34 1991), and *Handbook of American Women's History* (Ref HQ 1410.H36 1990) are located on the LSU libraries' reference shelves. Both works provide charts and financial background information on women's work throughout history.

Some reference departments keep frequently used materials on *ready reference* shelves or on special index tables, making it necessary to browse in several different areas.

Consult a Guide to Reference Books

The guides list reference sources by subject and often include subdivisions by type such as encyclopedias, handbooks, and manuals. Listed below are some of the more useful guides.

◆ *American Reference Books Annual.* Englewood, CO: Libraries Unlimited, 1970–.
   Lists both general and subject reference books. Comprehensive review of each work with author/title index and subject index.

◆ Balay, Robert, ed. *Guide to Reference Books.* 11th ed. Chicago: American Library Association, 1996.
   A comprehensive, annotated work that includes broad subject headings with further subdivisions according to type of source. Includes specific subject headings, and/or geographical subdivisions. The index incorporates author, title, subject, editors, compilers, and sponsoring bodies.

◆ Ryan, Joe. *First Stop: The Master Index to Subject Encyclopedias.* Phoenix: Oryx, 1989.
   Subject and keyword indexes allow easy searching for a broad range of topics. Includes encyclopedias, dictionaries, handbooks, and yearbooks.

◆ Walford, Albert J., ed. *Guide to Reference Material.* 7th ed. Rev. 3 vols. London: Library Association, 1996.
   Each volume is devoted to a different discipline: science and technology; social and historical sciences, philosophy and religion; generalia, language and literature, and the arts. Each entry is annotated. Includes author/title index and a subject index in each volume.

Consult Reference Sources on the Internet

Electronic sources are becoming more numerous and more important as components of the library's reference collection. Access to CD-ROMs, online databases, and the Internet is usually available in the reference area (as well as remotely). Reference sources such as *Bartlett's Familiar Quotations*, *Webster's Dictionary*, *Roget's Thesaurus*, *800 Number Directory*, and thesauri formerly available only in paper copy are readily available on the Internet. You can also find stock market prices, subject bibliographies, directories for e-mail addresses, instructions on resume writing, current employment opportunities, and current federal and state legislation quickly on the Internet. Many types of reference sources discussed earlier in this chapter (manuals, handbooks, dictionaries, etc.) can now be found on the Internet and searched using the basic search techniques discussed in Chapter 4. Chapter 6 discusses the use of search engines to find information on the Internet. However, finding reference materials on the Internet can be frustrating, so it is advisable to use one of the many guides to reference sources and that are available.

GUIDELINES FOR FINDING INTERNET REFERENCE MATERIAL

▼ type in the URL for a specific reference source

> EXAMPLE: ■
>
> http://britannica.com for the *Encyclopaedia Britannica* online.

▼ use a search engine to conduct a subject search, combining the topic with "reference"

> EXAMPLE ■
>
> "biology reference" or "education resources"
> Although this usually brings up a large list, you should be able to locate several relevant Web sites compiled by others on the subject.

▼ use a directory search engine like Yahoo and search on "Reference" as a category

> EXAMPLE: ■
>
> http://dir.yahoo.com/Reference/

▼ go to a university site and look for reference and subject guides

> EXAMPLE ■
>
> http://www.lib.lsu.edu/ref/readyref.html—ready reference sites selected by the reference staff at the LSU Libraries
> http://ithaca.edu/library/htmls/readyref.html—provides links to directories, calculators, style manuals, and consumer advice.

▼ use a "one-stop shopping" reference site

EXAMPLE ■

RefDesk.com (http://www.refdesk.com)
   OR
Internet Public Library (http://www.ipl.org/)
Both provide links to reference material by topic. You can find such things as the quote of the day; what happened today in history; and links to encyclopedias, dictionaries, almanacs, movie reviews, and newspapers from around the world.

Although much information is available online, most researchers still use a combination of articles from databases, Internet documents, books, and reference sources from the library. The lists of Selected Internet Sources at the end of this chapter present a representative sampling of Internet sites that may be used for reference purposes.

Ask the Reference Librarian for Assistance

Reference librarians are information specialists who are trained to analyze patrons' research needs and assist them in locating different sources of information. Most computers and electronic products are located near the Reference Desk. Librarians can assist patrons not only in locating information, but in providing guidance in developing search strategies for specific projects. Typical reference questions are changing from "Where do I find . . ." to "How do I log in to the campus network?" and "Which database should I use to find articles on this topic?" Because librarians have become more knowledgeable about computers and technology in general, they can serve the remote user as well as the in-house one.

Many libraries now provide electronic mail (e-mail) reference service, allowing patrons to submit questions. The answers are often returned by the library with complete bibliographic citations or full articles attached. This service is especially valuable for distance education and other users who cannot come to the library.

Document Delivery is another service provided by many libraries; patrons request printed or electronic materials, which is then delivered to them either in paper, microform, or electronic format, usually for a small fee. In most libraries, document delivery service is provided by the interlibrary loan office.

◆ EVALUATING REFERENCE SOURCES

A final step in the search for appropriate reference materials is to evaluate the sources. Once you have located the particular reference work that meets your information needs it is essential that you evaluate it. The criteria for evaluating reference sources is consistent with evaluating research materials in general and is discussed in detail in Chapter 3.

◆ SELECTED REFERENCE SOURCES BY TYPE

Many of these sources are now available electronically on CD-ROM or on the Internet.

Almanacs and Yearbooks

Almanacs

◆ *Information Please Almanac, Atlas and Yearbook*. New York: Simon and Schuster, 1947–.
A one-volume work arranged into broad subjects areas such as astronomy, economics and business, nutrition and health, religion, and science. Articles include both discussion and statistical material. Some signed articles on important issues of the period. Maps and some pictures are included. Topical arrangement with a subject index.

◆ *The World Almanac and Book of Facts*. New York: World Almanac, 1868–.
Covers a wide variety of subjects. An excellent source for statistics. Features a chronology of events that took place during the preceding year. Contains biographical information on U.S. presidents. Includes a few maps and some pictures. Index located at the front of the book.

◆ *World Factbook*. Washington: CIA, 1971–.
Created by the Central Intelligence Agency to support basic worldwide intelligence information. Includes a list of countries with reference maps, notes and definitions of terms.

Yearbooks

◆ *Americana Annual: an Encyclopedia of Events*. New York: Encyclopedia Americana, 1923–.
A supplement to the encyclopedia. Long signed articles discuss the year's political, economic, scientific and cultural developments. Includes a list of significant monthly events. Extensive biographical material on people in the news and of major figures who have died during the year.

◆ *Britannica Book of the Year*. Chicago: Encyclopaedia Britannica, 1938–.
Annual supplement to the encyclopedia. Includes several feature articles on newsworthy events. The "Year in Review" section covers the major events of the year as well as biographical information on people in the news. A separate section entitled "Britannica World Data" provides up-to-date statistical information on all countries of the world. Articles are signed and a list of contributors is provided.

◆ *Europa Year Book*. 30th ed. 2 vols. London: Europa Publications, 1926–.
The new edition represents a change of title from previous volumes subtitled *A World Survey*. Provides information on the organization and activities of the United Nations and other international organizations. Chapters on the major countries of the world discuss such things as government, economic affairs, social welfare, education, and recent history.

◆ *Statesmen's Year Book: Statistical and Historical Annual of the States of the World*. New York: St. Martin's, 1864–.
Handy reference source for information on various countries of the world. Gives brief history, statistical information, area and population, climate, constitution and government, and natural resources. For the United States, the information is not only for the whole country, but also for each state.

◆ *Statistical Abstract of the United States*. Washington: GPO, 1879–.
Issued annually by the U.S. Bureau of the Census. Consists of a compilation of social, political, and economic statistics gathered from both private and government sources. Most tables give comparative information from prior years. Many of the statistics are from primary sources; all information is documented.

Atlases, Gazetteers, and Guidebooks

Atlases

◆ Goode, J. Paul. *Goode's World Atlas*. 20th ed. Chicago: Rand McNally, 1999.
Easy-to-use volume arranged in four major divisions: (1) world thematic maps dealing with the world's climate, raw material distribution, landform, languages, and religions; (2) regional maps that cover the political and topographical features of the continents and the countries within those continents; (3) plate tectonics and ocean floor maps; and (4) maps covering the major cities of the world. Comprehensive index.

◆ *National Geographic Atlas of the World*. 7th ed. Washington: National Geographic Society, 1999.
Published for more than 35 years, this latest edition has been expanded to include full page maps for political, physical, and satellite images. Political maps reflect wars, revolutions, treaties, elections and other events.

◆ *Rand McNally Commercial Atlas and Marketing Guide*. Skokie, IL: Rand McNally, 1876–.
Contains business and commercial data. Useful for information on transportation, communication, economic conditions, and population. State and national maps are included along with maps of some American and Canadian cities. International in scope, but emphasis is on the United States. Supplemented by the *Rand McNally Road Atlas*. Includes highway maps, airlines, railroads, postal information, zip code service map, major military installations, state maps and index of places with statistics.

◆ *Rand McNally Road Atlas 1999*: United States, Canada, Mexico. 75th ed. Skokie, IL: Rand McNally, 1998.
Includes maps of states, provinces and counties, plus many city maps.

◆ Shepherd, William R. *Historical Atlas*. 9th ed. rev. New York: Holt, 1980.
Collection of chronologically arranged maps of the world dating from approximately 3000 BC to the 20th century. Includes plans of Rome (350 AD) and Athens (420 BC). Contains both political and physical maps.

Gazetteers

◆ Canby, Courtlandt. *Encyclopedia of Historic Places*. 2 vols. New York: Facts on File, 1984.
Lists in alphabetical order names of places of historical significance such as battle sites, archaeological sites, shrines, cities, towns, and countries. Gives geographic location and historical significance. Cross references from former names to present ones. Some illustrations.

◆ *Merriam-Webster's Geographical Dictionary*. 3rd ed. Springfield, MA: Merriam-Webster, 1998.
Alphabetically arranged list of place names with locations and pronunciations. Information for each state of the U.S. includes list of counties, products manufactured, and natural resources. Other countries of the world have similar listings under the country's name. Some maps.

◆ Munro, David. *Chambers World Gazetteer: An A–Z of Geographical Information*. 5th ed. Edinburgh: Chambers, 1988.
Alphabetical list of countries, towns, cities, and areas with descriptions of each. Helpful preface notes with specimen entry. Some maps and measurement conversion charts.

Guidebooks

◆ *Baedeker Guidebooks*. Englewood Cliffs, NJ: Prentice-Hall, 1828–.
One of the oldest series of guidebooks still being published. Provides information about individual countries, groups of countries, and cities. Gives the history of the area, places to see, places to stay, and restaurants. Many pictures and maps.

- *Fodor's Travel Guides.* New York: McKay, 1936–.

    Volumes cover various regions and cities of the United States, Europe, Asia, South America, and the Caribbean. Offers suggestions for transportation to and from an area and places of interest to visit. Discusses local customs and history. Maps of cities and lists of lodging places and restaurants. Well illustrated. Frequently revised.

Bibliographies

- *Books in Print.* New York: Bowker, 1948–.

    Lists books currently available from publishers. Contains separate author, title, subject, and publisher lists.

- *Cumulative Book Index.* New York: Wilson, 1933–1988.

    Author, title, and subject listing of books published in the English language throughout the world. Bibliographic information along with standard numbers useful for ordering books.

Concordances

- *New American Standard Exhaustive Concordance of the Bible.* Nashville: Holman, 1998.

    Lists words and phrases found in the *New American Standard Bible*; gives the book, chapter, verse, and reference number to the words listed in the Hebrew/Aramaic and Greek dictionaries found in the back of the book.

Dictionaries

Unabridged Dictionaries

- *The Random House Dictionary of the English Language.* 2nd ed. New York: Random House, 1999.

    Up-to-date, easy to read dictionary with good illustrations. Supplement includes French, Spanish, Italian, and German dictionaries; a style manual; and a world atlas. Names of people are included.

- *Webster's Third New International Dictionary of the English Language.* Springfield, MA: Merriam-Webster, 1996.

    Comprehensive dictionary containing all the principal words used in the English language. Provides pronunciations as well as definitions. A separate pronunciation guide is found in the front.

Abridged Dictionaries

- *The American Heritage Dictionary.* 3rd Office ed. Boston: Houghton Mifflin, 1994.

    Dictionary designed for "American English." Definitions often accompanied by illustrations. Contains several essays on the use of language. Features a separate style manual, list of abbreviations, geographic entries, and biographical entries.

- *Merriam-Webster's Collegiate Dictionary.* 10th ed. Springfield, MA: Merriam, 1999.

    Chronological within definitions. In some cases quotations are used to clarify the meanings of words. Contains a guide to pronunciation and explanatory notes. Lists of abbreviations, chemical symbols, foreign words and phrases, personal names, geographical names, colleges and universities, and a style manual are found in the back of the book.

Historical Dictionaries

Historical dictionaries place emphasis on the historical perspectives of words and phrases. These often contain useful information about words not found in the traditional dictionary.

◆ *Oxford English Dictionary.* 2nd ed. 20 vols. New York: Oxford University Press, 1989.
    Comprehensive record of the words used in the English language from the twelfth century to contemporary times. Quotations demonstrate how words were used during different time periods. Excellent source for quotations using words in a particular context.

Specialized Dictionaries

In addition to the traditional dictionaries, there are a great number of specialized dictionaries that approach the study of words from a different perspective. For example, a thesaurus groups synonyms together.

◆ *Dictionary of Crime: Criminal Justice, Criminology and Law Enforcement.* New York: Paragon House, 1992.
    Previously published as volume 5 of the *Encyclopedia of World Crime.*
◆ Chapman, Robert L. *American Slang.* New York: Harper Collins, 1994.
    Abridged edition of *The New Dictionary of American Slang,* 1986. Terms with definitions, parts of speech, examples, and, in some cases, the date of origin. Good introductory essay on slang.
◆ Kepfer, Barbara Ann. *Roget's 21st Century Thesaurus in Dictionary Form: The Essential Reference for Home, School or Office.* New York: Delta, 1999.
    Based on *Thesaurus of English Words and Phrases* by Peter Mark Roget. Includes an index.

Subject Dictionaries

Subject dictionaries are devoted primarily to a subject field and give the terminology most useful in that field. Many of these dictionaries are updated frequently to keep current with changing terminology and new developments.

◆ Black, Henry Campbell. *Black's Law Dictionary.* 7th ed. St. Paul: West, 1999.
    Comprehensive dictionary defining terms used in law and related subjects. Good cross references. Pronunciation guide arranged alphabetically.
◆ *Dorland's Illustrated Medical Dictionary.* 28th ed. Philadelphia: Saunders, 1994.
    Defines medical terms giving pronunciations, alternate definitions, if any, and origin of the word. Numerous plates showing detailed drawings of parts of the human body.

Foreign Language Dictionaries

Foreign language dictionaries can be found for virtually every written language. They may be written entirely in the language covered, or they may be English-foreign language.

◆ *Collins-Robert French-English, English-French Dictionary.* 3rd ed. Glasgow: Collins, 1996.
    Emphasizes contemporary rather than classical terms in both languages. "Style labels" indicate when a term may have stylistic complexities, e.g., local idioms that cannot be literally translated. Includes phrases as well as single words.

Directories

◆ *Encyclopedia of Associations*. Detroit: Gale, 1956–.
   Multivolume directory of active organizations in the United States and Canada. Has a separate volume for international organizations. Arranged by broad subject areas with separate organization name, executive name, keyword, and geographic indexes.

◆ *Thomas' Register of American Manufacturers*. New York: Thomas Publishing, 1905/06–.
   Lists of products and services available from American companies. Includes product and brand name indexes, company profiles, and a file of company catalogs. Available online, through *Thomas' Register CD-ROM*, and as *Thomas' Register Database*.

◆ *United States Congress. Official Congressional Directory*. Washington: GPO, 1809–.
   Published for each session of Congress. Contains names, addresses, committee assignments, and biographical sketches of members of Congress. Also includes names and addresses of top officials in all government agencies, international organizations, diplomatic missions, and the press corps. Contains maps of each Congressional district.

◆ *The World of Learning*. London: Europa, 1947–.
   Directory of research organizations, libraries and archives, colleges and universities, learned societies, museums, and art galleries found throughout the world. Arranged alphabetically by country. Includes names, addresses and some annotations.

Encyclopedias

General Encyclopedias

◆ *Encyclopedia Americana*. 30 vols. Danbury, CT: Grolier. 2000.
   The first encyclopedia published in the United States. It covers the arts and humanities as well as scientific development. Signed articles by experts in the field. Unique feature is the "century"' articles that discuss the outstanding events and trends of various time periods. Long articles contain a table of contents for easy reference. Supplemented by *Americana Annual*.

◆ *The Grolier Multimedia Encyclopedia*. Database. Danbury, CT: Grolier, c1995–.
   First of the CD-ROM encyclopedias. Full text of the printed *Academic American Encyclopedia*. Enhanced 1995 edition includes additional audio-visual effects.

◆ *The New Encyclopaedia Britannica*. 30 vols. Chicago: Encyclopaedia Britannica, 1998.
   Consists of three parts with a two-volume index. Volume 30, the *Propaedia* is an "Outline of Knowledge," that serves as a topical approach to the articles in volumes 1–12, the *Micropaedia,* and in volumes 13–29, the *Macropaedia*. The twelve-volume *Micropaedia* contains brief entries with cross references to the longer articles in the *Macropaedia*. The *Macropaedia* volumes contain long comprehensive articles complete with bibliographies. Articles are signed with initials that can be identified by referring to volume 30. Supplemented by *Britannica Book of the Year. Britannica CD-ROM* includes full text of the print encyclopedia plus a version of *Merriam-Webster Dictionary and Thesaurus.*

◆ *World Book Encyclopedia*. 22 vols. Chicago: World Book, 2000.
   Designed for elementary through high school students, but because of its extremely wide coverage, it is excellent for general reference. Major articles provide subject headings for related articles, an outline of the subject, and review questions. Numerous diagrams and pictures, good cross references, and signed articles. Updated by *World Book Yearbook*.

Subject Encyclopedias

◆ *Encyclopedia of Bioethics*. Rev. ed. New York: Simon & Schuster, 1995.
   Lengthy signed articles with good cross references and bibliographies. Covers the ethical concerns with human problems such as abortion, aging, human experimentation, population policies, and reproductive technologies.

◆ *Encyclopedia of Psychology*. Washington: American Psychological Association, 2000.
   Alphabetically arranged by specific topics. Includes bibliographical references and index.

◆ *International Encyclopedia of the Social Sciences*. 19 vols. New York: Macmillan, 1968–1991.
   Long scholarly articles with bibliographies covering all aspects of the social sciences from anthropology to statistics. Treats narrow subjects within the broad subjects. Good cross references. The *Biographical Supplement* contains a classified subject list to the alphabetically arranged biographies.

◆ *McGraw-Hill Encyclopedia of Science and Technology*. 7th ed. 20 vols. New York: McGraw-Hill, 1992.
   Covers all aspects of science and technology. Scholarly, yet nontechnical articles, most of which are signed. Illustrations, bibliographies, and cross references. Volume 20 contains topical and analytical indexes and a section on scientific notation. Kept up-to-date by *McGraw-Hill Yearbook of Science and Technology*.

Handbooks and Manuals

Handbooks

◆ *Benét's Reader's Encyclopedia*. 4th ed. New York: Harper & Row, 1996.
   Primarily concerned with literature but useful for identifying movements and important people in art and music. Contains references to literary characters and plot summaries. International in scope, but emphasis is on American and British works.

◆ De Vries, Mary Ann. *The New Robert's Rules of Order*. 2nd rev. ed. New York: Penguin, 1998.
   Guide to standard parliamentary procedure used by organizations to conduct business meetings. Introduction explains the history and development of parliamentary rules; a center section codifies procedures for conducting meetings. Other chapters explain the duties of organization officers, committee members, and board members. An index is included.

◆ *McGraw-Hill's National Electrical Code Handbook*. 23rd ed. New York: McGraw-Hill, 1998.
   Based on the 1996 code, written in conversational style. Presents information in easy-to-read format for safe installation of electrical wiring and equipment.

Manuals

◆ *United States Government Manual*. Washington: GPO, 1935–.
   Official guide to the organization of the United States government. Lists all of the government agencies, both official and semiofficial, along with the names, addresses, and phone numbers of their top personnel. Contains a copy of the U.S. Constitution, a list of abbreviations useful for identifying government agencies, an index of names, and an agency/subject index.

◆ SELECTED CURRENT EVENTS SOURCES

Following is a list of sources covering politics, contemporary issues, and news events. Many are loose-leaf services; some are shelved in Reference or Ready Reference collections.

- *Almanac of American Politics.* 1972–.

  Surveys of congressional districts, state and national politics. Published biennially.

- *Congressional Digest.* 1921–.

  Monthly publication that explores the pros and cons of major Congressional issues.

- *CQ Researcher* (formerly *Editorial Research Reports*). 1967–.

  In-depth analysis of current events and issues. Provides historical background, chronology of events, and opposing views on controversial issues written by experts on the subject. Includes extensive bibliographies for further research.

- *CQ Weekly Report.* 1961–.

  Congressional Quarterly publication that tracks the major legislation, floor action, events on Capitol Hill, and every major policy issue in Congress. Includes current bills before Congress, Supreme Court decisions, campaigns, and speeches.

- *Editorials on File.* 1970–.

  Published twice a month. Collects newspaper editorials on topics of current interest. Provides editorials for each topic presented.

- *Europa Year Book.* 1966–.

  Detailed information on country politics and organizations. Includes statistical surveys and names of officials.

- *Facts on File Yearbook.* 1945–.

  A weekly world news digest summarizing newspaper articles. Emphasis is on U.S. events and international affairs of American interest.

- *Keesing's Contemporary Archives.* 1965–.

  Monthly news summary published in Great Britain. Provides international coverage.

◆ SELECTED INTERNET SITES

General

CNN. http://www.cnn.com

For current news information. ABC, NBC, and other networks have similar sites.

Britannica Online. http://www.eb.com

Electric Library's Free Encyclopedia. http://www.encyclopedia.com/

Free Tutorials. http://www.learn2.com/

Freeweb Central. http://www.freewebcentral.com/

Internet Public Library. http://www.ipl.org/

A free online public service library. Collections include reference, associations, native authors, literary criticisms, newspapers, serials, and information for young people. Online text collection provides over 11,000 titles that can be browsed by author, title, or Dewey Decimal classification. Has forms to fill out so users can ask reference questions.

Refdesk.com. http://www.refdesk.com

A one-stop shopping site for locating current events and reference sites. Includes links to wire services, newspapers, magazines, columns, businesses, weather, quick reference, tutorials, and books.

Business

AnyWho Toll-Free Directory. http://anywho.com/

Better Business Bureau. http://www.bbb.org/

Bureau of Labor Statistics. http://stats.bls.gov/

Census Bureau. http://www.census.gov/

CEO Express. http://www.ceoexpress.com

Edgar. http://www.edgar-online.com

Search corporate annual reports and SEC filings.

Northern Light. http://northernlight.com
Business full-text articles and information.

Small Business Administration. http://www.sba.gov/

Yahoo Business and Economy. http://dir.yahoo.com/Business_and_Economy/

Zip Codes. http://www.usps.gov/ncsc/welcome1.htm

Career Guidance

Americas Job Bank. http://www.ajb.dnl.us

Career Mosaic. http://www.careermosaic.com (search by job type and location)

Federal Jobs Digest. http://www.jobsfed.com/

JobBank-USA. http://www.jobbankusa.com

Monster Board. http://www.monster.com

Occupational Outlook Handbook. http://stats.bls.gov/ocohome.htm

Riley Guide. http://www.dbm.com/jobguide

Virtual Job Fair. http://www.vjf.com

What Color is Your Parachute?. http://www.washingtonpost.com/parachute

Citation Guides

http://www.lib.duke.edu/libguide/citing.htm
Easy to follow guide gives specific examples of each electronic format.

http://www.lib.umich.edu/libhome/Documents.center/cite.html
Provides links to a variety of style manuals and guides.

Consumer Resources

Consumer Alert!. http://www.ftc.gov/ftc.consumer.htm

Consumer Information Center. http://www.pueblo.gsa.gov/
Government publications online.

Consumer Resources. http://www.lib.lsu.edu/ref/consumer.html

Kelly Blue Book. http://www.kbb.com/
Automobile prices.

U.S. Consumer Gateway. http://www.consumer.gov/

U.S. Postal Service. http://www.usps.gov/consumer/
Consumer information from the U.S. Postal Service.

Grants and Funding

Catalog of Federal Domestic Assistance. http://www.cfda.gov/

Foundation Center. http://fdncenter.org/
Tutorials and guides on getting funding

GrantsWeb. http://sra.rams.com/cws/sra/resource.htm

Health

Consumer Health. HealthWeb. http://healthweb.org/

Legal *(Note additional sources in Chapter 9.)*

Code of Federal Regulations. http://www.access.gpo.gov/nara/cfr/index.html

FindLaw. http://www.findlaw.com

Statistics *(Note additional sources in Chapter 10.)*

County and City Data Book. http://fisher.lib.Virginia.EDU/ccdb/

Statistical Abstract of the United States. http://www.census.gov/statab/www/

World Factbook. http://www.cia.gov/cia/publications/factbook/

Weather

Old Farmer's Almanac. http://www.almanac.com/

Weather Channel. http://www.weather.com/

Weather Underground. http://www.wunderground.com

◆ SELECTED PRINT REFERENCE SOURCES BY SUBJECT

Agriculture

Farm Chemicals Handbook. 1990.

Handbook of Engineering in Agriculture. 3 vols. 1988.

Art and Architecture

A History of Western Architecture. 1996.

Art Across America. 1990.

Book of Art: A Pictorial Encyclopedia of Painting, Drawing and Sculpture. 1994.

Dictionary of Art. 1996.

Dictionary of Contemporary American Artists. 1994.

Encyclopedia of World Art. 1959–1987.

Gardner's Art Through the Ages. 10th ed. 1996.

The Oxford Dictionary of Art. 1997.

Biology/Botany/Zoology

Cambridge Encyclopedia of Life Sciences. 1985.

Concise Oxford Dictionary of Zoology. 1991.

A Dictionary of Botany. 1984.

A Dictionary of Plant Pathology. 1989.

Encyclopedia of the Animal World. 11 vols. 1980.

Fishes of the World. 1994.

Grzimek's Animal Life Encyclopedia. 13 vols. 1972–1975.

Grzimek's Encyclopedia of Mammals. 5 vols. 1990.

The New Larousse Encyclopedia of Animal Life. Rev. ed. 1980.

Business and Economics

Accountant's Handbook. 8th ed. 1996.

Data Sources for Business and Market Analysis. 3rd ed. 1983.

Dictionary of Accounting Terms. 1995.

Encyclopedia of Business. 2 vols. 1995.

Encyclopedia of Business Information Sources. 14th ed. 2000.

International Directory of Company Histories. 30 vols. 1988–.

Standard & Poor's Industry Surveys. 3 vols. 2000.

Standard & Poor's Register of Corporations. 3 vols. plus supplement. 1999.

Value Line Investment Survey. 3 part loose-leaf service. 1936–.

Ward's Business Directory. 1997.

Communication and Journalism

Communication and the Mass Media: A Guide to the Reference Literature. 1991.

Communication Yearbook. 1977–.

Editorials on File. 1970–.

Facts on File: A Weekly World News Digest with Cumulative Index. 1940–.

The Gallup Poll: Public Opinion. 1935–.

Keesing's Record of World Events. 1931–.

What They Said: A Yearbook of Spoken Opinion. 1969–.

Computers and the Internet

Computer Glossary: The Complete Illustrated Dictionary. 1998.

Dictionary of Computer and Internet Terms. 1998.

Criminal Justice

Child Abuse and Neglect: An Information and Reference Guide. 1990.

City Crime Rankings: Crime in Metropolitan America. 1997.

Crime and the Justice System in America: An Encyclopedia. 1997.

Dictionary of Crime: Criminal Justice, Criminology & Law Enforcement. 1992.

The Encyclopedia of Child Abuse. 1989.

The Encyclopedia of Psychoactive Drugs. 25 vols. 1985–1992.

Encyclopedia of World Crime. 6 vols. 1989.

The Police Dictionary and Encyclopedia. 1988.

Education

American Educators' Encyclopedia. 1991.

Education Yearbook. 1972/73–.

Encyclopedia of Careers and Vocational Guidance. 4 vols. 11th ed. 2000.

Encyclopedia of Educational Research. 4 vols. 1992.

International Encyclopedia of Education. 10 vols. 1985.

Mental Measurements Yearbook. 1941–.

Philosophy of Education: An Encyclopedia. 1996.

Engineering Technology

Civil Engineers Reference Book. 1989.

Electrical Engineering Handbook. 1997.

Handbook of Industrial Engineering. 2nd ed. 1992.

Metals Handbook. 1998.

SAE Handbook. 1998.

Genealogy

A Dictionary of Heraldry. 1999.

A Dictionary of Surnames. 1998.

Handybook for Genealogists. 9th ed. 1999.

Source: A Guidebook of American Genealogy. 1984.

Geography

Cambridge Encyclopedia of Africa. 1981.

Cities of the World. 4 vols. 4th ed. 1993.

Dictionary of Human Geography. 1994.

Harper Atlas of World History. 1992.

Worldmark Encyclopedia of the States. 3rd ed. 1995.

Government *see* Law and Government

Grants and Funding

Annual Register of Grant Support: A Directory of Funding Sources. 1997.

Foundation Center's User-Friendly Guide: A Grantseekers Guide to Resources. 1994.

Foundation Directory. 1993.

Grants and Awards. 1991–.

Grants Register. 1998.

The "How to" Grants Manual: Successful Grantseeking Techniques for Obtaining Public and Private Grants. 1995.

Health *see* Medicine/Health/Sports Medicine

History

Africa South of the Sahara. 29th ed. 2000.

Annals of America. 21 vols. 1976–1987.

The Annual Register: A Record of World Events. 1788–1997.

Dictionary of Indian Tribes of the Americas. 4 vols. 1980.

Dictionary of Mexican American History. 1981.

Dictionary of the Middle Ages. 13 vols. 1982–.

Documents of American History. 10th ed. 1988.

Encyclopedia of the Holocaust. 4 vols. 1990.

Encyclopedia of the United States in the Twentieth Century. 1996.

Encyclopedia of World Facts and Dates. 1993.

Encyclopedia of World History. 1998.

Great Soviet Encyclopedia. 31 vols. 3rd ed. 1982

Illustrated Encyclopedia of World History. 1997.

International Library of Afro-American Life and History. 10 vols. 1978.

International and Multicultural

African American Almanac. 8th ed. 2000.

Encyclopedia of Asian History. 4 vols. 1988.

Encyclopedia of Multiculturalism. 6 vols. 1994.

Encyclopedia of the Holocaust. 4 vols. 1990.

Encyclopedia of Violence, Peace, and Conflict. 3 vols. 1999.

Encyclopedia of World Cultures. 1987–.

Handbook of Hispanic Cultures in the United States. 4 vols. 1994.

Handbook of North American Indians. 1984–.

Kodansha Encyclopedia of Japan. 9 vols. 1983.

Storytelling Encyclopedia: Historical, Cultural, and Multiethnic Approaches to Oral Traditions Around the World. 1997.

Journalism *see* **Communication and Journalism**

Language and Literature

Afro-American Writing Today: An Anniversary Issue of the Southern Review. 1989.

American Folklore: An Encyclopedia of Beliefs, Customs, Tales, Music, and Art. 1997.

Bartlett's Familiar Quotations. 16th ed. 1992.

Cambridge Encyclopedia of Language. 1987.

Cambridge Guide to Literature in English. 1993.

Columbia Literary History of the United States. 1988.

Contemporary Literary Criticism. 8 vols. 1973–.

Harbrace College Handbook. Rev. 13th ed. With *MLA Style Manual* updates. 1998.

New Arthurian Encyclopedia. 1991.

Oxford Companion to English Literature. Rev. ed. 1995.

Something About the Author. 1971–.

Twentieth-Century Literary Criticism. 1978–.

Webster's Third New International Dictionary of the English Language. 1993.

Law and Government

Almanac of American Politics. 1972–.

Bieber's Dictionary of Legal Abbreviations: Reference Guide for Attorneys, Legal Secretaries, Paralegals, and Law Students. 1993.

Blackwell Dictionary of Political Science: A User's Guide to Its Terms. 1999.

Child Abuse and Neglect: An Information and Reference Guide. 1990.

Countries of the World and Their Leaders Yearbook. 1980–.

County Year Book. 1975–.

Dictionary of Government and Politics. 1997.

Dictionary of 20th Century World Politics. 1993.

Encyclopedias of Revolutions and Revolutionaries: From Anarchism to Zhou Enlai. 1996.

Guide to American Law. 10 volumes with supplements. 1983–.

Illustrated Dictionary of Constitutional Concepts. 1996.

Politics in America. 1982–.

West's Encyclopedia of American Law. 12 vols. 1998.

Literature *see* Language and Literature

Mathematics

Concise Handbook of Mathematics and Physics. 1997.

CRC Handbook of Mathematical Science. 1962–.

Dictionary of Mathematics. 2 vols. 1982.

Encyclopedic Dictionary of Mathematics. 2nd edition. 1987.

Medicine/Health/Sports Medicine

Alternative Health & Medicine Encyclopedia. 1995.

Anatomy of the Human Body. 1985.

Concise Dictionary of Biomedicine and Molecular Biology. 1996.

Encyclopedia of Aging: A Comprehensive Resource in Gerontology and Geriatrics. 1995.

Encyclopedia of Sports Science. 2 vols. 1997.

Merck Manual of Diagnosis and Therapy. 1899–.

Physician's Desk Reference Book. 1947–.

Stedman's Medical Dictionary. 25th ed. 1990.

Motion Pictures, Radio, and Television

Chronicle of the Cinema. 1995.

Film Anthologies Index. 1994.

International Television and Video Almanac. 1956–.

Radio's Golden Years: The Encyclopedia of Radio Programs, 1930–1960. 1981.

Music/Theater

American Musical Film Song Encyclopedia. 1999.

American Musical Theatre Song Encyclopedia. 1995.

ASCAP Biographical Dictionary. 1980.

Best Plays of . . . and the Yearbook of Drama in America. 1894–.

Cambridge Guide to World Theatre. 1988.

The Drama Dictionary. 1988.

The Encyclopedia of Folk, Country, and Western Music. 1983.

Historical Encyclopedia of Costume. 1988.

History of Women's Costume. 1984.

New Grove Dictionary of American Music. 4 vols. 1986.

New Grove Dictionary of Jazz. 2 vols. 1988.

Norton/Grove Concise Encyclopedia of Music. 1988.

Oxford Companion to Popular Music. 1991.

Philosophy/Religion

Cambridge Dictionary of Philosophy. 1999.

Chambers Dictionary of Beliefs and Religions. 1992.

Dictionary of Philosophy and Religion: Eastern and Western Thought. 1996.

Dictionary of the History of Ideas. 5 vols. 1980.

Encyclopedia of American Religions. 1996.

Encyclopedia of Ethics. 2 vols. 1992.

Encyclopedia of Judaism. 1989.

Encyclopedia of Psychology. 4 vols. 1994.

Encyclopedia of Religion and Society. 1998.

Encyclopedia of Religions in the United States: One Hundred Religious Groups Speak for Themselves. 1992.

Encyclopedia of the Paranormal. 1996.

Folklore of American Holidays. 1987.

Man, Myth, and Magic: The Illustrated Encyclopedia of Mythology, Religion, and the Unknown. New ed. 21 vols. 1997.

New Catholic Encyclopedia. 18 vols. 1967–1989.

Routledge Encyclopedia of Philosophy. 10 vols. 1998.

World Philosophy: Essay-reviews of 225 Major Works. 5 vols. 1982.

Psychology

American Handbook of Psychiatry. 2nd ed. 8 vols. 1974–1986.

Encyclopedia of Adult Development. 1993.

Encyclopedia of Relationships Across the Lifespan. 1996.

Encyclopedia of Phobias, Fears, and Anxieties. 1989.

Encyclopedia of the Paranormal. 1996.

Oxford Companion to the Mind. 1987.

Religion *see* **Philosophy/Religion**

Science

Beilstein's Handbook of Organic Chemistry. 4th ed. 1989.

Britannica Yearbook of Science and the Future. 1968–.

Cambridge Atlas of Astronomy. 1994.

Concise Dictionary of Physics. 1990

CRC Handbook of Chemistry and Physics. 1995–1996.

Dictionary of Geology. 6th ed. 1986.

Dictionary of the History of Science. 1981.

Encyclopedia of Astronomy and Astrophysics. 1989.

Encyclopedia of Climatology. 1987.

Handbook of Industrial Robotics. 1985.

International Encyclopedia of Astronomy. 1987.

International Petroleum Encyclopedia. 1994.

McGraw-Hill Concise Encyclopedia of Science and Technology. 1998.

McGraw-Hill Encyclopedia of the Geological Sciences. 2nd ed. 1988.

Van Nostrand's Scientific Encyclopedia. 7th ed. 1989.

The Weather Almanac. 6th ed. 1992.

Social Sciences

A Hundred Years of Anthropology. 1978.

Atlas of Archaeology. 1998.

Cambridge Encyclopedia of Archaeology. 1980.

Dictionary of Human Geography. 3rd ed. 1994.

Dictionary of Terms and Techniques in Archaeology. 1989.

Encyclopedia of Adolescence. 2 vols. 1990.

Encyclopedia of Aging. 1987.

Encyclopedia of American Social History. 3 vols. 1992.

Encyclopedia of Cultural Anthropology. 1996.

Encyclopedia of Homosexuality. 2 vols. 1990.

Encyclopedia of Human Behavior. 4 vols. 1994.

Encyclopedia of Human Evolution and Prehistory. 2000.

Encyclopedia of Social and Cultural Anthropology. 1996.

Encyclopedia of Social Work. 1995 + supplements.

Handbook of American Popular Culture. 1989.

International Encyclopedia of Sociology. 1995.

Larousse Encyclopedia of Archaeology. 1997.

Social Science Encyclopedia. 2 vols. 1996.

Sports Medicine *see* Medicine/Health/Sports Medicine

Statistics *(Note additional resources in Chapter 10.)*

America's Top-Rated Cities: A Statistical Handbook. 1998.

Demographic Yearbook. 1949–.

Handbook of Key Economic Indicators. 1998.

Illustrated Book of World Rankings. 1991.

Places, Towns and Townships. 1998.

Statistical Abstract of the United States. 1878–.

Statistical Handbook of Women in America. 1996.

Statistical Record of Women Worldwide. 1995.

Theatre *see* Music

Women's Studies

International Who's Who of Women. 1992.

Statistical Handbook of Women in America. 1996.

W.I.S.H.: The International Handbook of Women's Studies. 1993.

Women: A Bibliography of Bibliographies. 1986.

Women's Studies Encyclopedia. 1999.

Reference Sources

Instructor: _____ Course/Section: _____

Name: _____

Date: _____ Points: _____

Review Questions

1. Give three characteristics of reference sources.

   a.

   b.

   c.

2. How are reference sources used in research?

3. Name and define three different types of reference sources.

   a.

   b.

   c.

4. What types of reference sources would you use for an overview on a topic?

5. Explain the difference between *direct* and *indirect* reference sources.

6. Which discipline would you look under to find information on each of the following?

   Topic   *Discipline*

   a. medicine

   b. religion

   c. computer science

   d. agriculture

   e. education

   f. music

7. Name five possible strategies you might consider in locating reference sources.

   a.

   b.

   c.

   d.

   e.

8. Why is it important to determine the date of the reference source being used in research?

9. Why is it important to look for signed articles in a reference book?

10. Why are bibliographies useful additions to articles found in reference sources?

11. Why is it important to have cross references in a reference source?

12. What advantages do you see in using the Internet to locate reference material?

13. If you had the choice between an in-house visit and sending an e-mail for a reference question, which would you choose and why?

Exercise 7.2 Reference Sources

7

Instructor: _____ Course/Section: _____

Name: _____

Date: _____ Points: _____

Selecting Types of Reference Sources

Various kinds of information may be obtained from many different reference sources. Name the type of reference source or sources in which you would likely find the following information. A source may be used more than once and may include non-book sources discussed in earlier chapters (see Figure 7.1).

EXAMPLE: Meaning and pronunciation   **Dictionary**

1. Brief, miscellaneous facts about Russia. _____

2. A list of sources about one author. _____

3. A published list of sources on political science. _____

4. Broad survey of atomic energy. _____

5. Recent map of Bosnia. _____

6. Brief description of the Mississippi River. _____

7. A brief survey of art history. _____

8. A short description of the current economy in Peru. _____

9. Illustrations of famous works of art. _____

10. Materials published by the American Sociological Association. _____

11. Events or trends of the last year. _____

12. List of manufacturers of air conditioners. _____

13. The population of Alaska in 1990. _____

14. The latitude and longitude of the Alps. _____

15. How to conduct an experiment in physics. _____

16. Short discussion of the function of the U.S. Department of the Interior. _____

17. Addresses of U.S. government officials. _____

18. Location of words used in Shakespeare's plays. _____

19. Diagram of an engine of a 1984 Ford. _____

20. Definitions of terms in anthropology. _____

21. A brief survey of education. _____

22. The capital of North Dakota. _____

23. Brief, miscellaneous facts about Haiti. _____

24. Your congressman's phone number in Washington. _____

25. A list of articles published by a biology professor. _____

26. A book covering all aspects of engineering. _____

27. Major happenings in the field of science last year. _____

28. Location of the word "marriage" in the Bible. _____

29. Major events at the United Nations last year. _____

30. The correct spelling of a medical term. _____

31. A current picture of a famous actor. _____

32. A book illustrating how to change the oil in your car. _____

33. A list of newspaper articles on a particular topic. _____

34. Pictures of the U.S. flag throughout history. _____

35. The number of currently employed males in
    your state. _____

36. The medical procedure involved in laser surgery. _____

37. A quotation from a poem when you only know the
    first line. _____

38. The exact dates of the Korean War. _____

39. A detailed description of hiking trails in England. _____

40. The correct spelling of the highest mountain in
    Tanzania. _____

Reference Sources

7

Instructor: _____ Course/Section: _____

Name: _____

Date: _____ Points: _____

Finding Reference Books

Locate a reference book that contains information on a topic. <u>DO NOT</u> use an abstract, index, bibliography, biographical dictionary, concordance, general dictionary or a general encyclopedia. Give the information requested below.

1. Topic:

2. Since reference books often are not listed under specific subject headings, what broad subject heading would be appropriate for your topic?

3. How did you locate this book? (e.g., library catalog or browse reference shelves)

Give the following information about the book.

4. If you used the online catalog, the exact command you used:

5. Title of the book you located:

6. Call number and location:

7. Author (or) editor of the book:

8. Date of publication:

9. Single or multivolume:

10. Arrangement of the book (alphabetical, topical, chronological):

11. Subjects covered in the book:

12. Title of an article on your topic:

13. Author of article (if any):

14. Volume number (if applicable) and inclusive pages of article:

15. Write the correct bibliographic citation for an article you found in the reference book, or cite the book itself if it is a single volume. Use the bibliographic examples given in Appendix A.

Reference Sources

Instructor: _____ Course/Section: _____

Name: _____

Date: _____ Points: _____

Locating Reference Books in the Online Catalog

1. Select a subject you are interested in to locate information in a reference book. What subject did you select?

2. Select one of the categories appropriate for that subject from the list of selected subject reference titles provided at the end of this chapter, and search your library catalog to determine which (if any) publications your library owns. Give the results of your search below.

3. Titles and dates of each of the works you found: (Use back of this page if necessary.)

   Write the exact library location next to these titles.

4. List the titles and dates of any works you did not find.

5. Locate one of the titles you found in Question 3 and give the following information.

   Title:

   Arrangement of the work:

   Does it have information that is appropriate for your topic? Explain.

6. Write a bibliographic citation to an article or chapter (or to the entire book if that is appropriate) for the title you located in Question 5. Use the examples in Appendix A.

Reference Sources

Instructor: _____ Course/Section: _____

Name: _____

Date: _____ Points: _____

Evaluating Reference Books

Select a topic of your choice. Locate information on the topic in each of the types of reference sources listed below and give the requested information about each.

Topic:

1. *Abridged dictionary*
   Title and date:

   Unabridged dictionary
   Title and date:

   Compare the two sources. How is the information similar? How does it differ?

   Write a bibliographic citation for each of the sources used. Use the examples given in Appendix A.

2. *General encyclopedia*
   Title and date:

   Subject encyclopedia
   Title and date:

   Compare the two sources. How is the information similar? How does it differ?

   Write a bibliographic citation for each of the sources used. Use the examples given in Appendix A.

3. *Subject or general bibliography*
   Title and date:

   Arrangement (alphabetically, topically, chronologically):

   Number of references in bibliography:

   Write a correct bibliographic citation. Use the examples given in Appendix A.

4. *Handbook or manual*
   Title and date:

   Write a brief summary of the information located.

   Write a correct bibliographic citation. Use the examples in Appendix A.

5. Using a state or a city as a topic, look up information in each of the types of reference sources listed below and give the requested information about each.

   Topic:

   Almanac
   Title and date:

   Population:

   Yearbook
   Title and date:

   Population:

   Compare the two sources. How is the information similar? How does it differ?

   Write a correct citation for each of the sources used. Use the bibliographic citations in Appendix A.

6.   Using a country as a topic, look up information in each of the types of reference sources listed below and give the requested information about each.

Topic:

Atlas
Title and date:

Population:

Gazetteer
Title and date:

Population:

Compare the two sources. How is the information similar? How does it differ?

Write a bibliographic citation for each of the sources used. Use the examples of bibliographic citations given in Appendix A.

Reference Sources

7

Instructor: _____ Course/Section: _____

Name: _____

Date: _____ Points: _____

Finding Reference Sources Online

Use a search engine to find a reference source on the Internet on a topic. See pages 140–142 in Chapter 6 for hints on using a search engine to find reference information.

1.   Which topic did you select? Why did you select this topic?

2.   Which search engine did you use?

3.   Give the search term(s) you used.

4.   How much information did you find?

5.   Select an appropriate reference source for your topic and give the URL and title page below.

6.   How would you classify the reference source you found, according to the types of reference sources discussed in this chapter?

7.   Is there an author for your entry on this topic? If so, give the name.

8. What is the publication date of this Web page? When was it last revised?

9. Describe briefly the information you find, or print out the first page and attach it to this exercise.

Reference Sources

7

Instructor: _____ Course/Section: _____

Name: _____

Date: _____ Points: _____

Finding Legal and Business Information Online

A. Legal Sources

Go to *Findlaw* at http://www.findlaw.com

1. Find the constitution of your home state. Give the URL for the constitution.

2. Use the "Legal Subject Index" of Findlaw to select a topic.

   a. What topic did you select?

   b. Give at least two citations for the topic you selected.

3. Find the Nebraska Unicameral online. What exactly is a "unicameral" form of state government?

4. What types of information can you find about the Supreme Court at http://supct.law.cornell.edu/supct/

B. Business Sources

5. Using the Google search engine, search for "SIC code."

   a. What does "SIC" stand for?

   b. Is this the current system in use today? If not, what is the new one called?

   c. Why is this system important for business and company information?

6.　Locate the Small Business Administration site on the Internet.

　　a.　What is the URL of this site?

　　b.　What type of information does this government agency provide for assistance to those beginning or involved in a small business?

7.　Go to the Subject Guides page at the LSU Libraries site at http://www.lib.lsu.edu/weblio.html. Scan this site to find a directory that lists Fortune 500 companies. Give the URL for the most recent listing that you find.

Reference Sources

Instructor: _____ Course/Section: _____

Namo: _____

Date: _____ Points: _____

Using Online Encyclopedias

Compare the results of a search on the Internet for information on the "holocaust."

1. Go to http://britannica.com. Briefly describe the search strategy you used, what types of results you found, and your overall evaluation of this site.

2. Go to http://encyclopedia.com next. Briefly describe the search strategy you used, what types of results you found, and your overall evaluation of this site.

3. Go to http://encarta.msn.com/Default.asp, the free *Encarta* site on the Internet. Briefly describe the search strategy you used, what types of results you found, and your overall evaluation.

4. Compare the three sites in terms of:

    Ease of use

    Clarity of instructions

    Number of results found

    Type of results found

5. Which of the three would you use the next time you need similar information? Why?

Reference Sources

7

Instructor: _____   Course/Section: _____

Name: _____

Date: _____   Points: _____

Using the *American Memory* Collection at the Library of Congress

From the Library of Congress page located at http://www.loc.gov/, click on "American Memory."

1. Browse the collections listed to see what is available. Select one collection of special interest to you. Which one did you select? Why did you select this one?

2. Select an appropriate subject to search within this collection, or read the list of contents provided and select one of them. Which subject did you select?

3. Describe the results of your search. How many entries did you find? What types of information did you find? (film, text, or recordings)

Go back to the *American Memory* home page and use the search feature to locate a copy of the design of the telephone drawn by Alexander Graham Bell.

4. Does your library have a copy of this design? How would you proceed to look for it in your library.

5. Would you use the *American Memory* collection again for research? Why?

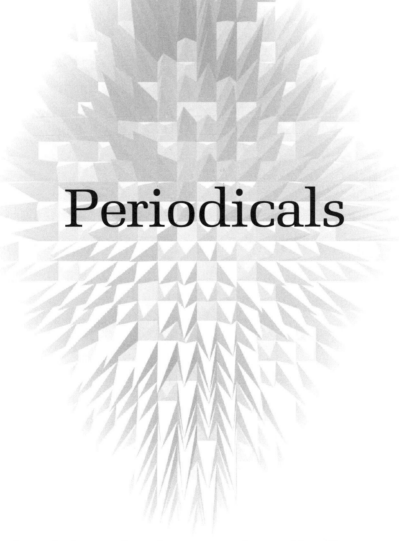

Periodicals

"The hand that rules the press, the radio, the screen and the far-spread magazine, rules the country."

LEARNED HAND

INTRODUCTION

Serials are publications that are issued on a continuing basis at regularly stated intervals. They include periodicals, newspapers, annuals and yearbooks, and the proceedings, transactions, and memoirs of societies and associations. The term *periodical* is usually used to refer to magazines and journals. Since newspapers appear periodically, for ease of discussion, this chapter will discuss magazines, journals and newspapers under the broad definition of periodicals.

Just as you may think of the library catalog as an index to its holdings, a large variety of indexes and databases serve the same purpose for the contents of individual periodical titles. Effective and critical use of information sources often depends on a mastery of these access tools for finding articles in newspapers, magazines and journals. It is the goal of this chapter to demystify this subject by describing and analyzing the major types of periodical indexes and databases and their use.

◆ WHY USE PERIODICALS FOR RESEARCH?

Information found in periodicals is valuable in research for several reasons.

- ◆ Information appearing in periodicals constitutes the bulk of published information; there are thousands of periodicals published regularly, each containing an abundance of articles on different topics.
- ◆ The material found in newspapers, magazines, and journals is the most recent printed information you can find outside of the Internet.
- ◆ Information in periodicals, particularly newspapers, reflects contemporary opinion. Articles written shortly after an event occurred, whether it was in the nineteenth century, the 1930s, or the 1990s, convey what people thought of the event at the time it occurred.
- ◆ Periodical literature reflects the constantly evolving nature of information. No matter when an event occurred, the facts surrounding it and the event's significance are constantly being reinterpreted.
- ◆ Periodical literature provides comparative information for different periods. Compare, for example, the concepts of the role of women in the workplace in the 1920s with those of the 1990s.
- ◆ Sometimes periodical literature is the only information available—the topic may be too faddish ever to appear in a book. The findings of researchers and scholars in particular fields are usually published in journals rather than in books.

◆ UNDERSTANDING PERIODICAL LITERATURE

As you can see, periodicals are important sources to use in the research process. How do you go about selecting appropriate periodical literature? How do you know which periodicals have the information that you need for your research purposes? You are probably familiar with a large number of periodicals—either you subscribe to one or more, or you have seen them on the display shelves at newsstands, grocery stores, or libraries. It is not unusual to stumble across information in a periodical that is exactly the answer to a research question that you might have. Although browsing is one way to find information in periodicals, it is neither the most efficient nor the most effective way. Because there are thousands of periodicals, you have to depend on something more than chance to find the most appropriate source for your needs. Finding and using periodical literature involves knowing something about the types of literature you can expect to find, the kinds of subjects covered, the formats, and the appropriate finding tools.

Types of Periodical Literature

There are two basic types of periodical literature: *popular* and *scholarly.*

Popular Periodical Literature

Magazines are designed to appeal to a broad segment of the population. They are characterized by relatively short articles written in nontechnical language, usually by staff writers. The style of writing is easy to understand and concise. The articles are especially useful for information on current events or for the contemporary treatment of a topic. Magazines are usually published weekly or monthly.

Newspapers provide short articles written in nontechnical language. Newspaper articles are usually *primary* sources of information because they provide firsthand accounts of an event. They are useful both for current and historical perspectives on a topic. Newspapers are usually published daily or weekly.

Scholarly Periodical Literature

Journals are scholarly publications intended for a more limited readership. The articles are written by scholars or experts in a field. The vocabulary is often technical, and the style of writing is more complex than that found in popular magazines. They provide research articles on specific topics, and may include charts and graphs. Journal articles usually include extensive bibliographies, reflecting the fact that the author has researched the topic. Journals are usually published monthly, quarterly, semiannually, or annually.

Subject Focus of Periodical Literature

In addition to the two types of periodical literature described above, you also need to consider the subject focus of periodical literature. Some periodicals are *general* in coverage while others are *subject* based—that is, they cover subjects that can then be categorized into broader subject *disciplines.*

THREE PRIMARY *DISCIPLINES* FOR SUBJECT-BASED LITERATURE
◆ **Humanities**—architecture, art, classical studies, history, journalism, literature, music, philosophy, poetry, and religion.
◆ **Social Sciences**—anthropology, business, criminal justice, economics, education, geography, law, management, political science, psychology, social work, and sociology.
◆ **Sciences**—agriculture, biology, chemistry, computer science, engineering, environment, health, mathematics, medicine, petroleum, and physics.

Format of Periodical Literature

Print

The traditional format of periodical literature is print on paper, although many libraries purchase microform (microfilm or microfiche) copies of newspapers and other periodicals. With the advent of computer technology as a storage and retrieval medium for information we are seeing more and more periodicals in electronic format.

E-Journals

Electronic journals (e-journals) have come into widespread use in the last few years. These publications are produced directly online, with or without a paper counterpart, and distributed over the Internet. An e-journal may include the full text of all articles in the periodical, or it may have only selected articles. Most e-journals are available by subscription, and some publishers require paper subscriptions along with electronic access. The e-journals that are available for free quite often have only current issues or selected articles. An example of an e-journal that provides selective articles is *Working Woman*, located at http://www.workingwoman.com/.

◆ FINDING INFORMATION IN PERIODICALS

Finding appropriate information in periodicals is a multistep process that begins by determining a topic and deciding which subjects or keywords might be used to find articles about the topic. The second step is to determine the type of information needed—whether popular or scholarly publications would be most relevant to the topic. Next you must decide what is to be the focus of your research and which subject discipline might be most appropriate. Then you must determine which indexes or databases to use to find the information. It is a good idea in doing a thorough search of the literature to use both general and subject indexes, abstracts, and databases. Figure 8.1 outlines the steps for finding information in periodicals.

Indexes and Abstracts

The library catalog lists the cataloged works contained in the library and gives location information, but it does not include individual articles in periodicals. For this you must use an *index, abstract* or *database*. An *index* to periodical literature is a guide that provides *citations* to articles in periodicals. A citation includes:

- ◆ the name of the author;
- ◆ the title of the article;
- ◆ the title of the periodical; and
- ◆ the volume number, date, and pages of the periodical in which the article appears.

An *abstract* is a type of index that gives the citation and includes a summary of each item. Abstracts are important reference sources because the summary will tell you whether or not the literature is appropriate for your needs. While the summaries in abstracts vary in length, there is usually sufficient information to determine the main ideas presented in the original work.

Although many indexes and abstracts continue to be published in printed form, indexes and abstracts in electronic format (either Web-based or CD-ROM) have become the norm.

◆ Steps for Finding Information in Periodical Literature	
Step 1	Decide on a topic. What keywords would you use to find articles about your topic?
Step 2	Decide if the information you need will be found in popular magazines or in scholarly journals.
Step 3	Determine which discipline or broad subject area would be most suitable for the topic—humanities, science, or social science.
Step 4	Based on your approach in steps 2 and 3, select an appropriate index for your subject. Explore the various printed indexes, abstracts, and databases available at your library, or select from the lists included in this chapter. A brief selection of indexes and abstracts is listed below.

Humanities
America: History & Life
Historical Abstracts
Humanities Index
MLA International
  Bibliography
Music Index
Art Index
Arts & Humanities
  Citation Index

Science
Agricola
Biological Abstracts
Biological & Agricultural
  Index
General Science Index
Science Citation Index
Computer Select
ACM Guide to Computing
Engineering Index
Medline

Social Sciences
ABI/INFORM
Education Index
ERIC
PsycLit
Social Sciences Index
Social Sciences Citation
  Index
PAIS International

Multi-Disciplinary Sources
Academic Universe; EBSCOhost; InfoTrac and *Electric Library* are all full-text databases that can be used for both popular and scholarly full-text articles in newspapers, magazines, and journals.

The reference librarian can also advise on the appropriate index to use.

Step 5	Interpret the citation correctly. Identify the full title of the magazine or journal, the volume, issue, pages, and date for the articles you select.
Step 6	Copy, download, or print the citations or articles you need.
Step 7	If necessary, check the library catalog to see if the library has the magazine or journal title you need. Review the holdings record for the title to see the correct location for your issue.

Figure 8.1. Finding information in periodicals.

Databases

A *database* is a collection of information that is stored electronically in such a way as to provide easy and quick search and retrieval capabilities. There are generally two types of databases, *bibliographic* and *full-text*. Databases have a distinct advantage over print sources in that they can be searched more quickly and more effectively. Basic search techniques for electronic searching are discussed in Chapter 4.

◆ *Bibliographic databases* are those that provide only citations to information in other sources. Currently the lines between bibliographic and full-text databases (described below) are blurred in that many databases provide both full-text and bibliographic information in a single database.

◆ *Full-text databases*, in the context of periodical literature, are those that provide, as the term implies, the full text of periodical articles along with citations and abstracts. Subscription services such as *Aca-*

demic Universe, InfoTrac, EBSCOhost, WilsonWeb, ProQuest Direct, and *Electric Library* include both full-text and bibliographic information. Some of the full-text articles have charts, graphs, photographs, and other images. Many full-text databases are multidisciplinary—they cover a broad spectrum of articles. Others, such as *ABI/INFORM*, are limited to specific subject areas.

Most of the databases are Web-based, but many are still available on CD-ROM. The entries on the CD-ROM versions usually display a labeled screen much like the catalog records discussed in Chapter 5. CD-ROM databases, for the most part, are available only in the library, although some libraries make them available campus-wide.

Using the various databases is relatively simple since most contain the same basic information. However, each database has its own particular search engine and way of searching. It is always advisable when you use a database for the first time to go to the help screen. Some libraries provide online tutorials and "quick guides" to the databases. You want to be sure that you understand how to search in order to derive maximum benefits for your efforts.

The most well-known databases are available on the Web. Most of these are an aggregation of databases. That is, they provide a selection of databases, based on the type of coverage. Some include only the more popular periodical titles; others are more subject specific.

The better known of these databases are described below.

Multidiscipline: General

The following databases include both general and subject databases.

◆   *Academic Universe*. Bethesda, MD: CIS, dates vary.
    Web-based service that provides access to news, business and legal information. It includes nearly 6,000 full-text publications, including company financial information, industry and market news, foreign and U.S. newspapers, magazines and trade journals, federal and state case law, accounting information, medical news and abstracts, law reviews, and state and country profiles.

    Use the following procedures to searching *Academic Universe*.

    ◆   Enter the database by clicking on the icon or selecting the title from your library's listing of databases.

    ◆   After entering the database, determine the appropriate category for your needs by selecting one of the following categories: News, Business, Legal Research, Medical, or Reference.

    ◆   Once you make the initial selection, you will be given another range of choices. For example, in the News category, you would select from: General News, Today's News, U.S. News, World News, Wires, Transcripts, Arts & Sports, Campus, or Foreign Language News.

    ◆   Once that selection is made, you then conduct a search by keyword or subject to find articles on your topic. Once articles are found, you can then read, print, download, or e-mail them to your address for later disposition.

◆   *EBSCOhost*. Birmingham, AL: EBSCO Subscription Services, dates vary.
    A "one-stop online reference system accessible via the Internet." *EBSCOhost* offers multiple databases in an easy-to-use interface. Among the database selections are: *Academic Search Elite, Business Source Premier, Clinical Reference Systems, Health Source Plus* and *Newspaper Source*. *Academic Search Elite* has full text for over 1,250 journals with many dating back to 1990 and abstracts and indexing for nearly 2,880 scholarly journals, with many dating back to 1984.

- *InfoTrac*. Gale Group: Los Altos, CA, dates vary.

   Features full-text articles and citations on academic and general topics, and is comprised of several databases, depending on the library's subscription. Some of the databases are *General Reference Center, General Business File, General Health Center, Expanded Academic Index*, and *National Newspaper Index*. Includes citations, abstracts and full-text articles from more than 1,000 popular magazines, business and professional journals, and newspapers.

- *Electric Library*. Wayne, PA: Infonautics, dates vary.

   Full-text online research service includes hundreds of magazines, journals, newspapers, and reference works. More suitable for high school level than college, but useful for transcripts and pictorial works not found elsewhere.

- *FirstSearch*. Dublin, OH: OCLC, dates vary.

   A collection of many of the online databases available from other sources. May include *ABI/INFORM, Agricola, Aids and Cancer Research, Applied Science & Technology Abstracts, Art Abstracts, Biography Index, Book Review Digest, Books in Print, CINAHL, Consumers Index, Dissertation Abstracts, OCLC, ERIC, GenderWatch, Humanities Abstracts* and many others, depending on library selection. Entries and dates of coverage vary depending on database selected. Some databases have citations only, others include full text.

- *WilsonWeb*. New York: H.W. Wilson, dates vary.

   OmniFile databases include full-text articles in business, humanities, science, education, and the social sciences, plus *Readers' Guide to Periodical Literature*. Indexes all Wilson products in one database. Includes full text, depending on subscription.

Multidiscipline: Scholarly

The following databases cover multiple subjects also, but they are limited to the more scholarly journals.

- *Cambridge Scientific Abstracts*. Bethesda, MD: CSA, dates vary.

   Provides access to more than 35 databases. Includes physical sciences, biological sciences, and computer science, *Sociological Abstracts,* and *Linguistics & Language Behavior Abstracts*, and *Medline*. Has citations and abstracts only, no full text, although there are direct links to any e-journals to which the library subscribes. May also provide local holdings information.

- *Carl UnCover*. Denver: Carl UnCover, 1988–. Also known as *UnCoverWeb*, it is available at: http://uncweb.carl.org/.

   This service provides free access to its periodical database of nearly 9 million article citations in over 18,000 multidisciplinary journals. *CARL UnCover* can be used either to order the document itself or to obtain citations to order material through an interlibrary loan process.

- *Web of Science*. Philadelphia: Institute for Scientific Information, dates vary.

   Provides Web access to *Arts & Humanities Citation Index, Social Sciences Citation Index*, and *Science Citation Index Expanded*, giving the serious researcher cross-disciplinary access in one source. The database contains citations only; no full text articles are available. The *citation* indexes, as these databases are known, are unique in coverage in that they are the only source that indexes the cited sources. If an author wants to know how many times his article was cited, and in which sources, he has to check one of the citation indexes. The various parts of *Web of Science* are:

   - *Science Citation Index Expanded,* covering the journal literature of the sciences. It indexes more than 5,700 major journals across 164 scientific disciplines, including agriculture, neuroscience, astronomy, oncology, biochemistry, pediatrics, biology, pharmacology, biotechnology, physics, chemistry, plant sciences, computer science, psychiatry, materials science, surgery, mathematics, veterinary science, medicine, and zoology.

◆ *Social Sciences Citation Index*, an index to the journal literature of the social sciences, covering more than 1,725 journals spanning 50 disciplines. Some of the disciplines covered include anthropology, political science, history, public health, industrial relations, social issues, information and library science, social work, law, sociology, linguistics, substance abuse, philosophy, urban studies, psychology, women's studies, and psychiatry.

◆ *Arts & Humanities Citation Index*, an index to 1,144 leading arts and humanities journals, as well as covering individually selected, relevant items from over 6,800 major science and social science journals. Some of the subjects covered include archaeology, linguistics, architecture, literary reviews, art, literature, Asian studies, music, classics, philosophy, dance, poetry, folklore, radio/television/film, history, religion, language, and theater.

Printed Indexes and Abstracts

Although indexes to periodical literature have existed since the middle of the nineteenth century, the number of indexes to periodical literature has increased considerably over the past few years. It is necessary to acquire a basic knowledge of indexes in order to take advantage of the wealth of information they provide.

Most of the paper versions of periodical indexes are published monthly with an annual cumulation in which all of the articles included throughout the year are arranged in a single list. A section in the front of each index usually lists alphabetically all the periodical titles indexed and gives the abbreviations used in the entries.

◆ *Readers' Guide to Periodical Literature* has long been a standard index to the most popular general-interest magazines published in the United States and Canada. It is one of only a few sources available for historical research. Published since 1900 by the H.W. Wilson Co., it covers current events and the popular literature in all subject areas. In some cases, *Readers' Guide* may be the only source available for contemporary information on a topic or event. For example, if you wanted to find articles on the signing of the original Panama Canal Treaty in 1903, the print copy of *Readers' Guide* would be an excellent place to start. (The electronic version of *Readers' Guide* dates back to 1984. In the current version there are about 136 full-text journals with coverage back to 1994.)

Each issue of the printed version of *Readers' Guide* is divided into several important sections. These are:

1. a list of the periodicals indexed;
2. a list of other abbreviations used in the index;
3. the main body of the index consisting of subject and author entries; and
4. a listing of book reviews by authors with citations.

Figures 8.2–8.4 show representative pages from the print version of *Readers' Guide*. These illustrations are provided to show a typical printed index to periodical literature.

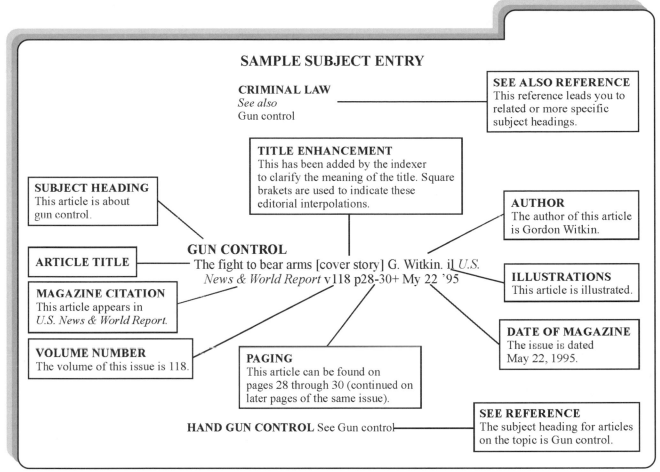

Figure 8.2. Sample subject entry from *Readers' Guide to Periodical Literature*.

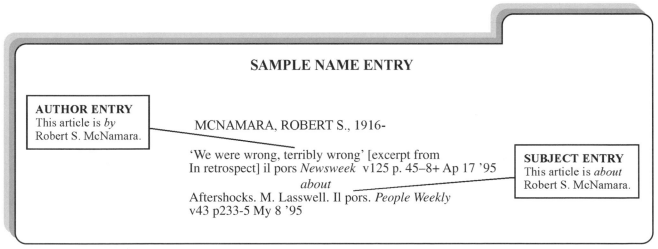

Figure 8.3. Sample name entry from *Readers' Guide to Periodical Literature*.

WOLVES—cont.
Wolves, moose, and tree rings on Isle Royale. B. E. McLaren and R. O. Peterson. bibl f il *Science* v266 p1555-8 D 2 '94

Control
Wolves: shoot first, investigate second [wolf shot dead after being released into River of No Return Wilderness] *Newsweek* v125 p60 Mr 27 '95

Photographs and photography
In the company of wolves. J. Brandenburg. il *National Wildlife* v33 p4-11 D '94/Ja '95
Pro profiles [R. McIntyre] K. McGee. il *Petersen's Photographic Magazine* v23 p46 N '94

WOMAN *See* Women

WOMAN SUFFRAGE

Canada
A battle not yet won. R. J. Taylor. il *Canada and the World Backgrounder* v60 no4 p4-7 '95

SUBJECT HEADING → **WOMEN**
See also ——— CROSS REFERENCES
Alcohol and women
Beauty, Personal
Black women
Computers and women
Cuban American women
Drugs and women
Eskimos—Women
Farm women
Feminism
Heroes and heroines
Hispanic American women
Jewish women
Lebanese American women
Married women
Muslim women
Sex differences
Single women
Young women
1994 in review: the good news. K. Golden and G. Kirshenbaum. il *Ms.* v5 p46-53 Ja/F '95
Wonder women. il *Gentlemen's Quarterly* v65 p152-3 F '95

Anatomy and physiology
See also
Breast
Menstruation
The great shape debate [fat and diseases] D. Points. il *Mademoiselle* v100 p77 Je '94
High heelhell [women's shoes] R. Berg. il *Vogue* v185 p224-5 F '95

Attitudes
Are there harder times ahead? [views of Albert Sidlinger] J. Schor. il *Working Woman* v20 p22 Mr '95
In our January/February 1994 issue, we asked: does women's equality depend on what we do about pornography? [survey results] J. Furio. il *Ms.* v5 p24-8 Ja/F '95

Clothing and dress
See Clothing and dress

Conferences
See also
World Conference on Women

Crimes against
See also
Abused women
Rape
Self defense for women
Sex crimes
Mosadi [worldwide mistreatment of women] R. J. Taylor. il *Canada and the World Backgrounder* v60 no4 p29-31 '95
Women and crime: do your fears fit the facts? D. Christiano. il *Glamour* v92 p134 S '94

Diseases
See also
AIDS (Disease) and women
Anorexia nervosa
Breast—Cancer
Bulimia
Menstruation—Disorders
Osteoporosis
Premenstrual syndrome
Sexually transmitted diseases
Hormonal havoc [effects on women's oral health] L. B. McGrath. il *American Health* v14 p23 Ja/F '95
Science by quota [NIH guidelines mandating inclusion of women and minorities in clinical research] S. Satel. *The New Republic* v212 p14+ F 27 '95

Too tired too often? Surprising new culprits. K. Feiden. il *McCall's* v121 p42+ S '94

Economic conditions
See also
Wages and salaries
Buoying women investors. P. J. Black. il *Business Week* p126-7 F 27 '95
The feminization of poverty. L. E. Taylor. il *Canada and the World Backgrounder* v60 no2 p16-18 '94
Mind over money [study by National Center for Women and Retirement Research; cover story] C. Willis. il *Working Woman* v20 p30-4+ F '95
Stop living paycheck to paycheck. C. E. Cohen. il *Working Woman* v20 p40-3+ Ja '95
What's your money personality? [quiz] C. L. Hayes. *Working Woman* v20 p35-7 F '95

Education
See also
Archer School for Girls (Los Angeles, Calif.)
Brearley School (New York, N.Y.)
Coeducation
Sex discrimination in education
Boys + girls together. M. Sajbel. il *Los Angeles* v40 p88-94+ Mr '95
Keep culture from keeping girls out of science. S. Tobias. *The Education Digest* v60 p19-20 S '94
Math challenged? [women tend not to excel in math] L. E. Taylor. il *Canada and the World Backgrounder* v60 no4 p20-1 '95
Riveters to rocket scientists: exploring the gender gap in quantitative fields [hard sciences] il *Change* v26 p41-4 N/D '94
The smarter sex? [academic performance of girls surpasses boys in British schools] L. Grant. il *World Press Review* v42 p45 Ja '95

Employment
See also
Black women—Employment
Married women—Employment
Mothers—Employment
Single mothers—Employment
Women—Occupations
1994 Hall of Shame [individuals, companies and organizations that hindered working women; cover story] il *Working Woman* v19 p28-31 D '94

TITLE OF ARTICLE
MAGAZINE
VOLUME PAGES DATE
ILLUSTRATED

The divorce backlash [judgments against working women] L. Mansnerus. il *Working Woman* v20 p40-5+ F '95
Joining the old boys' club [Canada] L. E. Taylor. il *Canada and the World Backgrounder* v60 no4 p12-13+ '95
Pregnant—and now without a job [discrimination] M. Lord. il *U.S. News & World Report* v118 p66 Ja 23 '95
What about women? [affirmative action] B. Cohn and others. il *Newsweek* v125 p22-5 Mr 27 '95
Women: where they stand in today's Los Angeles [study by the Los Angeles Women's Foundation] N. P. Jacoby. il *Los Angeles* v39 p74-84 Jl '94
Women working a third shift. H. Hartmann. il *Working Woman* v19 p16 D '94

History
Present since the creation [Alumnae Advisory Center] A. G. King. *American Heritage* v45 p24-6 D '94

Equal rights
See also
Sex discrimination
Woman suffrage
Women—Employment
Culture and women's rights: time to choose. L. D. Howell. *USA Today (Periodical)* v123 p53 Ja '95
Empowering women [discussion of December 1994 article] G. H. Brundtland. il *Environment* v37 p2-3+ Ja/F '95
Empowering women: an essential objective [International Conference on Population and Development] il *UN Chronicle* v31 p47 S '94
In our January/February 1994 issue, we asked: does women's equality depend on what we do about pornography? [survey results] J. Furio. il *Ms.* v5 p24-8 Ja/F '95
Invest in our future, invest in women. J. D. Hair. il *International Wildlife* v25 p26 Ja/F '95
The U.N. & women [World Conference on Women] M. Tax. *The Nation* v260 p405 Mr 27 '95
Women empowered: the earth's last hope [interview with N. Sadik] L. Conners. *New Perspectives Quarterly* v11 p13-15 Fall '94
Women, politics, and global management. L. C. Chen and others. bibl f il *Environment* v37 p4-9+ Ja/F '95

Figure 8.4. Sample page, *Readers' Guide to Periodical Literature,* December 1995, p. 758.

Newspaper Indexes/Databases

Newspapers are good sources for information on local, state, national, and international levels. Periodical indexes such as *Readers' Guide* provide references to many different publications, but a printed newspaper index usually access only one newspaper. Newspaper Indexes generally have subject entries and do not give the exact title of an article; instead, they give a brief description of the article.

Many newspaper indexes and the full text of newspapers are now available electronically. One of the most comprehensive databases of full-text newspapers is *Academic Universe*. (See the description under Multidiscipline: General.) *ProQuest Direct,* available from Bell and Howell Information and Learning Division, has an electronic collection of over 1,000 full-text newspapers. Subscribers can subscribe to a single online newspaper or can customize a database of selected newspapers. Selected indexing and full text of some newspapers are available in *EBSCOhost, InfoTrac,* and *Electric Library.* Some newspapers are available free on the Web, including the *New York Times.* Most of the directory-type search engines have a "news" category, linking major news stories to their site. CNN.com and other services offer full articles from current newspapers. Some services include back files.

Below is a description of the *New York Times Index.*

New York Times Index. New York: New York Times Company, 1913–.
> Earlier series covers the years 1851–1912. Subject index to *The New York Times* newspaper. Published twice monthly with annual cumulations. Most general databases now include citations from *The York Times.*

A sample page from *The New York Times Index* (Figure 8.5) is typical of the format of most newspaper indexes. Notice that in the November, 1995, issue, the index lists several subject headings for articles on "women." An article dealing with "Affirmative Action" and women will be found in the November 20 issue of *The New York Times.* The description gives additional information: the length of the article, the section, page, and column where the article may be found.

Since newspaper indexes usually cover only one newspaper, the year and title of the newspaper is located only on the front cover of the index, rather than listed in each individual citation. You must be careful to record the exact year and title of the newspaper index as part of the note-taking process. Once you select an article, you will need to search the online catalog to determine whether or not the library subscribes to the publication. Remember to check the holdings record to determine the exact location of this issue. Older issues of newspapers will most likely be kept on microfilm in the library.

Following are some representative indexes to major newspapers. Many of the large city newspapers are indexed, either in print or electronic format; they will not be listed here. You should check your online catalog to ascertain whether the newspaper in your city or another major newspaper that interests you is indexed.

Index to the Christian Science Monitor International Daily Newspaper. Boston: Christian Science Monitor, 1960–.
> Titles of articles are listed under subject with day, month, section, page and column noted.
> Selected articles from the *Christian Science Monitor* are available at http://www.csmonitor.com/.

USA Today. Arlington, VA: Gannett, 1982–.
> Daily newspaper featuring short articles. Has widespread readership. Selected coverage available at http://www.usatoday.com.

ADVERTISING AGE (MAGAZINE)
Advertising Age dismisses editor Steve Yahn (S). N 29.D.4:2
AEG AG
German rail and engineering company AEG AG says that it will split off its power transmission and industrial automation units on Jan 1; says rest of company will be reorganized to form holding company (S). N 29.D.3:1
AEROMEXICO. See also
Airlines and Airplanes. N 29
AERONAUTICS. See also
Aerospace Industries and Sciences
Airlines and Airplanes
Balloons
Helicopters
AEROSPACE INDUSTRIES AND SCIENCES. See also
Airlines and Airplanes
Space
AETNA LIFE & CASUALTY CO. See also
Aetna Life & Casualty Co. N 30
Aetna Life & Casualty Co to sell its property and liability insurance business to Travelers Group Inc for $4 billion in cash and concentrate on health care and life insurance; Travelers plans to merge Aetna businesses with its own property and liability insurance units, cutting $300 million of costs and some 3,300 jobs; Travelers chief executive Sanford I Weill says merged units, which will form new company and later sell stock to public, will run initially under both names; table; graphs (M). N 30.D.1:5
AFFIRMATIVE ACTION. See also
Labor, N 26
Drive to outlaw California's affirmative action programs runs into serious financial and political difficulties, and similar efforts nationwide have also lost momentum; push to kill programs outright has failed to stir much definitive legislative action or to draw large amounts of money and manpower needed to conduct petition drives; legislators, at strong combined insistence of civil rights and women's organizations, are increasingly assuming different approach, calling for elimination of fixed race and sex quotas and goals, but urging retention of outreach programs (M). N 20.A.1:1
AFGHANISTAN. See also
Egypt. N 23
AFIFI MOHAMMAD. See also
Murders and Attempted Murders, N 16
AFRICA. See also
Animals, N 16
Archeology and Anthropology, N 16
Electronic Information Systems, N 17
Photography, N 24
Only 12 of Africa's 54 countries are linked to Internet and list does not include Ivory Coast, although by African standards it has well-developed telephone network; this seen as a major obstacle to continent's economic development (M). N 17.A.5:1
AFRICAN-AMERICANS. Use Blacks
AFRICAN NATIONAL CONGRESS. See also
South Africa, N 27
AGASSI, ANDRE. See also
Tennis, N 19.29
AGE, CHRONOLOGICAL. See also
Computer and Video Games, N 24
Heart, N 21
Police, N 28
AGED. See also
Age, Chronological
Blood Pressure, N 28
Exercise, N 30
Heart, N 21
Housing, N 17,19
Jews, N 19
Medicare
Medicine and Health, N 28
Nursing Homes
Pensions and Retirement Plans
Robberies and Thefts, N 19
Stocks and Bonds, N 18
Travel and Vacations, N 26
Southington, Conn. police force is undertaking 2-day sensitivity course that offers insights on dealing with problems that face elderly (M), N 26.XIII-CN.1:1
Residents of luxury cooperative that was once Police Headquarters protest New York City's plan to locate Project Open Door, Chinatown's largest senior center, in the basement of the building; building fell into city's hands after its developers defaulted on real-estate taxes; photos (M), N 26.XIII-CY.6:3

p.3

CROSS REFERENCE

WOLF, MATT. See also
Theater, N 26
WOLFE, GEORGE C., See also
Theater—Bring in Da Noise, Bring in Da Funk Revue), N 16.26
WOLFF, FRANCIS. See also
Books and Literature—Blue Note Years. The (Book), N 19
WOLIN, WENDY SUE. See also
Murders and Attempted Murders, N 30
WOLRAICH, MARK L (DR). See also
Hyperactivity, N 22
WOLTERS KLUWER NV. See also
CCH Inc. N 28

SUBJECT HEADING

WOMEN. See also
Abortion
Affirmative Action, N 20
Archeology and Anthropology, N 21
Basketball, N 19
Colleges and Universities, N 16,17,20
Gambling, N 26
Hunting and Trapping, N 24
Jews, N 21
Labor, N 23.26
Millionaires and Billionaires, N 19
Motion Pictures—American President, the (Movie), N 29
Motion Pictures—Toy Story (Movie), N 29
Philanthropy, N 26
Police, N 19
Pregnancy and Obstetrics
Restaurants, N 16
Roman Catholic Church, N 19,21,25,26
Sex Crimes, N 26
Stocks and Bonds, N 19
Tennis, N 20
United States Armament and Defense, N 19,22
Virginia Military Institute, N 20,27
Westchester County (NY), N 19
Natalie Angier comment on revived use of word 'gal,' after years of dangling in feminist lexical limbo; photo (S), N 19.IV.2:1
Frank Rich Op-Ed column says two new movies. The American President and Toy Story, suggest all is not well as far as American family is concerned: says American President reflects uneasiness about women in power, such as Hillary Clinton, while Toy Story reinforces with a vengeance pre-eminent role of women in home (M). N 29.A.23:1
WOMEN'S PHILANTHROPIC COUNCIL. See also
Philanthropy, N 26
WOOD AND WOOD PRODUCTS
Metropolitan Lumber draws people in construction to 11th Avenue between 45th and 46th Streets; photo (M). N 26.XIII-CY.9:1
WOOL AND WOOLEN GOODS. See also
Apparel

p.20

DESCRIPTION OF ARTICLE

LENGTH

DATE

SECTION

PAGE, COLUMN

Figure 8.5. Sample page from *The New York Times Index*, November 16–30, 1995. (Copyright © 1995 by The New York Times Co. Reprinted by permission.)

Wall Street Journal Index. New York: Dow Jones, 1959–.

    Emphasizes financial and business news. Includes *Barron's Index,* a subject and corporate index to *Barron's Business and Financial Weekly.* The online version is available by subscription only.

The Washington Post Newspaper Index. Ann Arbor, MI: UMI, 1978–.

    Useful for coverage of news from the nation's capital. Selective coverage available at http://www.washingtonpost.com/.

 ## SELECTED SUBJECT INDEXES TO PERIODICAL LITERATURE

The citations below describe the print version. All of the titles are available on the Internet.

Agriculture

Agricola. Beltsville, MD: National Agricultural Library, 1972–.

    The holdings and index of the National Library of Agriculture. Includes agricultural literature primarily in both journals and book chapters, but also includes some monographs, series, microforms, audio-visuals, maps, and other types of materials.

Biological Abstracts. Philadelphia, PA: BIOSIS, 1989–.

    Bibliographic database containing citations with abstracts to the world's biological and biomedical literature. Updated quarterly.

Biological and Agricultural Index. New York: H.W. Wilson, 1964–. (Continues *Agricultural Index.* 1916–1964.)

    A cumulative subject index to 226 English-language periodicals in the fields of biology, agriculture, and related sciences.

Arts and Humanities

American History & Life. Santa Barbara, CA: ABC/CLIO, 1964–.

    Scholarly material in American history and culture. Indexes journal articles, books, book chapters, films, videos, microforms, and dissertations. Citations and abstracts.

Art Index. New York: H.W. Wilson, 1933–.

    Includes citations to articles in painting, sculpture, architecture, ceramics, graphic arts, landscape architecture, archaeology, and other related subjects.

Arts and Humanities Citation Index. Philadelphia: Institute for Scientific Information, 1976–.

    Accesses about 6,900 journals in literature, poetry, short stories, music, film, radio, dance, and theater.

Historical Abstracts. Santa Barbara, CA: CLIO Press, 1971–.

    Research in world history but not American. Two sections: Modern History 1450–1914, and Twentieth Century 1914 to the present. Citations from journals, books, dissertations, and audio-visual materials.

Humanities Index. New York: H.W. Wilson, 1974–.

    Author and subject index to articles in more than 300 English language periodicals in the humanities: archaeology, classical studies, folklore, history, language and literature, theology, and related subjects.

Social Sciences Index. New York: H.W. Wilson, 1974–.

    Author and subject index for articles in more than 300 periodicals in anthropology, area studies, economics, environmental science, geography, law and criminology, political science, psychology, public administration, sociology and related subjects.

MLA International Bibliography. New York: Modern Language Association of America, 1981–.

    Scholarly research in over 3,000 journals and series; covers relevant monographs, working papers, proceedings, bibliographies and other formats.

Business

ABI/INFORM. Ann Arbor, MI: UMI, 1971–.
>Indexes over 1,500 business and trade journals. Citations and abstracts to articles in all business-related topics, economics, and managerial science. Allows keyword searching and several print options.

Business Index. Los Altos, CA: Gale Group, 1979–.
>Provides cumulative author/subject access to over 800 business periodicals, including articles in the *Wall Street Journal, Barron's,* and the financial section of *The New York Times.* Also covers articles relating to business appearing in over 1,100 general and legal periodicals.

Business Periodicals Index. New York: H.W. Wilson, 1958–. (Continues *Industrial Arts Index.* 1913–1957.)
>Magazines and journals in advertising, banking and finance, marketing, accounting, labor and management, insurance, and general business. Good source for information about an industry and about individual companies.

Education

Education Index. New York: H.W. Wilson, 1929–.
>Subject index to educational literature including 339 periodicals, pamphlets, reports, and books. Includes counseling and personnel service, teaching methods and curriculum, special education and rehabilitation, and educational research.

ERIC. Rockville, MD: Department of Education, Office of Educational Research and Improvement, 1966–.
>Contains a combination of the *Resources in Education* (RIE) file of ERIC document citations and the *Current Index to Journals in Education* (CIJE) journal article citations from over 750 professional journals. Includes all aspects of education.

Public Affairs

PAIS International. New York: Public Affairs Information Service, 1915–. (Previous title *PAIS Bulletin.*)
>Citations to articles in international affairs, public administration, political science, history, economics, finance, and sociology. Both U.S. and U.N. government documents are included, as well as books, pamphlets, society publications, and periodicals. Published twice monthly; cumulated annually.

Science and Technology

Applied Science and Technology Index. New York: H.W. Wilson, 1958–. (Continues *Industrial Arts Index,* 1913–1957.)
>Citations to articles in the fields of aeronautics, automation, construction, electricity, engineering, and related subjects.

Biological Abstracts. (*See* Agriculture.)

Biological and Agricultural Index. (*See* Agriculture.)

Chemical Abstracts. Columbus, OH: American Chemical Society, 1907–.
>Contains literature related to chemistry appearing in books, reports, annotated documents, and about 14,000 journals and conferences.

Engineering Index. Baltimore: Engineering Index, 1984–.
>Contains abstracts of literature published in engineering journals, technical reports, monographs, conference proceedings. Issued monthly and cumulated annually. Annual volumes are divided into subject volumes and an author index volume. Available online and on CD-ROM as COMPENDEX.

GEOREF. Alexandria, VA: American Geological Institute, 1990–.

    Comprehensive coverage of more than 4,500 international journals, books, proceedings, dissertations, and maps in geology and geography. Covers 1785– (North American), 1967– (worldwide).

Index Medicus. Washington: GPO, 1960–.

    Created by the National Library of Medicine primarily for the medical professional, but it is also useful to lay persons interested in medical-related topics. Available online as *Medline*.

INSPEC. Stevage, Herts., England: Institution of Electrical Engineers, 1993–.

    Indexes scientific and technical literature in electrical engineering, electronics, communications, control engineering, computers and computing, and information technology. Covers 1969–.

MathSciNet. Providence, RI: American Mathematical Society, 1973–.

    Includes information relating to mathematics, statistics, physics, and computer science.

SCI, Science Citation Index. Philadelphia: Institute for Scientific Information, 1965–

    Bimonthly with calendar year cumulations. Published in three sections:

        Source Index—lists all journals indexed with abbreviations used in the entries. Used to locate authors.

        Permuterm Subject—has the full information on the article (title of article, name of journal, volume, issue number, pages and date).

        Citation Index—used to locate authors' names cited in other publications.

    Available on the Internet as *Web of Science*.

Social Sciences

NCJRS Documents Database. Washington: National Institute of Justice/National Criminal Justice Reference Service, 1972–.

    Contains references to periodical articles, research reports, books and unpublished materials from private sources as well as from local, state, and national governments.

Psychological Abstracts. Arlington, VA: American Psychological Association, 1927–.

    Abstracts of journal articles, monographs, and reports on psychology and related studies arranged by major classification groups. Includes author and subject index. Issued monthly. Available online and on CD-ROM as *PsycLit* and *PsycInfo*.

Sociological Abstracts. New York: Sociological Abstracts, 1952–.

    International in scope; covers articles from journals concerned with sociology. Electronic version covers 1977–.

 # ELECTRONIC JOURNALS

Humanities

JSTOR. JSTOR, 2000.

    Retrospective collection of over 100 journal titles representing core titles in each discipline of social sciences and humanities; some science and mathematics titles will be added during the year 2000. Available only by subscription.

Project Muse. Baltimore, MD. Johns Hopkins UP.

    Full-text articles in the humanities and social sciences: literature and criticism, history, visual and performing arts, cultural studies, education, political science, gender studies. Available only by subscription.

Social Sciences

(See *JSTOR* and *Project Muse*)

http://www.socioweb.com/~markbl/socioweb/
journals/
  sociology

http://www.unf.edu/~ebrady/persubus.html
  business

http://node.on.ca/ltreport
  education

http://www-sul.stanford.edu/collect/ejourn/
psa.html
  political science

Sciences

http://www.egj.lib.uidaho.edu/index.html
  environment

http://www.heartweb.org
  health

http://library.gsfc.nasa.gov/
  space

http://www.ou.edu/cas/botany-microjournals/
  botany

Periodicals

Instructor: _____ Course/Section: _____

Name: _____

Date: _____ Points: _____

Review Questions

1. Give three reasons why periodical materials are important sources for research.

   a.

   b.

   c.

2. List three different formats of periodical literature.

   a.

   b.

   c.

3. What is the difference in scope between a magazine or journal index and a newspaper index?

4. What is meant by the term "e-journal"?

5. How does an abstract differ from an index?

6. Explain the differences between a bibliographic database and a full-text database.

7. Name two electronic databases that could be useful in searching for popular articles.

   a.

   b.

8. Explain the difference between a popular and a scholarly index.

9. List three multidisciplinary subject databases.

10. What is the difference between a multidisciplinary index or database and a subject index?

11. How would you locate periodical articles in the library after the information has been found in an index?

Periodicals

8

Instructor: _____ Course/Section: _____

Name: _____

Date: _____ Points: _____

Selecting Databases

1. Select a topic of your choice or one provided by your instructor for research.

    Topic:

2. Write a preliminary thesis statement for this topic.

PART A. *EBSCOhost* and *InfoTrac* are examples of a general database that may include both popular and scholarly articles. Answer the following questions using one of the general databases available at your library.

1. Title of the database you selected:

2. Subject heading or keyword term(s) you used for your topic:

3. If you found citations under this heading, how many were listed?

4. If none were found, did the database give you other terms to select? If so, what were the terms?

5. Select one article from a popular magazine relevant to your topic and give the following information.

    Author:

    Title of the article:

    Full title of the periodical:

    Volume/issue: Pages of article: Date:

6. Write the correct citation of the article here, using examples from Appendix A.

7. Give two reasons why you selected this as a popular source.

    a.

    b.

8. Does the database give just the citation, or the full text of the article?

9. How would you determine if this article is also available in the library?

PART B. *WilsonWeb* and *FirstSearch* are examples of discipline-related periodical databases. Each includes a group of databases covering different subjects. Answer the following questions using the database you found related to your subject.

1. Title of the database you used:

2.   Subject heading or keyword you used for your topic:

3.   Did you find citations in this database under this heading?
     If not, which cross references did the database send you to?

4.   Give the following information for one article on your topic.

     Author:

     Title of magazine/journal:

     Title of the article:

     Volume/issue: Pages of article: Date:

5.   Did this database give you the citation only, the citation and abstract, or the full text of the
     article you retrieved?

6.   Write the correct citation of the article here, using examples in Appendix A.

7.   Would you consider this article popular or scholarly?
     Give two reasons to justify your answer.

     a.

     b.

8. How do articles you found in Part B compare to those you found in Part A above, the "general" databases? Give at least two differences you found.

a.

b.

9. How would you determine if this article could be found in your library? Give specific steps and tools you would use.

PART C. Besides general databases, such as those listed in Part A, and discipline-related data-bases, such as those in Part B, there are also many subject-specific or specialized databases on a variety of subjects, such as *ERIC* (education), *ABI/INFORM* (business), and *PsycInfo* (Psychology). Select an appropriate specialized database available in your library for your topic and complete the questions below.

1. Title of database you used:

2. Subject heading or keyword used for your topic:

3. Did you find citations in this database under this heading?
   If not, which cross references did the database send you to?

4. Give the following information for one article on your topic.

   Author:

   Title of magazine/journal:

   Title of the article:

   Volume/issue: Pages of article: Date:

5. Did this database give you the citation only, the citation and abstract, or the full text of the article you retrieved?

6. Write the correct citation of the article here, using examples from Appendix A.

7. Would you consider this article popular or scholarly?

   Give two reasons why.

   a.

   b.

8. How do articles in this database compare to those you found in Parts A and B above?

   Give at least two differences you found.

   a.

   b.

9. How would you determine if this article is available in the library?

PART D. Retrieve one of the articles you found in either Part A, Part B, or Part C above. Consider each of the following points as you read the article.

1. Does the author use primary or secondary sources to write the article?

2. Would you consider the author to be knowledgeable in this field? Why?

3. How current is the material covered in the article?

4. What type of language is used in the article? (Popular or scholarly?)

5. Who is the intended audience?

6. Is there any indication of bias on the part of the author?

7. What is the source of the author's information? (e.g., survey, personal knowledge, or interviews.)

8. If you were writing a research paper on this topic, would you consider using this article:

   a. at the beginning of your paper as an introduction?

   b. as a major point in your argument or presentation?

   c. as a supporting point of a thesis?

   d. at the conclusion of your paper?

9. Explain your choice for Question 37.

Periodicals

8

Instructor: _____ Course/Section: _____

Name: _____

Date: _____ Points: _____

Finding E-Journals

Select one of the following sites and answer the questions below.

http://www.adage.com   http://www.wired.com

http://www.newscientist.com/   http://www.pw.org/

1. Which Web site did you select?

2. What is the name of the page you selected?

3. Is the site full text or does it only provide information about the journal?

4. Does the site give archival information or current issue information only? Other?

5. Is the site free to search, or do you need a subscription or have to login?

6. Is this publication also available in print or other format? If so, give the formats.

7. Would you find articles from this publication indexed in full-text databases, indexes, or abstracts? How do you know, or what sources would you use to find out?

Periodicals

8

Instructor: _____ Course/Section: _____

Name: _____

Date: _____ Points: _____

Using *Readers' Guide to Periodical Literature*

Answer the following questions based upon the entries taken from *Readers' Guide to Periodical Literature*, Figure 8.4.

1. What subject heading would you use to locate additional information on women and employment?

2. Who wrote the article on "Woman Suffrage"?

3. Is the first article about women's employment illustrated? What determines this?

4. In which magazines can you locate some articles on equal rights for women?

5. Where would you find information on clothing and dress for women?

6. Which magazines contain articles on women's attitudes?

7. What is the best subject heading for articles dealing with women and smoking?

8.   What does the p46+ mean in the first article by Tobias Wolff?

9.   Who wrote the article on women's history?

10.   What do you consult in your library to locate call numbers or titles of magazines?

11.   List the steps you would need to take to retrieve one of these articles.

Periodicals

8

Instructor: _____ Course/Section: _____

Name: _____

Date: _____ Points: _____

Using Printed Periodical Indexes

Locate a periodical index or abstract that you could use to locate information on topic that interests you or that has been assigned by your instructor. Give the following information.

Topic:

1. Describe the strategy you used to find this index/abstract. Be specific in your answer. (Used library catalog, searched under . . ., browsed reference shelves, index shelves, etc.)

2. Call number and location of index/abstract:

3. Title of index/abstract:

4. What subjects are included in this source?

5. Describe the arrangement of the source (alphabetical, topical, etc.).

6. What subject heading(s) are used in this index/abstract for your topic?

7. Give the following information for one article on your topic.

   Author:

   Title of magazine/journal:

   Title of the article:

   Volume/issue: Pages of article: Date:

8. Does the library subscribe to this periodical?

10. If the library subscribes (or has this periodical in a full-text database), give the call number and location or title of the database here.

11. Write the correct bibliographic citation for this article, using the examples in Appendix A.

Periodicals

Instructor: _____ Course/Section: _____

Namo: _____

Date: _____ Points: _____

Selecting Printed Periodical Indexes

1. Select a topic of your choice, or use one provided by your instructor.

   Topic:

2. Write a preliminary thesis statement for this topic.

Examine the following printed indexes and respond to each question.

PART A. *Readers' Guide to Periodical Literature* is an example of a general, popular, periodical index. Answer the following questions using *Readers' Guide*.

1. Subject heading you used for your topic:

2. Did you find citations under this heading?
   If not, which cross references did the index send you to?

3. Give the following information for one article on your topic.

   Author:

   Full title of the magazine/journal:
   (Use the abbreviation list in the front of the index if necessary.)

   Title of the article:

   Volume/issue: Pages of article: Date:

4. Would you label this article as popular or scholarly?

5. Give two reasons why you think this would be a popular or scholarly article.

   a.

   b.

6. Could you find this article in the library?

7. If so, is it available in print, or only electronically?

8. Write the correct citation to this article, using the examples from Appendix A.

PART B. *Social Sciences Index*, *Humanities Index*, and *General Science Index* are examples of discipline-related periodical indexes. Each covers a group of related subjects in one particular area of knowledge. Answer the following questions using the appropriate discipline index for your thesis statement.

1. Title of index used:

2. Subject heading you used for your topic:

3. Did you find citations under this heading?

   If not, which cross references did the index send you to?

4. Give the following information for one article on your topic.

   Author:

   Full title of the magazine/journal:
   (Use the abbreviation list in the front of the index if necessary.)

   Title of the article:

   Volume/issue: Pages of article: Date:

5. Would you label this article as popular or scholarly?

6. Give two reasons why you think this would be a popular or scholarly article.

   a.

   b.

7. How do articles in this index compare to those you found in *Readers' Guide*? Give at least two differences you noted.

9. Could you find this article in the library?

   If so, is it available in print, or only electronically?

PART C. Besides general indexes, such as *Readers' Guide,* and discipline-related indexes, such as *Humanities Index,* there are also many subject-specific or specialized periodical indexes on a variety of subjects, such as *Education Index, PAIS,* and *Psychological Abstracts.* Find an appropriate specialized index to develop your thesis and answer the following questions.

1.   Index used for your topic:

2.   Subject heading you used for your topic:

3.   Did you find citations under this heading?

     If not, which cross references did the index send you to?

4.   Give the following information for one article on your topic.

     Author:

     Full title of the journal:
     (Use the abbreviation list in the front of the index if necessary.)

     Title of the article:

     Volume/issue: Pages of article: Date:

5.   Would you label this article as popular or scholarly?

6.   Give two reasons why you think this would be a popular or scholarly article.

     a.

     b.

7. How do articles in this index compare to those you found in *Readers' Guide* and the discipline index? Give at least two differences you noted.

8. Would you find this article in the library?

   If so, is it available in print, or only electronically?

9. Write the correct bibliographic citation for this article, using examples from Appendix A.

Periodicals

8
Instructor: _____ Course/Section: _____

Name: _____

Date: _____ Points: _____

Abstract Indentification

1. Identify the parts of this entry from the printed entry from *Sociological Abstracts*. Write the correct number next to the entry.

9505360	**2**	**3**	**4**

1   **Levine, Phillip B. & Zimmerman, David J**. (Wellesley Coll, MA 02181). **A comparison of the Sex-Type of Occupational Aspirations and Subsequent Achievement,** UM *Work and Occupations*, 1995, 22, 1, Feb, 73–84.

5   **6   7   6   8**

Explores the connection between the sex-type of a girl's occupational aspirations & that of her achieved occupation, replicating previous work by Jerry Jacobs (see SA 35:5/87R9890) & building on it by using more recent data & an alternative methodology. Two cohorts of data (1968 & 1979) from the National Longitudinal Surveys are employed to

9   estimate transition probability matrices between the sex-types of aspired & achieved occupations. Then, multivariate models of the probability of entering a traditional (ie, female-dominated or nontraditional (ie, male-dominated) occupation are estimated. Findings indicate that Jacobs actually overestimated the relationship between aspirations & achievement, & that this relationship has, in some ways, grown weaker over time.

10   2 Tables, 18 References. Adapted from the source document. (Copyright 1995, Sociological Abstracts, Inc., all rights reserved.)

a.   date of publication   _____

b.   abstract (summary) of the article   _____

c.   title of the journal (publication)   _____

d.   author of article   _____

e.   title of the article   _____

f.   supplementary material provided in article   _____

g.   volume and issue number of journal   _____

h.   abstract (accession) number   _____

i.   author's affiliation   _____

j.   page in journal where article appears   _____

2. Is this a popular or a scholarly work? Give three reasons to justify your answer.

    a.

    b.

    c.

3. Write the correct bibliographic citation for this article. Use examples from Appendix A.

Periodicals

Instructor: _____ Course/Section: _____

Name: _____

Date: _____ Points: _____

Using a Printed Newspaper Index

Use the sample page from *The New York Times Index* (Figure 8.5) to find articles on the subject of women and give the following information. (Remember, the name of the newspaper and the year are taken from the cover of the index.)

1. Month:

2. Day:

3. Year:

4. Section:

5. Column:

6. Page(s):

7. How would you locate this article in the library?

8. Write the correct bibliographic citation for this article, using the examples in Appendix A.

Periodicals

Instructor: _____   Course/Section: _____

     Name: _____

     Date: _____   Points: _____

Using Online Newspapers

Today many full-text newspapers are available online. Find a recent article from either *The New York Times* or another major newspaper and answer the following questions.

1. Give the name of the newspaper you found.

2. Give the URL for the newspaper.

3. Give the name of the author of the article, if given. If not, mark N/A for not applicable.

4. Give the exact title of the article.

5. How long is the article (number of words or number of pages)?

6. Write the correct bibliographic citation for this article, using the examples in Appendix A.

7. Were there any other references listed in this article for related information? If so, give one other entry here.

8. How would you determine if your library receives this newspaper? Be specific in your answer.

9

Government Information

"Just be thankful you're not getting all the government you're paying for."
WILL ROGERS

INTRODUCTION

In the United States it is an elementary—but all important—principle that the operations of government are to be open to scrutiny and criticism. This makes it possible for citizens to participate in government and to contribute to the advancement of society. Indeed, the American political system, and to a large extent the educational system, rests on the widespread acceptance of ready and fair access to information about government and information produced by the government. This principle has led local, state, national, and even international governing bodies to produce large quantities of information. Publications produced by governing bodies encompass a broad range of topics—not only on the government itself and how it is run, but also on many subjects of interest to citizens. This chapter is designed to serve as a guide for locating government information, both in traditional and electronic format. The emphasis is on U.S. government publications, which are more numerous than those of the other entities; there are brief introductions to local, state, and international documents.

◆ GOVERNMENT INFORMATION IN THE RESEARCH PROCESS

Government information is useful for research in many disciplines, but especially in the social sciences and the natural sciences. Although it is possible to find government information covering topics in the humanities, that is not the norm. Aside from the intrinsic value of contributing to an informed citizenry, government publications have a number of distinctive characteristics that add to their value as information sources.

ADVANTAGES OF USING GOVERNMENT PUBLICATIONS

◆ *Cover a broad spectrum of subjects.* Since the government is responsive to public needs, the subjects covered in government publications range from those that are useful only to specialists to those that are of interest to consumers.

◆ *Ready availability.* Government publications are inexpensive or, in many cases, free. One can write or call government agencies to acquire many of the publications. However, this is usually not necessary since most government publications can be found in libraries or on the Internet.

◆ *Primary sources of information.* Much of the information disseminated by the government is considered to be a primary source. Statistics that are gathered firsthand fit into this category as do myriads of government publications.

◆ *Free of bias.* The individuals who work for government agencies are not supposed to represent a particular viewpoint, political party, or special interest group; as a result, government information is generally considered to be objective.

◆ *Up-to-date information.* Because the government is the primary source for much of the information in non-government publications, information from a government source is often more current than that in a non-government publication. This is especially true today with information that is available through the Internet.

◆ *Only source of information on many topics.* Much of the information available from governmental agencies is not available from any other source. For example, the federal government is the sole provider of information on the amounts of toxic air released by various industries; the state government is the unique source for expenditures on state services.

As part of your search strategy, you should consider whether the information you need might be found in a government source.

ASK YOURSELF

◆ Are statistics needed?

◆ Is there a social issue involved, such as world hunger, overpopulation, abortion, or unemployment?

◆ Is it an issue that was discussed in Congress, such as use of seat belts or sexual harassment?

◆ Does it concern historical events, such as the war in Vietnam?

◆ Is it a local issue, such as the funding of public education?

◆ Is it scientific research that has been sponsored by the government?

Information produced by government agencies may show up in some of the tools you use to conduct a search. For example, if government documents are included in the library's online catalog along with other materials, they will show up in the results of many subject and keyword searches. Some periodical indexes include government periodicals and reports among the sources they index. For example, *PAIS International* includes both U.S. and international government publications. A keyword search on the Internet is also likely to turn up government sources. Even so, to find specific government information you need to know what type of information is available, what formats you can expect to encounter, and which tools to use to locate the information.

◆ UNITED STATES GOVERNMENT PUBLICATIONS

The United States government is the single largest producer of information in the world. The information sources from the federal government are as varied as they are numerous. They come in all sizes and shapes—from one-page leaflets to works of several thousand pages and many volumes. They vary in scope from highly technical scientific research reports to popular pamphlets on such topics as weight loss and caring for pets. Included in government publications are all the official documents such as laws, regulations, court decisions, presidential documents, treaties, congressional proceedings, military records, and census reports. The government issues a large number of reference books including indexes, abstracts, bibliographies, directories, atlases, handbooks, yearbooks, and almanacs. Approximately 1,200 government periodicals are published on a regular basis.

Format

The format of government information is almost as varied as its scope. Until recently, government publications were published in traditional formats: paper, microfiche, film, video and cassette tapes, photographs, maps, charts, and posters. The federal government has always been a leader in utilizing new technologies to produce, store, and retrieve information, and was the first publisher to make widespread use of the CD-ROM as a publication medium. There are thousands of government titles in CD-ROM format. These include statistical sources, maps, government regulations, and reference sources such as the *Statistical Abstract of the U.S.*

Today the Government Printing Office (GPO), which is the chief publisher of U.S. government information, is in a state of transition from a paper publisher to an electronic publisher. In 1996 Congress issued a mandate that the GPO formulate a plan to cease publishing and distributing government information in paper and microfiche format and move to electronic format. It was anticipated that before the end of the century all government information, with the exception of a few titles, would be available only in electronic format—primarily through the Internet. While this did not happen, it is true that large numbers of U.S. government publications are now available only on the Internet.

Depository Libraries

The Government Printing Office (GPO) was established in 1861 for the purpose of publishing the official publications of the federal government. Prior to that time private firms printed the official documents of the U.S. government. Consequently, we have historical documents published by authority of the federal government dating back to the Continental Congress. The GPO is still the official publisher and/or distributor of all the documents of the legislative, executive, and judicial branches of the federal government that are considered by law to be in the public interest—the Congressional debates, laws, executive orders, annual reports, court decisions, regulations, reports, and special studies.

In 1895, Congress enacted legislation that provided for the free distribution of documents to designated libraries and institutions. The libraries receiving documents free of charge from the GPO are called *depository libraries.* There are approximately 1,400 depository libraries in the United States. Of these, about 50 are *regional depository libraries,* which receive all the publications distributed by GPO. Other libraries are *selective depository libraries,* so designated because they can choose the items that they wish to receive. The depository library provides the facilities for housing documents and the staff needed to administer the collections. The only other obligations of the depository library are to assure that the materials are cared for according to guidelines established by the GPO and to make the documents available to the public.

Because government information is in a state of transition from paper and microfiche format to electronic format, the status of depository libraries is being questioned. The role of the depository library in a predominately Internet environment will no doubt change. With government information being available primarily through the Internet, the need to house and preserve government information in libraries throughout the country will cease to exist. Depository libraries will probably maintain their retrospective paper and microfiche collections, but will assume different roles with regard to current information. They will be expected to provide the means for the public to access government information on the Internet—

computers, printers, and Internet connectivity. They will also continue to provide bibliographic access to all publications—catalog records in the online catalog or some other index to government publications. And librarians knowledgeable about government information sources will still be available to assist users.

Finding U.S. Government Information

Most discussions of finding government information inevitably begin by acknowledging the difficulty of identifying and locating material published by the government. In most libraries, government publications are housed in a separate collection and shelved by SuDocs number (see Figure 9.1.). This of itself is not a problem. The problem is the fact that traditionally there have been very few tools to help users identify and locate these publications. It was not until the early 1990s that libraries began including government publications in their online catalogs; many library catalogs still do not include them. Even those libraries that do include government publications in the online catalog list only materials published since 1976 when GPO began creating records in machine readable format. Government publications traditionally have not been included in the usual indexing tools such as *Readers' Guide* and *Social Sciences Index*. Although many of the barriers to finding government information were lifted in the 1990s when libraries began including government publications in their online catalogs and government information became available on the Internet, it is still difficult to find government information. The tools listed below are helpful in getting you started. Beyond that you should consult a librarian who is familiar with government information.

General Finding Aids

You need to be aware of whether or not government documents are included in the online catalog in your library and what years of coverage are included. The records in the online catalog are based on entries from the *Monthly Catalog of United States Government Publications,* regarded as the primary access point for government publications distributed to depository libraries. The print version of the *Monthly Catalog* and its online counterpart, the *Catalog of United States Government Publications,* are described below.

Monthly Catalog of United States Government Publications. Washington: GPO, 1895–.
    The *Monthly Catalog* is the comprehensive index to government publications. Because government publications are now listed in online catalogs, it is used chiefly to search for retrospective government publications (pre-1976) that are not cataloged, but are shelved by SuDocs call number. The main entries are arranged alphabetically by issuing agency in the main body of the catalog. Each issue contains separate indexes for subjects, titles, title keywords, authors, series reports, contract numbers, stock numbers, and SuDocs numbers (see Figures 9.2 and 9.3). Since 1976, the GPO has been creating the *Monthly Catalog* from MARC records. Prior to this date, the bibliographic entries in the *Monthly Catalog* contained less detail. Figures 9.4 and 9.5 are examples of an index entry and a bibliographic record from a pre-1976 *Monthly Catalog.* The *Monthly Catalog* from 1976 to date is also available on the Internet by subscription from vendors such as DIALOG, OCLC *FirstSearch*, and MARCIVE.

Catalog of United States Government Publications. GPO, 1994–. 2 Nov. 1999. 5 Apr. 2000 <http://www.gpo.gov/catalog>.
    The online version of the *Monthly Catalog,* this is a search and retrieval service that contains bibliographic records of U.S. government information resources. It provides direct links to online resources from federal agencies and identifies print and CD-ROM materials distributed to depository libraries. Coverage begins with January 1994, and new records are added daily.

Figure 9.1.
Instructions for
locating a U.S.
government
publication.

How to find a U.S. Government Publication

As a Federal Depository Library, we receive many publications issued by agencies of the U.S. Government. These publications, which may include books, maps, posters, pamphlets, and periodicals, contain information on careers, business opportunities, space exploration, health and nutrition, energy, and many other subjects.

Federal Government publications in this collection are arranged by the Superintendent of Documents classification number. Publications are grouped together by issuing agency." To ensure that you find all of the materials available on a particular subject, be sure to check the indexes recommended by the librarian.

The example below shows how the Superintendent of Documents classification number C 61.34:987 is constructed for the publication *U.S. Industrial Outlook:*

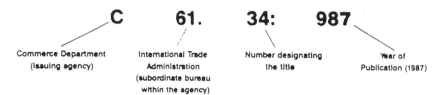

C	**61.**	**34:**	**987**
Commerce Department (issuing agency)	International Trade Administration (subordinate bureau within the agency)	Number designating the title	Year of Publication (1987)

Here are the prefixes from the Superintendent of Documents classification numbers for some other agencies that you may be interested in:

A	Agriculture Department
C 3.	Census Bureau (Commerce Department)
D	Defense Department
E	Energy Department
ED	Education Department
GA	General Accounting Office
GS	General Services Administration
HE	Health and Human Services Department
I	Interior Department
I 19.	U.S. Geological Survey (Interior Department)
J	Justice Department
Ju	Judiciary
L	Labor Department
LC	Library of Congress
NAS	National Aeronautics and Space Administration
S	State Department
SI	Smithsonian Institution
T 22.	Internal Revenue Service (Treasury Department)
X, Y	Congress
Y 4.	Congressional Committees .

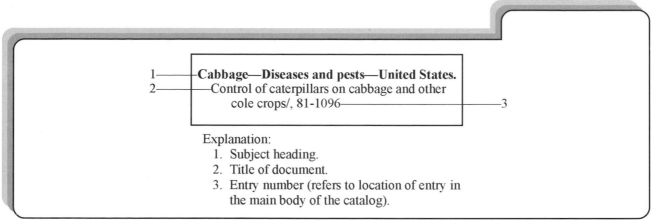

Explanation:
1. Subject heading.
2. Title of document.
3. Entry number (refers to location of entry in the main body of the catalog).

Figure 9.2. Excerpt from Subject Index in *Monthly Catalog.*

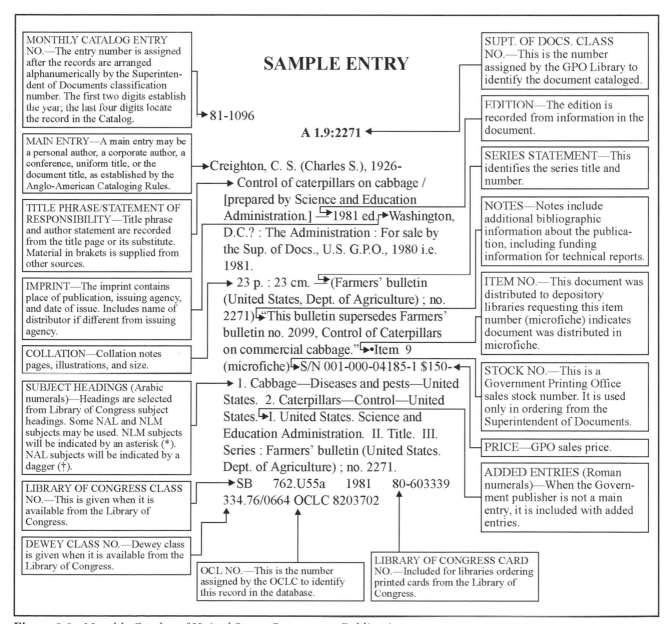

Figure 9.3. *Monthly Catalog of United States Government Publications.*

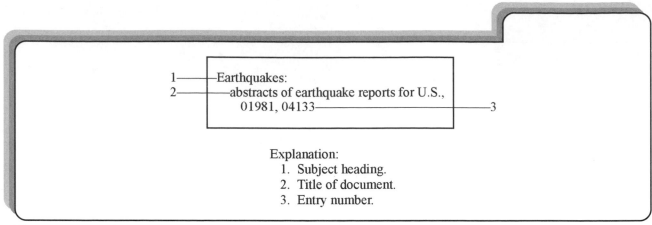

Figure 9.4. Sample entry from Subject Index.

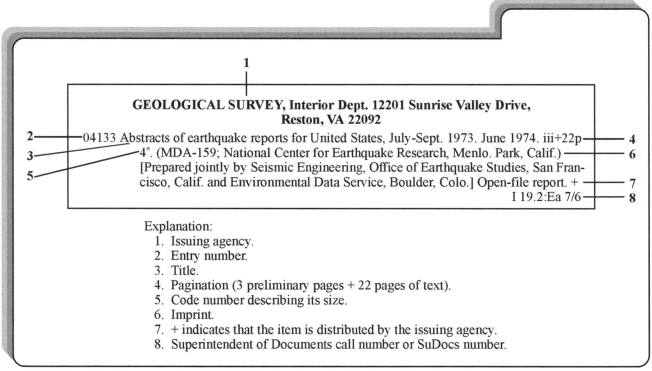

Figure 9.5. Main entry section of the catalog.

Internet Sites

Academic Universe. CIS/Lexis/Nexis. n.d. 14 Apr. 2000 < http://www.cispubs.com/>. Available by subscription only.

Although not devoted exclusively to government publications, *Academic Universe* does include a vast amount of information, most of it full text, by and about the U.S. government, including Congressional hearings, summaries of legislative actions, committee markups, television transcripts, presidential campaign materials, tax information, laws, regulations, attorney general opinions, the U.S. Code, and the Constitution.

Browse Government Resources. Library of Congress. Dec. 1999. 14 Apr. 2000 <http://lcweb.loc.gov/rr/news/extgovd.html>.

A list of government sources prepared and maintained by the Serial and Government Publications Division of the Library of Congress.

Federal Government Resources on the Web. Comp. Grace York. University of Michigan Documents Center. 23 Mar. 2000. 15 April 2000 <http://www.lib.umich.edu/libhome/Documents.center/federal.html>.

An excellent site for federal government information listed under the following categories: Bibliographies, Budget, Civil Service, Copyright, Directories, Executive Branch, Executive Orders, FOIA, GAO, Grants, Historic Documents, Legislative Branch, Judicial Branch, Laws, OMB, Patents, President, Regulations, Taxes, Trademarks, Web Site Directories, and White House.

GOVBOT: Database of Government Web Sources. The Center for Intelligent Information Retrieval. University of Massachusetts, Amherst. 1999–2000. 14 Apr. 2000 <http://ciir2.cs.umass.edu/Govbot/>.

A collection of over 1.5 million Web pages from U.S. government and military sites around the country. Has a form for easy searching.

Government Information Connection: Catalogs, Indexes, and Databases. Comp. Melody Kelly. University of North Texas Libraries. 11 Nov. 1999. 14 Apr. 2000 <http://www.library.unt.edu/govinfo/subject/catsindx.html>.

An alphabetical list to both general and subject-specific Internet catalogs, indexes and databases.

Government Information Locator Service (GILS). GPO. 10 January 2000. 14 Apr. 2000 <http://www.access.gpo.gov/su_docs/gils/gils.html>.

The federal government initiative to make government information accessible using computer and networking technology. As part of the federal role in the National Information Infrastructure, GILS records identify public information resources within the federal government and describe the information available in these resources.

GPO Access. GPO. 7 Apr. 2000. 14 Apr. 2000 <http://www.access.gpo.gov/su_docs/index.html>.

This free service is funded by the Federal Depository Library Program as a result of Public Law 103-40, known as the Government Printing Office Electronic Information Enhancement Act of 1993. It provides free online use of over 1,000 databases of federal information in over 70 applications. It is possible to search one database or multiple databases in a single search. A help page tells how to search *GPO Access.*

U.S. Federal Government Agencies Directory. Baton Rouge: Louisiana State University Libraries. 20 Jan. 2000. 14 Apr. 2000 <http://www.lib.lsu.edu/gov/fedgov.html>.

A directory of U. S. government agencies on the Internet as represented in the *United States Government Manual.*

Retrospective Government Information (Pre-1976)

Cumulative Subject Index to the Monthly Catalog of United States Government Publications, 1900–1971. Comp. William W. Buchanan, and Edna M. Kanely. 15 vols. Washington: Carrolton, 1973–1975.

A subject index to the titles listed in *Monthly Catalog* for the years 1900–1973.

Cumulative Title Index to United States Public Documents, 1789–1976. Comp. Daniel W. Lester, Sandra K. Faull, and Lorraine E. Lester. 16 vols. Arlington: United States Historical Documents Institute, 1979–1983.

An alphabetical listing of the titles of publications distributed by the Government Printing Office. Useful for locating a pre-1976 publication if the title is known.

Congressional Information

Congressional Information Services Index to Publications of the United States Congress (CIS/Index). Bethesda: CIS, 1970–.
> The paper counterpart to *Congressional Universe*.

Congressional Masterfile. Bethesda: CIS, 1789–1969.
> A CD-ROM-based database, it provides most of the same information as *Congressional Universe*, for the earlier years.

Congressional Universe. (Formerly *Congressional Compass*). CD-ROM. Bethesda: CIS/Lexis/Nexis, 1970–. 14 Apr. 2000 <http://www.cispubs.com>.
> A Web-based service that provides access to the full text of Congressional reports, hearings, committee prints, documents, bills, the *Congressional Record*, the *Federal Register*, and the *Code of Federal Regulations*. Has a bill tracking feature that allows users to research or monitor current public policy issues. Also includes legislative histories. Available by subscription only.

CQ Library. Washington: Congressional Quarterly, 1998–. 14 Apr. 2000 <http://libraryip.cq.com>.
> A subscription service that provides Web access to the full text of two of Congressional Quarterly's (CQ) print publications, the *CQ Weekly* and the *CQ Researcher*. The *CQ Weekly* covers all articles published from 1983 to the present; the *CQ Researcher* covers 1991 to the present. The *CQ Weekly* provides summaries of the most important legislative actions. The *CQ Researcher* provides in-depth analysis and insight into controversial issues. Available by subscription only.

Thomas. Library of Congress. Washington, n.d. 14 Apr. 2000 <http://thomas.loc.gov/>.
> Primary point of entry for information on current U.S. federal legislative information. It is fully searchable and includes the full text of bills, laws, the *Congressional Record* (the verbatim record of sessions of the U.S. Congress), reports, and links to other government information.

Scientific and Technical Information

DOE Information Bridge. Oak Ridge: Department of Energy, 1995–. 14 Apr. 2000 <http://home.osti.gov/bridge/home.html>.
> A subset of the *Energy Files,* this database contains the full text and bibliographic records of DOE-sponsored report literature. It includes over 49,000 reports that have been received and processed by OSTI since January, 1995.

Energy Files. Oak Ridge: Department of Energy. 14 Apr. 2000. 15 Apr. 2000 <http://home.osti.gov/EnergyFiles>.
> Home page to a vast array of information and resources pertaining to energy, science, and technology. Developed and maintained by the Department of Energy's Office of Scientific and Technical Information (OSTI), it provides searching across a number of energy-related databases.

Government Reports Announcements and Index. Springfield, VA: National Technical Information Service, 1970–. Bimonthly. The paper counterpart to the NTIS database.

NTIS: National Technical Information Service Electronic Catalog. Springfield, VA: National Technical Information Service, 1990–. 14 Apr. 2000 <http://www.ntis.gov/search.htm#free>.
> The National Technical Information Service is a clearinghouse for government-sponsored scientific, technical, engineering, and business research. It also includes some reports from state and local government agencies and from countries outside the U.S., as well as reports from over 200 federal agencies that are not distributed free of charge through the depository library program. The *Catalog* indexes and abstracts the reports in the NTIS collection. All the documents listed in the *Catalog* are available for sale. The *Catalog*, with records going back to 1964 is available by subscription from a number of vendors, including DIALOG and Biblioline.

Statistical Information

See Chapter 10.

 # STATE GOVERNMENT INFORMATION

State governments and the federal government have similar missions: to keep the public informed. Although state governments publish less information than the national government, they too are prolific publishers of information. Each state provides descriptions of its governmental activities, reports of special developments in industry and economics, maps, laws, and statistics on education, crime, health, employment, and business. The information found in state documents is especially useful because of its timeliness. Statistics on employment, housing construction, crime, and health, for example, are gathered by the states and published in state documents before they appear in federal documents.

Most states do not have funds to provide for widespread distribution of their publications. Rather, certain libraries are designated as depository libraries for state documents and automatically receive the state's publications. The way that depository collections are organized varies among libraries. Some libraries keep their documents in a separate state collection with other special materials on the state; others house them as a separate collection within the government documents department. Still other libraries integrate state documents with their general collection. Access to state documents varies among libraries. Many states publish checklists and bibliographies listing currently available publications; a few libraries catalog state documents along with other library materials; and many states are now publishing state documents online. Even though technology has improved access to state information, it is still difficult to identify and locate state publications. For that reason, in most libraries with state documents collections, a librarian with special training and experience is usually available to assist patrons in locating state information.

State Government Information on the Internet

FindLaw. State Resources. FindLaw, Inc. 1994–2000. 5 Apr. 2000. <http://www.findlaw.com/11stategov/index.html>.
  A state-by-state listing of legal information on the Internet.

State and Local Government on the Net. Piper Resources. 2000. 14 Apr. 2000 <http://www.piperinfo.com/state/index.cfm>.
  A guide to government sponsored Internet sites.

State and Local Governments. Library of Congress. 17 Mar. 2000. 5 Apr. 2000 <http://lcweb.loc.gov/global/state/stategov.html>.
  Library of Congress Web site listing state and local government information under two categories: *Meta-Indexes for State and Local Government Information* and *State Government Information.*

State Government and Politics. Comp. Grace York. University of Michigan. 14 Feb. 2000. Apr. 2000 <http://www.lib.umich.edu/libhome/Documents.center/state.html>.
  A comprehensive guide to state information on the Internet.

The State Web Locator. Center for Information Law and Policy. 1995–2000.
  14 Apr. 2000 <http://www.infoctr.edu/swl/>.
  A state by state listing for government information Web sites.

◆ LOCAL GOVERNMENT INFORMATION

In the United States there are many local units of government–towns, cities, counties, and special districts. Although information about local governmental units appears in federal government as well as in commercial publications, most of the key information is produced by local governmental units. Publications from local governments include records of their official activities, such as charters, laws, regulations, financial reports, city plans, maps, statistics, budgets, and decisions. Local publications are an important primary source of information. These documents usually are not widely distributed, making them difficult to locate and access. One way to get information from local governments is to request it directly from the local agency. Another way is through the library. Libraries, especially college and university libraries, often serve as depositories for local documents. The way local documents are handled varies among libraries. Some libraries catalog local documents along with the other materials in the library, others keep them in separate collections, which may or may not be cataloged. Since there are no quick and easy guides to local government publications, one should ask the librarian for assistance when seeking local documents or information about a local governmental unit.

Local Government Information on the Internet

GovLinks Index: Local Government. Governing.Com. Congressional Quarterly. n.d. 14 Apr. 2000 <http://www.governing.com/local.htm>.
    A guide to Internet resources for local government, including city and county home pages.
State and Local Government on the Net. Piper Resources. 2000. 14 Apr. 2000 <http://www.piperinfo.com/state/index.cfm>.
    A guide to government sponsored Internet sites.
State and Local Governments. Library of Congress. 17 Mar. 2000. 5 Apr. 2000 <http://lcweb.loc.gov/global/state/stategov.html>.
    Library of Congress Web site listing state and local government information. Local information found under the category *Meta-Indexes for State and Local Government*.

◆ INTERNATIONAL ORGANIZATIONS AND FOREIGN GOVERNMENTS

International government organizations (IGOs) refers to those institutions that are created as a result of formal agreements between two or more sovereign states. The agreements are designed to address and regulate (within the bounds of international law) matters of common concern to all the parties–peace keeping, human rights, or economic development. Included in the agreements are arrangements for maintaining facilities and providing for the ongoing activities of the members. IGOs vary greatly in their goals, structures, and geographic scope. Some focus on single issues while others deal with broader concerns. There are hundreds of IGOs, the most notable being the United Nations and its allied organizations such as World Health Organization, International Labour Organization, Food and Agriculture Organization, and World Bank. Other well-known international organizations include the European Union (EU), the North Atlantic Treaty Organization (NATO), the Organization of American States (OAS), and the Organization of the Petroleum Exporting Countries (OPEC).

The Internet has opened the door to finding information not only about IGOs but also about the governments of many individual countries of the world. The number of governments using the Internet to disseminate information is increasing at a phenomenal rate. Thanks primarily to government documents librarians, there are many sites that identify international government information at all levels. A few of the sites will be identified below. Others can be found by using one of the Internet search engines. Search for the term "international government information" or the name of a country or an organization.

United Nations

The United Nations is the largest of all the international government organizations. Headquartered in New York, it issues a large quantity of documents in print and electronic formats. The primary purpose of United Nations documents is to serve the immediate needs of the delegates to the United Nations. However, publications of the United Nations and its allied agencies are of great value because they deal with important issues in international affairs. They provide statistics and other types of information gathered from all over the globe on all facets of human endeavors. They also document world problems such as hunger, illiteracy, and human rights.

The publications of the United Nations and its allied agencies may or may not be listed in the main catalog along with the other resources of a library. In either case they may be shelved in a separate collection. Libraries that serve as depository libraries for United Nations documents usually keep the publications in a separate collection shelved by the series symbol, composed of capital letters in combination with numerical notations. The elements in the numbers are separated by slash marks. The example below is the call number for the 1985 *Report on the World Social Situation*.

EXAMPLE

ST/ESA/165

ST=United Nations Secretariat

ESA=Department of International and Social Affairs

165=Series number designation

UN Information on the Internet

Access UN. 1956–. Readex Corp. 4 Apr. 2000 <http://infoweb.newsbank.com/>.
    Provides access to current and retrospective United Nations documents and publications issued since 1956. (Dates may vary, depending on individual library subscriptions.) Searchable by author, country, type of document (official record, sales publication), subject, title, text, and date. It includes the full text of General Assembly plenary meetings and its committees since the 45th session. Articles appearing in UN periodicals are individually indexed. Includes citations to all the bilateral and multilateral treaties in the UN Treaty Series. Covers topics such as peacekeeping and security, world hunger, human rights, economic development, the environment, atomic energy, and other issues addressed by the United Nations. For older publications, see:
    Checklist of United Nations Documents. New York: United Nations, 1946–1949.
    United Nations Documents Index. (*UNDI*). New York: United Nations, 1950–1973. *Access UN* available by subscription only.

United Nations Documents and Publications. Comp. Chuck Eckman. Guide to Government Publications Series. Stanford University Jonsson Library of Government Documents. 8 Sept. 1998. 4 Apr. 2000 <http://www.stanford.edu/group/Jonsson/un.html>.
    An excellent guide to the UN, this site includes links to the Internet sites as well as print sources.

United Nations. New York: United Nations. 2000. 5 Apr. 2000 <http://www.un.org/>.
> Excellent starting point for current information by and about the UN. Contains links to many full-text documents, databases, e-journals, maps and geographic information.

Other International and Foreign Governments on the Internet

International Documents. Northwestern University Library, Government Publications and Maps. n.d. 4 Apr. 2000 <http://www.library.nwu.edu/govpub/resource/internat/foreign.html>.
> Includes links to international government organizations, foreign governments, and research guides.

Web Links. ALA GODORT, International Governments Task Force. 9 Dec. 1999. 14 Apr. 2000 <http://govinfo.ucsd.edu/idtf/links.html>.
> Useful collection of links to foreign national governments, IGOs, Non-Governmental Organizations (NGOs), and others.

The WWW Virtual Library: International Affairs Resources. Elizabethtown College, Elizabethtown, PA. 18 May 2000. 20 May 2000 <http://www.etown.edu/vl/>.
> Excellent site for international government information at all levels.

Government Information

Instructor: _____ Course/Section: _____

Name: _____

Date: _____ Points: _____

Review Questions

1. What is the importance of government information to the public?

2. Name four characteristics of government information that add to its value as a reference source.

   a.

   b.

   c.

   d.

3. Discuss the ways in which U.S. government publications vary (a) in scope and (b) in format.

   a.

   b.

4. What are federal depository libraries?

   Why were they established?

5. Describe how electronic publishing has affected depository libraries.

6. Which classification system is used to classify U.S. government publications in many academic libraries?

7. What is the purpose of the *Monthly Catalog of United States Government Publications*?

8. Name two indexes that one can use to find retrospective (pre-1976) U.S. government publications.

9. Give the URLs (Internet addresses) for two Web sites that serve as general guides to U.S. government publications.

10. What is meant by "local government" publications? What is the value of these publications?

11. Why are publications of the United Nations and its allied agencies important sources of information?

12. What system is used to classify UN documents?

13. Is there a depository for U.S. documents at your institution?

    If so, what type depository is it?

Government Information

9

Instructor: _____ Course/Section: _____

Name: _____

Date: _____ Points: _____

Finding Government Publications in the *Monthly Catalog*

Use the print version of the *Monthly Catalog* to locate information on a topic that interests you or one that your instructor assigns.

Provide the following information.

Topic:

1. Date of the *Monthly Catalog* used:

2. Subject heading used in the index to look up topic:

3. Give the following information on the source.

    Author:

    Title:

    No. of pages in the document:

    Publication date:

    Agency that issued the document:

    SuDocs call number:

4. Locate the document and write a brief summary describing the content and relevance to the topic.

5. Write the correct bibliographic citation for the document. Use the examples found in Appendix A for a model.

Use the online version of the *Monthly Catalog* (Catalog of United States Government Publications) to locate recent information on the same topic.

6. Keyword(s) used in search (give exact phrase used to search):

7. Give the following information for the source you find.

   Author:

   Title:

   No. of pages in the document:

   Publication date:

   Agency that issued document:

   SuDocs call number:

8. Does your library have this document?

   Which other libraries in your state have this document?

   Name the closest library to you that has this document.

Government Information

Instructor: _____ Course/Section: _____

Name: _____

Date: _____ Points: _____

Finding Government Publications in the Online Catalog

Use the online catalog in your library to determine whether or not your library has any government documents on a topic that you select or use one assigned by your instructor. Search by subject or keyword, as shown in the examples below.

    s=drugs--law and legislation
    k=drugs and hearing

Topic:

1.   Give the exact command you typed.

2.   Did you discover any government publications related to the topic?
     How can you tell that these are government publications?

3.   What classification system was used for these sources?

4.   Where are these items located in your library?

5.   Locate one of the items you found and give the following information.

     Title of the publication:

     SuDoc number: Date:

     Author/agency of publication:

6.	If you were writing a research paper, how would this publication be useful in developing your topic:

   a.	as a background source? Why?

   b.	as a source for developing a major point in your outline? Why?

   c.	as supportive evidence? Why?

   d.	as concluding remarks? Why?

7.	Write the correct bibliographic citation for this work. Use the bibliographic examples in Appendix A.

Government Information

Instructor: _____ Course/Section: _____

Name: _____

Date: _____ Points: _____

Finding U.S. Government Publications Online

Use the Internet to find an appropriate government site for each of the following. Write the correct URL for each site. (Hint: Start with an overall site for U.S. government information, such as one of those listed below.)

University of Michigan Documents Center: http://www.lib.umich.edu/libhome/Documents.center/

U.S. Federal Government Agencies Directory: http://www.lib.lsu.edu/gov/fedgov.html

FedStats: http://www.fedstats.gov

Thomas: http://thomas.loc.gov/home/textonly.html#s

American Memory: http://memory.loc.gov/ammem/amhome.html

Bureau of Labor Statistics: http://www.bls.gov/

GPO Access: http://www.access.gpo.gov/su_docs/aces/aaces002.html

1. Find an image of the Declaration of Independence. Give the URL.

2. Find the official site for the White House. Give the URL.

3. During each session of Congress, Senators and Representatives introduce bills on many issues of public concern, such as abortion, domestic violence, social security reform, income tax reform, and gun control. Select a topic from the bills that were introduced in the most recent Congressional session. Give the following information.

    Bill title:

    Bill no.:

    Date introduced:

4. The *Congressional Record* is the verbatim record of action that takes place in Congress. Locate the *Congressional Record* in *GPO Access* and find a discussion on background checks for guns at gun shows that took place in 1999. Give the following information.

    Search terms used in *GPO Access* to find information:

    Date of *Congressional Record* in which article appears:

    Pages:

5. Find a copy of state income tax forms for your state. Give the state name.

    Give the URL for a Web site with individual income tax forms.

    If your state does not tax personal income, locate the page that indicates this, and give the URL.

6. Find the address of the U.S. Ambassador to Russia.

    How did you locate this information?

7. Find current regulations for automotive emissions. Give the URL. Print the first page of the information you located and turn it in with this assignment.

8. Describe briefly the steps you took to locate this information.

9. Go to the LSU Libraries' *Federal Agency Directory* page (http://www.lib.lsu.edu/gov/ fedgov.html) and locate the federal government agency that would be most likely to give you the latest unemployment figures, the average hourly earnings, and cost of living index figures.

    What agency did you select?

    What are the latest figures for:

    unemployment?

    average hourly earnings?

    cost of living?

10. The following two articles relate to the issue of tanning.

    a. http://www.lotionbarn.com/tanning-facts.html

    b. http://vm.cfsan.fda.gov/~dms/cos-tan.html

    Using the criteria in Chapter 3 for evaluating information on the Internet, examine each of the sites. Which do you consider to be the most reliable? Explain your answer.

Government Information

9

Finding State Government Information Online

Go to the State and Local Government Web site at http://www.piperinfo.com/state/index.cfm.

Click on your home state and answer the questions below.

1. Which state did you select?

2. Under what broad categories would you find information about your state?

3. Where would you find driver's license information for your state?

4. What is the phone number for the governor of your state?

5. What is the URL for general tourist information for your state? How did you locate this link?

Return to the *State and Local Government* page at http://www.piperinfo.com/state/index.cfm.

6. What is the URL for a site that lists federal job opportunities?

7. What is the URL for a site that has census information?

Government Information

9

Instructor: _____ Course/Section: _____

Namo: _____

Date: _____ Points: _____

Finding International Government Information Online

Using the URLs listed in this chapter under **International Organizations and Foreign Governments** (pages 256–258), answer the following questions.

1. Name a journal related to Africa that is published by the United Nations and is available for free online.

   To which URL did you go to find this information?

2. Who is the prime minister of Australia?

   Does he have a home page? If so, give the URL.

3. Explain the steps you went through to find the information in Question 2 above, beginning with the URL you selected.

4. Who is the Mexican Ambassador to the United States?

   What is the address of the Mexican Embassy in the United States?

   What steps did you take to arrive at this information?

CHAPTER

10

Statistical Sources

"There are three kinds of lies: lies, damned lies, and statistics."
BENJAMIN DISRAELI

INTRODUCTION

Many agree with the notion expressed in the quotation on page 273. On the other hand, we know of people who believe that statistics don't lie. It is safe to say that neither of these two positions is altogether true. The fact is that statistics are used to prove and support research. It is also true that the researcher must evaluate statistical sources (just as they would any other information) as to reliability and usefulness.

There are generally two definitions of statistics: (1) the science that deals with the collection, classification, analysis, and interpretation of numerical facts and data; and (2) the actual numerical facts or data. Some sources present raw data, such as population or test scores, etc.; others have data that has been massaged, or interpreted by others, then presented to prove or verify a hypothesis. The United States government is the chief source for statistics gathered in the United States, but it is not the only source. Every level of government gathers statistics: international, national, state, and local. Organizations and businesses also collect them.

This chapter serves as a guide to finding statistical data and offers suggestions for evaluating statistical information. Many of the examples focus on the topic of women and employment to illustrate a search for statistical information on an actual topic.

WHY USE STATISTICS?

Statistics are a vital element in effective research. Scientists use statistical data to support or refute a hypothesis; businesses use statistics to survey market potential; economists analyze present conditions and forecast economic trends by using statistics; and social scientists use statistical data to understand and predict many types of human behavior. In the day-to-day conduct of our human activities we all use statistics in one form or another. We may want to know, for example, what is the best-selling software program for word processing; where are the top paying jobs in the country; what are the highest ranked graduate programs in business in the United States; what is the best city to live in the United States; which airline has the safest record. All rankings are based on statistics—the reliability of the statistics determines whether one can rely on the rankings.

FINDING STATISTICAL INFORMATION

Statistical data covering a wide range of topics appear in many sources. Many publications are dedicated exclusively to statistical data. Other publications might include statistics along with other information. This is especially true of data in magazine and journal articles.

- ◆ use the Internet;
- ◆ use an index to statistical sources;
- ◆ use a periodical index; or
- ◆ use the library's catalog.

Use the Internet

The Internet is a great source for statistics from local, state, national, and international agencies, and from business and professional organizations. The U.S. government has begun a policy requiring that federal agencies produce and distribute information in electronic format. The result is a wealth of government-produced statistical data on the Internet.

GUIDELINES TO FINDING STATISTICAL DATA ON THE INTERNET

▼ **Go to a well-maintained Web page with links to statistical sources.**

Search "statistic resources" on one of the search engines to locate a Web site listing statistical sources. An excellent site for statistical sources can be found on the University of Michigan Documents Center page at http://www.lib.umich.edu/libhome/Documents.center/stats.html.

There is a list of additional sites at the end of this chapter. Use them as a starting point until you find several sites you prefer.

▼ **Go directly to a government site using the URL.**

The Bureau of Labor Statistics page provides information on labor and employment in the United States.

http://stats.bls.gov

(This would be an appropriate site for statistical information on the topic of women and employment.)

Other levels of government also have links to statistical information (see Chapter 9).

Stat-USA: http://www.stat-usa.gov/stat-usa.html is an excellent source for statistical information. It is available in depository libraries or to individual subscribers.

▼ **Search the Internet for a specific statistical topic.**

Statistics of all kinds can be found on the Internet. Some statistics are located at specific government sites such as the Bureau of Labor Statistics. You can also use one of the search engines to locate statistical information. Chapter 6 discusses creating phrases to keep related terms together in an electronic search.

EXAMPLE ■

"employment statistics"
OR
"women statistics salar?"

Use an Index to Statistical Sources

There are a number of indexes to statistics. Use the online catalog to locate these.

EXAMPLE ■

s=united states--statistics--abstracts
   OR
s=statistics--indexes
   OR
use one of the indexes listed below.

American Statistics Index (ASI). Bethesda: CIS, 1973–.
> A two-part (index and abstracts) guide to statistical information published by the U.S. government. Citations include the Superintendent of Documents call number as well as a microfiche reference number to the microfiche collection published by Congressional Information Service (CIS) to accompany the index.

Index to International Statistics (IIS). Bethesda: CIS, 1983–.
> A similar index to *ASI*, covering statistical sources of the United Nations and its allied agencies, foreign governments, and international government organizations.

Statistical Abstract of the United States. Washington: GPO, 1878–.
> Published by the Bureau of the Census since 1878, it is considered by many to be the single most useful reference book on statistics. It provides a large number of statistics covering social and economic conditions in the United States as well as selected data for states, counties, cities and foreign countries. Although not an index in the true sense of the word, *Statistical Abstract* does serve as a guide to more extensive data that is published in reports from government and private agencies. The statistics are presented in tabular form with the source indicated below each table. *Statistical Abstract* is available in paper and CD-ROM format and on the Internet. The book is arranged by broad topics with a subject index at the end. Many of the tables provide statistical data for more than one year, usually 10 or more. Figure 10.1 is taken from the index of the 1991 edition of *Statistical Abstract*. The numbers in the index refer to table numbers instead of page numbers as in most indexes. Note the references to tables under the subject "Labor force, Female." Figure 10.2 shows Table 656, depicting the number of workers by occupation, earnings, and sex. Note that the source for this table is indicated below the table.

Statistical Reference Index (SRI). Bethesda: CIS, 1980–.
> Covers statistical publications of state and local governments, professional and trade organizations, and some commercial publishers.

Statistical Universe. Bethesda: CIS, 1973–.
> The Web-based version of the *American Statistics Index (ASI)*, the *Statistical Reference Index (SRI)* and the *Index to International Statistics (IIS)*, it abstracts and indexes federal, state and local, and international statistical publications. It fully replaces the CD-ROM version of *Statistical Masterfile*.

Use a Periodical Index

Although you could probably find statistics in a print index, it is much more effective to search for statistical sources in an electronic source. Periodical indexes, abstracts, and databases are discussed in detail in Chapter 8.

▼ STEPS TO FINDING STATISTICS IN PERIODICALS

1. Find an appropriate periodical index.
   Example:
   for business, use *ABI/INFORM* or *Business Index.*

   ▶▶ 2. Execute a keyword search:
   Example:
   in *ABI/INFORM* CD-ROM, search **women and salar? and statistics**

Figure 10.3 depicts the citation and abstract from the CD-ROM version of *ABI/INFORM.* To see if your library has the periodical cited, *Working Woman,* you would have to check the online catalog. The Web version of *ABI/INFORM* provides the full text of the article. Once it appears on the screen you can download, e-mail, or print it.

```
         Access No: 00958328 ProQuest ABI/INFORM (R) Research
Title:       16th annual salary survey 1995
Authors:  Harris, Diane; Holliday, Taylor; Hermelin, Francine G
Journal:  Working Woman [WKW] ISSN: 0145-5761
          Vol: 20 Iss: 1 Date: Jan 1995 p: 25-34 Illus: Charts
Reprint:  Contact UMI for article reprint (order no. 11494.00).
          Restrictions may apply.
Subjects: Polls & surveys; Women; Workforce; Wages & salaries; Wage
          rates; Statistical data
Geo Places: US
Codes:    9190 (United States); 6400 (Employee benefits &
          compensation); 9140 (Statistical data)
Abstract: Currently, professional and managerial women are leading
          the work force in wage growth. During the 5-year period ending 1993,
          salaries of executive and managerial women rose 2.3% when adjusted
          for inflation, while wages of professional women increased 2.2%,
          according to an analysis of Census Bureau data in the State of
          Working America, 1994-95. At the same time, men's salaries in nearly
          all occupations and at all wage and educational levels declined, as
          did pay from women in the bottom 20% wage bracket. The results of
          Working Woman's 16th annual salary survey support the notion that
          women in higher-level jobs are doing much better than previously
          reported. In at least half of the 24 fields for which gender
          statistics were available, women typically took home 80 to 90 cents
          for every dollar made by a man in the same position, which is a big
          improvement for working women as a whole, who on average still
          receive just 72% of what men earn. Moreover, many of these women
          appear to be narrowing the wage gap at a rate at least twice as great
          as the roughly penny-a-year pace recorded during the 1970s and 1980s.
```

Figure 10.3. Search in a periodical index *(ABI/INFORM)* (Copyright © 1996 by UMI Company. All Rights Reserved. Further distribution or reproduction is prohibited without prior written permission from UMI.)

Use a Periodical Index

Although you could probably find statistics in a print index, it is much more effective to search for statistical sources in an electronic source. Periodical indexes, abstracts, and databases are discussed in detail in Chapter 8.

▼ STEPS TO FINDING STATISTICS IN PERIODICALS

1. Find an appropriate periodical index.
   Example:
   for busin s use *ABI/INFORM* or *Business Index*.

▶▶ 2. Execute a keyword search:
   Example:
   in *ABI/INFORM* CD-ROM, search **women and salar? and statistics**

Figure 10.3 depicts the citation and abstract from the CD-ROM version of *ABI/INFORM*. To see if your library has the periodical cited, *Working Woman,* you would have to check the online catalog. The Web version of *ABI/INFORM* provides the full text of the article. Once it appears on the screen you can download, e-mail, or print it.

Figure 10.3. Search in a periodical index *(ABI/INFORM)* (Copyright © 1996 by UMI Company. All Rights Reserved. Further distribution or reproduction is prohibited without prior written permission from UMI.)

Figure 10.1. Index page from the *Statistical Abstract of the United States.*

Index

Federal outlays 495, 498
Juices 206, 207
Juveniles:
  Arrest 302
  Correction facilities 74, 327
  Court cases 325, 326

K

Kansas. See State data.
Kentucky. See State data.
Kenya. See Foreign countries.
Keogh plans, payments to 510
Kidney disease and infections, deaths 113, 114
Kiwi fruit 1119
Korea. See Foreign countries.
Korean conflict 536
Korean population 16, 24
Kuwait. See Foreign countries.

L

Laboratories, medical and dental 1308, 1309
Labor force, employment, and earnings (see also
1990 Census Sample Data p.xii, and individual
industries or occupations):
  Accidents and fatalities 665, 666, 667
  Work time lost 666
  Average pay, States 652
    Metro areas 653
  City government 488, 489, 490
  Civilian labor force:
    American Indian, Eskimo, Aleut population .. 42
    Asian and Pacific Islander population 42
    Black population .. 41, 609, 611, 612, 616, 617,
                         622, 629
    Educational attainment 611, 616, 631
    Employed .. 608, 610, 612, 613, 614, 616, 617,
           620, 627, 630, 631, 632, 633, 634
    Female 612, 613, 615, 616, 617, 618, 619,
                 620, 621, 622, 627

Educational attainment 221, 616, 637
Elderly 40, 609, 615, 618, 622, 623, 635
Employee benefits 576, 660, 661, 662
  Government employees 484
Employees 643, 644, 645
  States 644
Employment cost index 657
Employment projections 630, 633
Employment taxes and contributions 492
Farm population 1073, 1075, 1076
Female .. 612, 613, 615, 616, 617, 618, 619, 620,
  621, 622, 623, 624, 625, 626, 627, 629, 631,
    632, 636, 637, 638, 654, 655, 656
Foreign-owned firms 1323, 1391
Government. See Government.
Help wanted advertising 642
High school graduates and dropouts 255
High tech employment 634
Hispanic origin population 44, 609, 610, 612,
                      632, 635
Hours 643
Indexes of compensation 647
International comparisons 1385, 1386, 1387,
               1391, 1392, 1394
Job creation 851
Job openings and placements 642
Metropolitan areas 614, 653
Minimum wage workers 658, 659
Multimedia users 870
Occupational groups. See Occupations and
  individual occupations.
Occupational safety 665, 666, 667, 668
Production workers 645, 1243, 1244
Productivity 646, 647
Social insurance coverage ... 568, 569, 571, 589
State data 613, 641, 644, 652
Unemployed workers (see also Unemployment):
  Age 617, 622, 626, 635
  Alternative measures 640

NOTE: Index citations refer to table numbers, not page numbers.

Figure 10.2. Statistical table from the *Statistical Abstract of the United States,* referenced in Figure 10.1.

414   Labor Force, Employment, and Earnings

No. 656. Number of Workers With Earnings and Median Earnings, by Occupation of Longest Job Held and Sex: 1990

[Covers civilians 15 years old and over as of **March 1991.** Based on Current Population Survey; see text, section 1, and Appendix III. For definition of median, see Guide to Tabular Presentation]

MAJOR OCCUPATION OF LONGEST JOB HELD	ALL WORKERS				YEAR ROUND FULL-TIME				Ratio: Women to men	
	Women		Men		Women		Men			
	Number (1,000)	Median earnings	Number (1,000)	Median earnings	Number (1,000)	Median earnings	Number (1,000)	Median earnings	Number	Median earnings
Total [1]	61,732	$12,250	72,348	$21,522	31,682	$19,822	49,171	$27,678	0.64	0.72
Executive, administrators, and managerial.............	6,577	22,551	9,244	37,010	4,857	25,858	7,873	40,541	0.62	0.64
Professional specialty	8,814	23,113	8,035	36,942	4,982	29,181	6,192	41,100	0.80	0.71
Technical and related support ..	2,044	20,312	2,053	28,042	1,284	23,992	1,595	30,897	0.81	0.78
Sales....................	8,393	7,307	7,871	22,955	3,223	16,986	5,594	29,652	0.58	0.57
Admin. support, incl. clerical....	16,728	14,292	4,141	20,287	9,760	18,475	2,835	26,192	3.44	0.71
Precision production, craft and repair	1,395	13,377	13,448	22,149	795	18,739	9,412	26,506	0.08	0.71
Machine operators, assemblers, and inspectors	3,773	10,983	5,389	19,389	2,103	14,652	3,736	22,345	0.56	0.66
Transportation and material moving	511	10,805	5,056	20,053	174	16,003	3,241	24,559	0.05	0.65
Handlers, equipment cleaners, helpers, and laborers	995	8,270	4,885	9,912	412	13,650	2,065	18,426	0.20	0.74
Service workers.............	11,722	5,746	7,801	10,514	3,769	12,139	4,106	18,550	0.92	0.65
Private household	1,007	2,166	43	(B)	183	7,309	9	(B)	20.33	(X)
Service, except private household............	10,716	6,173	7,758	10,549	3,586	12,288	4,097	18,574	0.88	0.66
Farming, forestry, and fishing ...	680	3,810	3,548	7,881	241	10,007	1,736	14,452	0.14	0.69

B Base less than 75,000.   X Not applicable.   [1] Includes persons whose longest job was in the Armed Forces.
Source: U.S. Bureau of the Census, *Current Population Reports,* series P-60, No. 174.

Figure 10.4 illustrates a citation to a full-text article from the *Monthly Labor Review*, a useful statistical source from the Bureau of Labor Statistics. Note that the current issues of the *Monthly Labor Review* as well as archives, or back issues, are available and are fully searchable. It is possible to download articles in PDF format so statistical information is presented as it appears in the printed version.

Use the Library Catalog

Statistical information can also be found in the library catalog.

GUIDELINES TO RETRIEVE THE TYPE OF INFORMATION REQUIRED

▼ **Check the *Library of Congress Subject Headings (LCSH)*.**

▼ **Search the online catalog** to find the authorized subject heading. Figure 10.5 shows the authorized subject headings for "statistics." Note the "search also under" references.

▼ **Use the topic with the subdivision—statistics** for a subject search in the library catalog. (Remember that statistical information in books listed in the online catalog might not be current.)

EXAMPLE ■

s=education--statistics

In the online catalog of the Nebraska State College System, a subject search for "education—statistics" produced a number of titles as well as a cross reference to "see also 'Educational Indicators.'" A subject search for "crime statistics" produced the following message: "Crime statistics is not used in this library's catalog. 'Criminal statistics' is used instead." Thus, information for crime statistics will be found under the standardized subject heading "criminal statistics."

Figure 10.6 depicts the results of a search in the LSU catalog for **women—statistics**.

◆ **Use statistics as a subdivision for a geographical area.** Figure 10.7 illustrates a catalog screen using United States as the subject and statistics as the subdivision. This format may be used for city, state, national, or international areas.

EXAMPLE ■

New Orleans--statistics
France--statistics

◆ EVALUATING STATISTICAL SOURCES

It is easy to fall into a trap with statistics—researchers tend to look for data that will support a hypothesis or a position regardless of its reliability. It is always important to evaluate any information used in

Related BLS programs | Related articles

ABSTRACT

December 1999, Vol. 122, No. 12

Marriage, children, and women's employment: what do we know?

Philip N. Cohen
Assistant professor in the Department of Sociology, University of California, Irvine, Ca.

Suzanne M. Bianchi
Professor at the Center on Population, Gender, and Social Inequality, Department of Sociology, University of Maryland, College Park, Md.

Estimates of the level of women's full-time employment are greatly affected by the choice of reference period and universe; as States attempt to move poor mothers from welfare to work, a tendency may arise to overestimate how much mothers of young children actually work for pay.

▶ Read excerpt ▶ Download full article in PDF (81K)

Related BLS programs
Current Population Survey

Related *Monthly Labor Review* articles
Are women leaving the labor force?—July 1994.
Married mothers' work patterns: the job-family compromise.—June 1994.

Within *Monthly Labor Review Online* :
Welcome | Current Issue | Index | Subscribe | Archives

Exit *Monthly Labor Review Online* :
BLS Home | Publications & Research Papers

Figure 10.4. Sample entry from the *Monthly Labor Review,* available from the U.S. Bureau of Labor Statistics.

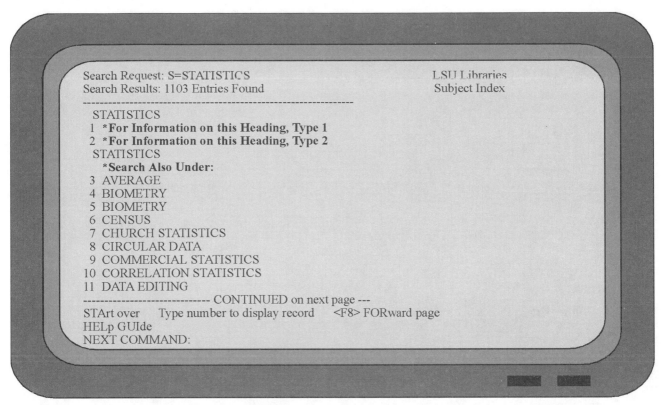

Figure 10.5. A broad search to determine the authorized headings.

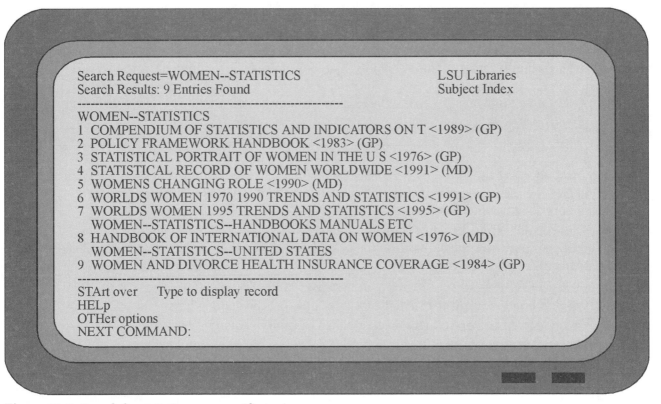

Figure 10.6. Search for statistics on a specific topic.

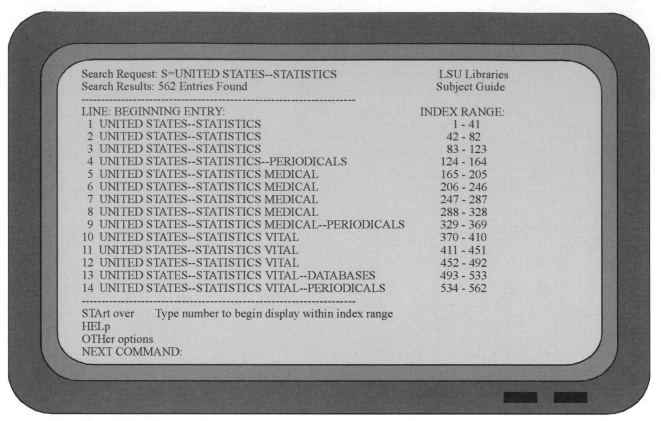

```
Search Request: S=UNITED STATES--STATISTICS          LSU Libraries
Search Results: 562 Entries Found                    Subject Guide
------------------------------------------------------------
LINE: BEGINNING ENTRY:                               INDEX RANGE:
  1 UNITED STATES--STATISTICS                           1 - 41
  2 UNITED STATES--STATISTICS                          42 - 82
  3 UNITED STATES--STATISTICS                          83 - 123
  4 UNITED STATES--STATISTICS--PERIODICALS            124 - 164
  5 UNITED STATES--STATISTICS MEDICAL                 165 - 205
  6 UNITED STATES--STATISTICS MEDICAL                 206 - 246
  7 UNITED STATES--STATISTICS MEDICAL                 247 - 287
  8 UNITED STATES--STATISTICS MEDICAL                 288 - 328
  9 UNITED STATES--STATISTICS MEDICAL--PERIODICALS    329 - 369
 10 UNITED STATES--STATISTICS VITAL                   370 - 410
 11 UNITED STATES--STATISTICS VITAL                   411 - 451
 12 UNITED STATES--STATISTICS VITAL                   452 - 492
 13 UNITED STATES--STATISTICS VITAL--DATABASES        493 - 533
 14 UNITED STATES--STATISTICS VITAL--PERIODICALS      534 - 562

------------------------------------------------------------
STArt over     Type number to begin display within index range
HELp
OTHer options
NEXT COMMAND:
```

Figure 10.7. Search using "statistics" as a subdivision for a geographical heading.

research; with statistics this is even more critical. General information concerning evaluating informational sources is discussed in Chapter 3. Statistical information requires a few additional considerations.

Before accepting statistical sources at face value we should ask ourselves a few questions.

 ASK YOURSELF

◆ **Who collected the data?** Is it a business that has a "vested" interest in its publication, such as the manufacturer of a particular product who might have gathered data to support an advertising claim?

◆ Do the statistics reflect a **bias?** Political polls, for example, might be biased to reflect certain strengths or weaknesses of the candidates, depending on the bias of the pollsters. In this case, it is necessary to find out something about the agency conducting the poll.

◆ Is the data **timely?** Check the dates of coverage and the publication date.

◆ Is the coverage **complete?** In polls, for example, was the sample large enough?

◆ Has the data been **repackaged** several times so as to distort its reliability? Government data is frequently repackaged by a commercial entity, and might not include all of the original data.

- ◆ Is this a "time" series? Data gathered over a long span of time is referred to as a ***time series***. It is usually considered to be a reliable source. In many cases, the research project calls for data that has a timeline.
- ◆ Is the data from a ***primary*** or a ***secondary*** source? If it is from a secondary source (for example, a periodical article), is the source documented?

The following two examples illustrate the importance of evaluating statistical information:

At first glance these sites might appear to be authentic, scholarly presentations. Upon careful examination, however, you will note errors, incorrect citation formats, and inaccurate information. These two sites are obviously designed to be used to teach the importance of evaluating statistical sites, but there are many such sites of similar merit that do not have the same honorable intention. With the wealth of information now available in a vast array of formats, it is becoming more important than ever that you learn to be critical in selecting information sources. Statistical information, whether it is to introduce, support, or draw conclusions about your research, must be accurate, current, and appropriate for your needs to be effective.

◆ SELECTED INTERNET SITES FOR STATISTICS

Guides

Chance. http://www.geom.umn.edu/docs/education/chance/
    Information on basic statistical concepts.
Internet Glossary of Statistical Terms. http://www.animatedsoftware.com/statglos/statglos.htm
    Glossary with links to related sites.
Statistics Every Writer Should Know. http://nilesonline.com/stats/

General

Economics and Statistics. http://www.lib.lsu.edu/bus/economic.html
FedStats. http://www.fedstats.gov
    Maintained by the Federal Interagency Council on Statistical Policy. Over 70 agencies.
State and Local Government on the Net. http://www.piperinfo.com/state/index.cfm
Statistical Resources on the Web. http://www.lib.umich.edu/libhome/Documents.center/stats.html
Statistical Universe. Subscription service available from CIS.
    Index plus links to statistics pages.

STAT-USA. http://www.stat-usa.gov
> Provides economic, business, social, and environmental program data produced by more than 50 Federal sources. Available free through depository libraries.

Uncle Sam. http://www.lib.memphis.edu/gpo/statis1.htm

Selected Sites by Subject

Business and Economics

Bureau of Labor Statistics. http://stats.bls.gov/datahome.htm

Economic Statistics Briefing Room. http://www.whitehouse.gov/fsbr/employment.html
> Employment and unemployment statistics from the White House.

Regional Economic Information System (REIS). U.S. Department of Commerce, Bureau of Economic Analysis. http://fisher.lib.virginia.edu/reis/
> State, county, and metropolitan area statistics for the period 1969–1997.

Crime and Criminals

Bureau of Justice Statistics. http://www.ojp.usdoj.gov/bjs/

Crime & Justice Electronic Data Abstracts. http://www.ojp.usdoj.gov/bjs/dtdata.htm

FBI Crime Statistics. http://www.fbi.gov/crimestats.htm

NCJRS Abstracts Database. http://www.ncjrs.org/database.htm

Sourcebook of Criminal Justice Statistics. http://www.albany.edu/sourcebook/

State Crime Data. http://www.ojp.usdoj.gov/bjs/datast.htm

Demographics

CIA World Fact Book. http://www.odci.gov/cia/publications/factbook/index.html

State and Metropolitan Area Data Book, 1997–98: http://www.census.gov/prod/3/98pubs/smadb-97.pdf

State Population Projections. http://www.ire.org/training/vnet/stproj.htm

U.S. Census Bureau. http://www.census.gov/

Education and Youth

Condition of Education. http://nces.ed.gov/

Education at a Glance. http://www.oecd.org/els/edu/EAG98/

Youth Indicators. http://nces.ed.gov/pubs/yi/

Health

Centers for Disease Control and Prevention. http://www.cdc.gov

MMWR—Morbidity and Mortality Weekly Report. http://www2.cdc.gov/mmwr/

National Center for Health Statistics. http://www.cdc.gov/nchs/default.htm

National Institute for Occupational Safety and Health. http://www.cdc.gov/niosh/homepage.html

SAMHSA Statistical Data. http://www.samhsa.gov/
> Includes: Mental Health and Substance Use/Abuse, Treatment Services System and its Utilization, etc.

International

Eurostat. http://europa.eu.int/comm/eurostat/
   The Statistical Office of the European Communities.
United Nations Development Program. http://www.undp.org/

Public Opinion

The Gallup Organization. http://www.gallup.com
Roper Center for Public Opinion Research. http://www.lib.uconn.edu/RoperCenter/

 # SELECTED LIST OF PRINT STATISTICAL SOURCES

(Note: Many titles are now available electronically.)

General

Historical Statistics of the United States: Colonial Times to 1970. Washington: GPO, 1976.
   Two volume source that contains a wide range of historical statistics for the U.S. Includes economic, political, and demographic data. Some tables start with the colonial period.
Historical Statistics of the United States: Two Centuries of the Census, 1790–1990. Comp. Donald B. Dodd. Westport, CN: Greenwood, 1993.
   This work includes bibliographical references.
Statistical Abstract of the United States. Washington: GPO, 1878–.
   An annual summary of data collected by the government; this publication provides statistics on a vast array of topics. The documentation following each table serves as a guide to more extensive data on the topic.
World Almanac and Book of Facts 2000. New York: Primedia, 1893–.
   Contains a wide variety of statistical information.

Subject

Business and Economics

Agricultural Statistics. Washington: GPO, 1936–.
   A concise collection of data such as crop yields, market value, price, number of farms, and export/import.
Annual Energy Review. Washington: GPO, 1982–.
   Detailed data on energy production, consumption, prices, imports, exports.
The Dow Jones Averages, 1885–1995. Chicago: Professional Publications, 1996.
   Compilation of averages.
Economic Report of the President. Washington: GPO, 1979–.
   An annual report containing detailed tables showing national income, manufacturing and commercial activity, government finance, and international trade.
Monthly Labor Review. Washington: GPO, 1918–.
   In addition to employment related articles, the publication features regular compilations of data related to labor/employment. It is included in a number of indexing services.

Standard and Poor's Statistical Service. New York: Standard and Poor, 1941–.

> Monthly publication with annual cumulations that contains statistics covering bank and finance, production and labor, price indexes, income and trade, building, electric powers and fuels, metals, transportation, textiles, paper products, and agricultural products. Cites data source.

Survey of Current Business. Washington: GPO, 1921–.

> A monthly publication of the U.S. Bureau of Economic Analysis. Provides current and historical data on business, industry, agriculture, and manufacturing.

U.S. Exports of Merchandise. Washington: U.S. Department of Commerce, 1998–.

> Monthly data, plus historical summary on separate CD-ROMs.

USA Trade. Washington: U.S. Department of Commerce. 1998–.

> Monthly accumulations of tabular data for exporting. Includes country and district information and four year annual history. Includes time series analysis with four years of data. CD-ROM.

Crime and Criminals

Sourcebook of Criminal Justice Statistics. Washington: GPO, 1973–.

> Tables give figures on prisons, prisoners, types of crimes, arrests, money spent on law enforcement and much more.

Uniform Crime Reports. Washington: GPO, 1930–.

> Formerly known as *Crime in the United States: FBI Uniform Crime Reports*. Statistics on numbers of arrests, types of crimes, etc. Annual.

Demographics

Census of Population and Housing. GPO, 1999.

> The U.S. Bureau of the Census "counts" the citizens of the United States every ten years. The data gathered includes social and economic characteristics of the population as well as head counts. The first decennial census was taken in 1790 and has continued ever since. In between the ten-year periods, the Bureau of the Census conducts surveys to obtain ongoing estimates of the population.

County and City Data Book. Washington: GPO, 1949–.

> Supplement to the *Statistical Abstract of the United States*, gives a wide variety of demographic, social, and economic statistics for regions, divisions, states, counties, and SMSAs (Standard Metropolitan Statistical Areas).

Current Population Reports. Washington: GPO, dates vary.

> Series of reports from the U.S. Census Bureau. P-20 series deals with population characteristics; P-23 covers special subjects.

Sourcebook of County Demographics. CACI Marketing Systems, 1990–.

> Continues *Sourcebook of Demographics and Buying Power for Every County in the USA*.

Education

The Core Data Task Force Report. Washington: U.S. Department of Education, 1997.

> Report prepared by the Core Data Task Force of the National Education Statistics Agenda Committee, National Forum on Education Statistics.

Digest of Education Statistics. Washington: GPO, 1975–.

> Detailed coverage of public, private, vocational, and higher education statistics.

Education in States and Nations: Indicators Comparing U.S. States with Other Industrialized Countries in 1991. Phelps, Richard P. and others. Washington: National Center for Education Statistics, 1996.

Projections of Education Statistics to 2009. Ed. William J. Hussar. Washington: Dept. of Education, Office of Educational Research and Improvement, National Center for Education Statistics, 1999.

International

United Nations Statistical Yearbook. New York: United Nations, 1948–.
   Statistics on a wide range of topics for countries of the world.

World Factbook. Washington: CIA, 1981–.
   Information on countries of the world gathered from a variety of sources: the Bureau of the Census, Central Intelligence Agency, Department of State, and others.

World Tables. Baltimore: Johns Hopkins UP for World Bank, 1976–.
   A detailed time series of data compiled from the files of the World Bank. Country statistics include balance of trade, balance of payments, and manufacturing output.

Statistical Sources

10

Instructor: _____ Course/Section: _____

Name: _____

Date: _____ Points: _____

Review Questions

1. What are the two definitions of statistics?

   a.

   b.

2. Why are statistics useful in research?

3. Name four ways to locate statistical information.

   a.

   b.

   c.

   d.

4. Name three methods you might use to locate statistical information on the Internet.

   a.

   b.

   c.

5.   Why would you expect to find many U.S. government statistics on the Internet?

6.   Construct a search command to use in a periodical index or database to find articles containing statistical information for each of the following.

   a.   Current population figures for China:

   b.   Rate of crime in U.S. cities:

   c.   Number of deaths by alcohol-related accidents per year:

7.   Give the commands (author, title, subject, or keyword) you would use in the online catalog to find each of the following. (Write the exact command, e.g., k=statistics and crime.)

   a.   Indexes to statistics

   b.   Statistics about women

8.   Give three criteria you would use to evaluate statistical sources.

   a.

   b.

   c.

Statistical Sources

Instructor: _____ Course/Section: _____

Name: _____

Date: _____ Points: _____

Finding Statistical Information Online

Find one of the following sites on the Internet.

University of Michigan. http://www.lib.umich.edu/libhome/Documents.center/stats.html

Louisiana State University. http://www.lib.lsu.edu/soc/stats.html

Fedstats. http://www.fedstats.gov

Give an appropriate URL for each of the questions listed below.

1. Which site would you use to find statistics on safety?

2. Which site would be most appropriate for statistics on health?

3. Which two sites would help you locate crime statistics?

4. Which site would you use to find the current economic situation of the United States?

5. Which site would you use to find educational statistics?

6. Which site would you use to find population information about your home state?

7. Print out the first page of the last site you visited and attach it to this assignment.

8. Write the correct bibliographic citation for the last web site you visited. (See examples in Appendix A.)

Statistical Sources

10

Instructor: _____ Course/Section: _____

Name: _____

Date: _____ Points: _____

Using *Statistical Abstract of the United States*

Use a current print copy of ***Statistical Abstract of the United States*** (usually located in the Reference area) to find statistics on a topic you select or one assigned by your instructor. Answer the questions below.

Topic:

1. Which year of *Statistical Abstracts of the United States* did you use?

2. Which subject heading(s) did you use to look up your topic in the index?

3. Did you find listings of tables under this heading?

    If so, list the numbers of the tables here.

    If not, which cross references did the index send you to?

4. Select one table for your topic and write the number of the table here.

5. What is the title of the table you selected?

6. Does the table use primary or secondary information? How do you know?

7. Write the correct bibliographic citation to one table on your topic. (See Appendix A, example XI.B.)

Statistical Sources

Instructor: _____ Course/Section: _____

Name: _____

Date: _____ Points: _____

Using Statistical Indexes

Use a volume of *ASI (American Statistics Index)*, *SRI (Statistical Reference Index)*, *IIS (International Index to Statistics)*, *Statistical Universe* or another statistical index to locate statistics on a topic of your choice or one assigned by your instructor.

1. Topic:

2. Title of statistical index used:

3 Year of index you used:

4. Subject heading(s) you used:

5. Abstract number/accession number/table you found, if applicable:

If you used a print index volume, find the matching abstract and look for the abstract number or accession number for the publication you found.

6. Write the title of the publication you found in the abstract or table.

7. Give the date of the publication.

8. Write the correct bibliographic citation for the publication you found. Use the examples in Appendix A.

Statistical Sources

10

Instructor: _____ Course/Section: _____

Name: _____

Date: _____ Points: _____

Finding Statistics in the Library Catalog

Use your library's catalog to find a statistical source on a topic you select or one assigned by your instructor. (Refer to the methods discussed in this chapter.)

Topic:

1. Subject heading(s) used for your topic:

2. Did you find any statistical sources under this heading?

   If not, which "cross references" did the index send you to?

3. Give the following information for source on your topic.

   Title:

   Author:

   Call number: Date:

4. If this item is located at your library, find it and examine it for information on your topic.

   a. Would you label this item as popular or scholarly?

   b. Give two reasons why you think this would be considered popular or scholarly.

5.   Write the correct bibliographic citation to this source. Use the examples in Appendix A.

6.   Explain why the statistical information found in this source would be useful in a research paper on this topic.

Instructor: _____ Course/Section: _____

Name: _____

Date: _____ Points: _____

Evaluating Statistical Information

Using an appropriate database with **full-text** articles, find two magazine or journal articles dealing with statistics on a topic of your choice or one assigned by your instructor. (Hint: Consider using "statistics" and your topic in the search command.)

1. Database used:

2. Write a citation to first article you found on your topic. Use examples in Appendix A.

3. Evaluate the data in the article in terms of:

    a. Who collected the data?

    b. Any bias present? Justify.

    c. Timely?

       Date of coverage?

    d. Complete or adequate coverage?

    e. Any distortion from repackaging?

    f. Time series (data gathered over a long span of time)?

    g. Data from primary or secondary sources?

    h. If secondary sources are used, is documentation provided?

4. Write a citation to the second article you found on your topic. Use examples in Appendix A.

5. Evaluate the data in the article in terms of:

    a. Who collected the data?

    b. Any bias present? Justify.

    c. Timely?

        Date of coverage?

    d. Complete or adequate coverage?

    e. Any distortion from repackaging?

    f. Time series (data gathered over a long span of time)?

    g. Data from primary or secondary sources?

    h. If secondary sources are used, is documentation provided?

6. Write a brief summary in which you compare the two articles, using the criteria you used for each in Questions 3 and 5 above.

Biographical Information

"There has rarely passed a life of which a judicious and faithful narrative would not be useful."

SAMUEL JOHNSON

INTRODUCTION

A biography is a written history of a person's life and accomplishments. Questions dealing with biographical information are among the most frequently asked in a library. People want to know about the lives of other people, both the famous and the not-so-famous. Popular literature is rich with sources that satisfy that need. Biography makes for wonderful reading, but more than that, it is an important source in the research process. We can approach research on most subjects through the lives of individuals who have shaped developments in the field. For example, to learn about the development of the polio vaccine, one must read about Jonas Salk.

Biographical information is so important to the contribution of knowledge that it can be found in most reference sources, including dictionaries, almanacs, and encyclopedias. There are many books written about people's lives; information about individuals appears in the daily newspapers and in magazines and journals. In addition, there are dictionaries devoted exclusively to presenting facts about the lives of individuals. The Internet is a rich source of biographical information. Biographical information on the Internet ranges from well-written and researched biographical articles to home pages of fan clubs and family album pages for individuals.

◆ FINDING BIOGRAPHICAL INFORMATION

Finding biographical information on noteworthy persons is not difficult. Articles about famous persons appear in many sources, including encyclopedias and dictionaries. It is the not-so-famous that cause problems. Selecting the appropriate source requires the researcher to determine certain basic information about the person—his or her nationality and profession and whether the person is living or not. The search strategy for finding biographical information depends on the question being asked and the information needed.

GUIDELINES FOR FINDING BIOGRAPHICAL INFORMATION

- ▼ Search the Internet.
- ▼ Search an online database.
- ▼ Look in the appropriate biographical dictionary.
- ▼ Use a specialized biographical index such as *Biography Index* or *Biography and Genealogy Master Index*.
- ▼ Check the general and/or appropriate periodical indexes and abstracts to find articles by or about the individual.
- ▼ Consult the library catalog to see if the library owns a book by or about the individual.
- ▼ Try a reference book such as a general or subject encyclopedia.
- ▼ Ask a reference librarian for help.

Internet

The Internet is a great source for biographical information. It is possible to find information on the lives of famous composers, actors, authors, and television personalities by executing a simple name search in one of the search engines such as Google or Lycos. For a broad search on biographical information, use search phrases such as "science biography," or "biography resources." This will take you to pages with numerous links to biographical information.

There are many excellent guides to biographical information on the Web that have been created by librarians. These include the *Biography* site from the University of Michigan and the *Biography* page available from the *Ready Reference* site on the LSU Libraries' home page. (The URLs for these sites can be found in the listing at the end of this chapter.) These sites are useful in that they provide links to categories of biographical databases and Web sites. It is always a good idea to use Web-based guides that are developed by librarians because they apply standard criteria in evaluating the sites for inclusion on the pages. Some libraries catalog Web sites that the librarians select for inclusion in their online catalogs, including Web sites for biographical information.

Many reference works, including dictionaries, encyclopedias, and indexes, are now available free on the Internet. These include *Biographical Dictionary, Encyclopedia.com*, and *Biographical Directory of the U.S. Congress*.

Databases

Full-text databases often include biographical information. You can find both works written by an individual and those written about his/her life by doing a name search in one of the full-text databases such as *Academic Universe*, InfoTrac's *General Reference Center* or EBSCOhost's *Academic Search Elite*. Biographical information frequently appears in book review and literary criticism material, which are discussed in Chapter 12.

Two full-text databases devoted exclusively to biographical information are available on the Web: *Gale Biography Resource Center* and *Wilson Biography Plus*. Since these are available only by subscription, you will have to check to see if your library is a subscriber to either or both of these.

Figure 11.1 shows a record retrieved as a result of a search in EBSCOhost's *Academic Search Elite* using the search phrase: "jonas salk and biography."

Title: The 50 most famous people of the century.

> **Subject(s):** CELEBRITIES; ONASSIS, Jacqueline Kennedy; DIANA, Princess of Wales; EINSTEIN, Albert; MOTHER Teresa
>
> **Source:** *Biography*, Dec99, Vol. 3 Issue 12, p74, 43p, 30c, 30bw
> Author(s): Cawley
>
> **Abstract:** Profiles the selected 50 most famous people of the 20th century. Includes Jacqueline Kennedy Onassis; Princess Diana; Marilyn Monroe; John F. Kennedy; Hillary Rodham Clinton; Elizabeth Taylor; Elvis Presley; Grace Kelly; Prince Charles; Helen Keller; Mother Teresa; Charles Lindbergh; Coco Chanel; Estee Lauder; Martin Luther King Jr.; Marie Curie; **Jonas Salk**; Albert Einstein; Muhammad Ali.
> **AN:** 2526138 **ISSN:** 1092-7891 **Database:** Academic Search Elite

Figure 11.1. Results of a search in *EBSCOhost's, Academic Search Elite* database.

Figure 11.2 shows a sample page resulting from a general search "women and biography" in the *ERIC* database.

[Return to search screen] [Previous] [Next]

199 documents found (25 returned) for query : *(women) :Descriptors AND (biography)*

Score	Document Title
628	ED272408. Beamer, Catharine, Comp.. Women's History: Re-Focusing the Past. A Selective Bibliography of Books at Mt. San Antonio College Library. . 1986
624	EJ092299. Allsop, Joan W.. Joan Tully--A Tribute Australian Journal of Adult Education; 13, 3, 146-50, Nov 73. 1973
613	ED095742. Graham, Patricia Albjerg. Women in Higher Education: A Biographical Inquiry. . 1974
611	ED141836. Bloom, Lynn Z.. Definitions of Feminist and Sexist Biographies of Women. . 1976
607	ED256657. Searing, Susan, Comp.; Shult, Linda, Comp.. Women and Science: Issues and Resources [and] Women and Information Technology: A Selective Bibliography. . 1985
606	ED260996. . Women at Work, Home and School. First Grade Social Studies: Susan LaFlesche, M.D., Mary McLeod Bethune, Dorothea Lange, Rachel Carson, Chien-Shiung Wu, [and] Nancy Lopez. . 1985
605	ED313702. Merrick, Beverly G.. Two Case Histories, Ishbel Ross and Emma Bugbee: Women Journalists Ride the Rail with the Suffragettes. . 1989
604	ED246001. Bonifanti, Georgeanne. Women's History Bibliography. . 1982
603	ED267936. Bellanger, Patricia; Reese, Lillian. Contemporary American Indian Women: Careers And Contributions. . 1983
602	EJ460105. Meyer, Alberta L.. Later Leaders in Education: Jennie Wahlert. Woman of Achievement. Childhood Education; v69 n3 p164-67 Spr 1993. 1993
601	ED231676. Styer, Sandra. Selecting Women's Biographies for the Social Studies. . 1983
601	ED161729. Schacher, Susan. Hypatia's Sisters: Biographies of Women Scientists - Past and Present. . 1976
601	ED135675. Rosenfelt, Deborah Silverton, Ed.. Strong Women: An Annotated Bibliography of Literature for the High School Classroom. . 1976
599	EJ451070. Mann, Sarah; And Others. Special Issue: Biography in Management and Organisational Development. Management Education and Development; v23 n3 p181-289 Fall 1992. 1992
597	EJ126721. Watson, Jane M.. Three Women of Mathematics Australian Mathematics Teacher; 30, 5, 153-160, Oct 74. 1974
596	ED319676. Eisenberg, Bonnie; And Others. Women in Colonial and Revolutionary America. . 1989
592	ED127217. Faxon, Pookie, Comp.; Bolint, Mary, Comp.. Films by and/or about Women, 1972: Directory of Filmmakers, Films, and Distributors; Internationally; Past and Present. . 1972
590	EJ124651. Gell, Marilyn. Five Women Library Journal; 100, 19, 1977-1983, Nov 1 75. 1975
590	ED340637. Sawyer, Kem Knapp. Lucretia Mott: Friend of Justice. With a Message from Rosalynn Carter. Picture-book Biography Series. . 1991
590	EJ370085. Henry, Susan. "Dear Companion, Ever-Ready Co-Worker": A Woman's Role in a Media Dynasty. Journalism Quarterly; v64 n2-3 p301-12 Sum-Fall 1987. 1987

Figure 11.2. Results of a search in the *ERIC* database on "women and biography." From ERIC Database. Copyright © 2000 by Information Institute of Syracuse. Reprinted by permission.

The results of a search in *Wilson Biography Plus* (a subscription database) for Maya Angelou are shown in Figure 11.3. The lengthy article contains a photograph and a listing of "Works by Subject" and "Works about Subject." Figure 11.4 shows an article on Maya Angelou available for free on the Internet from the Women's International Center.

◆ Wilson BiographiesPlus Illus UPDATED AUG 7

◆ **Full Record**

▶ *Back* ▶ *Print* ▶ *Save* ▶ *Email*
◆

<u>MORE INFORMATION</u>
<u>MORE IMAGES</u>

Copyright
Article Heading
Angelou, Maya
Apr. 4, 1928-
Publication Statement
1985 Biography from
WORLD AUTHORS 1975-1980
Pronunciation
(AN-jel-oh, MIE-yuh)
Full Text
ANGELOU, MAYA (April 4, 1928-), American memoirist and poet, was born Marguerite Ann Johnson in St. Louis, the daughter of Bailey Johnson, a doorman and later a naval hospital worker, and Vivian Baxter Johnson, a woman of extraordinary energy and resourcefulness. At the age of three, she and her four-year-old brother, Bailey, were sent by their parents, who had divorced, from Long Beach, California, to Stamps, Arkansas, to live with their paternal grandmother. Maya--her brother gave her the name--was brought up in this entirely segregated community (as well as for a short while in St. Louis), graduated from the Lafayette County Training School at the age of twelve, then moved with her brother back to San Francisco to live with their mother, who had remarried. She graduated from Mission High School at sixteen. Two months later, in the summer of 1944, she gave birth to a son, Guy--"the best thing that ever happened to me," she has said. "One would say of my life," she told an interviewer in 1972, "born loser, had to be; from a broken family, raped at eight, unwed mother at sixteen.... It's a fact but it's not the truth. In the black community, however bad it looks, there's a lot of love and so much humor."
She wrote eloquently of this childhood in her first volume of memoirs, I Know Why the Caged Bird Sings, a classic of American autobiography and an immediate critical and popular success. James Baldwin sensed after reading it "the beginning of a new era in the minds and hearts and lives of all Black men and women." The book, to him, "liberates the reader into life simply because Maya Angelou confronts her own life with such moving wonder, such a luminous

Figure 11.3. Results of a search in *Wilson Biography Plus* for information about Maya Angelou. Used by permission of Woman's International Center. www.wic.org

Maya Angelou

Greatness Through Literature

Internationally respected poet, writer and educator, Maya Angelou has given us such best-selling titles as I Know Why the Caged Bird Sings, Gather Together in My Name, Singin' and Swingin' and The Heart of a Woman. Multi-talented, she produced and starred in the great play Cabaret for Freedom and starred in The Blacks. She wrote the original screenplay and musical score for the film Georgia, Georgia and was both author and executive producer of a five-part television miniseries, Three Way Choice.

Miss Angelou's accomplishments have earned her the La Home Journal Woman of the Year award in communication an Matrix Award in the field of books from Women in Communication She received the Golden Eagle Award for her documentary, Americans in the Arts, produced by PBS. She is one of the women admitted into the Director's Guild. In 1974, she was appointed by Gerald Ford to the Bi-Centennial Commission and later by Jimmie Carter to the Commission for International Woman of the Year.

Her personal outreach to improve conditions for women in Third World, primarily in Africa, has helped change the live thousands less privileged. Here is where she gives with all her heart and soul.

[WIC Main Page | Biographies | Words of Wisdom | Newsletter | Birthdates | Living Legacy Awards]

Figure 11.4. Results of a search on the Women's International Center site for information on Maya Angelou.

Biographical Indexes

One way to locate biographical information, particularly retrospective biographical information, is to use an index devoted exclusively to biographical information. *Biographical indexes* are indirect sources of information; that is, they do not contain information about people; rather they provide references to sources that do. They index the biographical literature that appears in books, periodicals, newspapers and reference sources.

Biographical indexes may be general in coverage, or they may cover a particular subject. *Biography and Genealogy Master Index* covers persons of all professions, occupations, nationalities, and time periods. *Performing Arts Biography Master Index* provides references to articles about people who are outstanding in the theater arts. The coverage of some biographical indexes is limited to certain types of literature. *People in History* indexes only history journals and dissertations, while *Biography Index* is very broad in scope and indexes both periodicals and books.

Figures 11.5 and 11.6 show excerpts from *Biography and Genealogy Master Index (BAGMI)* in the print and CD-ROM formats, respectively. *BAGMI* is also available by subscription on the Internet. It offers the advantage (as does the CD-ROM version) of being able to search all years at once. For example, a search in the online version of *BAGMI* for Claudia Goldin points to 24 references that provide information about Ms. Goldin. With the print version it is necessary to determine which years to search and perhaps to search multiple volumes.

Most printed biographical indexes include citations to articles about individuals, including obituaries. Articles are listed alphabetically, with the individual's name as the subject. Figure 11.7 represents a sample page from *Biography Index* and is typical of the format of this type of biographical index.

Goldin, Barbara Diamond 1946-	IntAu&W	= International Authors and Writers
Int Au&W93		Who's Who
Goldin, Claudia Dale 1946- WhoAm95,	WhoAm	= Who's Who in America
WhoAmW 95	WhoAmW	= Who's Who of American Women
Goldin, Daniel S 1940- AmMWSc95,	AmMWSc	= American Men & Women of Science
BioIn18,-19,WhoAm95,WhoWor95	WhoWor	= Who's Who in the World

Figure 11.5. Entries from *Biography and Genealogy Master Index, 1996.* (Reprinted by permission of Gale Research, Inc.)

Goldin, Claudia Dale
1946-

American Economic Association, Directory of Members, 1974. Edited by Rendigs Fels. Published as Volume 64, Number 5 (October, 1974) of The American Economic Review.

American Men & Women of Science. A biographical directory of today's Leaders in physical, biological, and related sciences. 13th edition, Social & Behavioral Sciences. One volume. New York: R.R. Bowker Co., 1978.

Who's Who in America. 48th edition, 1994. New Providence, NJ: Marquis Who's Who, 1993.

Figure 11.6. Sample entry from *Biography and Genealogy Master Index (BAGMI)* CD-ROM. (Reprinted by permission of Gale Research, Inc.)

Biography Index

A

Abbey, Edward, 1927-1989, author
Obituary
  Natl Parks por 63:42 My/Je '89
  Sierra 74:100-1 My/Je '89
Abbot, Willis John, 1863-1934, author and journalist
Biographical dictionary of American journalism; edited by Joseph P. McKerns. Greenwood Press 1989 p1-3 bibl
Abbott, Jim, baseball player
Brofman, R. One for the Angels. il pors *Life* 12:118+ Je '89
Abbott, Lyman, 1835-1922, clergyman
Biographical dictionary of American journalism; edited by Joseph P. McKerns. Greenwood Press 1989 p3-4 bibl
Abbott, Robert S., 1868-1940, journalist
Biographical dictionary of American journalism; edited by Joseph P. McKerns. Greenwood Press 1989 p4-6 bibl
Abdul-Jabbar, Kareem, 1947-, basketball player
Kareem Abdul-Jabbar: what will he do after basketball? il pors *Jet* 76:46-8+ Je 26 '89
Lyons, D. C. Kareem's last hurrah. il pors *Ebony* 44:102+ My '89
Renaud, L. A fitting farewell. por *Macleans* 102:51 My 22 '89
Abel, Elie, Canadian journalist and educator
Biographical dictionary of American journalism; edited by Joseph P. McKerns. Greenwood Press 1989 p6-7 bibl
Abernathy, Ralph D., clergyman and civil rights leader
Abernathy, Ralph D. And the walls came tumbling down; an autobiography. Harper & Row 1989 638p il
A fight among Dr. King's faithful. por *Newsweek* 114:31 O 23 '89
Hampton, H. Dr. King's best friend. por *N Y Times Book Rev* p3 O 29 '89
Tattletale memoir. por *Time* 134:42 O 23 '89
Able, David, handicapped child
Grant, M. When the spirit takes wing. il pors *People Wkly* 31:50-5 My 15 '89
Abraham, F. Murray, actor
Copelin, D. "F" is for Farid: an interview with F. Murray Abraham. pors *Cineaste* 17 no1:[supp] 14-16 '89
Abraham, Gerald, 1904-1988, English musicologist
Obituary
  19th Century Music 12:188-9 Fall '88
Abu Nidal, Palestinian revolutionary
Brand, D. Finis for the master terrorist? por *Time* 134:69 D 11 '89
Abu Suud, Khaled, Kuwaiti government official
Master of the money game. por *Fortune* 120:184+ Jl 31 '89
Acevedo Díaz, Eduardo, 1851-1921, Uruguayan author
Ruffinelli, Jorge. Eduardo Acevedo Díaz. (In Latin American writers. Scribner 1989 p299-303) bibl
Achitoff, Louis, d. 1989, aviation expert and government employee
Obituary
  N Y Times p44 N 26 '89
Achucarro, Joaquin, 1932-, Spanish pianist
Elder, D. Joaquin Achucarro: the spirit and passion of Spain. il por *Clavier* 28:10-13 My/Je '89
Ackerley, J. R. (Joe Randolph), 1896-1967, English author
Jenkyns, R. New Repub days. *New Repub* 201:31-4 D 18 '89
Lurie, A. Love with the perfect dog. por *N Y Times Book Rev* p12 N 12 '89
Parker, Peter. Ackerley; the life of J.R. Ackerley. Farrar, Straus & Giroux 1989 465p il
Ackerley, Joe Randolph *See* Ackerley, J. R. (Joe Randolph), 1896-1967
Ackerman, Arthur F., 1903-1989, pediatrician
Obituary
  N Y Times pD-17 Ag 25 '89

Acosta, Joseph de, 1540-1600, Spanish missionary and historian
Arocena, Luis A. Father Joseph de Acosta. (In Latin American writers. Scribner 1989 p47-51) bibl
Adams, Abigail, 1744-1818, wife of John Adams and mother of John Quincy Adams
Gelles, E. B. Gossip: an eighteenth-century case. *J Soc Hist* 22:667-83 Summ '89
Juvenile literature
Lindsay, Rae. The presidents' first ladies. Watts 1989 p29-37 bibl il pors
Adams, Abigail, d. 1813, daughter of John and Abigail Adams
Gelles, E. B. Gossip: an eighteenth-century case. *J Soc Hist* 22:667-83 Summ '89
Adams, Ansel, 1902-1984, photographer
Biographical dictionary of American journalism; edited by Joseph P. McKerns. Greenwood Press 1989 p7-8 bibl
Adams, Brooks, 1848-1927, historian
Auchincloss, Louis. The Vanderbilt era; profiles of a gilded age. Scribner 1989 p163-74 il pors
Adams, Charles Francis, 1835-1915, lawyer, railroad executive and historian
Auchincloss, Louis. The Vanderbilt era; profiles of a gilded age. Scribner 1989 p163-74 il pors
Adams, Franklin P. (Franklin Pierce), 1881-1960, humorist
Biographical dictionary of American journalism; edited by Joseph P. McKerns. Greenwood Press 1989 p8-10 bibl
Adams, Gerry, Irish political leader
Fletcher, B. Interview with Sinn Fein President Gerry Adams. *Mon Rev* 41:16-26 My '89
Adams, Henry, 1838-1918, historian
Auchincloss, Louis. The Vanderbilt era; profiles of a gilded age. Scribner 1989 p163-74 il pors
Brogan, H. Faithful to his class. *N Y Times Book Rev* p22 N 19 '89
Delbanco, A. The seer of Lafayette Square. por *New Repub* 201:32-8 O 16 '89
Samuels, Ernest. Henry Adams. Belknap Press 1989 504p bibl
Adams, John, 1735-1826, president
Gelles, E. B. Gossip: an eighteenth-century case. *J Soc Hist* 22:667-83 Summ '89
Juvenile literature
Dwyer, Frank. John Adams. Chelsea House 1989 109p bibl il
Adams, John F. (John Franklin), 1919-1989, professor of insurance
Obituary
  Natl Underwrit (Life Health Financ Serv Ed) 93:5 Mr 20 '89
Adams, Julius J., d. 1989, newspaper editor
Obituary
  N Y Times Biogr Serv 20:741 Ag '89
Adams, Louisa Catherine, 1775-1852, president's wife
Juvenile literature
Lindsay, Rae. The presidents' first ladies. Watts 1989 p56-61 bibl il pors
Adams, Ralph E., d. 1989, seaman
Obituary
  N Y Times Biogr Serv 20:402 My '89
Adams, Samuel, 1722-1803, statesman
Biographical dictionary of American journalism; edited by Joseph P. McKerns. Greenwood Press 1989 p10-11 bibl
Pencak, W. Samuel Adams and Shays's Rebellion. *N Engl Q* 62:63-74 Mr '89
Adams, Samuel Hopkins, 1871-1958, author and journalist
Adams, Samuel Hopkins. Grandfather stories. Syracuse Univ. Press 1989 312p
Biographical dictionary of American journalism; edited by Joseph P. McKerns. Greenwood Press 1989 p11-13 bibl
Adams-Ender, Clara, general
Cheers, D. M. Nurse Corps chief. il pors *Ebony* 44:64+ Je '89

Figure 11.7. Selected reference from *Biography Index*. (Copyright © 1990 by the H.W. Wilson Company. Material reproduced by permission of the publisher.)

Biographical Dictionaries

Biographical dictionaries are works that contain limited information about people. They may be published either in a single volume or in multiple volumes. Some are monographs published only once, while others are serial publications issued on a monthly, quarterly, annual, or biennial basis. The *Biographical Directory of the American Congress*, 1774–1989, is an example of a single volume monographic work; the *Dictionary of American Biography* is a monograph published in multiple volumes. *Who's Who in America* and *Current Biography* are serial publications issued biennially and monthly, respectively.

A short biography of Claudia Goldin, the author used as an example in Figures 11.5 and 11.6 was found in *Who's Who in America* (see Figure 11.8). This entry is typical of many of the "Who's Who" series of biographical dictionaries.

Some biographical dictionaries such as *Twentieth Century Authors* and *Current Biography* contain pictures of the subjects. The length of the entries in biographical dictionaries may vary. Entries in the *International Who's Who* consist of a few brief facts about the person; those in the *Dictionary of National Biography* are long, descriptive, signed articles with bibliographies. *Current Biography* usually provides a picture with a narrative of the individual being discussed. Monthly issues highlight prominent people in the news in a wide variety of occupations, including national and international affairs.

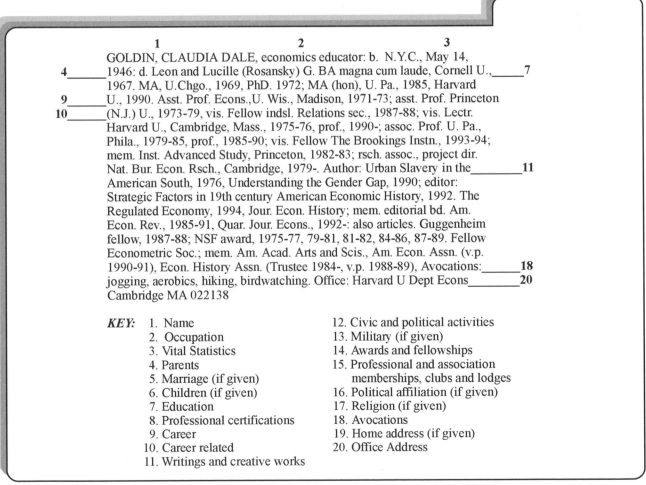

1   **2**   **3**

GOLDIN, CLAUDIA DALE, economics educator: b. N.Y.C., May 14,
4_____ 1946: d. Leon and Lucille (Rosansky) G. BA magna cum laude, Cornell U., _____**7**
1967. MA, U.Chgo., 1969, PhD. 1972; MA (hon), U. Pa., 1985, Harvard
9_____ U., 1990. Asst. Prof. Econs.,U. Wis., Madison, 1971-73; asst. Prof. Princeton
10_____ (N.J.) U., 1973-79, vis. Fellow indsl. Relations sec., 1987-88; vis. Lectr.
Harvard U., Cambridge, Mass., 1975-76, prof., 1990-; assoc. Prof. U. Pa.,
Phila., 1979-85, prof., 1985-90; vis. Fellow The Brookings Instn., 1993-94;
mem. Inst. Advanced Study, Princeton, 1982-83; rsch. assoc., project dir.
Nat. Bur. Econ. Rsch., Cambridge, 1979-. Author: Urban Slavery in the_____**11**
American South, 1976, Understanding the Gender Gap, 1990; editor:
Strategic Factors in 19th century American Economic History, 1992. The
Regulated Economy, 1994, Jour. Econ. History; mem. editorial bd. Am.
Econ. Rev., 1985-91, Quar. Jour. Econs., 1992-: also articles. Guggenheim
fellow, 1987-88; NSF award, 1975-77, 79-81, 81-82, 84-86, 87-89. Fellow
Econometric Soc.; mem. Am. Acad. Arts and Scis., Am. Econ. Assn. (v.p.
1990-91), Econ. History Assn. (Trustee 1984-, v.p. 1988-89), Avocations:_____**18**
jogging, aerobics, hiking, birdwatching. Office: Harvard U Dept Econs_____**20**
Cambridge MA 022138

KEY:

1. Name	12. Civic and political activities
2. Occupation	13. Military (if given)
3. Vital Statistics	14. Awards and fellowships
4. Parents	15. Professional and association
5. Marriage (if given)	memberships, clubs and lodges
6. Children (if given)	16. Political affiliation (if given)
7. Education	17. Religion (if given)
8. Professional certifications	18. Avocations
9. Career	19. Home address (if given)
10. Career related	20. Office Address
11. Writings and creative works	

Figure 11.8. Entry from *Who's Who in America, 1996.* (Copyright © 1996, Marquis *Who's Who,* a Reed Reference Publishing Co., a division of Reed Elsevier Inc., *Who's Who in America,* 50th edition, 1996.)

Retrospective biographical dictionaries such as *Webster's New Biographical Dictionary* include only persons who are no longer living; others such as *Contemporary Authors* contain information on persons of today. Some biographical dictionaries list both living and nonliving persons.

Library Catalogs

The library catalog is another useful source for finding biographical works. Usually biographies about individuals are listed by the name of the individual with nothing following it. Use the individual's last name as the subject.

EXAMPLE

SALK JONAS

Biographical dictionaries are listed under the heading:

BIOGRAPHY--DICTIONARIES

Figure 11.9 illustrates a typical subject search for a specific author (Shakespeare).

```
Search Request: S=SHAKESPEARE                           LSU Libraries
Search Results: 4377 Entries Found                      Subject Guide
-----------------------------------------------------------------
LINE:  BEGINNING ENTRY:                                 INDEX RANGE:
  1    SHAKESPEARE. GERVINUS GEORG GOTTFRIED 1805-1871      1 - 313
  2    SHAKESPEARE WILLIAM 1564-1616--ALLUSIONS          314 - 626
  3    SHAKESPEARE WILLIAM 1564-1616--BIOGRAPHY          627 - 939
  4    SHAKESPEARE WILLIAM 1564-1616--CHILDHOOD AND YOUTH  940 - 1252
  5    SHAKESPEARE WILLIAM 1564-1616--CRITICISM AND INTERPRETATIO
                                                        1253 - 1565
  6    SHAKESPEARE WILLIAM 1564-1616--CRITICISM AND INTERPRETATIO
                                                        1566 - 1878
  7    SHAKESPEARE WILLIAM 1564-1616--DRAMATIC PRODUCTION  1879 - 2191
  8    SHAKESPEARE WILLIAM 1564-1616--INFLUENCE          2192 - 2504
  9    SHAKESPEARE WILLIAM 1564-1616--LANGUAGE--GLOSSARIES ETC
                                                        2505 - 2817
 10    SHAKESPEARE WILLIAM 1564-1616--SONGS AND MUSIC    2818 - 3130
 11    SHAKESPEARE WILLIAM 1564-1616--STAGE HISTORY--1625 1800  3131 - 3443
 12    SHAKESPEARE WILLIAM 1564-1616--TRAGEDIES          3444 - 3756
 13    SHAKESPEARE WILLIAM 1564-1616. HAMLET             3757 - 4069
 14    SHAKESPEARE WILLIAM 1564-1616. MERCHANT OF VENICE  4070 - 4377
-----------------------------------------------------------------
STArt over      Type number to begin display within index range
HELp
OTHer options
NEXT COMMAND:
```

Figure 11.9. Subject guide screen. Results of search s=shakespeare.

Notice that there are several subheadings on the Subject Guide screen that would be useful in researching an account of Shakespeare's life:

EXAMPLE ■

--BIOGRAPHY

--CHILDHOOD AND YOUTH

--CRITICISM AND INTERPRETATION

--INFLUENCE

Figure 11.10 illustrates the results of a search in the online catalog for general biographical information about women.

Additional Sources for Biographical Information

Biographical information may be found in newspapers and in periodicals. Selected lists of sources for general and topical Internet sites, indexes, and dictionaries are provided at the end of this chapter.

```
Search Request: S=WOMEN--BIOGRAPHY              LSU Libraries
Search Results: 162 Entries Found               Subject Guide
-----------------------------------------------------------
LINE:  BEGINNING ENTRY:                          INDEX RANGE:
  1    WOMEN--BIOGRAPHY                              1 -  12
  2    WOMEN--BIOGRAPHY                             13 -  24
  3    WOMEN--BIOGRAPHY                             25 -  36
  4    WOMEN--BIOGRAPHY                             37 -  48
  5    WOMEN--BIOGRAPHY                             49 -  60
  6    WOMEN--BIOGRAPHY                             61 -  72
  7    WOMEN--BIOGRAPHY                             73 -  84
  8    WOMEN--BIOGRAPHY                             85 -  96
  9    WOMEN--BIOGRAPHY                             97 - 108
 10    WOMEN--BIOGRAPHY                            109 - 120
 11    WOMEN--BIOGRAPHY                            121 - 132
 12    WOMEN--BIOGRAPHY                            133 - 144
 13    WOMEN--BIOGRAPHY--ANCIENT                   145 - 156
 14    WOMEN--BIOGRAPHY--INDEXES                   157 - 162
-----------------------------------------------------------
STArt over      Type number to begin display within index range
HELp
OTHer options
NEXT COMMAND:
```

Figure 11.10. OPAC Subject Guide screen for biographies of women.

EVALUATING BIOGRAPHICAL INFORMATION

Selecting the right source for biographical information is just as important as selecting any other type of research material. Use the criteria in Chapter 3 (Table 3.2) to evaluate any biographical material you find. Remember that some sources will be more suited to your needs than others. For example, if you need detailed information on an individual's life, the short biographies in *Who's Who* would not be suitable. Compare, also, the detailed article from the *Wilson Biography Plus* database with the article on Maya Angelou in the Women's International Center (WIC) Web site, which gives only a small photograph and limited information about the writer (see Figures 11.3 and 11.4). It is a good practice to look at more than one biographical source to compare information.

 ## SELECTED INTERNET SITES FOR BIOGRAPHICAL INFORMATION

Guides

Biography. The Michigan Electronic Library Reference Desk. University of Michigan. http://mel.lib.mi.us/ reference/REF-biog.html

Ready Reference: Biography. Louisiana State University. http://www.lib.lsu.edu/ref/biography.html

General

Biographical Dictionary. http://www.s9.com/biography/

Biography.com. http://www.biography.com

Dead People Server. http://dpsinfo.com/dps/howtofind.shtml

Find a Grave. http://www.findagrave.com/

Lives. http://members.home.net/klanxner/lives/

Who's Alive and Who's Dead. http://www.neosoft.com/~davo/livedead/

Who's Who Online. http://whoswho-online.com/

World Biographical Index. http://www.biblio.tu-bs.de/acwww25u/wbi_en/log_li.html

Special Interests

AMG All-Music.Com Biographies. http://www.allmusic.com

Celebration of Women Writers. http://www.cgi-cs.cmu.edu/afs/cs.cmu.edu/user/mmbt/www/women/ celebration.html

Faces of Science: African Americans in the Sciences. http://www.lib.lsu.edu/lib/chem

Forbes List of the World's Richest People. http://www.forbes.com/tool/toolbox/billnew/index.asp

Internet Movie Database (IMDb). http://imdb.com

Jewish Heroes and Heroines in America. http://www.fau.edu/library/brodytoc.htm

Lists of US Presidents. http://www.fujisan.demon.co.uk/USPresidents/preslist.htm

Literary Menagerie. http://sunset.backbone.olemiss.edu/~egcash/

Nobel Prize Archive. http://www.nobelprizes.com/

Patron Saints Index. http://www.catholic-forum.com/saints/indexnt.htm

Political Graveyard. http://politicalgraveyard.com

Presidents of the United States. http://www.state.de.us/facts/ushist/intrpres.htm

Rock and Roll Hall of Fame and Museum. http://www.rockhall.com/induct/index.html

Uncle Sam: Who's Who in the Federal Government. http://www.lib.memphis.edu/gpo/whos3.htm

 SELECTED PRINT SOURCES FOR BIOGRAPHICAL INFORMATION

(Some sources may also be available online.)

Indexes

General Biographical Indexes

Author Biographies Master Index. 2 vols. Gale Biographical Index Series No. 3. Detroit: Gale, 1984.
> Useful source for references to biographical information on authors of all nationalities and all periods. Indexes biographical information in biographical dictionaries, encyclopedias, and directories. Includes information found in bibliographies and criticisms.

Biography and Genealogy Master Index. 2nd ed. 8 vols. Gale Biographical Index Series No.1. Detroit: Gale, 1980. *Annual Supplement,* 1981–. Also available on CD-ROM.
> Name index to biographical dictionaries, subject encyclopedias, literary criticism, and other biographical indexes such as *Biography Index.* Provides names and dates of biography sources. Universal in scope.

Biography Index. New York: H.W. Wilson, 1947–.
> Quarterly index to biographical information appearing in books and periodicals. Covers wide range of occupations. Arranged alphabetically, entries include birth and death dates (if available), occupation, and contributions to society. A separate index by occupations is located in the back of the book.

Historical Biographical Dictionaries Master Index. Gale Biographical Index Series No. 7. Detroit: Gale, 1980.
> Alphabetically arranged index to information on prominent persons now deceased. Indexed sources include biographical dictionaries, encyclopedias, and other reference sources. Coverage is primarily American, but a few non-Americans are also included.

Marquis Who's Who Index to Who's Who Books. Wilmette, IL: Marquis, 1985–.
> Annual index to the various Marquis *Who's Who* biographical dictionaries. Each volume lists names of individuals covered in the series during the prior year. If the person is listed in more than one dictionary, the references are given in chronological order. This index eliminates the need to go through all of the Marquis publications to find a particular reference.

Subject Biographical Indexes

Artist Biographies Master Index. Gale Biographical Index Series No. 9. Detroit: Gale, 1986.
> Provides references to biographical material on artists working in all aspects of art—fine arts, illustration, ceramics, craft, folk art, and architecture. Sources include biographical dictionaries, encyclopedias, directories, and indexes. Both historical and contemporary artists are included.

Business Biography Master Index. Gale Biographical Index Series No. 10. Detroit: Gale, 1987.
> Lists prominent persons in the field of business. Coverage is primarily contemporary, but includes a few historical figures. Sources include biographical dictionaries, encyclopedias, and directories. Predominately American in scope with a few international figures.

Journalist Biographical Master Index. Gale Biographical Index Series No. 4. Detroit: Gale, 1979.
   Indexes biographical information for people working in either the print or the broadcast media. Includes historical as well as contemporary journalists. Sources include biographical dictionaries and
   directories.

People in History: An Index to U.S. and Canadian Biographies in History Journals and Dissertations. 2 vols.
   Santa Barbara, CA: ABC-CLIO, 1988.
   Arranged alphabetically by name, each entry includes the author and title of the article, title of the
   source, and a brief abstract of the article. Volume 2 contains separate author and subject indexes.

*People in World History: An Index to Biographies in History Journals and Dissertations Covering All Countries
   of the World Except Canada and the U.S.* 2 vols. Santa Barbara, CA: ABC-CLIO, 1989.
   Each entry gives the author and title of the article, the title of the source, subject, and a brief abstract.
   Entries are arranged alphabetically by the subject of the article. Separate subject and author indexes in
   the second volume.

Performing Arts Biography Master Index. 2nd ed. Gale Biographical Index Series No. 5. Detroit: Gale, 1981.
   References to biographical information on persons working in the theater, films and television, or
   the concert stage. Sources indexed include biographical dictionaries, subject encyclopedias, and
   directories.

Twentieth-Century Authors Biographies Master Index. Gale Biographical Index Series No.8. Detroit: Gale,
   1984.
   Similar to the *Author Biographies Master Index*, but includes only contemporary authors. International
   in scope. Indexes biographical dictionaries, encyclopedia articles, and periodicals.

Biographical Dictionaries

General Biographical Dictionaries

Current Biography. New York: H.W. Wilson, 1940–.
   Features people in the news: politicians, sports figures, entertainers, and scientists. The articles about
   the individuals are noncritical but comprehensive. Each article is accompanied by a photograph and a
   short bibliography. The annual cumulative volume includes a section of obituaries and a multiyear
   cumulative index.

International Who's Who. 1935–. London: Europa, 1935–.
   Contains information on people from all over the world. Articles are short and unsigned. Includes an
   obituary section listing those persons who have died since the preceding volume was published. Includes a list of the world's reigning royal families.

Who's Who: An Annual Biographical Dictionary. New York: St. Martin's, 1897–.
   Alphabetical listing of outstanding British subjects as well as some prominent international figures.
   Gives pertinent personal and professional data. Contains a list of obituaries and a list of the present
   royal family.

Who's Who in America. Chicago: Marquis, 1899–.
   Published biennially with a supplement issued on the off year. Lists notable Americans and some international figures. Arrangement is alphabetical with geographic, professional area, retiree, and necrol-
   ogy indexes. Entries are brief and noncritical.

Retrospective Biographical Dictionaries

American National Biography. Ed. John A. Garraty and Mark C. Carnes. 24 vols. New York: Oxford, 1999.
   Biographies of more than 17,400 men and women—from all eras and walks of life—whose lives have
   shaped the nation. An online version is also available.

Dictionary of American Biography. 20 vols. New York: Scribner, 1928–1936. *Supplements* 1–8, 1944–1988.

Published under the auspices of the American Council of Learned Societies, this scholarly and comprehensive work provides biographical information about notable Americans no longer living. Long scholarly signed articles; extensive bibliographies. Includes noteworthy persons from the colonial period to 1970. Supplement 8 was published in two volumes and includes specialized indexes to all of the preceding volumes.

Dictionary of National Biography. 22 vols. London: Oxford, 1950. *Supplements* 2–8, 1912–1990.

Originally published in 1895; reprinted at irregular intervals along with supplements. Premier source for historical biographical information on outstanding British subjects. Includes some non-British persons who are important in British history. Long, scholarly, signed articles with extensive bibliographies.

Webster's New Biographical Dictionary. Springfield, MA: Merriam, 1988.

This new edition contains biographical information on approximately 30,000 notable personages beginning with the year 3100 BC to the twentieth century. Worldwide in scope but most useful for American, British, and Canadian subjects. Articles are short and include birth and death dates, notable accomplishments, and pronunciations of names.

Who Was Who, 1907–1980. 7 vols. New York: St. Martin's, 1929–1981.

Companion volumes to *Who's Who;* contains reprints of articles about people listed in *Who's Who* who have died since the last compilation. Usually only the death date has been added but occasionally supplemental new material is included. Cumulative index to all seven volumes published in 1981.

Who Was Who in America. Historical Volume, 1607–1896. Chicago: Marquis, 1963.

Short biographical sketches of both Americans and non-Americans who were influential in the history of the United States. Contains lists of the names of the early governors, the U.S. presidents and vice-presidents, Supreme Court Justices, and cabinet officers.

Who Was Who in America with World Notables, 1897–1989. Wilmette, IL: Marquis, 1942–1989.

Compilation of the biographies of people no longer living that originally appeared in *Who's Who in America*. Death dates and, in some cases, other new information have been added. An index to all volumes of *Who Was Who in America 1607–1989* was published in 1989.

Subject Biographical Dictionaries

American Men and Women of Science. New York: Bowker, 1971–.

Multivolume biographical dictionary listing people who are prominent in the physical and biological sciences. Articles are short and list personal data, accomplishments, and publications. Unsigned and noncritical.

Biographical Directory of the United States Congress, 1774–1989. Washington: GPO, 1989.

Short biographical sketches of the members of Congress beginning with the Continental Congress and continuing through the 100th Congress. Some entries have bibliographies. Contains listings of the executive officers and cabinet members beginning with the administration of George Washington and going through that of Ronald Reagan. Available on the Internet with up-to-date listings at http://bioguide.congress.gov/biosearch/biosearch.asp.

Contemporary Authors. Detroit: Gale, 1962–.

Comprehensive source for biographical as well as bibliographical information on current writers of both fiction and nonfiction. Includes authors who are currently writing for newspapers, magazines, motion pictures, theater, and television. Separate annual cumulative index contains references to all previous volumes as well as other biographical sources published by Gale.

Directory of American Scholars. 8th ed. 4 vols. New York: Bowker, 1982.

Contains profiles of American and Canadian scholars who are actively working in the humanities and the social sciences. Each volume is devoted to a different subject area—Volume I: history; Volume II:

English, speech and drama; Volume III: foreign languages, linguistics, and philology; Volume IV: philosophy, religion, and law. Each volume contains a geographic index. In addition, Volume IV has a cumulative index to the scholars listed in all volumes.

Twentieth Century Authors. New York: H.W. Wilson, 1941. *First Supplement*, 1955.

Universal in scope, but limited to authors working in this century. Provides photograph, list of works completed, and a bibliography of sources used to compile the article. Articles are unsigned. Alphabetically arranged by author's name.

World Authors, 1975–1980. New York: H.W. Wilson, 1985.

Continues *Twentieth Century Authors* with a similar arrangement and scope. Set includes three separately issued volumes covering the years 1950–1970, 1970–1975, and 1975–1980.

Biographical Information

Instructor: _____ Course/Section: _____

Name: _____

Date: _____ Points: _____

Review Questions

1. Why are biographies important sources for research?

2. Name four possible steps (other than consulting the reference librarian) that you could take to find information about the lives of people.

   a.

   b.

   c.

   d.

3. What information about a person is useful in helping to select the appropriate biographical source?

4. Why is the Internet a good source for biographical information?

5. Name two biographical sources that are now free on the Internet.

6. What is the difference between a biographical index and a biographical dictionary?

7. What subject heading would be used to find a general biographical dictionary in the library catalog?

8. What subject heading would you use to find a biographical dictionary listing people in psychology?

9. How does a retrospective biographical dictionary such as the *Dictionary of American History* differ from a current one such as *Who's Who in America?*

10. What types of sources are indexed in *Biography Index?*

Biographical Information

Instructor: _____ Course/Section: _____

Name: _____

Date: _____ Points: _____

Finding Biographies in Periodical Databases

Locate biographical information for one of the following individuals using either a CD-ROM or an online database such as *EBSCOhost, InfoTrac, WilsonSelect, FirstSearch,* or *SilverPlatter.*

Albert Camus	Bill Gates	Sean Connery
Bob Dole	Chuck Yeager	William (Bill) Clinton
Robert Kennedy	Whoopie Goldberg	Michael J. Fox

1. Circle the name you selected.

2. Which database(s) did you use to find information?

3. Write your search statement the exact way you typed it.

4. How many results did you find for this person?

5. Are any of the articles full text? If so, select one and print the first page.

6. Does the list contain articles that are not full text?

7.   Describe how you would locate the articles in Question 6 in your library holdings.

8.   Give the correct bibliographic citation for two entries you found on your individual (use the sample citations in Appendix A).

Exercise 11.3 Biographical Information

11

Instructor: _____ Course/Section: _____

Name: _____

Date: _____ Points: _____

Finding Biographies on the Internet

Locate biographical information on the Internet on two of the individuals listed below using either *Biography.com* at http://www.biography.com or *Biographical Dictionary* at http://www.s9.com/biography/.

Albert Einstein	Ann Landers	Michael Jackson
Pope John XXIII	John Lennon	Charles Schulz
John F. Kennedy	Princess Diana	Mother Teresa

1. Circle the names you selected.

2. Which Web site(s) did you use? (Give the URL.)

3. Describe the type and amount of information you found for each individual (e.g., short, detailed, references given).

Use two of the following sites for additional information on the same two individuals:

Dead People Server	http://dpsinfo.com/dps/howtofind.shtml
Who's Alive and Who's Dead	http://www.neosoft.com/~davo/livedead/
Lives	http://members.home.net/klanxner/lives/

4. Circle the sites you selected.

5. Give the birth date and/or death date (if applicable) for each individual that you researched.

                                                                  Birth date   Death date

    a. Name of first individual:

    b. Name of second individual:

6. Compare the information you found in this last group of Web sites with that found in the first group. Did you retrieve more information from this set or the first?

7. Which site was more useful? Why?

Biographical Information

Instructor: _____ Course/Section: _____

Name: _____

Date: _____ Points: _____

Using Biographical Indexes

Biographical indexes contain citations to articles about individuals who are outstanding or well-known for their accomplishments. Using one of the biographical indexes mentioned in this chapter or one you find in the library catalog, look up information on the life of an individual about whom you are interested or one assigned by your instructor.

Name of Person:

When you have found your reference, note the following information.

1. Title of the biographical index used:

2. Call number of the biographical index used:

3. Identify at least three publications in which you would find information about this individual. (Make sure you find the full title of the publication.)

4. Look in the library catalog to see whether your library has any of the sources you listed in Question 3. Write the call numbers you find for each of these.

5. Locate one of the articles you found. Copy the first page and return it to your instructor with this assignment.

6. Write the correct bibliographic citation for the article you found on this individual. (Use the bibliographic citation examples in Appendix A.)

Biographical Information

11   Instructor: _____   Course/Section: _____

Namo: _____

Date: _____   Points: _____

Using Biographical Dictionaries

Biographical dictionaries give information on the lives of individuals who are outstanding or well-known for their accomplishments. Using the *Biographical Directory of the American Congress, 1774–1989*, find a biography of Thomas Jefferson and give the following information.

1. What is the call number of the *Biographical Directory of the American Congress, 1774–1989?*

2. Was Thomas Jefferson the second president of the United States? If not, which one was he?

3. List three of his major achievements.

    a.

    b.

    c.

4. When did he die? Where is he buried?

5. Describe any civic involvements mentioned in the entry.

6. What educational level did he achieve?

7. From which school did he graduate?

Using a different biographical dictionary, look up information on the life of an individual in whom you are interested or one assigned by your instructor. Give the following information:

8. Name of person you selected:

9. Title of biographical dictionary used:

10. How did you find this biographical dictionary? (Library catalog, browse reference, ask for help?)

11. Call number of the biographical dictionary used:

12. Identify the individual's:

    Place of birth:

    Date of birth, and death if not living:

    Occupation or profession:

13. Write a bibliographic entry for the article you have found. Use the examples in Appendix A.

14. Write a brief paragraph giving a few facts about the person's accomplishments.

Exercise 11.6 Biographical Information

11

Instructor: _____ Course/Section: _____

Name: _____

Date: _____ Points: _____

Finding Biographies in the Online Catalog

Use your library's online catalog to find biographical information on one of the following individuals. Circle the name of the individual you look up.

Malcolm X	John Keats	Frank Lloyd Wright
Simon Bolivar	Genghis Khan	Benjamin Franklin
Ralph Bunche	Jawaharial Nehru	Cleopatra
Adolf Hitler	Carl Schurz	Joseph Stalin
Sitting Bull	Ho Chi Minh	

1. Locate at least one work **about** the individual you selected.
   Record the title and call number.

2. What command did you use to find the biography of this individual?

3. Retrieve one biography of the individual above. Write a bibliographic citation to the work that you locate. (Use the examples given in Appendix A.)

4. Briefly describe a few of the major accomplishments of that individual.

12

Book Reviews, Literary Criticism, and Literature in Collections

"What we become depends on what we read after all of the professors have finished with us. The greatest university of all is a collection of books."

THOMAS CARLYLE

INTRODUCTION

Have you ever looked for a poem that you learned when you were a child but have not seen in print since? Or a short story that you read several years ago but can't recall where it appeared? Or a review of a current book? Or a critique of a novel? This chapter reviews a variety of sources that would help you find this type of information.

Just as you use indexes to find individual articles in magazines, journals, and newspapers, so also must you use special finding aids to find book reviews, individual poems, stories, essays, plays, speeches, and articles or essays that criticize or analyze an author's literary work. Becoming familiar with some key finding aids for these types of materials is extremely useful.

◆ BOOK REVIEWS

Reviews of most new books and of forthcoming books are published in newspapers and magazines and on the Internet. Written by critics and journalists, book reviews provide descriptions and critical evaluations of books. The success or failure of a book's sale frequently depends on whether or not it receives positive reviews.

GUIDELINES FOR FINDING BOOK REVIEWS

▼ Search the Internet.
▼ Use an index to book reviews.
▼ Search a periodical index or database.

Internet

An advantage of the Internet over printed sources for book reviews is that book reviews often appear online before they appear in print. Following are sites to help locate book reviews on the Internet.

ACQWEB's Directory of Book Reviews on the Web. ACQWEB. 1994–2000. 28 Apr. 2000 <http://www.library.vanderbilt.edu/law/acqs/bookrev.html>.
   Extensive list of sites for book reviews, arranged by categories.
Amazon.com. Amazon.com, c1996–2000. 23 Apr. 2000 <http://www.amazon.com/>.
   Often includes a table of contents, editorial reviews, and customer reviews of books available for sale.
BookReviews.net. n. d. 24 Apr. 2000 < http://www.bookreviews.net/>.
   Provides general links, children's books, newspaper book reviews, etc. Includes many links for librarians and others for book review sources online. Included are nonbook sites as well as subject links.
Book Spot. StartSpot Mediaworks. 1997–2000. 24 Apr. 2000 <http://www.bookspot.com/bookreviews.htm>.
   Links to book reviews for current titles in *Booklist*, the *New York Times*, and *New York Review of Books*, among others. Includes a list of top choices for the year.

Indexes to Book Reviews

Indexes to book reviews are good sources for reviews of books appearing in periodicals and newspapers. Some of these indexes have excerpts from the reviews, while others only list the sources.

To find book reviews in an index, you must have the publication date and either the author's name or title of the work. Three sources for book reviews are:

Book Review Digest. New York: H.W. Wilson, 1905–.
> An alphabetical listing by authors of books. Each entry includes the title of the book, bibliographical information, and publisher's note. The publisher's note is followed by references to the reviews that appear in periodicals. Some of the references include excerpts from the book reviews. Also includes a subject and title index. A list of periodicals indexed is located in the front. Issued monthly with annual cumulation.

Book Review Index, a Master Cumulation. Detroit: Gale, 1955–.
> Provides citations for book reviews and includes both author and title indexes. Includes list of abbreviated journal titles.

Combined Retrospective Index to Book Reviews in Humanities Journals, 1802–1974. Ed. Evan Ira Farber. 10 vols. Woodbridge, CT: Research Publications, 1983–1984.
> An author and title access to about 500,000 reviews from 150 humanities journals. Names of reviewers are also given. Volume 10 has a title index.

Figure 12.1 illustrates a page from *Book Review Index* with citations to reviews of Claudia Goldin's work, *Understanding the Gender Gap*.

Note that a review of *Understanding the Gender Gap* is in *American Historical Review (AHR)* and *Journal of Literary History (JLH)*. A list of abbreviations for the journals listed in the entries can be found at the beginning of *Book Review Index*.

The title entry for the book, *Understanding the Gender Gap*, is shown in Figure 12.2.

Fire! The Beginnings of the Labor Movement
(Illus. by James Watling)
 c   BL - v88 - My 1 '92 - p1600 [51-250]
 c   CCB-B - v45 - Ap '92 - p206 [51-250]
 c   HB - v68 - Jl '92 - p474 [51-250]
 c   KR - v60 - My 15 '92 - p677 [51-250]
 c   LT - v5 - S '92 - p23 [51-250]
 c   SLJ - v38 - Jl '92 - p73 [51-250]
Just Enough Is Plenty
 c   Inst - v101 - N '91 - p23

Goldin, Claudia - *Strategic Factors in Nineteenth
Century American Economic History*
   Choice - v30 - S '92 - p185 [51-250]
Understanding the Gender Gap
   AHR - v96 - O '91 - p1271
   JEL - v29 - S '91 - p1153
   JIH - v22 - Win '92 - p477
   JPE - v99 - D '91 - p1332
   J Soc H - v25 - Win '91 - p430
   Signs - v17 - Aut '91 - p220

Goldin, Grace - *Speak Out for Age*
   Bloom Rev - v12 - Mr '92 - p23 [251-500]
Goldin, Ian - *Agricultural Trade Liberalization*
   Econ Bks - v18 - Sum '91 - p91
Golding, Sue - *Gramsci's Democratic Theory*
   UPBN - v4 - Je '92 - p25 [1-50]
Golding, William - *Lord of the Flies*
 y   BIC - v20 - O '91 - p26
 y   BL - v88 - F 15 '92 - p1100 [1-50]
   GW - v145 - S 29 '91 - p25
The Paper Men
   GW - v145 - S 29 '91 - p25
The Pyramid
   GW - v145 - S 29 '91 - p25
Rites of Passage
   GW - v145 - S 29 '91 - p25
The Spire
   GW - v145 - S 29 '91 - p25
Goldman, Alan H - *Empirical Knowledge*
   Phil R - v101 - Ap '92 - p428 + [501 +]
Goldman, Albert - *Elvis*
   Choice - v29 - Ap '92 - p1192 + [501 +]
Ladies and Gentlemen–Lenny Bruce!!
   Trib Bks - F 2 '92 - p8
The Lives of John Lennon
   Choice - v29 - Ap '92 - p1192 + [501 +]
Sound Bites
 y   BL - v88 - My 15 '92 - p1653 [51-250]
 y   BL - v88 - My 15 '92 - p1669 [1-50]
   BW - v22 - Ag 9 '92 - p6 [251-500]
   KR - v60 - Ap 15 '92 - p530 [51-250]
   LJ - v117 - My 1 '92 - p83 [51-250]
   PW - v239 - Ap 13 '92 - p51 [51-250]
Goldman, Alvin I - *Liaisons: Philosophy Meets the
Cognitive and Social Sciences*
   Choice - v29 - Jl '92 - p1693 [51-250]
Goldman, Ari L - *The Search for God at Harvard*
   CC - v109 - Ja 1 '92 - p19
   Ch Today - v35 - N 25 '91 - p35
   Comt - v92 - O '91 - p54
   NL - v74 - N 4 '91 - p23
   NYTBR - v97 - Je 14 '92 - p32 [51-250]
   PW - v239 - Ap 20 '92 - p51 [1-50]
   TT - v48 - O '91 - p338
Goldman, Benjamin A - *The Truth about Where
You Live*
 r   BL - v88 - F 1 '92 - p1058
 r   Choice - v29 - My '92 - p1427 [51-250]
 r   LJ - v117 - Ap 1 '92 - p110 + [51-250]
 r   New Age - v9 - My '92 - p102 [51-250]
Goldman, Bob - *Death in the Locker Room*
 yr BL - v88 - Jl '92 - p1932 [51-250]
Goldman, Francisco - *The Long Night of White
Chickens*
   BL - v88 - My 15 '92 - p1660 [51-250]
   Boston R - v17 - S '92 - p38 [501 +]
   BW - v22 - Je 7 '92 - p9 [501 +]
   CSM - v84 - Jl 24 '92 - p14 [501 +]
   Esq - v117 - Je '92 - p42 [51-250]
   KR - v60 - Ap 15 '92 - p484 [51-250]
   LATBR - Jl 19 '92 - p3 + [501 +]
   LJ - v117 - Je 1 '92 - p176 [51-250]
   NYTBR - v97 - Ag 16 '92 - p20 [501 +]
   PW - v239 - Ap 13 '92 - p42 + [51-250]
   VV - v37 - Jl 21 '92 - p90 + [501 +]

   KR - v60 - Ja 15 '92 - p91
   LJ - v117 - F 15 '92 - p169
   NYTBR - v97 - Jl 12 '92 - p18 [51-250]
   Obs - Ag 30 '92 - p51 [51-250]
   PW - v239 - F 3 '92 - p74
   W&I - v7 - S '92 - p419 + [501 +]
Goldman, Judith - *The Early Pictures 1861-1964*
(Illus. by James Rosenquist)
   LJ - v117 - Ag '92 - p98 [51-250]
Goldman, Lawrence - *The Blind Victorian*
   AHR - v96 - D '91 - p1651
   VS - v35 - Aut '91 - p90
Goldman, Marshall I - *What Went Wrong with
Perestroika*
   BL - v88 - O 15 '91 - p404
   BW - v21 - N 10 '91 - p12
   Choice - v29 - Mr '92 - p1152 [51-250]
   CSM - v83 - N 8 '91 - p14
   Econ - v322 - Mr 21 '92 - p97 [501 +]
   LJ - v116 - O 15 '91 - p102
   NYRB - v38 - N 7 '91 - p53
   NYTBR - v97 - F 2 '92 - p15
Goldman, Martin E - *The Handbook of Heart
Drugs*
   BL - v88 - Ag '92 - p1985 [51-250]
 r   LJ - v117 - Jl '92 - p76 [51-250]
Goldman, Martin S - *Nat Turner and the
Southhampton Revolt of 1831*
 y   B Rpt - v11 - S '92 - p58 [51-250]
 y   KR - v60 - Ap 1 '92 - p465 [51-250]
 y   SLJ - v38 - Je '92 - p145 [51-250]
 y   VOYA - v15 - Je '92 - p123 + [501 +]
Goldman, Nahum - *Online Information Hunting*
 r   BWatch - v13 - My '92 - p3 + [1-50]
Goldman, Nathan C - *Space Policy*
   SciTech - v16 - Ag '92 - p35 [1-50]
Goldman, Ralph M - *From Warfare to Party
Politics*
   Pers PS - v21 - Spr '92 - p124 [501 +]
The National Party Chairmen and Committees
   APSR - v86 - Mr '92 - p237 + [501 +]
Goldman, Robert - *Mapping Hegemony*
   Choice - v29 - Jl '92 - p1671 [51-250]
Goldman, Robert M - *A Free Ballot and a Fair
Count*
   JSH - v58 - Ag '92 - p552 + [251-500]
Goldman, Roger - *Thurgood Marshall: Justice for
All*
   LATBR - Ag 9 '92 - p1 + [501 +]
   LJ - v117 - Jl '92 - p104 [51-250]
   PW - v239 - Je 1 '92 - p47 + [51-250]
Goldman, Steve - *Vibration Spectrum Analysis*
   New TB - v76 - N '91 - p1571 [51-250]
Goldman, Steven L - *Science, Technology, and
Social Progress*
   Isis - v83 - Mr '92 - p168 + [501 +]
Goldman, William - *Hype and Glory*
   Books - v5 - N '91 - p21 + [51-250]
   Obs - O 20 '91 - p61
Goldmann, Nahum - *Online Information Hunting*
   SciTech - v16 - Je '92 - p4 [1-50]
Goldoni, Luca - *Maria Luiga Donna in Carriera*
   BL - v88 - My 15 '92 - p1667 [1-50]
Goldratt, Eliyahu M - *The Goal: A Process of
Ongoing Improvement*
   Mgt R - v81 - Ja '92 - p63 [51-250]
Goldreich, Gloria - *Years of Dreams*
   BL - v88 - Ap 15 '92 - p1502 [51-250]
   KR - v60 - F 1 '92 - p131
   PW - v239 - F 3 '92 - p62
Goldring, Roland - *Fossils in the Field*
 r   New Sci - v134 - My 9 '92 - p40 + [501 +]
   SciTech - v15 - S '91 - p19 [1-50]
Goldsborough, Robert - *The Crain Adventure*
   R&R Bk N - v7 - O '92 - p37 [1-50]
Fade to Black
   Arm Det - v25 - Spr '92 - p251 [51-250]
 y   Kliatt - v26 - Ap '92 - p6 [51-250]
Fade to Black. Audio Version
   Arm Det - v24 - Fall '91 - p500
 y   Kliatt - v26 - Ap '92 - p58 [51-250]
Silver Spire
   KR - v60 - Ag 15 '92 - p1019 [51-250]
   PW - v239 - Ag 31 '92 - p67 [51-250]

   CS - v21 - Jl '92 - p444 + [501 +]
   CS - v21 - Jl '92 - p445 + [501 +]
   JMF - v54 - My '92 - p464 + [501 +]
   Wom R Bks - v9 - D '91 - p16
Goldschmidt, Arthur, Jr. - *A Concise History of the
Middle East. 4th ed., Rev. and Updated*
   MEJ - v46 - Win '92 - p122
   R&R Bk N - v6 - D '91 - p5 [1-50]
Goldschmidt, Bertrand - *Atomic Rivals*
   T&C - v33 - Ja '92 - p177 + [501 +]
Goldschmidt, Georges-Arthur - *Die Absonderung*
   TLS - Mr 6 '92 - p22 [251-500]
   WLT - v66 - Spr '92 - p331 [251-500]
Goldschmidt, Walter - *The Human Career*
   A Anth - v93 - D '91 - p977
Goldsmith, Alix - *Celebritest: Intimate Profiles of
Seventy Celebrities*
   FIR - v43 - Mr '92 - p130 + [51-250]
Goldsmith, Andrea - *Modern Interiors*
   Aust Bk R - S '91 - p15
Goldsmith, Arnold L - *The Modern American
Urban Novel*
   MFS - v37 - Win '91 - p760 [251-500]
Goldsmith, Arthur A - *Building Agricultural
Institutions*
   Pac A - v65 - Spr '92 - p116 + [501 +]
Goldsmith, Barrie - *Monitoring for Conservation
and Ecology*
   Choice - v29 - N '91 - p468
   ECOL - v73 - Je '92 - p1134 + [501 +]
   New TB - v76 - S '91 - p1290 + [51-250]
   QRB - v67 - Je '92 - p228 [251-500]
Goldsmith, Colin - *Extensions of Calculus*
   TES - O 11 '91 - p44
Goldsmith, Deward - *The Earth Report*
   HMR - S '90 - p9
Goldsmith, Donald - *The Astronomers*
 y   B Rpt - v10 - N '91 - p51
 y   WLB - v65 - Je '91 - p162
Goldsmith, Edward - *The Way: An Ecological
World View*
   TLS - S 11 '92 - p5 [501 +]
Goldsmith, Elizabeth C - *Writing the Female Voice*
   Can Lit - Aut '91 - p156 + [501 +]
Goldsmith, Emanuel S - *The American Judaism of
Mordecai M. Kaplan*
   Choice - v29 - D '91 - p652
Goldsmith, John A - *Autosegmental and Metrical
Phonology*
   MLJ - v76 - Sum '92 - p259 [501 +]
Goldsmith, Lynn - *Circus Dreams*
   Ant & CH - v96 - N '91 - p45
Goldsmith, Olivia - *The First Wives Club*
   BL - v88 - Mr 15 '92 - p1335 + [51-250]
   BW - v22 - Mr 1 '92 - p12 [1-50]
   KR - v59 - D 15 '91 - p1549
   LJ - v117 - Ja '92 - p174
   NYTBR - v97 - My 10 '92 - p17 [251-500]
   PW - v239 - Ja 6 '92 - p48
   Trib Bks - Mr 22 '92 - p6 [51-250]
The First Wives Club. Audio Version
   LJ - v117 - My 1 '92 - p132 [51-250]
   PW - v239 - My 4 '92 - p26 [51-250]
Goldsmith, Timothy H - *The Biological Roots of
Human Nature*
   Choice - v29 - Je '92 - p1568 [51-250]
Goldstaub, Sylvia - *Unconditional Love*
   Advocate - Je 16 '92 - p117 [51-250]
   Lam Bk Rpt - v3 - My '92 - p46 [1-50]
Goldsteen, Raymond L - *Demanding Democracy
after Three Mile Island*
   AJS - v98 - Jl '92 - p197 + [501 +]
   Choice - v29 - Ap '92 - p1290 [51-250]
   CS - v21 - Jl '92 - p487 [251-500]
Goldstein, Allan L - *Combination Therapies*
   SciTech - v16 - Je '92 - p17 [51-250]
Goldstein, Avery - *From Bandwagon to Balance-of-
Power Politics*
   Choice - v29 - N '91 - p515
Goldstein, Bobbye S - *What's on the Menu? (Illus.
by Chris L Demerest)*
 c   BL - v88 - Ap 15 '92 - p1534 [51-250]
 c   SLJ - v38 - Jl '92 - p68 [51-250]
Goldstein, Darra - *A Taste of Russia*

Figure 12.1. Entries from *Book Review Index.* (Reprinted by permission of Gale Research, Inc.)

UNDERSTANDING/ *Title Index*

Understanding the Fourth Gospel - Ashton,
  John
Understanding the Gender Gap - Golding,
  Claudia

Figure 12.2. Title Index, *Book Review Index,* 1992, *p. 1470.* (Reprinted by permission of Gale Research, Inc.)

Sample pages from *Book Review Digest* are shown in Figures 12.3–12.5. Figure 12.3 illustrates how to use *Book Review Digest.* Figure 12.4 is a page from the subject/title index of *Book Review Digest* showing entries for the subject "women—employment." Note the citation to a review of the book, *Gender & Racial Inequality at Work* by D. Tomaskovic-Devey.

Once you identify the full title of the periodical in which a review appears you can search the library catalog to see if it is in your library. Use a title search for the title of the periodical. Check the holdings screen for the specific issues you need.

EXAMPLE
t=booklist
t=choice

Periodical Indexes and Databases

Periodical indexes and databases, discussed in Chapter 8, can be useful in finding book reviews. To find reviews of books on certain topics you might search a database by using the search phrase "[subject] and book review." If you know the author of the book you might search for "[author] and book review." A search in *EBSCOhost* for "book review and literature" lists book reviews in a variety of publications on topics dealing with literature. You can also search by the title of the book.

Sample Entry

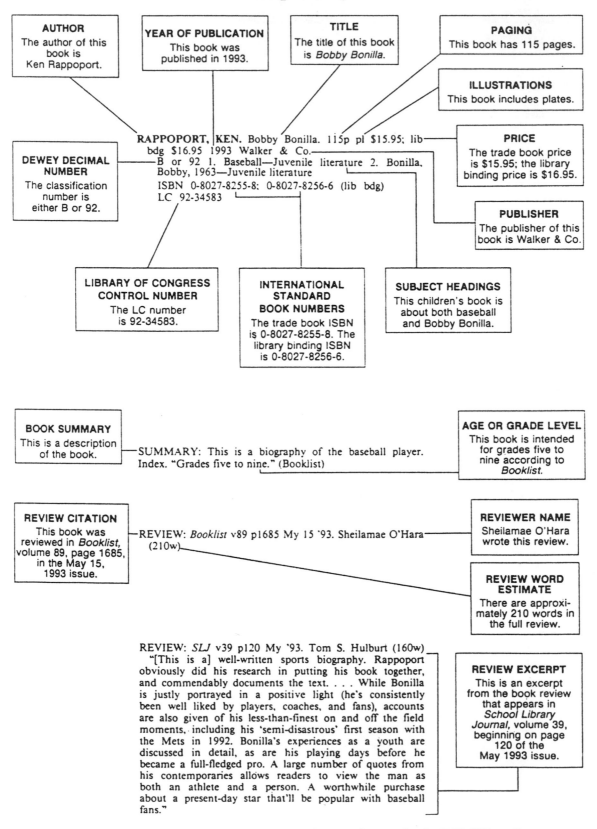

AUTHOR
The author of this book is Ken Rappoport.

YEAR OF PUBLICATION
This book was published in 1993.

TITLE
The title of this book is *Bobby Bonilla*.

PAGING
This book has 115 pages.

ILLUSTRATIONS
This book includes plates.

DEWEY DECIMAL NUMBER
The classification number is either B or 92.

PRICE
The trade book price is $15.95; the library binding price is $16.95.

PUBLISHER
The publisher of this book is Walker & Co.

RAPPOPORT, KEN. Bobby Bonilla. 115p pl $15.95; lib bdg $16.95 1993 Walker & Co.
B or 92 1. Baseball—Juvenile literature 2. Bonilla, Bobby, 1963—Juvenile literature
ISBN 0-8027-8255-8; 0-8027-8256-6 (lib bdg)
LC 92-34583

LIBRARY OF CONGRESS CONTROL NUMBER
The LC number is 92-34583.

INTERNATIONAL STANDARD BOOK NUMBERS
The trade book ISBN is 0-8027-8255-8. The library binding ISBN is 0-8027-8256-6.

SUBJECT HEADINGS
This children's book is about both baseball and Bobby Bonilla.

BOOK SUMMARY
This is a description of the book.

AGE OR GRADE LEVEL
This book is intended for grades five to nine according to *Booklist*.

SUMMARY: This is a biography of the baseball player. Index. "Grades five to nine." (Booklist)

REVIEW CITATION
This book was reviewed in *Booklist*, volume 89, page 1685, in the May 15, 1993 issue.

REVIEWER NAME
Sheilamae O'Hara wrote this review.

REVIEW WORD ESTIMATE
There are approximately 210 words in the full review.

REVIEW: *Booklist* v89 p1685 My 15 '93. Sheilamae O'Hara (210w)

REVIEW: *SLJ* v39 p120 My '93. Tom S. Hulburt (160w)
"[This is a] well-written sports biography. Rappoport obviously did his research in putting his book together, and commendably documents the text. . . . While Bonilla is justly portrayed in a positive light (he's consistently been well liked by players, coaches, and fans), accounts are also given of his less-than-finest on and off the field moments, including his 'semi-disastrous' first season with the Mets in 1992. Bonilla's experiences as a youth are discussed in detail, as are his playing days before he became a full-fledged pro. A large number of quotes from his contemporaries allows readers to view the man as both an athlete and a person. A worthwhile purchase about a present-day star that'll be popular with baseball fans."

REVIEW EXCERPT
This is an excerpt from the book review that appears in *School Library Journal*, volume 39, beginning on page 120 of the May 1993 issue.

Figure 12.3. Sample entry from *Book Review Digest*. (Copyright 1994 by the H.W. Wilson Company. Reprinted by permission.)

The wine-dark sea. O'Brian, P.
Winged victory. Perret, G.
Wingfield, George, 1876-1959
  Raymond, C. E. George Wingfield
The wings of a falcon. Voigt, C.
Wings of hope and daring. Stenberg, C.
Winik, Marion
  Winik, M. Telling
Winn-Dixie Stores, Inc.
  Staten, V. Can you trust a tomato in January?
The winner within. Riley, P.
Winnicott, D. W. (Donald Woods), 1896-1971
  Phillips, A. On kissing, tickling, and being bored
Winnicott, Donald Woods *See* Winnicott, D. W. (Donald Woods), 1896-1971
Winning the grand award. Iritz, M. H.
Winning ugly. Gilbert, B.
Winslow, Marcella Comès
  Winslow, M. C. Brushes with the literary
Winter
        Juvenile literature
  Honda, T. Wild horse winter
  Maass, R. When winter comes
Winter camp. Hill, K.
Winter fox. Brutschy, J.
The Winter Prince. Wein, E. E.
Winter sports
        See also
  Sleds and sledding
Winter's orphans. Farentinos, R. C.
Wipe your feet!. Lehan, D.
Wiretapping
        See also
  Eavesdropping
Wisconsin
        History
  Apps, J. W. Breweries of Wisconsin
        Politics and government
  Woliver, L. R. From outrage to action
        Rural conditions
  Pederson, J. M. Between memory and reality
Wise, Isaac Mayer, 1819-1900
  Temkin, S. D. Isaac Mayer Wise, shaping American Judaism
The wish for kings. Lapham, L. H.
Wishbones. Wilson, B. K.
Wit and humor
        See also ·
  American wit and humor
  Comedy
  Jokes
  Tall tales
  Grizzard, L. I took a lickin' and kept on tickin'
  James, S. The adventures of Stout Mama
  White, B. Mama makes up her mind
        Juvenile literature
  Talbott, H. Your pet dinosaur, an owner's manual
Witchcraft
  Gragg, L. D. The Salem witch crisis
  Hester, M. Lewd women and wicked witches
The witches and the singing mice. Nimmo, J.
The witch's face. Kimmel, E. A.
Witch's fire. Butler, B.
With a Black platoon in combat. Rishell, L.
With liberty and justice for some. Kairys, D.
With teeth in the earth. Tussman, M. H.
With women's eyes
Within reach
Without consent or contract
Without remorse. Clancy, T.
Without sin. Klaw, S. ·
Witness against the beast. Thompson, E. P.
Witness for freedom
Witness to disintegration. Hixson, W. L.
A witness to genocide. Gutman, R.
Wives
        See also
  Abused women
  Widows
The wives of Bath. Swan, S. E.
The wizard next door. Glassman, P.
A Wizard's dozen
Woiwode, Larry
  Woiwode, L. Acts
Wojnarowicz, David, 1954-1992
  Wojnarowicz, D. Memories that smell like gasoline
Wole Soyinka revisited. Wright, D.
Wolf, Hugo, 1860-1903
  Youens, S. Hugo Wolf

Wolf, Lucien, 1857-1930
  Levene, M. War, Jews, and the new Europe
The wolf. Bradshaw, J.
The wolf & the raven. Paxson, D. L.
Wolf at the door. Corcoran, B.
Wolf children *See* Wild children
Wolf whistle. Nordan, L.
Wolfe, Michael, 1945-
  Wolfe, M. The hadj
Wolfpack (Basketball team) *See* North Carolina State Wolfpack (Basketball team)
Wollstonecraft, Mary, 1759-1797
        Fiction
  Sherwood, F. Vindication
Wolves
        Juvenile literature
  Bradshaw, J. The wolf
  Brandenburg, J. To the top of the world
  Greene, C. Reading about the gray wolf
  Patent, D. H. Dogs
  Simon, S. Wolves
Wolves. Simon, S.
Woman at the edge of two worlds. Andrews, L. V.
A woman at war. Moore, M.
Woman changing woman. Rutter, V. B.
A woman doctor's guide to menopause. Jovanovic-Peterson, L.
The woman reader, 1837-1914. Flint, K.
A woman unafraid. Colman, P.
A woman's book of choices. Chalker, R.
The woman's heart book. Pashkow, F. J.
A woman's view. Basinger, J.
A woman's worth. Williamson, M.
Women ———————————— SUBJECT HEADING
        See also
  Abused women
  Black women   } —— CROSS REFERENCES
  Jewish women
  Social work with women
  White women
  Heidensohn, F. Women in control?
        Bibliography ———— SUBDIVISION
  Bindocci, C. G. Women and technology
        Biography
  Boyer, R. M. Apache mothers and daughters —— AUTHOR AND TITLE OF BOOK
  Notable Hispanic American women
  Shepherd, N. A price below rubies
        Dictionaries
  Mahoney, M. H. Women in espionage
  The Norton book of women's lives
        Books and reading
  Flint, K. The woman reader, 1837-1914
  Turner, C. Living by the pen
        Civil rights
        See also
  Pro-choice movement
  Pro-life movement
  Alonso, H. H. Peace as a women's issue
  Costain, A. N. Inviting women's rebellion
  Daniels, C. R. At women's expense
  Ferraro, G. A. Changing history
        Dictionaries
  Franck, I. M. The women's desk reference
        Diaries
  Clarke, P. Life lines
        Diseases
        See also
  Women—Health and hygiene
  Confronting cancer, constructing change
  Helfant, R. H. Women, take heart
  Lockie, A. The women's guide to homeopathy
  McGinn, K. A. Women's cancers
  Pashkow, F. J. The woman's heart book
        Education
  Powers, J. B. The "girl question" in education
  Unsettling relations
        Employment
  Agonito, R. No more "nice girl"
  Amott, T. L. Caught in the crisis
  Cook, A. H. The most difficult revolution
  Driscoll, D.-M. Members of the club
  Glazer, N. Y. Women's paid and unpaid labor
  Murphy, T. A. Ten hours' labor
  Sokoloff, N. J. Black women and white women in the professions
  Strom, S. H. Beyond the typewriter
  Tomaskovic-Devey, D. Gender & racial inequality at work
  Turbin, C. Working women of collar city

Figure 12.4. Subject and Title Index from *Book Review Digest, 1994,* p. 2545. (Copyright 1994 by the H.W. Wilson Company. Reprinted by permission.)

TOLKIN, MICHAEL—*Continued*
mall. In addition, Tolkin has no sense of humour at all. . . . [The novel] is consistently, stultifyingly dull, despite its graphic descriptions of trolleys of unmatched limbs, barrels of human viscera in the air-crash morgue. [It] might make a good film. As a novel, however, it is still-born."

TOLLEFSON, JAMES W. The strength not to fight; an oral history of conscientious objectors of the Vietnam War. 248p $22.95 1993 Little, Brown
    959.704   1. Vietnam   War,   1961-1975—
    Conscientious objectors
    ISBN 0-316-85112-4   LC 92-36335

SUMMARY: The author examines the "experiences of conscientious objectors (CO) during the Vietnam War. The personal histories resulting from the author's interviews . . . discuss why people resisted the war, how they were able to gain CO status, and what were the consequences of their actions." (Libr J) Bibliography.

REVIEW: *Choice* v31 p664 D '93. R.E. Marcello (180w)
    "Tollefson, himself a conscientious objector during the Vietnam War, has written this book based on in-depth interviews with 40 anonymous men who shared his convictions about that conflict. He does not pretend to have used a scientific sampling in selecting his subjects. Tollefson uses a clever format. Instead of writing a series of separate, individual stories, he organized the book around the major experiences of the conscientious objectors. His purpose, through these highly personal and sometimes emotional accounts, is to understand and convey accurately the experiences of his interviewees. . . . He makes no judgments, neither praising nor apologizing for nor condemning his interviewees. Good bibliography of secondary sources on conscientious objection."

REVIEW: *Libr J* v118 p154 Je 1 '93. Robert Favini (110w)
    "[Tollefson] lets the collective power of many varied stories provide a chronicle of the men who sought CO status as well as the society in which they lived. This book will serve as a fine complement to Christian Appy's oral history, Working-Class War: American Combat Soldiers and Vietnam [BRD 1993]. The extensive bibliography renders the book even more valuable. Recommended for all libraries."

TOLLISON, ROBERT D. The National Collegiate Athletic Association. See Fleisher, A. A.

TOM, LINDA C., il. Random House American Sign Language dictionary. See Costello, E.

TOMASKO, ROBERT M. Rethinking the corporation; the architecture of change. 213p il $22.95 1993 AMACOM
    658.4   1. Corporations 2. Management 3. Organizational change
    ISBN 0-8144-5022-9   LC 93-9246

SUMMARY: This book argues against "the unstructured reduction of managerial staff. . . . Downsizing for the purpose of saving funds without significant planning and consideration of human needs and aspirations, Tomasko asserts, can lead to long-term problems. Jobs within the enterprise need to be meaningful to the workers—especially to one of the corporation's most valuable resources, the middle manager. Tomasko stresses the necessity for teamwork in planning, a diminution of hierarchy, and the use of professional as well as managerial career paths." (Libr J) Index.

REVIEW: *Bus Horiz* v37 p87 My/Je '94. Henry H. Beam (1200w)

REVIEW: *Choice* v31 p644 D '93. G. Klinefelter (170w)
    "Tomasko focuses on two groups of readers; those in the organization who have the power and responsibility to bring about change and those who are on the receiving end of change. A renowned consultant in organizational structure and architectural structure, he approaches the subject of organizational planning from the perspective of an archi-

tect, covering such topics as construction of stable structures, dealing with constraints, and effectively combining several components into a unified entity. . . . An interesting and creative approach to an important topic for managers as they guide their organizations into the 21st century."

REVIEW: *Libr J* v118 p148 Je 1 '93. Littleton M. Maxwell (150w)
    "Tomasko (Downsizing: Reshaping the Corporation, 1990) . . . recommends a corporate structure that is strong and economical, but, above all, not too rigid. This thought-provoking book is recommended for public, academic, and corporate collections."

TOMASKOVIC-DEVEY, DONALD. Gender & racial inequality at work; the sources & consequences of job segregation. (Cornell studies in industrial and labor relations, no27) 212p $38; pa $16.95 1993 ILR Press
    331.13   1. Discrimination in employment 2. Sex discrimination 3. Race discrimination 4. Women—Employment 5. Blacks—Employment
    ISBN 0-87546-304-5; 0-87546-305-3 (pa)
    LC 93-16551

SUMMARY: This study is based on data from the 1989 North Carolina Employment and Health Survey. The author examines black-white and male-female inequalities in employment and job-level segregation by race and sex. "Within economic and sociological frameworks, he theorizes about such organizational and public policy issues as comparable worth and affirmative action." (Booklist) Bibliography. Index.

REVIEW: *Booklist* v89 p2019 Ag '93. David Rouse (150w)
    "Librarians need no reminder that one sex or the other is usually predominant in many jobs or professions. But if they are looking for empirical, scholarly evidence of both some of the sources and many of the consequences of so-called job segregation, Tomaskovic-Devey provides it. A North Carolina State University sociology professor, he uses a 1989 North Carolina employment and health survey, unique because it included a random sample of all occupations from the general population, to develop and support his conclusions. . . . Recommended for research-oriented collections."

REVIEW: *Choice* v31 p877 Ja '94. E. Hu-DeHart (180w)
    "Tomaskovic-Devey's study is a valuable contribution to what can be termed 'glass ceiling research'—that is, an inquiry into job segregation and subsequent barriers to upward mobility for groups of workers (as opposed to individuals) in the workplace. . . . [His] conclusions about race, however, are based on research concerning black workers only. Further, Tomaskovic-Devey does not thoroughly explore the intersection of gender and race. . . . Despite the obviously relevant and timely nature of this topic for the majority of American workers (women and minorities), those uninitiated in the technical discourse of social science research will not find this book very accessible."

CITATION TO BOOK BEING REVIEWED

PUBLISHER'S SUMMARY

CITATION TO REVIEW

EXCERPT FROM REVIEW

TOMASSI, NOREEN, ed. Money for international exchange in the arts. See Money for international exchange in the arts

TOMB, HOWARD, 1959-. MicroAliens; dazzling journeys with an electron microscope; [by] Howard Tomb and Dennis Kunkel; with drawings by Tracy Dockray. 79p il $16 1993 Farrar, Straus & Giroux
    578   1. Microorganisms—Juvenile literature 2. Electron microscope and microscopy—Juvenile literature
    ISBN 0-374-34960-6   LC 93-1403

SUMMARY: In this book, text and photographs taken with an electron microscope examine such items as bird feathers, fleas, skin, mold, and blood. "Grades four to eight." (SLJ)

Figure 12.5. Main entry section, *Book Review Digest, 1994,* p. 2074. (Copyright 1994 by the H.W. Wilson Company. Reprinted by permission.)

Other databases useful for finding book reviews include:

Arts & Humanities Citation Index (Web of Science). Philadelphia: ISI, 1989–.
 Updated weekly. Contains data on items from more than 1,144 journals, including individually selected relevant items from more than 6,800 science and social sciences journals. Searches can be limited to book reviews as a document type. Available by subscription only.

Humanities Abstracts. New York: H.W. Wilson, 1984–. Available from *WilsonWeb, FirstSearch, SilverPlatter,* and others.
 Updated monthly. Indexes more than 300 key humanities publications, including reviews of books, plays, ballets, musicals, and television and radio programs.

Readers' Guide Abstracts. New York: H.W. Wilson, 1984–. Available from *WilsonWeb, FirstSearch, SilverPlatter,* and others.
 Comprehensive abstracting and indexing for periodicals with full text of selected periodicals back to January 1994. Includes book reviews as well as reviews of movies and plays.

◆ LITERARY CRITICISM

Works of literary criticism contain articles or essays that evaluate, judge, describe, analyze, or compare an author's novel, poem, play, short story, or other literary work.

Defining Terms

Definitions are sometimes needed for particular literary terms, such as "allusion," "satire," etc. Below are three useful sources for this type of information.

Cuddon, J. A. *A Dictionary of Literary Terms and Literary Theory*. New York: Blackwell, 1998.

Harmon, William, and Hugh C. Holman. *A Handbook to Literature*. New York: Simon & Schuster, 1999.

Harris, Robert. *A Glossary of Literary Terms and A Handbook of Rhetorical Devices*. University of Kentucky, n.d. 24 Apr. 2000 <http://www.uky.edu/ArtsSciences/Classics/Harris/rhetform.html>.

Finding Literary Criticism

Since many of the finding aids for literary criticism are arranged by time periods, by type of literature, or other criteria, you must consider the following questions.

ASK YOURSELF

- ◆ Is the author living or dead?
- ◆ Where and when did the author live?
- ◆ What genre of literature is he/she known for: short stories, drama, poetry, novels, plays?
- ◆ What is the primary language of his/her writings?

To find literary criticism, you can search the Internet, use a database, search the online catalog, find a biography of the author that includes criticism, or use an index to literary criticism.

Internet

The *Online Literary Criticism Collection* of the Internet Public Library, available at http://www.ipl.org/ref/litcrit/guide.html, provides links to both literary criticism and summaries of many works. Northern Light, a search engine, available at http://www.northernlight.com/, allows searching by author as well as more specific searches for literary criticism of an author.

> **EXAMPLE** ■
>
> A search for "Toni Morrison criticism" (with the quotation marks) brings up 9 hits.
>
> The same search, without the quotation marks, results in 146 hits that are organized in "folders" such as: Morrison, Toni—works, studies, & biography; book reviews, and class notes and assignments.

Literary Index, produced by Gale Publishing Company, is a free online index to forty of Gale's printed sources. It can be found at http://www.galenet.com/servlet/LitIndex. The entries include location information only; no textual information is available. However, it is a quick and easy way to locate biographies of authors and critical essays on their writings found in the Gale literary series.

Other Internet sources will be identified with the finding aids discussed below.

Databases

Contemporary Authors. Gale Group, continuous updating. Web access.
> Covers more than 100,000 modern authors from a wide range of media who were active prior to 1960 and whose works continue to influence contemporary literature. Information is drawn from the entire *Contemporary Authors* print series. Available by subscription only.

Literature Research Center. Gale Group, continuous updating. Web access.
> Provides access to the full text of biographies, bibliographies, and critical analysis of authors from every age and literary discipline. It combines three of Gale's most used literary sources—*Contemporary Authors Online*, including more than 100,000 writers; *Contemporary Literary Criticism Select*, with entries on all authors appearing in *CLC* since vol. 95 of the print series and complete profiles of 266 most studied authors from editions prior to vol. 95; and the *Dictionary of Literary Biography Online*, which includes more than 10,000 critical essays on authors and their works written by academic scholars. It is searchable by author, title, genre, literary movement or literary themes. Available by subscription only.

Library Catalog

Commentaries, criticisms, interpretations, and explanatory information about all kinds of literature can be found through the online catalog. Use the author of the original work and selected subheadings of the work. The following two screens from an OPAC illustrate how critical interpretations of Shakespeare's works can be found.

From the Subject Guide screen, select the subheading "criticism and interpretation." Select line six to display entries dealing with criticism and interpretations of Shakespeare's works in general. The Subject Index screen displays individual titles of critical works.

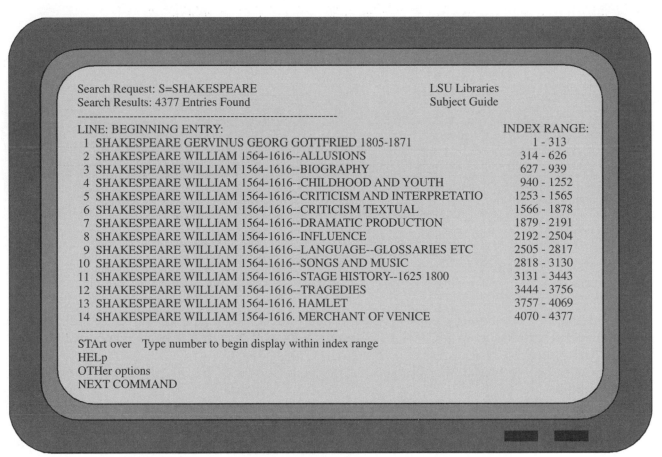

Search Request: S=SHAKESPEARE   LSU Libraries
Search Results: 4377 Entries Found   Subject Guide

LINE: BEGINNING ENTRY: INDEX RANGE:
 1 SHAKESPEARE GERVINUS GEORG GOTTFRIED 1805-1871   1 - 313
 2 SHAKESPEARE WILLIAM 1564-1616--ALLUSIONS   314 - 626
 3 SHAKESPEARE WILLIAM 1564-1616--BIOGRAPHY   627 - 939
 4 SHAKESPEARE WILLIAM 1564-1616--CHILDHOOD AND YOUTH   940 - 1252
 5 SHAKESPEARE WILLIAM 1564-1616--CRITICISM AND INTERPRETATIO   1253 - 1565
 6 SHAKESPEARE WILLIAM 1564-1616--CRITICISM TEXTUAL   1566 - 1878
 7 SHAKESPEARE WILLIAM 1564-1616--DRAMATIC PRODUCTION   1879 - 2191
 8 SHAKESPEARE WILLIAM 1564-1616--INFLUENCE   2192 - 2504
 9 SHAKESPEARE WILLIAM 1564-1616--LANGUAGE--GLOSSARIES ETC   2505 - 2817
10 SHAKESPEARE WILLIAM 1564-1616--SONGS AND MUSIC   2818 - 3130
11 SHAKESPEARE WILLIAM 1564-1616--STAGE HISTORY--1625 1800   3131 - 3443
12 SHAKESPEARE WILLIAM 1564-1616--TRAGEDIES   3444 - 3756
13 SHAKESPEARE WILLIAM 1564-1616. HAMLET   3757 - 4069
14 SHAKESPEARE WILLIAM 1564-1616. MERCHANT OF VENICE   4070 - 4377

STArt over   Type number to begin display within index range
HELp
OTHer options
NEXT COMMAND

Figure 12.6. OPAC subject search, Subject Guide screen.

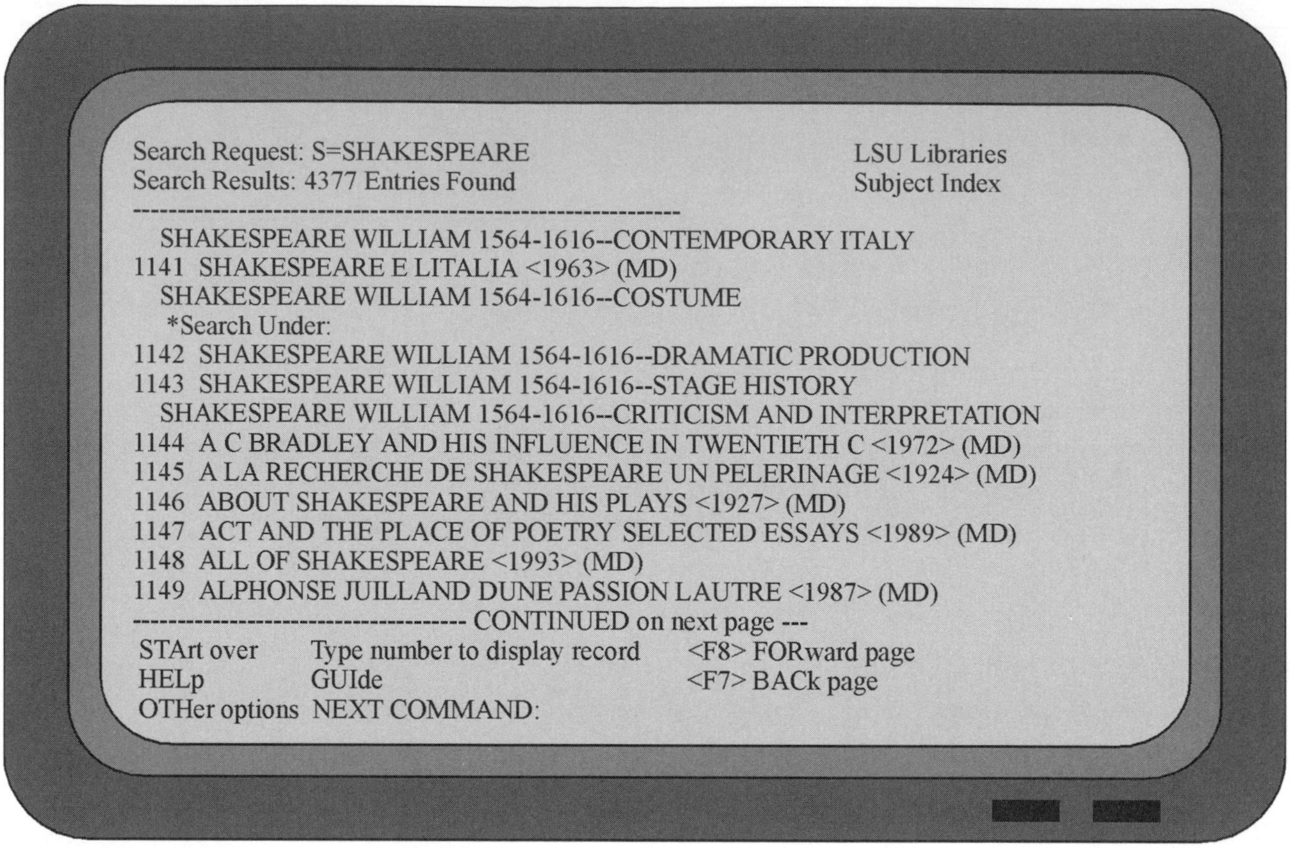

```
Search Request: S=SHAKESPEARE                              LSU Libraries
Search Results: 4377 Entries Found                         Subject Index
-------------------------------------------------------------
    SHAKESPEARE WILLIAM 1564-1616--CONTEMPORARY ITALY
1141  SHAKESPEARE E LITALIA <1963> (MD)
    SHAKESPEARE WILLIAM 1564-1616--COSTUME
  *Search Under:
1142  SHAKESPEARE WILLIAM 1564-1616--DRAMATIC PRODUCTION
1143  SHAKESPEARE WILLIAM 1564-1616--STAGE HISTORY
    SHAKESPEARE WILLIAM 1564-1616--CRITICISM AND INTERPRETATION
1144  A C BRADLEY AND HIS INFLUENCE IN TWENTIETH C <1972> (MD)
1145  A LA RECHERCHE DE SHAKESPEARE UN PELERINAGE <1924> (MD)
1146  ABOUT SHAKESPEARE AND HIS PLAYS <1927> (MD)
1147  ACT AND THE PLACE OF POETRY SELECTED ESSAYS <1989> (MD)
1148  ALL OF SHAKESPEARE <1993> (MD)
1149  ALPHONSE JUILLAND DUNE PASSION LAUTRE <1987> (MD)
-------------------------------- CONTINUED on next page ---
STArt over     Type number to display record     <F8> FORward page
HELp           GUIde                              <F7> BACk page
OTHer options  NEXT COMMAND:
```

Figure 12.7. OPAC Subject Index screen.

Author Biographies

Biographies of authors frequently provide analyses and criticisms of their works. In addition to the biographical sources discussed in Chapter 11, biographies of authors can also be found on the Internet.

Author Guides: Webliography. LSU Libraries. 1995–2000. 24 Apr. 2000 <http://www.lib.lsu.edu/hum/auth-main.html>.
Typical of university libraries' web pages for author information. Includes links to author and publication information.

Contemporary Authors: A Bio-bibliographical Guide to Current Writers in Fiction, General Nonfiction, Poetry, Journalism, Drama, Motion Pictures, Television and Other Fields. Detroit: Gale, 1963–.
Print version that includes articles and references to other sources for criticism.

Dictionary of Literary Biography. Gale Group, continuous updating. Web access.
Updated periodically. Outlines the lives and careers of authors from all eras and genres and summarizes the critical response to their work. Each entry contains personal information, a list of principal works and further readings about the author. Available by subscription only.

Online Literary Criticism Collection. Internet Public Library. 28 Apr. 2000 <http://www.ipl.org/ref/litcrit/>.
A selected list of over 3,000 Web sites providing biographies and criticisms. Can be browsed by author, title, or by nationality of authors.

Yahoo! Authors. Yahoo. 2000. 24 Apr. 2000 <http://dir.yahoo.com/Arts/Humanities/Literature/Authors/>.
Access to selected author biographies and criticisms of their works.

Indexes to Literary Criticism

Some of the following guides are limited to literature of a specific nationality, while others are international in their coverage. Both the titles and the annotations indicate in some measure the scope of the guide.

General

Contemporary Literary Criticism. Detroit: Gale, 1973–.
> Covers living writers and those who died after 1960, includes excerpts and citations from mystery and science fiction authors. Provides extensive annotated bibliographies.

Essay and General Literature Index. New York: H.W. Wilson, 1900/1933–.
> An excellent source for criticism of all types of literature.

Magill, Frank Northern. *Magill's Bibliography of Literary Criticism; Selected Sources for the Study of More than 2,500 Outstanding Works of Western Literature.* 4 vols. Englewood Cliffs, NJ: Salem, 1979.
> Criticisms in books, parts of books, and periodicals of poetry, drama, and fiction.

Modern Language Association International Bibliography. 1921–. CD-ROM version called *MLA* (database). Also available on the Internet.
> Coverage for the online version began with 1981 and is updated quarterly. Includes criticism of many literary works.

Nineteenth-Century Literary Criticism. Detroit: Gale, 1981–.
> Similar to *CLC* and *TCLC*, except it is limited to writers who lived between 1800 and 1900.

Twentieth-Century Literary Criticism. Detroit: Gale, 1978–.
> Similar to *CLC* and *NCLC* above, except it covers authors who died between 1900 and 1960.

Novels

Abernethy, Peter L., Christian J.W. Kloesel, and Jeffry R. Smitten. *English Novel Explication. Supplement.* 6 vols. Hamden, CT: Shoe String, 1976–1997.
> This work supplements and updates the Palmer and Dyson guide. Extends *English Novel Explication series* to 1998.

Gerstenberger, Donna, and George Hendrick. *The American Novel, a Checklist of Twentieth Century Criticism on Novels Written Since 1789.* 2 vols. Denver: Allan Swallow, 1961–1970. Vol. 1, *The American Novel 1789–1959.* Vol. 2, *Criticisms Written 1960–1968.*
> Criticisms are listed under major authors by titles of works. Includes citations from books and periodicals.

Kearney, E.I., and L.S. Fitzgerald. *The Continental Novel, a Checklist of Criticism in English 1967–1980.* Metuchen, NJ: Scarecrow, 1988.
> Critical entries are organized under the following categories: the French novel, the Spanish and Portuguese novel, the Italian novel, the German novel, the Scandinavian novel, and the Russian and East European novel.

Palmer, Helen H., and Anne Jane Dyson. *English Novel Explication: Criticisms to 1972.* Hamden, CT: Shoe String, 1973.
> Cites criticisms found in books and periodicals in English and foreign languages from 1958 to 1972.

Plays (Drama)

Breed, Paul F., and Florence M. Snideman. *Dramatic Criticism Index: A Bibliography of Commentaries on Playwrights from Ibsen to the Avante-Garde.* Detroit: Gale, 1972.
> Includes critical articles from over 200 periodicals and 630 books. Main entries under authors. Includes a title and a critic index.

Eddleman, Floyd Eugene. *American Drama Criticism: Interpretations, 1890–1977.* 2nd ed. Hamden, CT: Shoe String, 1979. *Supplement I,* 1984. *Supplement II,* 1989. *Supplement III* 1992.

Palmer, Helen H. *European Drama Criticism 1900–1975.* 2nd ed. Hamden, CT: Shoe String, 1977.
A source book to critical writings of representative European plays in selected books and periodicals. Information is organized in three parts: (1) alphabetical list of playwrights with critical articles that appear in periodicals and books, (2) a list of books used as sources and a list of periodicals searched, and (3) an author-title index.

Palmer, Helen H., and Anne Jane Dyson. *American Drama Criticism Interpretations, 1890–1965, Inclusive of American Drama since the First Play Produced in America.* Hamden, CT: Shoe String, 1967. *Supplement I,* 1970. *Supplement II,* 1976. *Supplement III,* 1990.
Lists critical articles of American plays located in periodicals, books, and monographs. Arrangement is alphabetical by playwright.

Poetry

Alexander, Harriet Semmes, comp. *American and British Poetry: A Guide to the Criticism.* 2 vols. Athens, OH: Swallow Press/Ohio University Press, 1984–.
Indexes criticisms located in 170 journals and 500 books published between 1925 and 1990. Volume 1 covers the years 1925–1978; volume 2 covers 1979–1990.

Cline, Gloria Stark, and Jeffrey A. Baker. *An Index to Criticisms of British and American Poetry.* Metuchen, NJ: Scarecrow, 1973.
Cites critical articles on poetry published in periodicals and books between 1960 and 1970. List of abbreviations of periodicals used in entries and a bibliography of books cited are found in the back of this work.

Shields, Ellen F. *Contemporary English Poetry: An Annotated Bibliography of Criticism to 1980.* New York: Garland, 1984.

Short Stories

Short Story Criticism. Detroit: Gale. 1988–. Annual.
Criticisms are listed in chronological order. Cumulative author and title indexes are included.

Walker, Warren S. *Twentieth-Century Short Story Explication: Interpretations 1900–1975 of Short Fiction since 1800.* 3rd ed. Hamden, CT: Shoe String, 1977. Supplements, 1961–1991.
Analysis of short stories appearing in books, periodicals, and monographs.

◆ LITERATURE IN COLLECTIONS (ANTHOLOGIES)

The term *anthology* refers to any collection of varied literary compositions. Anthologies can also include works from a period of history or works devoted to a particular subject or theme. Most anthologies include works of varied authorship, but it is not uncommon to have representative works of one author selected by an editor and collected in an anthology. The outstanding characteristic of an anthology is that it includes many different titles of shorter works under one title.

Finding Works Included in Anthologies

Library catalogs usually list the titles of anthologies that the library owns, but they do not include titles of the shorter works in the anthologies. For example, the title, *Ten Modern Masters: An Anthology of the Short Story,* would be listed in the catalog, but the short story, "I'm a Fool," which is included in the anthology, probably would not be listed. The Internet is an excellent source to locate materials that might be included in anthologies—short stories, poems, plays, or essays—or just to find individual titles of shorter literary works. Most of the materials from anthologies that are being published on the Internet are older, so there are no copyright restrictions prohibiting free public access. However, some newer materials are also included. The other way to find materials in anthologies is to use one of the indexes available for that purpose.

Internet

Many sites on the Internet might be considered "virtual anthologies," in that texts of individual writers or texts devoted to specific subjects are collected on one site. A "virtual anthology" can be found at http://4poetry.4anything.com/4/0,1001,5666,00.html. A collection of some of the works of Edgar Allen Poe can be found at http://www.pambytes.com/poe/poe.html. Science fiction buffs can find a collection of short stories at www.sfwriter.com/stindex.htm. Some universities' and special collections' sites now provide digitized full-text versions of short stories, biographies, and other literary works. The Electronic Text Center at the University of Virginia (http://etext.lib.virginia.edu/features.html) has digitized a number of collected works and made them available to the public.

The sites below contain general collections of literary works.

ARTFL Project: American and French Research on the Treasury of French Language. U of Chicago P. n.d. 24 Apr. 2000 <http://humanities.uchicago.edu/ARTFL/ARTFL.html#general>.
 Collection of nearly 2,000 texts, ranging from classic works of French literature to various kinds of non-fiction prose and technical writing. Includes eighteenth, nineteenth and twentieth century works and some seventeenth century texts as well as some medieval and Renaissance texts. Genres include novels, verse, theater, journalism, essays, correspondence and treatises. Subjects include literary criticism, biology, history, economics and philosophy. Available by subscription only.

Bartleby.com: Great Books Online. Bartleby.com. 2000. 28 Apr. 2000 <http://www.bartleby.com/>.
 Full-text short stories and poetry. Available free.

LION: Literature Online. Chadwyck-Healey. 2000. 23 Apr. 2000 <http://lion.chadwyck.co.uk/html/homenosub.htm>.
 A fully searchable library of over 250,000 full-text works of English and American literature. Includes several literary databases of poetry, plays and fiction as well as general reference works and links to other Internet sites. Available by subscription only.

Indexes

Besides the Internet, indexes to literature in collections can be found in a number of sources. The selected guides below are listed by type of literature.

Essays

Essay and General Literature Index is an index to essays and articles from anthologies and collections published in English. It is available both in paper and electronic format. The focus is primarily on the humanities and social sciences, with coverage of topics in history, political science, economics, and philosophy. Also includes criticism of literary works, drama, and film. The titles that are indexed are mostly monographs, but some annuals and serial publications such as *Proceedings of the American Antiquarian Society* and the *Dickens Studies Annual* are included. It is arranged alphabetically by subject and includes an author index and a "List of Books Indexed." Figure 12.8 is a sample page from the subject index showing a citation to an appropriate essay for the topic of "women and employment."

Women—*Continued*

~~Crime~~

See Female offenders

Crimes against

See also Rape

MacKinnon, C. A. Crimes of war, crimes of peace. (*In* On human rights; ed. by S. Shute and S. Hurley p83-109)

Morgan, R. A massacre in Montreal. (*In* Morgan, R. The word of a woman p199-205)

Segel, L. Does pornography cause violence? The search for evidence. (*In* Dirty looks: women, pornography, power; ed. by P. C. Gibson and R. Gibson p5-21)

Diseases

See also Gynecology; Women—Health and hygiene

Education

Bee, B. Critical literacy and the politics of gender. (*In* Critical literacy; ed. by C. Lankshear and P. L. McLaren p105-31)

Harris, S. K. Responding to the text(s): women readers and the quest for higher education. (*In* Readers in history; ed. by J. L. Machor p259-82)

Great Britain

Wolff, J. The culture of separate spheres: the role of culture in nineteenth-century public and private life. (*In* Wolff, J. Feminine sentences p12-33)

Ireland

Innes, C. L. 'Groups rather than individuals': women in politics and education. (*In* Innes, C. L. Woman and nation in Irish literature and society, 1880-1935 p110-27)

Middle East

Abadan-Unat, N. The impact of legal and educational reforms on Turkish women. (*In* Women in Middle Eastern history; ed. by N. R. Keddie and B. Baron p177-94)

Berkey, J. P. Women and Islamic education in the Mamluk period. (*In* Women in Middle Eastern history; ed. by N. R. Keddie and B. Baron p143-57)

Education (Higher)

Heilbrun, C. G. The politics of mind: women, tradition, and the university. (*In* Gender in the classroom; ed. by S. L. Gabriel and I. Smithson p28-40)

Kramarae, C., and Treichler, P. A. Power relationships in the classroom. (*In* Gender in the classroom; ed. by S. L. Gabriel and I. Smithson p41-59)

Lee, E. B. Reflections on the education of women. (*In* The Liberal arts in a time of crisis; ed. by B. A. Scott p135-40)

Emancipation

See Women's rights

Employment

See also Sex discrimination in employment

Coser, R. L. Power lost and status gained: a step in the direction of sex equality. (*In* The Nature of work; ed. by K. Erikson and S. P. Vallas p71-87)

California

Hossfeld, K. J. "Their logic against them": contradictions in sex, race, and class in Silicon Valley. (*In* Women workers and global restructuring; ed. by K. Ward p149-78)

Developing countries

Tiano, S. Maquiladora women: a new category of workers? (*In* Women workers and global restructuring; ed. by K. Ward p193-223)

Great Britain

Dupree, M. The community perspective in family history: the Potteries during the nineteenth century. (*In* The First modern society; ed. by A. L. Beier, D. Cannadine and J. M. Rosenheim p549-73)

Greece

Hadjicostandi, J. "Façon": women's formal and informal work in the garment industry in Kavala, Greece. (*In* Women workers and global restructuring; ed. by K. Ward p64-81)

Ireland

Pyle, J. L. Export-led development and the underemployment of women: the impact of discriminatory development policy in the Republic of Ireland. (*In* Women workers and global restructuring; ed. by K. Ward p85-112)

Italy

Cammarosano, S. O. Labouring women in northern and central Italy in the nineteenth century. (*In* Society and politics in the age of the Risorgimento; ed. by J. A. Davis and P. Ginsborg p152-83)

Japan

Carney, L. S., and O'Kelly, C. G. Women's work and women's place in the Japanese economic miracle. (*In* Women workers and global restructuring; ed. by K. Ward p113-45)

Java

Wolf, D. L. Linking women's labor with the global economy: factory workers and their families in rural Java. (*In* Women workers and global restructuring; ed. by K. Ward p25-47)

Taiwan

Gallin, R. S. Women and the export industry in Taiwan: the muting of class consciousness. (*In* Women workers and global restructuring; ed. by K. Ward p179-92)

United States

Gabin, N. F. Time out of mind: the UAW's response to female labor laws and mandatory overtime in the 1960s. (*In* Work engendered: toward a new history of American labor; ed. by A. Baron p351-74)

Kessler-Harris, A. Law and a living: the gendered content of "free labor". (*In* Gender, class, race and reform in the Progressive Era; ed. by N. Frankel and N. S. Dye p87-109)

Enfranchisement

See Women—Suffrage

Health and hygiene

See also Clothing and dress

Jacobson, J. L. Improving women's reproductive health. (*In* State of the world, 1992 p83-99)

Figure 12.8. Sample page from *Essay and General Literature Index, 1990–1994*, p. 1794.

Note the work listed under the heading "women" and the subheading "employment" by R.L. Coser entitled "Power Lost and Status Gained: A Step in the Direction of Sex Equality." This essay is found in a work entitled *The Nature of Work*, edited by K. Erikson and S. P. Vallas. To retrieve this essay, you would conduct a title search in the library catalog for "nature of work," or search for "coser r l" as the author. The essay will be found on pages 71 through 87.

Individual essays can also be found under the author's name in *Essay and General Literature Index*. Figure 12.9 shows a citation to a work coauthored by Claudia Goldin and Stanley L. Engerman. Figure 12.10 illustrates the full entry listed under the author Engerman in the same index.

Short Stories

To find a short story you should consult *Short Story Index* published by the H.W. Wilson Company. This index provides references to short stories written in or translated into English that have appeared in collections and selected periodicals. The periodicals are those indexed in *Readers' Guide to Periodical Literature* and *Humanities Index*. There is also an electronic version of the *Short Story Index*. It covers the years 1983 forward and includes links to some full-text short stories.

The print version includes both a subject and an author index. Figure 12.11 illustrates an example under the subject "women."

Goldhurst, William
  Of mice and men; John Steinbeck's parable
  of the curse of Cain. (*In* The Short novels
  of John Steinbeck: ed. by J. J. Benson
  p48-59)
Goldin, Claudia
  (jt. Auth) See Engerman, Stanley L.,
  and Goldin, Claudia

Figure 12.9. Excerpt from author index, *Essay and General Literature Index, 1990–1994*, p. 658.

Enger, John Van
  Faith as a concept of order in medieval
  Christendom. (*In* Belief in history;
  ed. by T. Kselman p19-67)
Engerman, Stanley L., and Goldin, Claudia
  Seasonality in nineteenth-century labor
  markets. (*In* American economic development
  in historical perspective; ed. by T. Weiss
  and D. Schaefer p99-126)

Figure 12.10. Excerpt from author index, *Essay and General Literature Index, 1990–1994*, p. 495.

ACTORS—*Continued*

Besant, Sir W., and Rice, J. The case of Mr. Lucraft
Bioy Casares, A. Cato
Bloch, R. Show biz
Boyd, W. Not yet, Jayette
Breen, J. L. Starstruck
Burns, C. Also starring
Crumley, J. The heavy
Goldman, E. S. Nelly Fallower's *Streetcar*
Goldsmith, O. Adventures of a strolling player
Hagedorn, J. T. Film noir
Hall, M. M. The pool people
Lombreglia, R. Jungle video
Mori, T. Japanese Hamlet
Nakayama, C. Good afternoon, ladies
Onetti, J. C. A dream come true
Palacio Valdés, A. Drama in the flies
Paul, B. Close, but no cigar
Runyon, D. Broadway complex
Saroyan, W. The man with the heart in the highlands
Schmidt, H. J. The honored guest
Slesar, H. Starring the defense
Spencer, D. Our secret's out
Spencer, S. Credit
Stoker, B. A criminal star
Thomas, G. An ample wish
Urbánek, Z. For dreams that now have ceased
Villanueva, M. The insult
Villiers de l'Isle-Adam, A., comte de. The desire to be a man
Zinnes, H. Wings

The **actors** company. Finney, E. J.
Actress. Oates, J. C.

ACTRESSES

See also Motion picture actors and actresses; Theater life

Aickman, R. The visiting star
Alcott, L. M. Hope's debut
Alcott, L. M. La Jeune; or, Actress and woman
Alcott, L. M. A laugh and a look
Alcott, L. M. The romance of a bouquet
Allen, S. The interview
Brennan, K. Jack
Carroll, J. The lick of time
Carter, A. The merchant of shadows
Cather, W. Coming, Aphrodite!
Cheever, J. The fourth alarm
Cliff, M. Screen memory
Compo, S. The continuity girl
DePew, A. Rita and Maxine
Fitzgerald, F. S. Last kiss
Frame, R. Switchback
Ganina, M. Stage actress
Haslam, G. W. Joaquin
Hébert, A. The first garden
Ingalls, R. The end of tragedy
Kinder, R. M. Witches
Kress, N. With the original cast
Lewis, S. As P. T.
Mason, B. A. A new-wave format
McGahern, J. Peaches
Minot, S. Île Sèche
Munro, A. Simon's luck
Nakayama, C. Star time
Norman, H. Whatever Lola wants
Oates, J. C. Actress
Onetti, J. C. Hell most feared
Orr, M. The wisdom of Eve
Palacio Valdés, A. Clotilde's romance
Poniatowska, E. Park Cinema

Pritchett, V. S. The chain-smoker
Salter, J. The cinema
Tagore, Sir R. Resistance broken
Tokareva, V. Thou shalt not make . . .
Turchi, P. Magician
Uvarova, L. Be still, torments of passion
Verlaine, M. J. The nude scene
Vidal, G. Erlinda and Mr. Coffin
Vivante, A. The last kiss
Walker, C. Z. The very pineapple
Wallace, D. F. My appearance
Whitebird, J. Mrs. Bruja

Acts of contrition. Binstock, R. C.
Acts of kindness. Wagner, M. M.
Acts of mercy. Coleman, J. C.
Actual oil. Steinbach, M.
Ad astra per aspera. Compo, S.
Adam, Christina
Fires
Birch Lane Press presents American fiction #3
Adam, one afternoon. Calvino, I.
Adamidou, Irena Ioannidou *See* Ioannidou Adamidou, Irena
Adams, Alice, 1926- ◄——— AUTHOR
1940: fall
Adams, A. After you've gone
Prize stories, 1990
After you've gone
Adams, A. After you've gone
Legal fictions; ed. by J. Wishingrad
Prize stories, 1989
Alaska
The Oxford book of American short stories; ed. by J. C. Oates
Alternatives
American stories II: fiction from the Atlantic monthly
Beautiful girl
The Invisible enemy; ed. by M. Dow and J. Regan
Child's play ◄—— SHORT STORY
Adams, A. After you've gone ◄ SOURCE
Earthquake damage
The New Yorker v66 p44-9 My 7 '90
Prize stories, 1991
The end of the world
Adams, A. After you've gone
Favors
Adams, A. After you've gone
Fog
Adams, A. After you've gone
The islands
Prize stories, 1993
The Sophisticated cat; comp. by J. C. Oates and D. Halpern
The last lovely city
The Best American short stories, 1992
The New Yorker v67 p33-9 Mr 11 '91
Prize stories, 1992
Lost cat
Adams, A. After you've gone
The Company of cats; ed. by M. J. Rosen
Love and work
Southwest Review v77 p466-79 Aut '92
Molly's dog
The Literary dog; ed. by J. Schinto
The oasis
The Rough road home; ed. by R. Gingher
Ocracoke Island
Adams, A. After you've gone

Figure 12.11. Author search, *Short Story Index*. From Short Story Index. Reprinted by permission.

```
WOMEN
              See also Black women; Jewish women;
        Muslim women; Single women
Adams, A.  Child's play
Adams, A.  The end of the world
Adams, A.  Molly's dog
Adams, A.  Return trips
```

Figure 12.12. Excerpt from Subject Index, *Short Story Index, 1989–1993*, p. 960.

To find the source where the short story can be found, consult the author index. An example is shown in Figure 12.12.

To retrieve the short story "A Child's Play" by Alice Adams, conduct an author search in the library catalog under "adams alice" or a title search under "after you've gone," the larger work that includes the short story.

Plays

Inter-Play: An On-line Index to Plays in Collections, Anthologies, and Periodicals. Comp. Robert Westover and Janet Wright. Portland State University. 23 Feb. 2000. 28 Feb. 2000 <http://www.portals.org/inter-play/>.
Index to approximately 18,026 citations to plays in several languages, many of which are not included in the standard printed play indexes such as *Ottemiller's Index to Plays in Collections* or H. W. Wilson's *Play Index*. The authors have not included separately published plays or works by familiar authors such as Shakespeare as these can be located through local library catalogs. The sources indexed range from the late 19th century through the current year. The database is frequently updated.

Keller, Dean H. *Index to Plays in Periodicals.* Metuchen, NJ: Scarecrow, 1971. Supplements, 1973, 1979, 1990.
Indexes about 10,000 plays located in 267 periodicals in one volume with supplements to 1990.

Ottemiller's Index to Plays in Collections, an Author and Title Index Appearing in Collections Published between 1900 and Early 1985. Rev. and enlarged by John M. Connor and Billie M. Connor. 7th ed. Metuchen, NJ: Scarecrow, 1988.
Index to full-length plays appearing in books published in England and the United States. It is divided into three sections: (1) author index with titles and dates of performance, (2) list of collections analyzed with key to symbols, and (3) title index.

Play Index. New York: H.W. Wilson, 1949–.
The key index in eight volumes covering the years 1949–1952, 1953–1960, 1961–1967, 1968–1972, 1973–1977, 1978–1982, 1983–1987, and 1988–1992. Each volume indexes thousands of plays for the time period covered. The index is divided into four parts. Part I lists plays under authors' names and anthologies in which the plays are found. Part II includes the cast analysis by number of male and female characters needed. Part III lists anthologies with full bibliographic information. Part IV includes a directory of publishers and distributors.

Poetry

American Poetry Index: An Author and Title Index to Poetry by Americans in Single Author Collections. Vol. 1, 1981–1982. Vol. 2, 1983. Vol. 3, 1984. New York: Grander Book Co., 1983.
An alphabetical index to authors and titles of over 10,000 poems published in 190 collections, which are identified by number after author's name in main index.

Caskey, Jefferson D., comp. *Index to Poetry in Popular Periodicals, 1955–1959.* Westport, CT: Greenwood, 1984.
Indexes 7,400 poems by title appearing in American periodicals from 1955 to 1959. Also includes a first-line index, author index, and subject index.

_____. *Index to Poetry in Popular Periodicals, 1960–1964.* Westport, CT: Greenwood, 1988.
An update of the earlier title.

The Columbia Granger's Index to Poetry. 11th ed. New York: Columbia UP, 1997.
Continues *Granger's Index to Poetry.* Indexes over 100,000 poems appearing in over 400 anthologies.

Granger, Edith. *Granger's Index to Poetry, 1970–1981.* Ed. William James Smith. 7th ed., completely rev. and enl., indexing anthologies published through December 31, 1981. New York: Columbia UP, 1982.
First published in 1904, this is considered the standard index to poetry. Each edition enlarges on the previous one, omitting some anthologies and adding new ones. Later editions arranged by sections as follows: (1) title and first-line index, (2) author index, and (3) subject index.

Poems: Research Guide. U of Delaware Library. 25 Oct. 1999. 28 Apr. 2000. <http://www2.lib.udel.edu/subj/engl/resguide/poems.htm>.

Poetry Archives. E-mule.com, 1997–2000. 28 Feb. 2000 <http://www.emule.com/poetry/>.
Large collection of free classical poetry on the Internet. Searchable by author, title, and first line of poem.

Speeches

Mitchell, Charity. *Speech Index: An Index to Collections of World Famous Orations and Speeches for Various Occasions.* Metuchen, NJ: Scarecrow, 1982. *Supplement,* 4th ed., 1966–1980.
Alphabetical arrangement of speeches by author, subject, and type of speech.

Representative American Speeches. H.W. Wilson, 1938–. Annual.
Collection of speeches. Has cumulative author index: 1937–1960 in 1959/60 volume; annual index since 1960/61.

Speech Resources. Virginia Commonwealth University. 23 Feb. 2000. 28 Apr. 2000 <http://www.library.vcu.edu/guides/speeches.html>.
Good site for identifying print and online sources for speeches. Includes: Indexes, Original Print Sources, Finding Speeches Online, Selected Speech Sites on the Web.

Sutton, Roberta Briggs. *Speech Index; an Index to 259 Collections of World Famous Orations and Speeches for Various Occasions.* 4th ed. Rev. and enl. New York: Scarecrow, 1966.

Vital Speeches of the Day. New York: City News, 1934–.
Excellent source for speeches on current issues and social trends in the United States and other countries. Published twice a month. Annual index published in November issue. Also indexed in *Readers' Guide* and in *ABI/INFORM.* Also has a 25-year (1934–1959) author/subject index.

Book Reviews, Literary Criticism, and Literature in Collections

12 Instructor: _____ Course/Section: _____

Name: _____

Date: _____ Points: _____

Review Questions

1. List the three types of sources discussed in this chapter.

    a.

    b.

    c.

2. What is the importance of using a book review for an author's work?

3. What is the difference between a book review and a literary criticism?

4. Name two book review indexes that would be useful.

5. What is the advantage of having book reviews available on the Internet?

6. Give the URLs for two Internet sites that have book reviews.

7. Can book reviews be located through periodical indexes? Justify your answer.

8. How does one locate book reviews or articles on literary criticism in the library after the reference to a review has been found in an index?

9. Name two sources you could use for finding literary criticism of a particular writer.

   a.

   b.

10. What is an anthology?

11. How would you locate a short story that is not listed in the online catalog?

12. Name an index you would use to find chapters or essays in books.

Book Reviews, Literary Criticism, and Literature in Collections

12 Instructor: _____ Course/Section: _____

Name: _____

Date: _____ Points: _____

Finding Book Reviews

Reviews of books may be obtained from *Book Review Index, Book Review Digest* or any other sources containing book reviews. Choose one of the reviews listed in Figure 12.5, *Book Review Digest, 1994*, and answer the following questions:

1. Analyze one reference you found by giving the following information.

    a. Author of book selected:

    b. Title of the book:

    c. Author of review (if unsigned, mark NA):

    d. Give the following information about the source in which the review appears.

        (1) Complete title of the magazine or journal:

        (2) Volume:

        (3) Pages:

        (4) Date:

        (5) Number of words in review:

        (6) How many other references to reviews were given?

Use your library catalog or periodicals holdings list to determine whether or not your library subscribes to the magazine or journal in which the review appears. If your library subscribes to the magazine or journal, answer the following questions.

2. What is the call number of the magazine or journal?

Retrieve the review article.

3. Read the complete review. Is this a book you would want to read? Justify your answer.

4. Write a bibliographic reference to the review. Use the bibliographic citations examples given in Appendix A.

Book Reviews, Literary Criticism, and Literature in Collections

Instructor: _____ Course/Section: _____

Name: _____

Date: _____ Points: _____

Finding Literary Criticism

Using a source described in this chapter, locate a reference to a criticism of a novel, poem, play, or short story that you have read, or select from the list below. Locate the criticism, read it, and complete the following questions.

For Whom the Bell Tolls by Ernest Hemingway
The Road Not Taken by Robert Frost
The Pit and the Pendulum by Edgar Allan Poe
The Client by John Grisham
Pet Sematary by Stephen King

1. Give the author and title of the literary work you selected.

2. What is the title of the index or other source you use to locate the criticism?

3. How did you locate the index or other source for Question 2?

4. Give the following information about the criticism.

   Title of the work in which criticism appears:

   If a periodical, give the date and volume of the periodical and the pages on which it appears.

   Indicate if a full-text database or another online source is used.

5. What is the call number of the book or periodical in which the criticism appears (if not full text)?

6. Briefly summarize some of the major points the author of the criticism makes about the work.

7. Write a bibliographical citation for the criticism you found. Use the bibliographic citations given in Appendix A.

8. Do you agree or disagree with the critic's assessment of the work? Justify your answer.

Book Reviews, Literary Criticism, and Literature in Collections

Instructor: _____ Course/Section: _____

Name: _____

Date: _____ Points: _____

Using *Essay and General Literature Index*

The *Essay and General Literature Index* is an index to materials in anthologies. Consult the index for information on a topic you select or one assigned by your instructor. After you have found your reference, answer the following questions.

1. What is the call number of the *Essay and General Literature Index?*

2. Give the date of the volume used.

3. Give the complete subject heading under which you located your topic.

4. Analyze the reference you located by giving the following information.

   a. Author of the article:

   b. Title of the article:

   c. Editor or author of the book (circle one or the other and record the name).

   d. Name of the book in which the article appears:

   e. Pages in the book in which the article appears:

   f. Place, publisher, and copyright or publication date of the book:

5.   Does the library own the book? If so, what is the call number?

6.   Write a bibliographic reference to the article you have found. Use the bibliographic citations examples in Appendix A for citing an essay in a collection or an anthology.

7.   Would this article be a good reference for your topic? Justify your answer.

Book Reviews, Literary Criticism, and Literature in Collections

12

Instructor: _____ Course/Section: _____

Name: _____

Date: _____ Points: _____

Exploring Literary Collections Online

Go to the Electronic Text Center at the University of Virginia at http://etext.lib.virginia.edu/features.html

Click on Poe Archives (http://etext.lib.virginia.edu/poe/).

Click on "About Poe" and read the "Brief Biography" located at http://etext.lib.virginia.edu/poe/poebiog.html. Then answer the following questions.

1. What were the occupations of Poe's parents?

2. Where did Poe attend college?

3. How long did he serve in the U.S. army?

4. Did he attend West Point? Why didn't he graduate there?

5. What was the title of his first attempt at publishing?

6. How did Poe die and where is he buried?

7. Are any references given here for further research on Edgar Allan Poe? If so, give one title and author.

At the bottom of the biography, click on "Fiction" to see a list of full-text works available at this site for the author. Scroll down to the list of short stories beginning with *The Assignation*. Select one that you would like to look at.

8. What is the title you selected?

9. When was this title published?

10. What it the title of the anthology in which this story originally appeared?

11. Click on the "Header" of this story and print out the page. Attach it to this assignment.

12. How does reading the story online compare with reading it in book form?

13. If given a choice of full-text online, cassette, or traditional book formats, which would you prefer and why?

Return to the home page for Poe. Select "Search the Poe Archives" to find a specific term in Poe's works.

14. Using the search engine on the page, find out how many times the words "despair" and "love" are mentioned in all the texts and summaries in the Poe Archives and answer the following questions.

Number of times in which the word appeared:

Total number of works in which the word "despair" appeared:

Number of works in which the word "love" appeared:

Total number of times the word "love" appeared:

Explain how this feature is useful to someone who might be doing research on Poe. Describe how this feature compares with a printed text of short stories.

Appendix A

◆ DOCUMENTING SOURCES (MLA STYLE)

Works Cited

The bibliographic entries below provide guidance for citing some of the more common sources in a *Works Cited* list. The examples are based on the *MLA Handbook*. For additional help consult the *MLA Handbook* or one of the other style manuals listed in Chapter 2 (if you use another style). Citation examples are provided for the following categories of materials.

1. Books
2. Reference Books
3. Periodical and Newspaper Articles
4. Unpublished Dissertation and Thesis
5. Class Lecture
6. Interview
7. Sound Recording
8. Videotapes
9. Microforms
10. Television or Radio Programs
11. Government Publications
12. Electronic formats

1.   Books

Items to include in documenting a book:

- ◆ Author's full name. If there are more than one, but less than four authors, all of the authors' names are included. When there are four or more authors, cite the first one listed on the title page followed by "et al." or by "and others."
- ◆ Title of part of book if only citing one part.
- ◆ The title of the book as it appears on the title page. In preparing a manuscript for publication, use italics to highlight titles of published works; underline titles in papers that are not being prepared for publication.
- ◆ Editor, translator, compiler (if any).
- ◆ The edition if other than the first.
- ◆ Volume if part of a multivolume set.
- ◆ The series (if any).
- ◆ Publication information.
  - ◆ The city of publication. If more than one place is listed on the title page, only the first one listed is used. The name of the state is included if the city is not well known.
  - ◆ The publisher. The shortened name of the publisher is used unless there is confusion in identification. The shortened forms of publishers' names are found in the *MLA Handbook* (6.5).

◆ The date of publication. Publication date is found on the title page. If there is no publication date given, the latest copyright date is used. If neither a publication date nor a copyright date is given, the abbreviation, n.d., is used.

Note that the first line of each entry begins at the left margin. Subsequent lines in each entry are indented five spaces to the right.

1.1. Book by one author

Kaufman, Martin. Homeopathy in America: the Rise and Fall of a Medical Heresy. Baltimore: Johns Hopkins UP, 1971.

1.2. Book by two or more authors

Powers, Scott K., and Stephen L. Dodd. Total Fitness: Exercise, Nutrition, and Wellness. 2nd ed. Boston: Allyn, 1999.

1.3. Book by two or more authors with the same last name

Durant, Will, and Ariel Durant. A Dual Autobiography. New York: Simon, 1977.

1.4. Book by more than three persons

Davis, James, et al. Society and the Law: New Meanings for an Old Profession. New York: Free, 1962.

Note: May also use Davis, James, and others, or give all names in full.

1.5. Two or more books by the same author

Mink, Gwendolyn. The Wages of Motherhood: Inequality in the Welfare State. Ithaca: Cornell UP, 1995.

---. Welfare's End. Ithaca: Cornell UP, 1998.

Note: When citing two or more books by the same author, give the author's name in the first entry. Use three hyphens followed by a period in place of the author's name in subsequent entries.

1.6. Book by a corporate author

Center for the Study of Democratic Institutions. Natural Law and Modern Society. Contrib. John Cogley, et al. Cleveland: World, 1973.

1.7. Book that is an edited work

Green, Phillip, and Michael Walzer, eds. The Political Imagination in Literature: A Reader. New York: Free, 1969.

1.8. Book that is part of a series

Hunt, Lacy H. Dynamics of Forecasting Financial Cycles: Theory, Technique, and Implementation. Contemporary Studies in Economic and Financial Analysis. Greenwich: JAI, 1976.

1.9. **Book that is one volume of a multivolume work, one author, each volume a different title**

Malone, Dumas. <u>Jefferson and the Ordeal of Liberty</u>. Boston: Little, 1962. Vol. III of <u>Jefferson and His Time</u>. 6 vols., 1948-1981.

1.10. **Book that is one volume of a multivolume work with one general title**

Warren, Charles. <u>The Supreme Court in United States History</u>. Rev. ed. 2 Vols. Boston: Little, 1926.

1.11. **Book that is a translation of an author's work**

Nietzsche, Frederick. <u>The Birth of Tragedy and the Genealogy of Morals</u>. Trans. Francis Golffing. Garden City: Doubleday, 1956.

1.12. **Short story in a collected work (anthology)**

Faulkner, William. "Dry September." <u>Ten Modern Masters: An Anthology of the Short Story</u>. Ed. Robert G. Davis. New York: Harcourt, 1953. 339-50.

Note: Elements cited are author of short story, title of short story, title of book in which story appears, editor of book, publication information, pages on which story appears.

1.13. **Essay or article in a collected work (anthology)**

Barker, James D. "Man, Mood, and the Presidency." <u>The Presidency Reappraised</u>. Ed. Rexford G. Tugwell and Thomas E. Cronin. New York: Prager, 1974. 205-14.

Note: Elements cited: author of article, title of article, title of book in which article appears, editors of book, publication information, pages on which article appears in book.

2. Reference Books

Items to include when citing articles from encyclopedias, yearbooks, biographical dictionaries, and other well known reference books:

- ◆ The author of the article, if known.
- ◆ The title of the article as it appears in the book.
- ◆ The title of the book in which the article appears.
- ◆ The edition, if other than the first, and the date of publication.
- ◆ The volume number if one of a multivolume set, unless entire set is alphabetically arranged.
- ◆ The inclusive paging of the article. If articles are arranged in alphabetical order in the work, page numbers should be omitted.

If the reference is not well known, or if there is confusion about the title, give full publication information.

2.1. **Article from a multivolume general reference book**

Vandam, Leroy D. "Anesthetic." <u>Encyclopaedia Britannica: Macropaedia</u>. 1974.

2.2. Article from a single volume general reference book

Betancourt, Romulo. "Latin America, Its Problems and Possibilities." <u>Britannica Book of the Year, 1966</u>. 1967.

2.3. Article from a multivolume subject reference book

Flexner, Eleanor. "Woman's Rights Movement." <u>Dictionary of American History</u>. Ed. Joseph G.E. Hopkins and Wayne Andrews. 6 vols. New York: Scribner's, 1961. VI, Supp. 1: 301-43.

Note: Since there is another reference book with the same or similar title, it is necessary to give full publication information.

2.4. Article from a biographical dictionary (unsigned)

"Sellers, Peter (Richard Henry)." <u>Who's Who 1976-1977</u>. 1976.

Note: Full name of subject of article is used as title of article.

2.5. Article from a biographical dictionary (signed)

Cole, Arthur C. "Webster, Daniel." <u>Dictionary of American Biography</u>. 1936.

2.6. Book of quotations

Johnson, Samuel. "He who praises everybody praises nobody. . ." <u>The Oxford Dictionary of Quotations</u>. 2nd ed. 237.

3. Periodical and Newspaper Articles

Items to include when citing articles from periodicals:

- The author of the article if it is a signed article.
- The title of the article.
- The title of the periodical.
- The volume number and/or issue number if it is a scholarly journal.
- The date of the periodical.
- The inclusive pages of the article. If an article is not printed on consecutive pages, that is, if it begins on one page and continues on later pages, cite the beginning page followed by a "+."

3.1. Article from a monthly magazine (signed)

Starr, Roger. "A Kind Word about Money." <u>Harper's</u> Apr. 1976: 79-92.

Note: For a monthly magazine, cite only the date and pages.

3.2. Article from a monthly magazine (unsigned)

"First National Data on Reading Speed." <u>Intellect</u> Oct. 1972: 9.

3.3. Article from a weekly magazine (signed)

Meindl, James D. "Microelectronics and Computers in Medicine." <u>Science</u> 12 Feb. 1982: 792-97.

3.4. Article from a weekly magazine (unsigned)

"Behind the Threat of More Inflation." <u>Business Week</u> 18 Nov. 1972: 76-78.

3.5. Article from a journal with continuously numbered pages throughout the volume

Runkle, Gerald. "Is Violence Always Wrong?" <u>Journal of Politics</u> 38 (1976): 247-91.

3.6. Article from a journal with separately numbered pages in each issue

Martin, Jay. "A Watertight Watergate Future: Americans in a Post-American Age." <u>The Antioch Review</u> 33.2 (1975): 7-25.

Note: 33.2 indicates volume 33, issue number no. 2.

3.7. Book review (signed)

Sherrill, Robert. Rev. of <u>The Time of Illusion</u>, by Jonathan Schell. <u>New York Times Book Review</u> 18 Jan. 1976: 1-2.

Note: Elements cited are the author of review, title of book, author of book, periodical in which review appears, date, page(s).

3.8. Book review with title (signed)

Hughes, Robert. "The Sorcerer's Apprentice." Rev. of <u>Journey to Ixtlan</u>, by Carlos Castaneda. <u>Time</u> 6 Nov. 1972: 101.

3.9. Book review (unsigned)

Rev. of <u>The Efficacy of Law</u>, by Harry W. Jones. <u>Choice</u> 7 (1970): 941.

3.10. Newspaper article (signed)

Goldstein, Tom. "New Federal Tax Law Could Foster Growth of Plans to Provide Pre-paid Legal Services." <u>New York Times</u> 28 Sept. 1976, eastern ed.: A36.

3.11. Newspaper article (unsigned)

"College Enrollment Decline Predicted for South in '80's." <u>Morning Advocate</u> [Baton Rouge] 28 Sept. 1976: B7.

3.12. Editorial from a newspaper

"Takeovers Yes, Hold-ups No." Editorial. <u>New York Times</u> 28 Nov. 1986, eastern ed.: A26.

4. Unpublished Dissertation and Thesis

Bolden, Anthony J. "All Blues: A Study of African-American Resistance Poetry." Diss. Louisiana State U, 1998.

Vogel, Amanda E. "Body Image by Association: Women's Interpretations of Aerobics and the Role of the Fitness Instructor." Thesis (M.A.). U of British Columbia, 1998.

5. Class Lecture

Wilson, John. "Women in the Labor Force." Sociology 101. Louisiana State U, Baton Rouge, LA. 18 Feb. 1996.

6. Interview

Harris, Michael. Personal interview. 3 Feb. 1996.

7. Sound Recordings

Monk, Thelonius. Live at the It Club. 2 compact discs. Sony Music Entertainment, 1998.

Wayne, Jeff. The War of the Worlds: Rock Musical. Narr. Richard Burton, with soloists, vocal and instrumental ensembles. LP. Columbia, n.d.

Note: Citation includes performer, title of recording, type of recording, producer, date.

8. Videotapes

Our National Parks. Videocassette. Prod. Wolfgang Bayer Productions. National Geographic Book Service, 1989.

9. Microforms

Spalter-Roth, Roberta M., and Heidi I. Hartmann. Increasing Working Mothers' Earnings. Washington: Institute for Women's Policy Research, 1991: ERIC Microfiche ED 370825.

10. Television and Radio Programs

Items to include when citing a television or radio program:

- Title of the episode (enclose in quotation marks).
- Title of the program (underline).
- Name of performers, narrators, etc. of the particular episode, if applicable.
- Title of the series, if any (do not use quotation marks or underlining).
- Name of producers, directors, etc. if applicable.
- Name of network.

- ◆ Identification of the station and the city where viewed or heard.
- ◆ Date broadcast.

```
"Sports, Fitness and the Brain." The Gray Matters. Prod. Mary Beth
     Kirchner and Robert Rand. Radio series produced for Public Radio In-
     ternational, in association with the Dana Alliance for Brain Initia-
     tives. PRI. WUMB-FM, Boston. 5 Mar. 1999.
```

11. Government Publications

Government publications are issued by many different types of government agencies from local to international. Often the names of the authors are not provided in the document. Generally the following items are included in a citation to a government publication.

- ◆ Author—if individual author is not given, cite the name of the government entity (a city, a state, a national government, or international organization) followed by the particular agency that is responsible for the publication.
- ◆ Title of the publication.
- ◆ Any publication information necessary for identification of the publication, such as special reports or parts of series.
- ◆ Publication information. (The Government Printing Office (GPO) is usually cited as the publisher for most U.S. government publications, regardless of the branch or agency that issues them.).

Note: Cite government periodicals as you would periodicals from commercial publishers.

The citation examples below are for various types of United States government publications.

11.1. Agency publication

```
Reid, William J., Jr., and F.P. Cuthbert, Jr. Aphids on Leafy Vegetables:
     How to Control Them. Agricultural Research Service, Farmers' Bulletin
     No. 2148. Washington: GPO, 1976.
```

11.2. Reference book

```
"Number of Workers with Earnings . . ." Statistical Abstract of the United
     States, 1991. Table 656.
```

11.3. Congressional hearings, reports, documents

```
United States. Cong. House. Committee on the Judiciary. Opposing the
     Granting of Permanent Residence in the United States to Certain
     Aliens. Report to accompany H. Res. 795. 95th Cong., 1st sess. H.R.
     no. 691. Washington: GPO, 1977.
---.---. Senate. Committee on Indian Affairs. Providing for Business
     Development and Trade Promotion for Native Americans, and for Other
     Purposes. Report to accompany S. 401. 106th Cong., 1st sess. S. Rept.
     106-149. Washington: GPO, 1999.
```

---.---.---. Committee on Agriculture, Nutrition, and Forestry. Better Nutrition and Health for Children Act of 1993, Hearings: March 1, 1994, May 16, 1994, June 10, 1994, and June 17, 1994. 103 Cong. 2nd sess. S. 1614. Washington: GPO, 1995.

Note: The entries appear in the order as they would in a *Works Cited* list. When citing more than one work by the same government agency, use three hyphens in place of the name of the agency in the next entry and any following one(s). In the second entry above, the author is the United States Congress, Senate, Committee on Indian Affairs. The author in the next entry is the United States Congress, Senate, Committee on Agriculture.

11.4. Laws, decrees, etc.

PL 96-5 11 (Dec. 11, 1980). Paperwork Reduction Act of 1980. 94 Stat. 2812.

Note: Citation to the *Statutes at Large*. Elements included in citation in the order given are: public law number, date approved, title of law, volume number of the *Statutes at Large*, abbreviation for *Statutes at Large*, page number.

20 U.S.C. 238 (1980).

Note: Citation to the *United States Code*. Elements in citation are number of code, abbreviation of *United States Code*, section number, and edition date.

11.5. Court case

Brewer v. Williams, 430 U.S. 389 (1977).

Note: Name of case, volume 430 of *U.S. Reports*, page 389, year of publication.

11.6. *Congressional Record*

Cong. Rec. 121 (1975): 40634.

12.   Electronic Format

When listing a source in electronic format originally printed in a book, journal, or other printed format, use the general guidelines you would use to cite the printed form. In addition, add the information that identifies the particular kind of format and, for Internet sources, the date of access and the Internet address.

12.1. CD-ROM

United States. Dept. of Commerce. Bureau of the Census. Data User Ser. Div. 1990 Census of Population and Housing: Equal Employment Opportunity File. CD-ROM. Disc. 1. Washington: Dept. of Commerce, 1993.

Dead Sea Scrolls Revealed. CD-ROM. Tel Aviv : Pixel Multimedia; London : A. Witkin; Oak Harbor, WA: Logos Research Systems, 1994.

"Dabble." The Oxford English Dictionary. 2nd ed. CD-ROM. Oxford: Oxford UP, 1992.

Woolf, Virginia. "The Captain's Death Bed." The Complete Works of Virginia Woolf Including Variant and Hard-to-Find Editions. Ed. Mark Hussey. CD-ROM . Woodbridge, CT: Primary Source Media, 1997.

Weninger, Robert. Rev. of <u>Passage Through Hell</u>, by David L. Pike. <u>The German Quarterly</u> 72.2 (1999): 194-95. <u>Humanities Abstracts FTX</u>. CD-ROM. SilverPlatter. Dec. 1999.

12.2. Internet

Because there are no standards for what is placed on the Internet, citing the sources can be confusing. Generally, you should include the following elements.

◆ Author, if given.

◆ Title of article, if it appears to be part of a larger work (in quotations).

◆ Title of work or Page (underlined).

◆ Title of the project (if any).

◆ Publication information: date of publication and name of sponsoring organization, if applicable.

◆ Date of access.

◆ Web address (URL).

In citing a service to which the library subscribes, you should complete the information as for the print source followed by the name of the database or service used (underlined); the library; the date of access; and the URL for the site (if it is too long, cite the vendor's home page).

12.2.1. Scholarly works

Lerman, Robert I. "Meritocracy without Rising Inequality?" <u>Economic Restructuring and the Job Market</u>. Policy and Research Report, no. 2. The Urban Institute. 2000. 23 Feb. 2000 <http://www.urban.org/econ/econ2.htm>.

United States. Dept. of Agriculture. Agriculture Research Service. Human Nutrition Information Service. <u>Provisional Table on the Vitamin K Content of Foods</u>. Prep. John L. Weihrauch and Ashok S. Chatra. HNIS-PT-104. Feb 1994. 23 Feb. 2000 <http://www.nal.usda.gov/fnic/foodcomp/Data/Other/pt104.pdf>.

12.2.2. Online books and selections from books

Twain, Mark. <u>A Double Barrelled Detective Story</u>. [New York: Harper, 1902]. The Naked Word Electronic Edition. 16 Jan. 2000. 23 Feb. 2000 <http://sr8.xoom.com/etcollective/nakedword/htmltext/dbdstory.html>.

Boswell, James. "Selections." <u>Life of Samuel Johnson</u>. Oxford, 1904. Ed. Jack Lynch. 23 Feb. 2000 <http://newark.rutgers.edu/~jlynch/Texts/BLJ/b272.html>.

12.2.3. Online journal articles

Kuang, Wembo. "The Development of Electronic Publication in China." <u>LIBRES: Library and Information Science Research</u> 9.1 (1999). 23 Feb. 2000 <http://aztec.lib.utk.edu/libres/libre9n1/wenbo.htm>.

Johnson, Glen M. Rev. of <u>Huckleberry Finn as Idol and Target</u>, by Jonathan Arac. <u>The Mark Twain Forum</u> 4 Nov. 1997. 23 Feb. 2000 <http://web.mit.edu/linguistics/www/forum/reviews/arac1.html>.

12.2.4. Online subscription services

Gartner, Scott Sigmund, and Gary M. Segura. "War, Casualties, and Public Opinion." <u>Journal of Conflict Resolution</u> 42.3 (1998): 278+. <u>Electronic Collections Online</u>. OCLC. Louisiana State U Lib., Baton Rouge. 23 Feb. 2000 <http://firstsearch.oclc.org/html/eco_frames.html>.

Lubove, Seth. "Subprime Borrower." <u>Forbes</u> 7 Feb 2000: 58. <u>ABI/INFORM Global</u>. ProQuest Direct. Delgado Community College Lib., New Orleans. 23 Feb. 2000 <http://proquest.umi.com/pqdweb>.

"Farming on the Edge of Chaos." <u>Whole Earth</u>. Summer. 1999: 72. <u>Health Source Plus</u>. EBSCOhost. Wayne State College, Wayne, NE. 23 Feb. 2000 <http://search.epnet.com/>.

Fiero, John W. "Anne Rice: Overview." <u>Contemporary Novelists</u>. 6th ed. 1996. Literature Resource Center. Gale Group. Wayne State College, Wayne, NE. 23 Feb. 2000 <http://www.galenet.com/servlet/LitRC?&u=LRC&u=CA&u=CLC&u=DLB>.

12.2.5. Newspaper articles

"Screening Newborns Can Defeat Hereditary Diseases." <u>New York Times on the Web</u>. 25 Feb. 2000. 26 Feb. 2000 <http://www.nytimes.com/library/national/science/health/022600hth-newborn-screening.html>.

12.2.6. Personal or professional home pages

Martin, Jan. <u>English Springer Spaniel</u>. 23 Feb. 2000. 26 Feb. 2000 <http://www.teleport.com/~ariel/essfaq.html>.

Immunization Action Coalition. Home Page. 25 Feb. 2000. 26 Feb 2000 <http://www.immunize.org/index.htm>.

12.2.7. E-mail

Sokolowski, Denise. "Re: textbook." E-mail to the authors. 1 June 1999.

12.2.8. Bulletin boards and other online discussions

Lange, Andre. "Anthology of Early Texts on Television." Online posting. 4 Feb. 2000. Broadcast News Forum. 25 Feb. 2000 <http://www.delphi.com/ab-broadcastnws/messages/?msg=235.1&ctx=1>.

Tomczak, Diane. "Re: Dyslexia and Laptops." Online posting. 23 Sept. 1999. ECPROFDEV-L: Early Childhood Professional Development Listserv. 24 Feb. 2000 <http://ericeece.org/listserv/ecprof-l.html>.

Appendix B

◆ GLOSSARY

abstract A type of index that gives the location of an article in a periodical or a book and a brief summary of that article.

Acceptable Use Policy (AUP) A policy for Internet users that defines the accepted use of the server and the network. Internet providers, both commercial and non-commercial, frequently have AUPs.

address Internet address that refers to the e-mail address or the IP (Internet Protocol) address.

analog Data that is encoded in continuous signals over a range or interval of values—for example, the signals transmitted via a telephone line as opposed to data on a digital computer that uses binary coding.

annotated bibliography A list of works with descriptions and a brief summary or critical statement about each.

annotation Critical or explanatory note about the contents of a book or article.

anthology Any collection of varied literary compositions; includes many different titles of shorter works under one title.

appendix Section of a book or other literary work containing supplementary materials such as tables or maps.

article A complete piece of writing that is part of a larger work.

ASCII (American Standard Code for Information Interchange) Standard character-to-number encoding widely used in the computer industry.

authentication The verification of the identity of a person or process, most often associated with the login (username) and password verification process for computer use. (*See also* authorization.)

authorization The process of granting or denying access to an Internet resource. Most computer security systems use a two-step process: (1) authentication, which verifies that a user is who he or she claims to be, and (2) authorization, which allows the user access to those resources to which he or she is entitled, depending on the preassigned privileges associated with the user's identity.

Backbone On the Internet, the top level in a hierarchical network; it connects regional and local networks.

bibliographic citation All the necessary information to find a particular source, for example, author, title, place of publication, publisher, and date for books and author of article, title of article, publication, volume, issue, date, and pages for periodical articles.

bibliography List of sources of information.

binary A code used in computing based on numbers. Once data is entered into a computer, it is converted into binary numbers consisting of the two digits 0 and 1 (bits).

bit Binary digit, the smallest amount of information that may be stored in a computer.

book number Last letter/number combination in a call number. Stands for the author of the book and sometimes the title.

Bookmark A page on the Netscape browser on which you can lists URLs or Web addresses. Bookmarks serve as links for easy access to Web addresses. In Internet Explorer such a page is called "Favorite Places."

Boolean A field of mathematical logic developed in the mid-19th century by the English mathematician George Boole; logic is applied in keyword searching in electronic sources by combining concepts using three commands or operators.

Boolean operators   The terms **and, or, not** used in keyword searching to broaden, narrow or limit a search.

Boolean search   A keyword search that uses Boolean operators to obtain a precise definition of a query.

browser   The software that allows you to locate, display, and use Web documents. Netscape and Internet Explorer are the most widely used browsers.

browsing   Refers to a search in a directory-type search engine on the Internet. Also, casually looking for information on the Internet.

Bulletin Board Service (BBS)   An Internet service that typically provides electronic mail services, exchange of ideas, data files, and any other services or activities of interest to the bulletin board system's operator. May be operated by hobbyists, government agencies, or educational and research institutions.

byte   One character of information, usually eight bits wide.

call number   The identification number that determines where a book or other library material is located in the library.

card catalog   Library holdings recorded on 3" x 5" cards, filed alphabetically.

CD-ROM (compact disk, read only memory)   A compact disk containing text and/or images that is accessed by computers.

Chat (Internet Relay Chat)   A world-wide "party line" protocol that allows individuals to converse with others in real time. (*See also* Talk.)

citation   A reference to an exact source of information.

class number   Top part of call number that stands for subject matter of the book.

client   A computer system or process that requests a service of another computer system or process.

client-server   A common way to describe the relationship between the computer that requests information (client) and the computer that houses the information (server).

commands   Symbols and/or terms used to retrieve computer-stored information.

concept search   A search for the broad meaning of a term, rather than its narrower aspect.

consortium   A group of libraries forming a cooperative for the purpose of sharing services and individual collections.

contemporary   Belonging to the same time period in history.

controlled vocabulary   Standardized or established terms used in databases or catalogs as subject headings or descriptors.

copyright   The legal right to control the production, use, and sale of copies of a literary, musical, or artistic work.

cross reference   A reference from one term or word in a book or index to another word or term.

cumulation   An index that is formed as a result of the incorporation of successive parts of elements. All the material is arranged in one alphabet.

current   Existing at the present time.

cyberspace   A term used to refer to the universe of computers and networks. Originally coined by William Gibson in his fantasy novel *Neuromancer*.

database   Units of information that are stored in machine readable form and retrieved by use of a computer.

depository library   Specially designated libraries that receive government publications free of charge.

descriptors   A term used in some indexes or databases to represent subject headings.

dialup   A temporary, as opposed to dedicated, connection between computers established over a standard phone line.

digital   Data transmitted as discrete and non-continuous pulses (off and on) in the form of binary digits 0 and 1 known as bits, as opposed to *analog* or continuous representation.

digital library   A collection of information in digital (machine-readable) format, rather than on paper or microform. (*See also* virtual library.)

digitization   The process of converting text or images to digital format so that they can be displayed on a computer screen.

direct source   Information presented in such a way that is not necessary to consult another source.

directory search engine   A search engine that presents information in broad subject categories and proceeds through increasingly more specific topics or subjects. It provides a means of focusing more closely on the object of the search. (*See also* mediated search.)

discipline   A branch of knowledge (e.g., humanities, social sciences, or science).

dissertation   Research that is completed in partial fulfillment of the requirements for a doctoral degree.

document delivery   Service provided by libraries to deliver copies of materials from other libraries or vendors to users usually for a fee. The service is often administered by the interlibrary loan department. In some libraries, document delivery consists of the physical or electronic delivery of materials to the office or place of business of a library user.

documentation   A reference to a source used or consulted in research.

domain   A domain, also known as a "domain name," is a unique name that identifies places on the Internet. An example of a domain name is webcrawler.com. Domains can be used as part of a Web site address (e.g., www.domain.com) or they can form part of an e-mail address (e.g., support@domain.com). Domain names are registered for use to avoid duplication of addresses. They allow the use of descriptive words that better enable people to remember Web sites or e-mail addresses.

download   To transfer data or program files from one computer to another for storage on a hard-drive, floppy disk, or other storage device.

DVD (digital versatile disk or digital video disk)   A small disk used for storing text, images, and sounds; similar to a CD-ROM, except that it holds much more information—enough for a full-length movie—and is much faster.

edition   All copies of a book printed from a single typesetting.

e-journal   Periodical published in electronic format; may require a subscription or login ID to use.

E-mail (electronic mail)   A system whereby a computer user can exchange messages with other computer users (or groups of users) via a communications network.

endnotes   Identification of sources used in a text, placed at the end of the text or, in a book, at the ends of chapters.

entry   Description of individual sources of information.

FAX *See* facsimile transmission.

facsimile A reproduction or copy of a work that replicates the exact appearance of the original.

facsimile transmission (FAX) Transmission of text or images, over telephone lines from one location to another, with output printed as a facsimile of the original. Requires a FAX machine with a scanner, a printer, and a modem that is connected to a telephone line.

field The different elements or access points by which records are retrieved in an online catalog or a database.

File Transfer Protocol (FTP) A protocol that allows a user on one host computer to transfer and access files to and from another host over a network.

finger A program that displays information about a particular user, or all users, logged on the local system or on a remote system. It typically shows full name, last login time, idle time, terminal line, and terminal location (where applicable).

flame A strong opinion and/or criticism of something, usually as a frank inflammatory statement, in an electronic mail message.

footnotes Identification of sources used in a text, placed at the bottom of the page.

free-text search A search for words regardless of where they appear in a record.

full-text database Database that provides the complete text of material from the original source.

FTP *See* File Transfer Protocol

gateway A communications device/program that passes data between networks on the Internet.

glossary A list with definitions of technical or unusual terms used in the text.

Gopher A menu-driven client-server computer information system. Gopher uses a simple protocol that allows a single Gopher client to access a Gopher server.

hacker A person who is skilled in the internal workings of computers and networks. The term usually refers to individuals who use this knowledge to penetrate systems to cause mischief.

hits A list of documents that are returned in response to a computer search; also called matches.

home page The first screen you see when you go to a site on the Web.

host A computer that allows users to communicate with other host computers on a network, such as by electronic mail, Telnet, and FTP.

hot links Links within a text on the internet that connect directly to another site.

HTML (Hypertext Markup Language) A standardized document-formatting language used in creating documents on the World Wide Web. With HTML, tags are embedded in the text to instruct the client how to display the document.

HTTP (Hypertext Transfer Protocol) The client-server protocol used to transfer HTML documents from one site to another on the Web.

hypertext Text that contains pointers, or links, to documents on other servers or to parts of the same document. Words or phrases in the document are highlighted, or underlined, to indicate links. The user can click on the highlighted word to display the document.

humanities Fields of knowledge concerned with human culture, such as art, philosophy, literature, and religion.

icon A small image or symbol on a computer screen representing a software program, a file, or other data element that is opened when clicked on with a mouse.

imprint Place of publication, publisher, and either publication or copyright date.

index Alphabetical list of the subjects discussed in a book with corresponding page number; also a separate publication that points to information found in other sources.

indirect source A guide to information that is located in other sources, such as an index.

information Knowledge in the form of ideas, facts, or data created by the human mind.

information processing All of the ways that humans transmit, record, store, retrieve and use information.

integrated catalog An online system that provides bibliographic records for periodical indexes in the same database as the online catalog.

interface The process that allows the user to communicate with the software program to perform certain operations; includes the screen display that tells the user how to communicate with the software system.

Internet A world-wide network that connects computers to one another, allowing for the free flow of information among them. Consists of a three level hierarchy—national (backbone) networks, regional networks, and local networks.

introduction Describes the subject matter and gives a preliminary statement leading to the main contents of a book.

IP (Internet Protocol) The protocol that allows a packet to travel through multiple networks on its way to its final destination.

IP address The address identifying the host computer.

italic Kind of type in which the letters usually slope to the right and which is used for emphasis.

journal Scholarly periodical usually issued monthly or quarterly.

keyword A term that a computer uses as the basis for executing a search.

keyword search "Free-text searching"; electronic searching using nonstandardized headings.

LAN (Local Area Network) A data network intended to serve a small area, usually users in close proximity.

library network Libraries linked together via telecommunication facilities for the purpose of sharing resources.

link A word or an image, which, when clicked, connects to a site on the Internet.

LISTSERV An e-mail distribution system in which mail is automatically distributed to all subscribers.

logon The process of identifying yourself and connecting to a computer system.

MARC Machine-readable cataloging records.

mediated search engine A search engine that has direct human intervention. Starts with a broad subject category and proceeds through increasingly more specific topics or subjects. It provides a means of focusing more closely on the object of the search. (*See also* Directory Search Engine.)

meta search A search that uses a number of search engines in parallel to provide a response to a query.

meta tag   HTML tag that provides information about a Web page. Unlike normal HTML tags, meta tags do not affect how the page is displayed. Instead, they provide information such as who created the page, how often it is updated, what the page is about, and which keywords represent the page's content. Many search engines use this information when building their indexes; also used to catalog Web pages.

microfiche   Microimages of text and other materials printed on a small plastic sheet, usually about 3" x 5" in size. Images must be viewed and printed using a special reader/printer. Magazines, journals, and many government documents are stored in this format.

microfilm   Microimages of text printed on a roll of film, allowing greater storage and archiving of materials. Requires special readers to view and/or print this material.

microform   Printed materials that are reduced in size by photographic means and can only be read with special readers.

Mosaic   A graphics Internet browser developed at the University of Illinois for use with Macintosh, Windows, and UNIX operating systems; has been superseded by Netscape and Internet Explorer.

multi-engine search   *See* meta search.

Netscape   One of the more widely used Internet browsers.

network   A communications system that connects computers at different sites.

notes   Identification of sources used in a text; also explanatory material.

online   Databases stored on a remote computer and accessed locally.

online catalog   Library catalog records in machine readable form which are accessed by use of computers.

online search   A search that is carried out by means of a computer.

OPAC (online public access catalog)   A computer-based source describing the holdings of a particular library; sometimes offers access to periodical databases and catalogs from other libraries.

packet   A small parcel of data by which information is transmitted over the Internet.

pamphlet file   A cardboard, plastic, or metal file for storing pamphlets, loose issues of periodicals, newspaper clippings, and other materials unbound materials. (*See also* vertical file.)

parenthetical references   Citations placed in the text and keyed to the list of *Works Cited*.

periodicals   Magazines and journals.

PDF (Portable Document Format)   A file format developed by Adobe that displays a file on the screen exactly as it looks in the original paper format.

plagiarism   Appropriation of ideas or the copying of the language of another writer without formal acknowledgment.

positional operators   Terms used to refer to the order in which words appear in a record–"adj," "adj#," "with," and "same."

preface   A part of a book that gives the author's purpose in writing the book and acknowledges those persons who have helped in its preparation.

primary source   A firsthand or eyewitness account of an event.

prompt   A message on a computer screen that asks the user for information or a command.

query   A search request consisting words or phrases that define the information that the user is seeking.

record   Individual entries in an online catalog or database.

relevance   The usefulness of a response to a computer-based query. Most search engines rank their hits from the best match to the query to the poorest.

reprint   Copies of the same edition printed at a later time.

robot   The software for indexing and updating Web sites. It operates by scanning documents on the Internet via a network of links. A robot is also known as a *spider, crawler,* or *indexer.*

route   The path that a message takes on the Internet from its source to its destination.

router   A device that forwards traffic among networks.

sciences   Fields of knowledge covering general truths especially as obtained and tested through scientific method; also fields of knowledge concerned with the physical world and its phenomena; includes chemistry, biology, physics, and medicine.

scope   The range of material covered in a book, article, or other information source.

search engine   A computer program that conducts searches in an electronic source.

search statement   Words or phrases that make up the search terms used to look up information in an electronic source.

search strategy   The process to be used in locating information.

secondary source   Literature that analyzes, interprets, relates, or evaluates a primary source or other secondary sources.

***see also* reference**   A listing of additional headings to consult for information.

***see* reference**   A reference from a term that is not used to one that is used.

serial   Publications issued on a continuing basis at regularly stated intervals.

series   Publications similar in content and format.

short-title   First part of a compound title.

site   *See* Web site.

social sciences   Fields of knowledge dealing with human social relationships, such as political science, anthropology, education, and criminal justice.

spider   The software that scans documents on the Internet and adds them to the search engine's database. A spider is the same as a robot.

stacks   Groups of shelves on which books are placed in a library.

stemming   The ability for a search engine to search for variations of a word based on its stem. For example, entering "catalog" might also find "catalogs" and "cataloging," depending on the search engine.

subheading   A subdivision of a major heading.

subject search   A search using controlled vocabulary (such as *LCSH*) to search a record.

subtitle   Second part of a compound title that explains the short-title.

surfing   Exploring sites on the Internet.

table of contents   A list of chapters or parts of a book in numerical order with the pages on which they are located.

Talk   A protocol that allows two or more people on remote computers to communicate in real-time fashion.

TCP   *See* Transmission Control Protocol.

TCP/IP (Transmission Control Protocol over Internet Protocol)   The abbreviation that refers to the suite of protocols sustaining the Internet.

Telnet   Software that allows the user to logon to a remote computer and use its software as if onsite. Telnet is designed to transmits ASCII text and is used in many libraries to provide access to text-based library catalogs. (*See also* WebPac.)

terminal   An computer device consisting of a keyboard and a monitor that can be used to enter or display data from a larger computer (a minicomputer or a mainframe), but is not capable of independent processing of information. Sometimes called a "dumb terminal."

thesis   A research project completed in partial fulfillment of the requirements for the master's degree.

thesis statement   A statement of purpose in a research paper.

title page   Page in front of a book that gives the official author, title, and often the imprint.

Transmission Control Protocol (TCP)   Internet standard transport protocol.

truncation   Abbreviation of words in the commands given to search an online database.

tunneling   The process by which data is transferred between domains on the Internet.

URL (Uniform Resource Locator)   The address of any resource on the Internet.

USENET   A collection of thousands of topically named newsgroups to which people contribute. Not all Internet hosts subscribe to USENET.

vendor   One who markets databases to subscribers.

vertical file   Files containing ephemeral materials such as pamphlets, pictures, and newspaper clippings.

virtual library   A library in which the collection is in electronic format rather than in a tangible form, such as paper or microform. Some libraries use the term to refer to that portion of their collection available on the Internet. (*See also* digital library.)

virus   A program that is spread by replicating itself on any computer system with which it comes in contact.

volume   Written or printed sheets put together to form a book. One book of a series. All the issues of a periodical bound together to make a unit.

WAN   *See* Wide Area Network

WebPAC   A Web-based OPAC (online public access catalog) with a graphics-based interface accessible through the Web, as opposed to a text-based catalog accessible via Telnet.

Web page   A Web document with a URL or Internet address. Also, a page within a Web site. When Web pages are part of the same document, they are also collectively known as a Web site.

Web site   A location on any server that contains hypertext documents.

Wide Area Network (WAN)   A network that covers a large geographic area.

wild card   In a query, a symbol that replaces a portion of a word to indicate that other word constructions are applicable.

World Wide Web (WWW, Web)   A hypertext-based, distributed information system that allows users to view, create, or edit hypertext documents. Documents are viewed using a browser.

WWW   *See* World Wide Web.

Definitions relating to the Internet were adapted from Gary Scott Malkin and Tracy LaQuey Parker, *Internet User Glossary*, http://www.kanren.net/kanren/internet_user_glossary.html; and David Wuolu, "Basic Internet Terminology." Unpublished paper (Baton Rouge: Louisiana State University), 1995. An excellent, frequently updated, glossary of Internet terms is Enzer Matisse, *Glossary of Internet Terms*, available at http://www.matisse.net/files/glossary.html.

Appendix C

The Research Project

Instructor: _____ Course/Section: _____

Name: _____

Date: _____ Points: _____

Topic and Outline

1. Select a topic you might want to use in a ten-page research paper.

    Topic:

    Write three questions or statements you can make about this topic based on what you already know about it.

    a.

    b.

    c.

2. Compile a thesis statement using your responses to Question 1 as a basis. (See Chapter 2 for example.)

3. Write a preliminary outline for your paper. To do this you should look for background information on this topic in sources such as a general encyclopedia, a magazine, or on the Internet. (See Chapter 2 for guidance.)

The Research Project

Instructor: _____ Course/Section: _____

Name: _____

Date: _____ Points: _____

Developing a Search Strategy

Using the thesis statement and outline from Project 1.1, develop a search strategy for your research project. Answer the following questions.

1. Would you approach this topic from a humanities, social science, or science perspective? Explain.

2. What subject headings do you propose to use to find books in your library catalog on your topic?

3. Look up the headings from Question 2 in the *LCSH* on this topic. List those that you locate. Also list any alternative subject headings in the *LCSH*.

4. What keywords do you propose to use to find additional books on the topic in your library catalog?

5. Which periodical indexes or databases will you use to locate citations for popular articles? Why did you choose these?

   What subject headings will you use in these indexes or databases?

6. Which scholarly periodical indexes or databases will you use? Why did you select these?

    What subject headings will you use in these indexes or databases?

7. List other sources you would consult as part of your search strategy and explain why you would consult each. (For example: statistical source—to find the number of . . .)

The Research Project

C Instructor: _____ Course/Section: _____

Name: _____

Date: _____ Points: _____

Works Consulted

After you have selected your topic, compiled an outline (Project 1.1), and defined a search strategy (Project 1.2), you are to locate sources that support your thesis statement and the points in your outline. At a minimum you should have:

1 reference work that provides background information, a definition, or an overview of your topic;

3 sources from the library's catalog (books or government documents);

2 Internet sources that you locate by using different search engines;

2 articles from popular magazines;

2 articles from scholarly journals; and

2 additional sources such as a reference book, biographical information, or book reviews.

As you identify and locate your sources, complete a Research Project Worksheet (p. 391) for each.

After you have located all of your sources, prepare a Works Consulted list that is to be turned in along with your worksheets. The Works Consulted list is to be typed using MLA style documentation. See the examples in Appendix A and the Works Cited list in Chapter 2.

The Research Project

Instructor: _____ Course/Section: _____

Name: _____

Date: _____ Points: _____

Research Project Worksheet

Use copies of this form to record information on the sources you locate for your research project. Items which do not apply should be labeled N/A. (Make a copy of the form to use with each source that you locate.)

1. Title of the source:

2. How did you locate the source? (library catalog, index or abstract, database, Internet)

3. Give the subject heading, keyword, or other command you used to locate the source.

4. If this is a reference work, give the subject heading used within the work.

5. If this is an article from a periodical, give the name of the index, abstract, or database you used to locate the article.

   What subject headings or keywords did you use to locate the article?

6. If this is an item you located on the Internet, give the name of the search engine you used to locate the article.

What search command did you use to locate the information?

7. If this is a print source, what is the call number and library location?

8. How does the information in this source support your thesis statement and outline? Give the headings in the outline which apply.

9. On the back of this sheet, write a bibliographic citation for this source. Use the examples in Appendix A.

10. Write a brief evaluation of the source using the criteria found in Chapter 3.
    (Use a separate sheet of paper if necessary.)

11. Write any notes you wish to take from this source. Paraphrase the words of the author or use direct quotes if needed for emphasis or authoritativeness. Enclose direct quotes in quotation marks. Record page numbers of materials used. (Use the back of the sheet.)

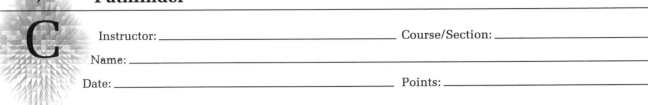

A pathfinder is a guide to information on a topic. It should help the reader identify information sources and the correct terminology to use to locate information. It also directs the reader to good books, the best indexes and databases, appropriate reference sources, information on the Internet, and other pertinent literature.

Create a pathfinder for a topic you select or one that is assigned by your instructor. Use the form below to record your information. You may wish to include more than the minimum number of sources requested. Cite each source that you select using the MLA style for documentation (see Appendix A).

Note: Write complete citations for any books, articles in reference books and periodicals, and Internet sites; it is not necessary to give complete citations for finding aids.

If you are unable to locate information in any of the categories, see your instructor.

1. Topic:

2. Write a brief summary of your topic in two or three sentences. The statements should reflect the scope of your research and which aspects of the topic are to be included with your pathfinder.

3. An introduction to the topic appears in:
    (Use a general or subject encyclopedia or another reference source such as a handbook, almanac, yearbook, a journal or magazine article, or information on the Internet. **(Cite at least one source.)**

4. Subject heading to use for finding information on this topic are:
    (Use the *LCSH (Library of Congress Subject Headings)* to find appropriate subject headings.)

    Broader term(s) (BT):

    Narrower term(s) (NT):

    Related term(s) (RT):

5. Some relevant books on this topic are: **(Cite at least three books.)**

6. Some reference books which contain information on this topic are:
    (Your sources must actually contain information on the topic, such as that found in manuals, texts, handbooks, gazetteers, atlases, subject dictionaries, or encyclopedias. <u>Do not use Indexes or bibliographies</u>. **(Cite at least two sources.)**

7. Indexes or databases to use for identifying articles in popular magazines on this topic are:

    a. **(List at least one)**

    b. Search term(s) to use in these indexes or databases to find information on the topic are:

    c. Some relevant periodicals articles from these indexes or databases are: **(Cite at least two articles.)**

8. Indexes or databases to be used to find articles on this topic in scholarly journals are:

    a. **(List at least two)**

    b. Search term(s) to use in these indexes or databases to find information on the topic are:

    c. Some relevant periodicals articles from these indexes or databases are: **(Cite at least two articles.)**

9. Search engines that can be used to locate free information on the Internet on this topic are: (Use at least two different search engines.)

   a. 1st search engine (name):

   b. search term(s) used:

   c. Some relevant Web sites found by using this search engine are: **(Cite at least two Web sites.)**

   d. 2nd search engine (name)

   e. search term(s) used:

   f. Some relevant Web sites found by using this search engine are: **(Cite at least two Web sites.)**

10. Finding aids useful for locating government documents on the topic are:

    a. **(List at least one):**

    b. Search term(s) used in this finding aid are:

    c. Some government documents with information on this topic are: **(Cite at least two.)**

11. Good sources for statistics on this topic are: **(Cite at least two.)**

12. One article with biographical information on an individual who has written on this topic or who is prominent in this field is: **(Cite at least one.)**

13. A review of a book on this topic appears in: **(Cite at least one.)**

C   Instructor: _____ Course/Section: _____

Name: _____

Date: _____ Points: _____

The assignment below is designed to have you select and evaluate sources of information for a research paper. Although you will not be writing a paper, you will identify library sources and the correct terminology to use in a literature search for information that you could use in a research paper on the topic. You will be locating books, indexes and databases, Internet sources and other relevant literature. Any of the sources you use can be in electronic format or in paper. You may wish to include more than the minimum of sources requested. Write complete bibliographic citations for each appropriate entry below. Use the examples in Appendix A for all bibliographic citations. **(If you are unable to locate material in any of these categories, see your instructor.)**

---

1. Select a **topic** for a hypothetical 10-page research paper, in which you will use a variety of sources.

    Topic:

2. Give a **brief summary** of your topic in two or three sentences. Define your subject as specifically as possible. The statement should reflect the scope of your research and which aspects of the topic are to be included in the search. It may include questions you would like to answer.

3. Use a general or subject encyclopedia to find an **introduction** to the topic. Alternate sources include handbooks or good general books on the subject. Give the correct bibliographic citation for the source you found.

4. Use the *LCSH (Library of Congress Subject Headings)* books to find terms dealing with your topic. Include a few of each of the following if found: .

Broader term(s) (BT):

Narrower term(s) (NT):

Related term(s) (RT):

5. Find at least three books that are relevant to your topic. Write the correct bibliographic citations below.

6. Find two **reference books** which contain information on this topic.
   (Choose your sources from the library catalog, by browsing in the reference stacks, or with the help of a librarian. Your sources must actually contain information on the topic, such as that found in manuals, texts, handbooks, gazetteers, atlases, subject dictionaries, or encyclopedias. <u>Do not use Indexes or bibliographies</u>.)

   Write the correct bibliographic citations for these works.

7. Give the names of three or four appropriate indexes or databases for your topic.

   a.

   b.

   c.

   d.

   Write the search term(s) you used in each one to get an article on your topic. (The letters below correspond to those in Question 7.)

   a.

   b.

   c.

   d.

8. Find one relevant article from each index or database on your topic. Print or copy the first page of each of the articles and attach the pages to this assignment. Write the correct bibliographic citations for each of the articles below. (The letters below correspond to the indexes or databases listed in Question 7.)

a.

b.

c.

d.

9. For each article above, write a brief evaluation. Indicate whether the article is popular or scholarly. Give specific examples to justify your answer. Indicate whether the article is a primary or a secondary source.

a.

b.

c.

d.

10. Use two different search engines to find two Web sites that are relevant to your topic.
1st search engine used:

search term(s):

results (number of "hits"):

Write the correct bibliographic citation for each source you select.

2nd search engine used:

search term(s):

results (number of "hits"):

Write the correct bibliographic citation for the sources you select.

11.   Compare the two search engines in terms of ease of use, accuracy, and results.

12.   Which Web source was more appropriate for your topic? Why?

13.   Find two government documents relevant to your topic.
      Which aid or index did you use? (Internet, library catalog, *Monthly Catalog, GPO Access*, etc.)

      Search term(s) used:

      Write the correct bibliographic citations for each document.

14.   You may select additional sources, such as statistics, biographies, or book reviews, that have not been included in the questions above. Write a correct bibliographic citation for each.

15.   Select two of the best sources you located and give a brief evaluation of their usefulness to your topic. Use the evaluation criteria in Chapter 3 to formulate your evaluation comments.

16.   Compile a Works Consulted list (a bibliography) from the sources you locate. Do not cite the finding aids you used to locate information such as online catalogs, indexes and databases, and the Internet. Rather, cite only the actual sources of information. The Works Consulted list is to be typed on a separate sheet. Use the Works Cited list in Chapter 2 as an example.

Selecting and Evaluating Sources

G   Instructor: _____ Course/Section: _____

   Name: _____

   Date: _____ Points: _____

The assignment below is designed to have you select and evaluate sources of information for a research paper. Although you will not be writing a paper, you will identify library sources and the correct terminology to use in a literature search for information that you could use in a research paper on the topic. You will be locating books, indexes and databases, Internet sources and other relevant literature. Any of the sources you use can be in electronic format or in paper. You may wish to include more than the minimum of sources requested. Write complete bibliographic citations for each appropriate entry below. Use the examples in Appendix A for all bibliographic citations. **(If you are unable to locate material in any of these categories, see your instructor.)**

1. Select a **topic** for a hypothetical 10-page research paper, in which you will use a variety of sources.

    Topic: **discrimination against women in employment**

2. Give a **brief summary** of your topic in two or three sentences. Define your subject as specifically as possible. The statement should reflect the scope of your research and which aspects of the topic are to be included in the search. It may include questions you would like to answer.

    Are women still discriminated against in the workplace? One area where this is clearly evident is in salary discrepancies. This paper will examine the extent of inequities in salaries of men and that of women in the workplace.

3. Use a general or subject encyclopedia to find an **introduction** to the topic. Alternate sources include handbooks or good general books on the subject. Give the correct bibliographic citation for the source you found.
    Sochen, June. "Women's Rights." Compton's Encyclopedia. 1991. 271–279

4. Use the *LCSH (Library of Congress Subject Headings)* books to find terms dealing with your topic. Include a few of each of the following if found:

    Broader term(s) (BT):   **discrimination; sex discrimination against women; women's rights; women--employment**

    Narrower term(s) (NT):   **sex discrimination; wages--women**

    Related term(s) (RT):   **equal pay for equal work**

5. Find at least three books that are relevant to your topic. Write the correct bibliographic citations below.

Bradley, Harriet. <u>Gender and Power in the Workplace: Analyzing the Impact of Economic Change</u>. New York: St. Martin's Press, 1999

McColgan, Aileen. <u>Just Wages for Women</u>. New York: Oxford UP, 1997.

Nash, Margaret A. <u>Changing Roles of Men and Women: Educating for Equity in the Workplace</u>. Madison, WI: U of Wisconsin, 1991.

Schneider, Dorothy, and Carl J. Schneider. <u>The ABC-CLIO Companion to Women in the Workplace</u>. Santa Barbara: ABC-CLIO, 1993.

6. Find two **reference books** which contain information on this topic.
    (Choose your sources from the library catalog, by browsing in the reference stacks, or with the help of a librarian. Your sources must actually contain information on the topic, such as that found in manuals, texts, handbooks, gazetteers, atlases, subject dictionaries, or encyclopedias. <u>Do not use Indexes or bibliographies</u>.)
    Write the correct bibliographic citations for these works.

"Sex Discrimination." <u>Handbook of American Women's History</u>. New York: Garland, 1990.

Taeuber, Cynthia M. <u>Statistical Handbook of Women in America</u>. Phoenix, AZ: Oryx, 1991

7. Give the names of three or four appropriate indexes or databases for your topic.

    a. <u>Academic Search Elite</u> (EBSCOHost)

    b. <u>ABI/INFORM</u> (ProQuest Direct)

    c. <u>Social Sciences Index</u>

    d. <u>Readers' Guide</u>

    Write the search term(s) you used in each one to get an article on your topic. (The letters below correspond to those in Question 7.)

    a. **women and employment and salaries**

    b. **gender differences and earnings**

    c. **wage differentials**

    d. **women--salaries**

8. Find one relevant article from each index or database on your topic. Print or copy the first page of each of the articles and attach the pages to this assignment. Write the correct bibliographic citations for each of the articles below. (The letters below correspond to the indexes or databases listed in Question 7.)

   a. Figart, Deborah M. "Equal Pay for Equal Work: The Role of Job Evaluation in an Evolving Social Norm." <u>Journal of Economic Issues</u> 34.1 (2000): 1–19. <u>EBSCOhost: Academic Search Elite</u>. EBSCOhost Web. LLN (Louisiana Library Network), Baton Rouge. 13 June 2000 <http://search.epnet.com/>.

   b. Stuhlmacher, Alice F., and Amy E. Walters. "Gender Differences in Negotiation Outcome: A Meta Analysis." <u>Personnel Psychology</u> 52.3 (1999): 653–77. <u>ABI/INFORM Global</u>. ProQuest Direct, LLN (Louisiana Library Network), Baton Rouge 23 Feb. 2000 <http://proquest.umi.com/pqdweb>.

   c. England, Paula, Melissa A. Herbert, and Barbara S. Kilbourne. "The Gendered Valuation of Occupations and Skills: Earnings in 1980 Census Occupations." <u>Social Forces</u> 73.1 (1994): 65–9.

   d. Sloan, Carrie, and Jessica Mehalic. "Pay Dirt! An Across-the-USA Salary Exposé." <u>Mademoiselle</u> Sept. 1999: 212+.

9. For each article above, write a brief evaluation. Indicate whether the article is popular or scholarly. Give specific examples to justify your answer. Indicate whether the article is a primary or a secondary source.

   a. In EBSCO Host I limited my search to refereed articles using the search terms above. The author relies primarily on secondary sources and does not include any primary materials. Figart is an Associate Professor of Economics at Richard Stockton College, Pomona, New Jersey.

   b. This is a scholarly article in which the authors present results of a study they conducted on negotiation outcomes (primary research). They also cite a number of other studies on the same subject. The language is rather technical, especially when describing the methodology used for the research. The study was partially funded by a University Research Council grant from DePaul University. A note indicated the article was reviewed by anonymous reviewers prior to publication.

   c. This is a scholarly article written by three authors who are university professors in the field of sociology. The article is extensively documented and cites data gathered from a number of primary sources such as the U.S. Census.

   d. This is a popular article appearing in a monthly magazine. Intended for an audience of young women, it presents an overview of salaries that women earn in different kinds of jobs—ranging from waitresses earning $10,000 to women in managerial positions earning $92,000. It is not documented, although it uses statistics from other sources. It would be considered a secondary source.

10. Use two different search engines to find two Web sites that are relevant to your topic.

    1st search engine used: Yahoo

    search term(s): **women salaries**

    results (number of "hits"): **20+**

    Write the correct bibliographic citation for each source you select.

    "Clinton's Pay Initiative Won't Pay Off for Women." <u>The Contrarian</u>, **4.3: 7 Feb. 2000. 13 June 2000 <http://www.pacificresearch.org/contrn/00-02-07.html>.**

    "Salary Gap Narrows for All, Women." <u>Detroit News</u>. **16 Jan. 1996. 13 June 2000 <http:// detroitnews.com/menu/stories/32277.htm>.**

    2nd search engine used: HotBot

    search term(s): **women salaries**

    results (number of "hits"): **10+**

    Write the correct bibliographic citation for the sources you select.

    "Working Women Making Strides: Earnings Grow; Gap Between Men and Women Shrinking." Channel 4000. 9 June 1998. 13 June 2000 <http://www.wcco.com/news/stories/ news-980609-210844.html>.

    United States. Dept. of Labor. Women's Bureau. "Ten Steps to an Equal Pay Self-Audit for Employers." 13 June 2000 <http://www.dol.gov/dol/wb/10step71.htm>.

11. Compare the two search engines in terms of ease of use, accuracy, and results.

    Both were easy to use, with menus that were self-evident. Yahoo's selections included a category for social science with a sub-category for women's studies. Although HotBot did not include a category for social science, it did have a category for society which included headings under women's rights and women's studies. All articles found were relevant and many were up-to-date.

12. Which Web source was more appropriate for your topic? Why?

    I found the article from the Department of Labor, Women's Bureau, to be the most pertinent in tracing the disparity between the salaries of men and women in the workplace. It indicated that the federal government is aware of a disparity between salaries and is making efforts to remedy the problem by working with employers.

13. Find two government documents relevant to your topic.
    Which aid or index did you use? (Internet, library catalog, *Monthly Catalog*, *GPO Access*, etc.)

    Online catalog

    Search term(s) used:

    women discrimination employment (keyword search)

    Write the correct bibliographic citations for each document.

    United States. Public Sector Programs. Office of Program Operations. Equal Employment Opportunity Commission. <u>Annual Report on the Employment of Minorities, Women & Handicapped Individuals in the Federal Government</u>. Washington: GPO: 1997–98.

    United States. Department of Labor. Employment Standards Administration. <u>The Glass Ceiling Initiative: Are There Cracks in the Ceiling?</u> Washington: GPO, 1997.

14. You may select additional sources, such as statistics, biographies, or book reviews, that have not been included in the questions above. Write a correct bibliographic citation for each.

    Ares, B. Drummond, Jr. "Efforts to End Job Preference Are Failing." <u>New York Times</u> 20 Nov. 1995:A 1.

    Lake, Karen. Interview with Marlene McDaniel, CEO, Women.com. <u>iBoost.com</u>. Published courtesy <u>StrategyWeek.com</u>. 1999–2000. 21 June 2000 <http://www.eboz.com/articles/ interviews/5005a.shtml>.

    McGlynn, Clare. Rev. of <u>Just Wages for Women</u>, by Aileen McColgan. <u>British Journal of Industrial Relations</u> 36 (1998):505+.

    "U. S. Wage and Salary Workers Paid Hourly Rates, Second Quarter 1998." <u>The World Almanac and Book of Facts</u>. 1999, 150.

    Walby, Sylvia. Rev. of <u>Gender and Power in the Workplace: Analyzing the Impact of Economic Change</u>, by Harriet Bradley. <u>American Journal of Sociology</u> 105 (1999): 859–60.

15. Select two of the best sources you located and give a brief evaluation of their usefulness to your topic. Use the evaluation criteria in Chapter 3 to formulate your evaluation comments.

From the index to <u>Compton's Encyclopedia</u> I was able to find "woman" as a subject heading, then a reference to women's rights. An article entitled "Women's Rights" included a full discussion of the history of women's role in society and was helpful in formulating the thesis for this assignment. One section, "Women at Work," was particularly helpful in giving an overview of the topic of discrimination against women in the workforce. The article was easy to read, longer than other encyclopedia articles I consulted, and was presented in chronological order. Several bibliographical references were given for further consideration.

The article, "Equal Pay for Equal Work: The Role of Job Evaluation in an Evolving Social Norm," discusses how job evaluations often reflect an employer's bias against family circumstances. The article presents a history and development of job evaluations, including the Equal Pay Act of 1963. It is interesting that even though some issues were addressed by the Act, more issues, such as gender influenced pay practices, quickly surfaced. Although job evaluation was not the primary focus of my research, the article provided some background information on wage discrepancies between women and men.

16. Compile a Works Consulted list (a bibliography) from the sources you locate. Do not cite the finding aids you used to locate information such as online catalogs, indexes and databases, and the Internet. Rather, cite only the actual sources of information. The Works Consulted list is to be typed on a separate sheet. Use the Works Cited list in Chapter 2 as an example.

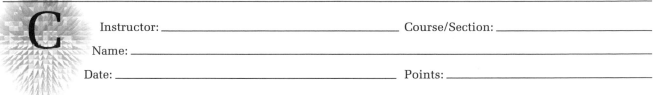

For this assignment you will work in groups of 2–5 persons to use various library tools (reference books, indexes, abstracts, databases, the online catalog, or the Internet) to gather information on a topic of your choice.

Each group will turn in the results of their research to the instructor, make a 5 to 10 minute presentation to the class, and prepare a Works Consulted list.

The group must decide how to divide up the work so that each member can make a meaningful contribution to the project. You are encouraged to include more than the minimum number of sources suggested in the instructions.

Each member of the group will receive the same grade for the project. Participation by each group member is required.

In your oral presentation, you should explain:

◆   why you selected the topic,

◆   what search strategy was used to find the various sources, and

◆   why you selected the particular sources.

Grading will be based on: The appropriateness of your topic
    The search strategy used
    The suitability of the sources you select for your topic
    Proper documentation of sources
    Class presentation

Select a broad topic such as literature, business, biology, agriculture, psychology, or music and narrow it down to a manageable topic. Use *LCSH*, the online catalog, or a general or subject encyclopedia.

1.   Identify the subject/topic you selected and tell why you selected it.

2. Find background information on this topic. List the sources you used to find the information.

3. Write a focused thesis statement describing the exact angle you are using to pursue your research.

4. Use the online catalog to locate three books on your topic. Write a citation for each below. (Follow the examples in Appendix A.)

   What command(s) did you use in the online catalog to locate the books?

5. Use an index or database to locate articles from popular magazines.

   What index or database did you use?

   What search terms did you use to look for information on your topic.

   Locate at least two relevant articles and write a citation for each. (Follow the examples in Appendix A.)

6. Select two indexes or databases that have information on your topic. What indexes or databases did you select?

What search terms did you use to locate information on your topic?

Locate at least two relevant articles from each of the indexes and write a citation for each. (Follow the examples in Appendix A.)

Find any of the following that applies to your thesis statement:

7. Statistics to support your thesis. (Cite the table or article you find.)

8. Biographical information, either on an author of one of your works, or on a person well known in your subject area. Write a citation for this biography.

9. Two Internet sites on your topic. (Write the citation for each.)

Which search engines did you use?

What search terms did you use?

10. Discuss the results of your search for this topic. Would you have enough information to write a 10 page research paper? Which source(s) would you use for:

    a. The introduction to your paper?

    b. The main points of your paper?

    c. The conclusion?

11. Compile a Works Consulted list (a bibliography) from the sources you located. Do not cite the finding aids you used to locate information such as online catalogs, indexes and databases, and the Internet. Rather, cite only the actual sources of information. Type the Works Consulted list on a separate sheet. Use the Works Cited list in Chapter 2 as an example.

Index

Note: For titles of reference books and indexes consult the lists at the end of the chapters.

ABI/INFORM, 216
ARPA (Advanced Research Projects Agency), 133
A–V
   see Audio-visual material
Abstracts, 206
Academic library, 3
Academic Universe, 208
Access points, 74–79
Access UN, 257
Agricola, 215
Agriculture
   indexes, 215
   reference books, 176
   statistics, 285
Almanacs, 162, 168
American Memory, 6
American Men and Women of Science, 315
American Novel, a Checklist of Twentieth Century
   Criticisms on Novels Written Since 1789, 341
American Poetry Index, 348
American Reference Book Annual, 165
American Slang, 171
American Statistics Index (ASI), 276
Americana Annual, 168
Annuals, 5
Anthologies
   definition of, 342
   indexes, 343–348
   Internet, 343
Appendix
   definition of, 4
Applied Science and Technology Index, 216
Architecture
   reference books, 176
Archives, 6
Archives and manuscripts department, 13
Art
   indexes, 215
   reference books, 176
Art Index, 215
Artist Biographies Master Index, 313
Arts and Humanities Citations Index, 210, 215, 337
Atlases, 169
Audio-visual material, 6
Author Biographies Master Index, 313
Author search, 74

Baedeker Guidebooks, 169
Benét's Readers Encyclopedia, 173
Bibliographic citations
   examples, 362–371
Bibliographic database, 207
Bibliographic references in text, 39–40
Bibliographies, 160, 170
Bibliography
   annotated 41
   arrangement, 41–42

   definition of, 41
   examples, 41–42
   types, 41
Biographical dictionaries, 309–310, 314–316
Biographical indexes, 306–308, 313–314
Biographical Directory of the American Congress,
   1774–1989, 315
Biographical sources, 313–316
Biography
   definition of, 302
   evaluating, 312
   indexes, 313–314
   Internet, 312–313
Biography and Genealogy Master Index, 313
Biography Index, 313
Biological Abstracts, 216
Biological and Agricultural Index, 216
Biology
   indexes, 215
   reference books, 176
   see Agriculture
Black's Law Dictionary, 171
Book
   definition of, 3
   documentation, 362–364
   features of, 4
Book catalogs, 97
Book Review Digest, 331, 334–336
Book Review Index, 331–332
Book reviews
   indexes, 331–337
   Internet, 330
Books in Print, 170
Boolean operators, 78
Botany
   reference books, 176
Branch libraries, 13
Britannica Book of the Year, 168
Business
   indexes, 216
   Internet, 174–175
   reference books, 176
   statistics, 278
Business Biography Master Index, 313
Business Index, 216
Business Periodicals Index, 216

CARL, 16
CARL UnCover, 209
CD-ROM, 11
   books, 5
   catalogs, 97
   databases, 11
   documentation, 369
COM (Computer Output Microform) catalogs, 97
Call number, 93–94
Cambridge Scientific Abstracts, 209

Card catalog, 97
    arrangement, 97
    definition of, 97
Career guidance
    reference books, 175
Catalog cards, 97–99
Catalog of United States Government Publications, 249
Chambers World Gazetteer, 169
Checklist of United Nations Documents, 257
Chemical Abstracts, 216
Christian Science Monitor, index, 213
Circulation, 15
Citation guides, 175
Citation indexes, 209
Classification, 88–91
Classification number, 91
Collins-Robert French-English, English-French Dictionary, 171
Columbia Granger's Index to Poetry, 348
Combined Retrospective Index to Book Reviews in Humanities Journals, 331
Commands, 73
Communication
    reference books, 176
Computers
    reference books, 176
Concordances, 162, 170
Congressional Digest, 174
Congressional Directory, 172
Congressional information, 254
Congressional Information Services Index, 271
Congressional Masterfile, 254
Congressional Universe, 254
Consumer resources
    reference books, 175
Contemporary Authors, 315
Contemporary English Poetry. . ., 342
Contemporary Literary Criticism, 341
Continental Novel, a Checklist of Criticism in English 1900–1966, The, 341
Copyright, 37
Criminal justice
    Internet, 284
    reference books, 176
Cross references, 97
Cumulative Book Index, 170
Current Biography, 314
Current events, 173–174

DVD
    definition of, 11
    documentation, 369
Database, 71, 207
    records, 73
Demographics
    Internet, 284
Depository libraries, 247
Dewey Decimal Classification System, 89
Dictionaries, 162, 170–171
Dictionary of American Biography, 315
Dictionary of Crime, 171

Dictionary of National Biography, 315
Directories, 162, 172
Directory of American Scholars, 315
Disciplines, 205
Dissertation
    definition of, 5
    documentation, 367
Document delivery, 15
Documentation, 38–42, 362–371
Dorland's Illustrated Medical Dictionary, 171
Dramatic Criticism Index, 341

E-book, 3
E-journal, 5, 206
E-mail, 136
ERIC, 216
EBSCOhost, 208
Economics
    reference books, 176
Edition, 4
Editorials on File, 174
Education
    indexes, 216
    reference books, 177
Education Index, 216
Electric Library, 209
Electronic format, 70–72
    documentation, 369
Electronic reference services, 15
Electronic searching, 73–82
Electronic sources, 8
Encyclopedia Americana, 172
Encyclopedia of Associations, 172
Encyclopedia of Bioethics, 173
Encyclopedia of Psychology, 173
Encyclopedias, 162, 172–173
Endnotes, 39
Engineering
    indexes, 216
    reference books, 127
Engineering Index, 216
English Novel Explication, 341
Entries, 99
Essay and General Literature Index, 343
Essays, 343–345
Europa Year Book, 168, 174
Evaluation of sources, 58–59
    Internet, 57, 60
    reference books, 167, 58–59
    statistics, 279, 282–283

Facts on File Yearbook, 174
Fields, 73, 99
Filing
    letter by letter, 97
    word by word, 97
FirstSearch, 209
Fodor's Travel Guides, 170
Footnotes, 39–40
Foreword, 4

Format
    definition of, 3
Full-text database, 73, 207

Gazetteers, 162, 169
Genealogy
    reference books, 177
Geography
    indexes, 217
    reference books, 177
GeoRef, 217
Glossary, 4
Goode's World Atlas, 169
Gopher, 137
Government information
    documentation, 368–369
    finding aids, 249–251, 253–254
    international, 256
    Internet, 252–253, 257–258
    local, 256
    national, 252–254
    reference books, 178
    research process, 246
    state, 255
Government Printing Office, 248
Granger's Index to Poetry, 348
Grants and funding
    reference books, 177
Grolier Multimedia Encyclopedia, 172
Guide to Reference Books, 165
Guide to Reference Material, 165
Guidebooks, 162, 169–170
Guides to reference books, 165

HTML, 138
Handbooks, 162, 173
Health
    Internet, 175
    reference books, 178
Historical Abstracts, 215
Historical Atlas, 169
Historical Biographical Dictionaries Master Index, 313
History
    indexes, 215
    reference books, 177
Holdings, 105
Home page, 137
Humanities Index, 215
Hypertext, 137

IP address, 135
Ibid., 40
Illustrations, list of, 4
Imprint, 4
Index, 162
Index Medicus, 217
Index to Plays in Periodicals, 347
Index to Poetry in Popular Periodicals, 348
Index to the Christian Science Monitor International Daily Newspaper, 213

Indexes
    see Periodical indexes
Indexes to book reviews, 331–337
Indexes to literary criticism, 341–342
Indexes to literature in collections
    see Anthologies
Indexes to periodicals
    see Periodical indexes
Information Please Almanac, 168
Information Superhighway, 133
Information transfer, 134
InfoTrac, 209
Inspec, 217
Interlibrary loan, 15
International
    government, 256–258
    reference books, 177
International Encyclopedia of the Social Sciences, 173
International Government Organizations (IGOs), 256
International Who's Who, 314
Integrated online system, 105
Internet
    definition of, 8, 72, 133
    documentation, 370
    evaluation of, 60, 144
    history, 133–134
    reference books, 176
    reference sites, 166, 174–175
    searching, 142–144
Internet Explorer, 138
Internet Protocol (IP), 134–135
Interview
    documentation, 367
Introduction, 4

JSTOR, 217
Journalism
    reference books, 176
Journals, 205
Journalist Biographical Master Index, 314

Kessing's Contemporary Archives, 174
Keyword search, 77–79, 143

LCSH (*Library of Congress Subject Headings*), 76
LAN
    see Local Area Network
Language
    reference books, 178
Law
    reference books, 178
    see also Government information
Lecture
    documentation, 367
LEXIS/NEXIS
    see Academic Universe
Librarians
    reference, 12, 14
    technical services, 14

Library catalog, 88
    access points, 99
Library cooperatives, 16
Library instruction, 15
Library networks, 16, 108
Library of Congress Classification System, 89–92
Library of Congress Subject Headings (LCSH), 75–76
Library services, 13–16
Listserves, 136
Literary criticism
    definition of, 337
    indexes, 341–342
    Internet, 338
    reference books, 340
Literature
    indexes, 215
    reference books, 178
Literature in collections, 342
Loc. cit., 40
Local Area Network (LAN), 134
Location symbol, 96

MARC (Machine Readable Catalog), 99
MLA International Bibliography, 215
MLA Handbook for Writers of Research Papers, 38
Magazines, 5, 205
Magill's Bibliography of Literary Criticism, 341
Manuals, 162, 173
Marquis Who's Who Index to Who's Who Books, 313
MathSciNet, 217
Mathematics
    indexes, 217
    reference books, 178
McGraw-Hill Encyclopedia of Science and Technology, 173
Medicine
    Internet, 175
    reference books, 178
Merriam-Webster's Collegiate Dictionary, 170
Merriam-Webster's Geographic Dictionary, 169
Microcard, 6
Microfiche, 6
Microfiche reader, 25
Microfilm, 6
Microfilm reader, 25
Microforms, 6
    documentation, 367
Microprint, 10
Monthly Catalog of United States Government Publications, 249
Mosaic, 138
Motion pictures
    reference books, 178
Multicultural
    reference books, 177
Music
    reference books, 178–179

NCJRS, 217
National Geographic Atlas of the World, 169

Natural language search, 143
Nebraska State College Library System, 108
Nested searches, 79
Netscape, 138
Networks, Internet, 134
New American Standard Exhaustive Concordance of the Bible, 170
New Encyclopedia Britannica, 172
New Roberts Rules of Order, 173
New York Times Index, 213–214
Newspaper article documentation, 366
Newspaper indexes, 213
Newspapers, 5
Nineteenth Century Literary Criticism, 341
Note taking, 36
Notes, 39
Novels
    criticism, 341

OPAC (Online Public Access Catalog), 99
Online catalog, 8, 70, 99
    screens, 100–104
    searching, 99
Online databases
    definition of, 8
    searching, 73–82
Op. cit., 40
Ottemiller's Index to Plays in Collections. . ., 347
Outline, 32
Oxford English Dictionary, 171

PAIS International, 216
Pamphlet file, 6
Paraphrase, 37
Parenthetical references, 39
People in History, 314
People in World History, 314
Performing Arts Biography Master Index, 314
Periodical articles
    documentation, 365–366
Periodical department, 12
Periodical indexes/abstracts
    electronic, 207–210
    integrated catalog, 105
    popular, 205
    printed, 206–207
    scholarly, 205
    selecting, 207
    using, 210–214
Periodical literature, 205
Periodicals, 5, 204
Philosophy
    reference books, 179
Phonograph recordings
    documentation, 367
Phrase search, 143
Plagiarism, 37
Play Index, 347
Plays, 347

Poetry, 348
Political science
    reference books, 178
Popular sources, 55, 205
Positional operators, 79
Preface, 4
Primary sources, 54
Project Muse, 217
Psychological Abstracts, 217
Psychology
    reference books, 179

Quotations
    documentation, 365
    use in research papers, 39–40

Radio
    documentation, 367
    reference books, 178
Rand McNally Commercial Atlas and Marketing Guide, 169
Random House Dictionary of the English Language, 170
Rare books department, 13
Readers' Guide to Periodical Literature, 210–211
Records, 72
Reference books, 168–174
    documentation, 364–365
Reference sources
    abstracts, 162
    almanacs, 162, 168
    atlases, 162, 169
    bibliographies, 162, 170
    biographical dictionaries, 314–316
    biographical indexes, 313–314
    characteristics, 159–160
    concordances, 162, 179
    dictionaries, 162, 170–171
    directories, 162, 172
    documentation, 364–365
    encyclopedias, 162, 172–173
    evaluating, 58, 167
    finding, 164–167
    gazetteers, 162, 169
    guidebooks, 162, 169
    guides to reference books, 165
    handbooks, 162, 173
    indexes, 162, 206, 210–217
    Internet, 166, 174
    manuals, 162, 173
    selection, 161
    types, 160, 162
    yearbooks, 162, 168
Reference department, 12
Reference interview, 14
Reference librarians, 167
Religion
    reference books, 179
Research paper
    bibliography, 41–42
    definition of, 30

documentation, 37–42
evaluation criteria, 36
notes, 39–40
outline, 32
search strategy, 34–35
selecting a topic, 31
selection criteria, 36
steps in preparing, 31
taking notes, 36
thesis statement, 32–33
works cited, 41–42
writing, 37
Reserve department, 12
Roget's 21st Century Thesaurus in Dictionary Form, 171

SCI (*Science Citation Index*), 217
SSCI (*Social Science Citation Index*), 210
SuDocs
    see Superintendent of Documents Classification
        System
Scholarly sources, 55, 205
Science
    indexes, 216–217
    reference books, 179
Science Citation Index, 217
Search engines,
    definition of, 141
    description, 68–69
    features, 145
    types, 142
Search strategy, 34–35
Secondary sources, 55
See also reference, 97
Selection criteria, 36
Serials, 5, 204
Short stories, 345–347
Short Story Index, 345
Social sciences
    indexes, 217, 219, 242
    reference books, 179–180
Social Sciences Citation Index, 210
Social Science Index, 215
Sociological Abstracts, 217
Sound recordings
    documentation, 367
Special collections, 13
Speech Index. . ., 348
Speeches, 348
Sports medicine
    Internet, 175
    reference books, 178
Stacks, 11
Statesmen's Year Book, 168
Statistical Abstract of the United States, 168, 276
Statistical Reference Index (SRI), 276
Statistical Universe, 276
Statistics
    definition of, 274
    evaluating, 279
    finding, 274–279

guides, 283
indexes, 276–278
Internet, 175, 275, 283–287
reference books, 180, 285–287
Stopwords, 82
Style manuals, 38
Subject headings, 75
Subject search, 74–75
Superintendent of Documents Classification system (SuDocs), 93

Table of contents, 4
Television
    reference books, 178
Term paper
    see research paper
Text-based catalog, 99
    sample screens, 100–104
Theater
    reference books, 178–179
Thesis
    definition of, 5
    documentation, 367
Thesis statement, 32
Thomas' Register of American Manufacturers, 172
Time series, 283
Title page, 4
Title search, 74
Topic, 31
Truncation, 77
Twentieth Century Authors, 315
Twentieth Century Authors Biographies Master Index, 314
Twentieth Century Literary Criticism, 341
Twentieth Century Short Story Explication, 342

URL
    see Uniform Resource Locator (URL),
USA Today, 213
Uniform Resource Locator (URL), 138
United Nations, 257
United Nations Documents Index, 257
United Nations symbol numbers, 93
United States Government Manual, 173

United States government publications, 249–254
Usenet news, 136

Vertical file, 6
Video materials, 6
Videotapes
    documentation, 366
Virtual library, 2

Wall Street Journal Index, 215
Weather
    Internet, 175
Web of Science, 209
Web-based catalog, 105
WebPac, 99
Webster's New Biographical Dictionary, 315
Webster's Third New International Dictionary of the English Language, 170
Who Was Who, 315
Who Was Who in America, 315
Who Was Who in America, Historical Volume 1607–1896, 315
Who Was Who in America, with World Notables, 315
Who's Who, 314
Who's Who in America, 314
Wide Area Network (WAN), 134
Women's Studies
    reference books, 180
Works cited, 41–42
Works consulted, 41–42
World Almanac and Book of Facts, 168
World Authors, 1970–1980, 315
World Book Encyclopedia, 172
WorldCat, 108
World FactBook, 168
World of Learning, 172
World Wide Web (WWW), 137–139

Yearbooks, 5, 162, 168

Zoology
    reference books, 176

the Research Process
books & beyond

How will we cope with the information explosion?

Quick and easy exposure to the vast wealth of information currently available has made it critical for people to understand the general process of how information is stored, accessed, and retrieved.

The Research Process: Books and Beyond will aid the researcher in:
- determining what information is needed
- knowing how to locate the necessary information
- evaluating and using information effectively

Persons using this book will be able to:
- understand the organization and services of libraries
- recognize the types and formats of information that are available
- execute the steps in writing a research paper by learning how to
  —select a topic for a research paper
  —write a thesis statement and outline
  —plan and execute a search strategy
  —synthesize what is learned with original ideas and interpretations
  —write and document the paper with special attention to ethical and legal use of information
- critically examine and evaluate information to determine authority, reliability, comprehensiveness, accuracy, and currency
- analyze information and determine suitability for research needs
- perform basic search techniques using author, title, subject, and keyword search strategies
- understand classification and organization of library materials
- interpret and use information from online catalogs effectively
- use various search engines to locate free information on the Internet
- select, locate, evaluate, and use various types of print and electronic information sources
- recognize and select specific information based on discipline and specific purpose (e.g., popular or scholarly, primary or secondary, current or historical)
- cite the various types of sources using a specific documentation style

Myrtle S. Bolner
Gayle A. Poirier

second edition

ISBN 0-7872-7329-5

90000

9 780787 273293

KENDALL/HUNT PUBLISHING COMPANY
Dubuque, Iowa